OpenGL 4 Shading Language Cookbook

Second Edition

Over 70 recipes demonstrating simple and advanced techniques for producing high-quality, real-time 3D graphics using OpenGL and GLSL 4.x

David Wolff

[PACKT] open source ✣
PUBLISHING   community experience distilled

BIRMINGHAM - MUMBAI

OpenGL 4 Shading Language Cookbook
Second Edition

First published: July 2011

Second edition: December 2013

Production Reference: 1171213

Published by Packt Publishing Ltd.
Livery Place
35 Livery Street
Birmingham B3 2PB, UK.

ISBN 978-1-78216-702-0

www.packtpub.com

Cover Image by Aniket Sawant (aniket_sawant_photography@hotmail.com)

Credits

Author

David Wolff

Reviewers

Bartłomiej Filipek

Thomas Le Guerroué-Drévillon

Muhammad Mobeen Movania

Dario Scarpa

Javed Rabbani Shah

Acquisition Editors

Gregory Wild

Edward Gordon

Usha Iyer

Lead Technical Editor

Neeshma Ramakrishnan

Technical Editors

Kunal Anil Gaikwad

Jinesh Kampani

Aman Preet Singh

Project Coordinator

Shiksha Chaturvedi

Proofreaders

Elinor Perry-Smith

Chris Smith

Indexer

Mariammal Chettiyar

Graphics

Sheetal Aute

Ronak Dhruv

Production Coordinator

Nilesh R. Mohite

Cover Work

Nilesh R. Mohite

About the Author

David Wolff is an associate professor in the Computer Science and Computer Engineering Department at Pacific Lutheran University (PLU). He received a PhD in Physics and an MS in Computer Science from Oregon State University. He has been teaching computer graphics to undergraduates at PLU for over 10 years, using OpenGL.

About the Reviewers

Bartłomiej Filipek is an experienced software developer with a passion for teaching. He has been leading OpenGL and graphics programming courses at Jagiellonian University in Cracow for around five years now. Additionally he gives lectures and workshops about modern C++ techniques at local universities.

His professional experience focuses mostly on native application development including rendering systems, large-scale software development, game engines, multimedia applications, user interfaces, GPU computing, and even biofeedback.

He shares his programming stories at his blog: `http://www.bfilipek.com/`.

Thomas Le Guerroué-Drévillon is a freshly graduated software engineer. Having a profound interest in mathematics and drawing, it came easily to him to mix together these two passions in one field: computer graphics.

Originally French, he used up all the opportunities given by his university to study and work all around the world. It allowed him to enjoy his first international experience in Estonia, the second in the prestigious KAIST in South Korea, and finally ending up now in Canada.

Even though his university provided the mathematical background, he got his experience with OpenGL and GLSL on his own. He believes that the link between the well documented API and the shader samples is missing. Thus he naturally accepted to review this cookbook, which for him is the material he would have loved to get a hand on when he started developing interests in OpenGL/GLSL.

Dr. Muhammad Mobeen Movania received his PhD degree in Advance Computer Graphics and Visualization from Nanyang Technological University, Singapore. After finishing his PhD, he joined Institute for Infocomm Research, A-Star, Singapore to work on Augmented Reality based Virtual Tryon and Cloth Simulation systems using GPU and OpenGL. Before joining NTU, he was a junior graphics programmer at Data Communication and Control (DCC) Pvt. Ltd., Karachi, Pakistan. He worked on DirectX and OpenGL API for producing real-time interactive tactical simulators and dynamic integrated training simulators. His research interests include GPU-based volumetric rendering techniques, GPU technologies, real-time soft body physics, real-time dynamic shadows, real-time collision detection and response, and hierarchical geometric data structures. He is also the author of the OpenCloth project (http://code.google.com/p/opencloth), which implements various cloth simulation algorithms in OpenGL. His blog (http://mmmovania.blogspot.com) lists a lot of useful graphics tips and tricks. When not involved with computer graphics, he composes music and is an avid squash player.

Dr. Mobeen has published several conference and journal papers on real-time computer graphics and visualization. Recently, he authored a book on OpenGL (*OpenGL Development Cookbook* by *Packt Publishing*, published in 2013) which details several applied recipes using modern OpenGL. He has also authored a book chapter in another book (*OpenGL Insights* by *AK Peters/CRC Press*, published in 2012).

Dr. Mobeen is currently an Assistant Professor at DHA Suffa University, Karachi, Pakistan where he is busy nurturing young minds to become outstanding programmers and researchers of tomorrow.

I would like to thank almighty ALLAH for bestowing his countless blessings on me and my family. After that, I would like to extend my gratitude towards my family, my parents (Mr. and Mrs. Abdul Aziz Movania), my wife (Tanveer Taji), my sisters (Mrs. Azra Saleem and Mrs. Sajida Shakir), my brothers (Mr. Khalid Movania and Mr. Abdul Majid Movania), all my nephews/nieces and my daughter (Muntaha Movania).

Dario Scarpa has been coding for fun and profit for the last 15 years, and has no intention to stop. Jumping around among IT jobs as developer/sysadmin, amateur video game programming, and CS exams at the University of Salerno (Italy), he also managed to work with Adventure Productions in building Zodiac, a digital delivery platform focused on adventure games. At the time of reviewing this book, he's about to get his Master's degree, with a thesis on computer graphics that got him working intensively with—guess what—OpenGL.

Javed Rabbani Shah received his degree in Electrical Engineering from the University of Engineering and Technology, Lahore, Pakistan in 2004. He started his professional career by joining Delta Indus Systems (now Vision Master Inc.), where he worked with solder paste inspection systems for statistical process control involving technologies such as Image Processing, 3D Machine Vision, and FPGAs. He then joined the Embedded Systems Division of Mentor Graphics in 2007 and got the opportunity to work with the Nucleus+ real-time operating system, USB 2.0 middleware, WebKit, and OpenGL ES 2.0. He spearheaded the effort to integrate OpenGL ES 2.0 features in Mentor's cross-platform Inflexion 3D user interface engine.

He is currently working at Saffron Digital in central London, where he is involved in work related to cross-platform secure video playback, DRM, and UltraViolet technologies.

In his spare time, he likes to learn emerging technologies like OpenGL ES 3.0 and OpenCL.

www.PacktPub.com

Support files, eBooks, discount offers and more

You might want to visit www.PacktPub.com for support files and downloads related to your book.

Did you know that Packt offers eBook versions of every book published, with PDF and ePub files available? You can upgrade to the eBook version at www.PacktPub.com and, as a print book customer, you are entitled to a discount on the eBook copy. Get in touch with us at service@packtpub.com for more details.

At www.PacktPub.com, you can also read a collection of free technical articles, sign up for a range of free newsletters and receive exclusive discounts and offers on Packt books and eBooks.

http://PacktLib.PacktPub.com

Do you need instant solutions to your IT questions? PacktLib is Packt's online digital book library. Here, you can access, read and search across Packt's entire library of books.

Why Subscribe?

- ▸ Fully searchable across every book published by Packt
- ▸ Copy and paste, print and bookmark content
- ▸ On demand and accessible via web browser

Free Access for Packt account holders

If you have an account with Packt at www.PacktPub.com, you can use this to access PacktLib today and view nine entirely free books. Simply use your login credentials for immediate access.

Table of Contents

Preface

The OpenGL Shading Language (GLSL) is now a fundamental and critical part of programming with OpenGL. It provides us with unprecedented flexibility and power by making the formerly fixed-function graphics pipeline programmable. With GLSL, we can leverage the Graphics Processing Unit (GPU) to implement advanced and sophisticated rendering techniques and even do arbitrary computation. With GLSL 4.x, programmers can do more with the GPU than ever before thanks to new shader stages such as tessellation shaders and compute shaders.

In this book, we cover the full spectrum of GLSL programming. Starting with the basics of shading with the vertex and fragment shaders, we take you from simple to advanced techniques. From textures, shadows, and image processing, to noise and particle systems, we cover practical examples to give you the tools you need to leverage GLSL in your projects. We also cover how to use geometry shaders, tessellation shaders, and the very recent addition to GLSL: compute shaders. With these, you can make use of the GPU for a variety of tasks that go beyond just shading. With geometry and tessellation shaders, we can create additional geometry or modify geometry, and with compute shaders we can do arbitrary computation on the GPU.

For those new to GLSL, it's best to read this book in order, starting with Chapter 1. The recipes will walk you through from basic through to advanced techniques. For someone who is more experienced with GLSL, you might find it better to pick out specific recipes and jump directly there. Most recipes are self-contained, but some may refer to other recipes. The introduction to each chapter provides important general information about the topic, so you might want to read through that as well.

GLSL 4.x makes programming with OpenGL even more rewarding and fun. I sincerely hope that you find this book to be useful and that you use these recipes as a starting point in your own projects. I hope that you find programming in OpenGL and GLSL as enjoyable as I do, and that these techniques inspire you to create beautiful graphics.

What this book covers

Chapter 1, Getting Started with GLSL, explains the steps needed to compile, link, and use GLSL shaders within an OpenGL program. It also covers how to send data to shaders using attributes and uniform variables, and the use of the GLM library for mathematics support. Every modern OpenGL program today requires a function loader. In this chapter, we also cover the use of GLLoadGen, a relatively new and easy-to-use OpenGL loader generator.

Chapter 2, The Basics of GLSL Shaders, introduces you to the basics of GLSL programming with per-vertex shading. In this chapter, you see examples of basic shading techniques such as the ADS (ambient, diffuse, and specular) shading algorithm, two-sided shading, and flat shading. It also covers examples of basic GLSL concepts such as functions and subroutines.

Chapter 3, Lighting, Shading, and Optimization, presents more advanced shading techniques, with a focus on the fragment shader. It introduces you to techniques such as spotlights, per-fragment shading, toon shading, fog, and others. We also discuss several simple optimizations to make your shaders run faster.

Chapter 4, Using Textures, provides a general introduction to using textures in GLSL shaders. Textures can be used for a variety of purposes besides simply "pasting" an image onto a surface. In this chapter, we cover the basic application of one or more 2D textures, as well as a variety of other techniques including alpha maps, normal maps, cube maps, projected textures, and rendering to a texture. We also cover sampler objects, a relatively new feature that decouples sampling parameters from the texture object itself.

Chapter 5, Image Processing and Screen Space Techniques, explains common techniques for the post-processing of rendered images and some other screen-space techniques. Image post-processing is becoming a crucially important part of modern game engines and other rendering pipelines. This chapter discusses how to implement some of the more common post-processing techniques such as tone mapping, bloom, blur, gamma correction, and edge detection. We also cover some screen-space rendering techniques such as deferred shading, multisample antialiasing, and order-independent transparency.

Chapter 6, Using Geometry and Tessellation Shaders, covers techniques that demonstrate how to use these new and powerful shader stages. After reading this chapter, you should be comfortable with their basic functionality and understand how to use them. We cover techniques such as geometry-shader-generated point sprites, silhouette lines, depth-based tessellation, Bezier surfaces, and more.

Chapter 7, Shadows, introduces basic techniques for producing real-time shadows. This chapter includes recipes for the two most common shadow techniques: shadow maps and shadow volumes. We cover common techniques for antialiasing shadow maps, as well as how to use the geometry shader to help produce shadow volumes.

Chapter 8, Using Noise in Shaders, covers the use of Perlin noise for creating various effects. The first recipe shows you how to create a wide variety of textures containing noise data using GLM (a powerful mathematics library). Then we move on to recipes that use noise textures for creating a number of effects such as wood grain, clouds, disintegration, paint, and static.

Chapter 9, Particle Systems and Animation, focuses on techniques for creating particle systems. We see how to create a particle system to simulate fire, smoke, and water. We also make use of the OpenGL feature called transform feedback, in order to gain additional efficiency by moving the particle updates onto the GPU.

Chapter 10, Using Compute Shaders, introduces you to several techniques that make use of one of the newest features in OpenGL, the compute shader. The compute shader provides us with the ability to do general computation on the GPU within OpenGL. In this chapter, we discuss how to use the compute shader for particle simulations, cloth simulation, edge detection, and the generation of a procedural fractal texture. After reading this chapter, the reader should have a good feel for how to use the compute shader for arbitrary computational tasks.

What you need for this book

The recipes in this book use some of the latest and greatest features in OpenGL 4.x. Therefore, in order to implement them, you'll need graphics hardware (graphics card or onboard GPU) and drivers that support at least OpenGL 4.3. If you're unsure about what version of OpenGL your setup can support, there are a number of utilities available for determining this information. One option is GLview from Realtech VR, available at: `http://www.realtech-vr.com/glview/`. If you're running Windows or Linux, drivers are readily available for most modern hardware. However, if you're using MacOS X, unfortunately, you may need to wait. As of this writing, the latest version of MacOS X (10.9 Mavericks) only supports OpenGL 4.1.

Once you've verified that you have the required OpenGL drivers, you'll also need the following:

- A C++ compiler. On Linux, the GNU Compiler Collection (gcc, g++, and so on) may already be available, and if not, it should be available through your distribution's package manager. On Windows, Microsoft Visual Studio will work fine, but if you don't have a copy, then the MinGW compiler (available from `http://mingw.org/`) is a good option.

- The GLFW library Version 3.0 or later, available from `http://www.glfw.org/`. This library provides OpenGL context creation, window support, and support for user input events.

- The GLM library Version 0.9.4 or later, available from `http://glm.g-truc.net/`. This provides mathematics support with classes for matrices, vectors, common transformations, noise functions, and much more.

Who this book is for

The primary focus of this book is the OpenGL Shading Language (GLSL). Therefore, we don't spend any time discussing the basics of programming with OpenGL. In this book I assume that the reader has some experience with programming in OpenGL, and understands basic 3D rendering concepts such as model coordinates, view coordinates, clip coordinates, perspective transforms, and the other associated transformations. There's no assumption of any experience with shader programming, however, so if you're new to GLSL, this is a great place to start.

If you're an OpenGL programmer looking to learn about GLSL programming, then this book is for you. Even if you have some shader programming experience, you will very likely find the recipes in this book to be valuable. We cover a range of simple to advanced techniques, using some of the newest features of OpenGL (such as compute shaders and tessellation shaders). So even experienced GLSL programmers, who are looking to learn how to use these new features, may also find this book to be useful.

In short, this book is for programmers who understand the basics of 3D graphics in OpenGL, and are interested in either learning GLSL, or taking advantage of some of the newest features in modern GLSL 4.x.

Conventions

In this book, you will find a number of styles of text that distinguish between different kinds of information. Here are some examples of these styles, and an explanation of their meaning.

Code words in text, database table names, folder names, filenames, file extensions, pathnames, dummy URLs, user input, and Twitter handles are shown as follows: "The number of work groups are determined by the parameters to `glDispatchCompute`."

A block of code is set as follows:

```
void main()
{
    Color = VertexColor;
    gl_Position = RotationMatrix * vec4(VertexPosition,1.0);
}
```

When we wish to draw your attention to a particular part of a code block, the relevant lines or items are set in bold:

```
void main()
{
    Color = VertexColor;
    gl_Position = RotationMatrix * vec4(VertexPosition,1.0);
}
```

Any command-line input or output is written as follows:

```
Active attributes:
1      VertexColor (vec3)
0      VertexPosition (vec3)
```

New terms and **important words** are shown in bold.

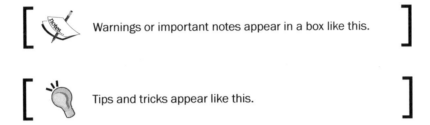

Warnings or important notes appear in a box like this.

Tips and tricks appear like this.

Reader feedback

Feedback from our readers is always welcome. Let us know what you think about this book—what you liked or may have disliked. Reader feedback is important for us to develop titles that you really get the most out of.

To send us general feedback, simply send an e-mail to feedback@packtpub.com, and mention the book title via the subject of your message.

If there is a topic that you have expertise in and you are interested in either writing or contributing to a book, see our author guide on www.packtpub.com/authors.

Customer support

Now that you are the proud owner of a Packt book, we have a number of things to help you to get the most from your purchase.

Downloading the example code

You can download the example code files for all Packt books you have purchased from your account at http://www.packtpub.com. If you purchased this book elsewhere, you can visit http://www.packtpub.com/support and register to have the files e-mailed directly to you.

Full source code for all of the recipes in this text is available on GitHub at: https://github.com/daw42/glslcookbook.

Downloading the color images of this book

We also provide you a PDF file that has color images of the screenshots/diagrams used in this book. The color images will help you better understand the changes in the output. You can download this file from: http://www.packtpub.com/sites/default/files/downloads/7020OS_Colorimages.pdf

Errata

Although we have taken every care to ensure the accuracy of our content, mistakes do happen. If you find a mistake in one of our books—maybe a mistake in the text or the code—we would be grateful if you would report this to us. By doing so, you can save other readers from frustration and help us improve subsequent versions of this book. If you find any errata, please report them by visiting http://www.packtpub.com/submit-errata, selecting your book, clicking on the **errata submission form** link, and entering the details of your errata. Once your errata are verified, your submission will be accepted and the errata will be uploaded on our website, or added to any list of existing errata, under the Errata section of that title. Any existing errata can be viewed by selecting your title from http://www.packtpub.com/support.

Piracy

Piracy of copyright material on the Internet is an ongoing problem across all media. At Packt, we take the protection of our copyright and licenses very seriously. If you come across any illegal copies of our works, in any form, on the Internet, please provide us with the location address or website name immediately so that we can pursue a remedy.

Please contact us at copyright@packtpub.com with a link to the suspected pirated material.

We appreciate your help in protecting our authors, and our ability to bring you valuable content.

Questions

You can contact us at questions@packtpub.com if you are having a problem with any aspect of the book, and we will do our best to address it.

1

Getting Started with GLSL

In this chapter, we will cover the following recipes:

- ▸ Using a function loader to access the latest OpenGL functionality
- ▸ Using GLM for mathematics
- ▸ Determining the GLSL and OpenGL version
- ▸ Compiling a shader
- ▸ Linking a shader program
- ▸ Sending data to a shader using vertex attributes and vertex buffer objects
- ▸ Getting a list of active vertex input attributes and locations
- ▸ Sending data to a shader using uniform variables
- ▸ Getting a list of active uniform variables
- ▸ Using uniform blocks and uniform buffer objects
- ▸ Getting debug messages
- ▸ Building a C++ shader program class

Introduction

The **OpenGL Shading Language** (**GLSL**) Version 4 brings unprecedented power and flexibility to programmers interested in creating modern, interactive, and graphical programs. It allows us to harness the power of modern **Graphics Processing Units** (**GPUs**) in a straightforward way by providing a simple yet powerful language and API. Of course, the first step towards using GLSL is to create a program that utilizes the latest version of the OpenGL API. GLSL programs don't stand on their own; they must be a part of a larger OpenGL program. In this chapter, we will provide some tips and techniques for getting a basic program up and running. First, let's start with some background.

The OpenGL Shading Language

The GLSL is now a fundamental and integral part of the OpenGL API. Going forward, every program written using the OpenGL API will internally utilize one or several GLSL programs. These "mini-programs" are often referred to as **shader programs**. A shader program usually consists of several components called **shaders**. Each shader executes within a different section of the OpenGL pipeline. Each shader runs on the GPU, and as the name implies, (typically) implement the algorithms related to the lighting and shading effects of an image. However, shaders are capable of doing much more than just implementing a shading algorithm. They are also capable of performing animation, tessellation, or even generalized computation.

 The field of study dubbed **GPGPU (General Purpose Computing on Graphics Processing Units)** is concerned with utilization of GPUs (often using specialized APIs such as CUDA or OpenCL) to perform general purpose computations such as fluid dynamics, molecular dynamics, cryptography, and so on. With compute shaders, introduced in OpenGL 4.3, we can now do GPGPU within OpenGL.

Shader programs are designed for direct execution on the GPU and are executed in parallel. For example, a fragment shader might be executed once for every pixel, with each execution running simultaneously on a separate GPU thread. The number of processors on the graphics card determines how many can be executed at one time. This makes shader programs incredibly efficient, and provides the programmer with a simple API for implementing highly parallel computation.

The computing power available in modern graphics cards is impressive. The following table shows the number of shader processors available for several models in the NVIDIA GeForce series cards (source: `http://en.wikipedia.org/wiki/Comparison_of_ Nvidia_graphics_processing_units`).

Model	Unified Shader Processors
GeForce GTS 450	192
GeForce GTX 480	480
GeForce GTX 780	2304

Shader programs are intended to replace parts of the OpenGL architecture referred to as the **fixed-function pipeline**. Prior to OpenGL Version 2.0, the shading algorithm was "hard-coded" into the pipeline and had only limited configurability. This default lighting/shading algorithm was a core part of the fixed-function pipeline. When we, as programmers, wanted to implement more advanced or realistic effects, we used various tricks to force the fixed-function pipeline into being more flexible than it really was. The advent of GLSL will help by providing us with the ability to replace this "hard-coded" functionality with our own programs written in GLSL, thus giving us a great deal of additional flexibility and power. For more details on the programmable pipeline, see the introduction to *Chapter 2, The Basics of GLSL Shaders*.

In fact, recent (core) versions of OpenGL not only provide this capability, but they require shader programs as part of every OpenGL program. The old fixed-function pipeline has been deprecated in favor of a new programmable pipeline, a key part of which is the shader program written in GLSL.

Profiles – Core vs. Compatibility

OpenGL Version 3.0 introduced a **deprecation model**, which allowed for the gradual removal of functions from the OpenGL specification. Functions or features can be marked as deprecated, meaning that they are expected to be removed from a future version of OpenGL. For example, immediate mode rendering using `glBegin`/`glEnd` was marked deprecated in version 3.0 and removed in version 3.1.

In order to maintain backwards compatibility, the concept of **compatibility profiles** was introduced with OpenGL 3.2. A programmer that is writing code intended to be used with a particular version of OpenGL (with older features removed) would use the so-called **core profile**. Someone who also wanted to maintain compatibility with older functionality could use the compatibility profile.

It may be somewhat confusing that there is also the concept of a **forward compatible** context, which is distinguished slightly from the concept of a core/compatibility profile. A context that is considered forward compatible basically indicates that all deprecated functionality has been removed. In other words, if a context is forward compatible, it only includes functions that are in the core, but not those that were marked as deprecated. Some window APIs provide the ability to select forward compatible status along with the profile.

The steps for selecting a core or compatibility profile are window system API dependent. For example, in GLFW, one can select a forward compatible, 4.3 core profile using the following code:

```
glfwWindowHint ( GLFW_CONTEXT_VERSION_MAJOR, 4 );
glfwWindowHint ( GLFW_CONTEXT_VERSION_MINOR, 3 );
glfwWindowHint (GLFW_OPENGL_FORWARD_COMPAT, GL_TRUE);
glfwWindowHint (GLFW_OPENGL_PROFILE, GLFW_OPENGL_CORE_PROFILE);

GLFWwindow *window = glfwCreateWindow(640, 480, "Title",
        NULL, NULL);
```

All programs in this book are designed to be compatible with a forward compatible OpenGL 4.3 core profile.

Using a function loader to access the latest OpenGL functionality

The OpenGL **ABI (application binary interface)** is frozen to OpenGL version 1.1 on Windows. Unfortunately for Windows developers, that means that it is not possible to link directly to functions that are provided in newer versions of OpenGL. Instead, one must get access to these functions by acquiring a function pointer at runtime. Getting access to the function pointers is not difficult, but requires somewhat tedious work, and has a tendency to clutter your code. Additionally, Windows typically comes with a standard OpenGL `gl.h` file that also conforms to OpenGL 1.1. The OpenGL wiki states that Microsoft has no plans to ever update the `gl.h` and `opengl32.lib` that come with their compilers. Thankfully, others have provided libraries that manage all of this for us by transparently providing the needed function pointers, while also exposing the needed functionality in header files. There are several libraries available that provide this kind of support. One of the oldest and most common is **GLEW (OpenGL Extension Wrangler)**. However, there are a few serious issues with GLEW that might make it less desirable, and insufficient for my purposes when writing this book. First, at time of writing, it doesn't yet support core profiles properly, and for this book, I want to focus only on the latest non-deprecated functionality. Second, it provides one large header file that includes everything from all versions of OpenGL. It might be preferable to have a more streamlined header file that only includes functions that we might use. Finally, GLEW is distributed as a library that needs to be compiled separately and linked into our project. It is often preferable to have a loader that can be included into a project simply by adding the source files and compiling them directly into our executable, avoiding the need to support another link-time dependency.

In this recipe, we'll use the **OpenGL Loader Generator** (GLLoadGen), available from `https://bitbucket.org/alfonse/glloadgen/wiki/Home`. This very flexible and efficient library solves all three of the issues described in the previous paragraph. It supports core profiles and it can generate a header that includes only the needed functionality, and also generates just a couple of files (a source file and a header) that we can add directly into our project.

Getting ready

To use GLLoadGen, you'll need **Lua**. Lua is a lightweight embeddable scripting language that is available for nearly all platforms. Binaries are available at `http://luabinaries.sourceforge.net`, and a fully packaged install for Windows (LuaForWindows) is available at:

`https://code.google.com/p/luaforwindows`

Download the GLLoadGen distribution from: `https://bitbucket.org/alfonse/glloadgen/downloads`. The distribution is compressed using 7zip, which is not widely installed, so you may need to install a 7zip utility, available at `http://7-zip.org/`. Extract the distribution to a convenient location on your hard drive. Since GLLoadGen is written in Lua, there's nothing to compile, once the distribution is uncompressed, you're ready to go.

How to do it...

The first step is to generate the header and source files for the OpenGL version and profile of choice. For this example, we'll generate files for an OpenGL 4.3 core profile. We can then copy the files into our project and compile them directly alongside our code:

1. To generate the header and source files, navigate to the GLLoadGen distribution directory, and run GLLoadGen with the following arguments:

```
lua LoadGen.lua -style=pointer_c -spec=gl -version=4.3 \
-profile=core core_4_3
```

2. The previous step should generate two files: gl_core_4_3.c and gl_core_4_3.h. Move these files into your project and include gl_core_4_3.c in your build. Within your program code, you can include the gl_core_4_3.h file whenever you need access to the OpenGL functions. However, in order to initialize the function pointers, you need to make sure to call a function to do so. The needed function is called ogl_LoadFunctions. Somewhere just after the GL context is created (typically in an initialization function), and before any OpenGL functions are called, use the following code:

```
int loaded = ogl_LoadFunctions();
if (loaded == ogl_LOAD_FAILED) {
  //Destroy the context and abort
  return;
}

int num_failed = loaded - ogl_LOAD_SUCCEEDED;
printf("Number of functions that failed to load: %i.\n",
    num_failed);
```

That's all there is to it!

How it works...

The lua command in step 1 generates a pair of files, that is; a header and a source file. The header provides prototypes for all of the selected OpenGL functions and redefines them as function pointers, and defines all of the OpenGL constants as well. The source file provides initialization code for the function pointers as well as some other utility functions. We can include the gl_core_4_3.h header file wherever we need prototypes for OpenGL functions, so all function entry points are available at compile time. At run time, the ogl_LoadFunctions() function will initialize all available function pointers. If some functions fail to load, the number of failures can be determined by the subtraction operation shown in step 2. If a function is not available in the selected OpenGL version, the code may not compile, because only function prototypes for the selected OpenGL version and profile are available in the header (depending on how it was generated).

The command line arguments available to GLLoadGen are fully documented here: `https://bitbucket.org/alfonse/glloadgen/wiki/Command_Line_Options`. The previous example shows the most commonly used setup, but there's a good amount of flexibility built into this tool.

Now that we have generated this source/header pair, we no longer have any dependency on `GLLoadGen` and our program can be compiled without it. This is a significant advantage over tools such as GLEW.

There's more...

`GLLoadGen` includes a few additional features that are quite useful. We can generate more C++ friendly code, manage extensions, and generate files that work without the need to call an initialization function.

Generating a C++ loader

GLLoadGen supports generation of C++ header/source files as well. This can be selected via the `-style` parameter. For example, to generate C++ files, use `-style=pointer_cpp` as in the following example:

```
lua LoadGen.lua -style=pointer_cpp -spec=gl -version=4.3 \
-profile=core core_4_3
```

This will generate `gl_core_4_3.cpp` and `gl_core_4_3.hpp`. This places all OpenGL functions and constants within the `gl::` namespace, and removes their `gl` (or `GL`) prefix. For example, to call the function `glBufferData`, you might use the following syntax.

```
gl::BufferData(gl::ARRAY_BUFFER, size, data, gl::STATIC_DRAW);
```

Loading the function pointers is also slightly different. The return value is an object rather than just a simple integer and `LoadFunctions` is in the `gl::sys` namespace.

```
gl::exts::LoadTest didLoad = gl::sys::LoadFunctions();

if(!didLoad) {
    // Clean up (destroy the context) and abort.
    return;
}

printf("Number of functions that failed to load: %i.\n",
  didLoad.GetNumMissing());
```

No-load styles

GLLoadGen supports the automatic initialization of function pointers. This can be selected using the `noload_c` or `noload_cpp` options for the `style` parameter. With these styles, there is no need to call the initialization function `ogl_LoadFunctions`. The pointers are loaded automatically, the first time a function is called. This can be convenient, but there's very little overhead to loading them all at initialization.

Using Extensions

GLLoadGen does not automatically support extensions. Instead, you need to ask for them with command line parameters. For example, to request `ARB_texture_view` and `ARB_vertex_attrib_binding` extensions, you might use the following command.

```
lua LoadGen.lua -style=pointer_c -spec=gl -version=3.3 \
-profile=core core_3_3 \
-exts ARB_texture_view ARB_vertex_attrib_binding
```

The `-exts` parameter is a space-separated list of extensions. GLLoadGen also provides the ability to load a list of extensions from a file (via the `-extfile` parameter) and provides some common extension files on the website.

You can also use GLLoadGen to check for the existence of an extension at run-time. For details, see the GLLoadGen wiki.

See also

▸ GLEW, an older, and more common loader and extension manager, available from `glew.sourceforge.net`.

Using GLM for mathematics

Mathematics is core to all of computer graphics. In earlier versions, OpenGL provided support for managing coordinate transformations and projections using the standard matrix stacks (`GL_MODELVIEW` and `GL_PROJECTION`). In recent versions of core OpenGL however, all of the functionality supporting the matrix stacks has been removed. Therefore, it is up to us to provide our own support for the usual transformation and projection matrices, and then to pass them into our shaders. Of course, we could write our own matrix and vector classes to manage this, but some might prefer to use a ready-made, robust library.

One such library is **GLM (OpenGL Mathematics)** written by *Christophe Riccio*. Its design is based on the GLSL specification, so the syntax is very similar to the mathematical support in GLSL. For experienced GLSL programmers, this makes GLM very easy to use and familiar. Additionally, it provides extensions that include functionality similar to some of the much-missed OpenGL functions such as `glOrtho`, `glRotate`, or `gluLookAt`.

Getting ready

Since GLM is a header-only library, installation is simple. Download the latest GLM distribution from `http://glm.g-truc.net`. Then, unzip the archive file, and copy the `glm` directory contained inside to anywhere in your compiler's include path.

How to do it...

To use the GLM libraries, it is simply a matter of including the core header file, and headers for any extensions. For this example, we'll include the matrix transform extension as follows:

```
#include <glm/glm.hpp>
#include <glm/gtc/matrix_transform.hpp>
```

Then the GLM classes are available in the `glm` namespace. The following is an example of how you might go about making use of some of them:

```
glm::vec4 position = glm::vec4( 1.0f, 0.0f, 0.0f, 1.0f );
glm::mat4 view = glm::lookAt( glm::vec3(0.0,0.0,5.0),
      glm::vec3(0.0,0.0,0.0),
      glm::vec3(0.0,1.0,0.0) );
glm::mat4 model(1.0f);   // The identity matrix
model = glm::rotate( model, 90.0f, glm::vec3(0.0f,1.0f,0.0) );
glm::mat4 mv = view * model;
glm::vec4 transformed = mv * position;
```

How it works...

The GLM library is a header-only library. All of the implementation is included within the header files. It doesn't require separate compilation and you don't need to link your program to it. Just placing the header files in your include path is all that's required!

The previous example first creates a `vec4` (four coordinate vector) representing a position. Then it creates a 4 x 4 view matrix by using the `glm::lookAt` function. This works in a similar fashion to the old `gluLookAt` function. Here, we set the camera's location at (0, 0, 5), looking towards the origin, with the "up" direction in the direction of the y-axis. We then go on to create the model matrix by first storing the identity matrix in the variable `model` (via the single argument constructor), and multiplying by a rotation matrix using the `glm::rotate` function. The multiplication here is implicitly done by the `glm::rotate` function. It multiplies its first parameter by the rotation matrix (on the right) that is generated by the function. The second parameter is the angle of rotation (in degrees), and the third parameter is the axis of rotation. Since before this statement, `model` is the identity matrix, the net result is that `model` becomes a rotation matrix of 90 degrees around the y-axis.

Finally, we create our modelview matrix (`mv`) by multiplying the `view` and `model` variables, and then using the combined matrix to transform the position. Note that the multiplication operator has been overloaded to behave in the expected way.

There's more...

It is not recommended to import all of the GLM namespace by using the following command:

```
using namespace glm;
```

This will most likely cause a number of namespace clashes. Instead, it is preferable to import symbols one at a time, as needed. For example:

```
#include <glm/glm.hpp>
using glm::vec3;
using glm::mat4;
```

Using the GLM types as input to OpenGL

GLM supports directly passing a GLM type to OpenGL using one of the OpenGL vector functions (with the suffix `v`). For example, to pass a `mat4` named `proj` to OpenGL we can use the following code:

```
glm::mat4 proj = glm::perspective( viewAngle, aspect, nearDist,
    farDist );
glUniformMatrix4fv(location, 1, GL_FALSE, &proj[0][0]);
```

See also

▶ The Qt SDK includes many classes for vector/matrix mathematics, and is another good option if you're already using Qt

▶ The GLM website `http://glm.g-truc.net` has additional documentation and examples

Determining the GLSL and OpenGL version

In order to support a wide range of systems, it is essential to be able to query for the supported OpenGL and GLSL version of the current driver. It is quite simple to do so, and there are two main functions involved: `glGetString` and `glGetIntegerv`.

How to do it...

The code shown as follows will print the version information to `stdout`:

```
const GLubyte *renderer = glGetString( GL_RENDERER );
const GLubyte *vendor = glGetString( GL_VENDOR );
const GLubyte *version = glGetString( GL_VERSION );
const GLubyte *glslVersion =
        glGetString( GL_SHADING_LANGUAGE_VERSION );

GLint major, minor;
glGetIntegerv(GL_MAJOR_VERSION, &major);
glGetIntegerv(GL_MINOR_VERSION, &minor);

printf("GL Vendor            : %s\n", vendor);
printf("GL Renderer          : %s\n", renderer);
printf("GL Version (string)  : %s\n", version);
printf("GL Version (integer) : %d.%d\n", major, minor);
printf("GLSL Version         : %s\n", glslVersion);
```

How it works...

Note that there are two different ways to retrieve the OpenGL version: using `glGetString` and `glGetIntegerv`. The former can be useful for providing readable output, but may not be as convenient for programmatically checking the version because of the need to parse the string. The string provided by `glGetString(GL_VERSION)` should always begin with the major and minor versions separated by a dot, however, the minor version could be followed with a vendor-specific build number. Additionally, the rest of the string can contain additional vendor-specific information and may also include information about the selected profile (see the *Introduction* section of this chapter). It is important to note that the use of `glGetIntegerv` to query for version information requires OpenGL 3.0 or greater.

The queries for `GL_VENDOR` and `GL_RENDERER` provide additional information about the OpenGL driver. The call `glGetString(GL_VENDOR)` returns the company responsible for the OpenGL implementation. The call to `glGetString(GL_RENDERER)` provides the name of the renderer which is specific to a particular hardware platform (such as the ATI Radeon HD 5600 Series). Note that both of these do not vary from release to release, so can be used to determine the current platform.

Of more importance to us in the context of this book is the call to `glGetString( GL_SHADING_LANGUAGE_VERSION)` which provides the supported GLSL version number. This string should begin with the major and minor version numbers separated by a period, but similar to the `GL_VERSION` query, may include other vendor-specific information.

There's more...

It is often useful to query for the supported extensions of the current OpenGL implementation. In versions prior to OpenGL 3.0, one could retrieve a full, space separated list of extension names with the following code:

```
GLubyte *extensions = glGetString(GL_EXTENSIONS);
```

The string that is returned can be extremely long and parsing it can be susceptible to error if not done carefully.

In OpenGL 3.0, a new technique was introduced, and the previous functionality was deprecated (and finally removed in 3.1). Extension names are now indexed and can be individually queried by index. We use the `glGetStringi` variant for this. For example, to get the name of the extension stored at index i, we use: `glGetStringi(GL_EXTENSIONS, i)`. To print a list of all extensions, we could use the following code:

```
GLint nExtensions;
glGetIntegerv(GL_NUM_EXTENSIONS, &nExtensions);

for( int i = 0; i < nExtensions; i++ )
    printf("%s\n", glGetStringi( GL_EXTENSIONS, i ) );
```

See also

▶ The GLLoadGen tool has additional support for querying version and extension information. Refer to the *Using a function loader to access the latest OpenGL functionality* recipe and the GLLoadGen website.

Compiling a shader

To get started, we need to know how to compile our GLSL shaders. The GLSL compiler is built right into the OpenGL library, and shaders can only be compiled within the context of a running OpenGL program. There is currently no external tool for precompiling GLSL shaders and/or shader programs.

 Recently, OpenGL 4.1 added the ability to save compiled shader programs to a file, enabling OpenGL programs to avoid the overhead of shader compilation by loading pre-compiled shader programs.

Compiling a shader involves creating a shader object, providing the source code (as a string or set of strings) to the shader object, and asking the shader object to compile the code. The process is roughly represented by the following diagram:

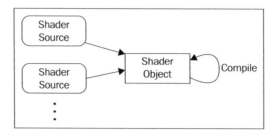

Getting ready

To compile a shader, we'll need a basic example to work with. Let's start with the following simple vertex shader. Save it in a file named `basic.vert`.

```
#version 430

in vec3 VertexPosition;
in vec3 VertexColor;

out vec3 Color;

void main()
{
    Color = VertexColor;
    gl_Position = vec4( VertexPosition, 1.0 );
}
```

In case you're curious about what this code does, it works as a "pass-through" shader. It takes the input attributes `VertexPosition` and `VertexColor` and passes them along to the fragment shader via the output variables `gl_Position` and `Color`.

Next, we'll need to build a basic shell for an OpenGL program using a window toolkit that supports OpenGL. Examples of cross-platform toolkits include GLFW, GLUT, FLTK, Qt, or wxWidgets. Throughout this text, I'll make the assumption that you can create a basic OpenGL program with your favorite toolkit. Virtually all toolkits have a hook for an initialization function, a resize callback (called upon resizing of the window), and a drawing callback (called for each window refresh). For the purposes of this recipe, we need a program that creates and initializes an OpenGL context, it need not do anything other than display an empty OpenGL window. Note that you'll also need to load the OpenGL function pointers (refer to the *Using a function loader to access the latest OpenGL functionality* recipe).

Finally, load the shader source code into a character array named `shaderCode`. Don't forget to add the null character at the end! This example assumes that the variable `shaderCode` points to an array of `GLchar` that is properly terminated by a null character.

How to do it...

To compile a shader, use the following steps:

1. Create the shader object as follows:

```
GLuint vertShader = glCreateShader( GL_VERTEX_SHADER );
if( 0 == vertShader )
{
  fprintf(stderr, "Error creating vertex shader.\n");
  exit(EXIT_FAILURE);
}
```

2. Copy the source code (perhaps from multiple locations) into the shader object:

```
const GLchar * shaderCode = loadShaderAsString("basic.vert");
const GLchar* codeArray[] = {shaderCode};
glShaderSource( vertShader, 1, codeArray, NULL );
```

3. Compile the shader:

```
glCompileShader( vertShader );
```

4. Verify the compilation status:

```
GLint result;
glGetShaderiv( vertShader, GL_COMPILE_STATUS, &result );
if( GL_FALSE == result )
{
  fprintf(stderr, "Vertex shader compilation failed!\n");

  GLint logLen;
  glGetShaderiv(vertShader, GL_INFO_LOG_LENGTH, &logLen);

  if( logLen > 0 )
  {
    char * log = new char[logLen];

    GLsizei written;
    glGetShaderInfoLog(vertShader, logLen, &written, log);

    fprintf(stderr, "Shader log:\n%s", log);
    delete [] log;
  }
}
```

How it works...

The first step is to create the shader object using the `glCreateShader` function. The argument is the type of shader, and can be one of the following: `GL_VERTEX_SHADER`, `GL_FRAGMENT_SHADER`, `GL_GEOMETRY_SHADER`, `GL_TESS_EVALUATION_SHADER`, `GL_TESS_CONTROL_SHADER`, or (as of version 4.3) `GL_COMPUTE_SHADER`. In this case, since we are compiling a vertex shader, we use `GL_VERTEX_SHADER`. This function returns the value used for referencing the vertex shader object, sometimes called the object "handle". We store that value in the variable `vertShader`. If an error occurs while creating the shader object, this function will return 0, so we check for that and if it occurs, we print an appropriate message and terminate.

Following the creation of the shader object, we load the source code into the shader object using the function `glShaderSource`. This function is designed to accept an array of strings (as opposed to just a single one) in order to support the option of compiling multiple sources (files, strings) at once. So before we call `glShaderSource`, we place a pointer to our source code into an array named `sourceArray`. The first argument to `glShaderSource` is the handle to the shader object. The second is the number of source code strings that are contained in the array. The third argument is a pointer to an array of source code strings. The final argument is an array of `GLint` values that contains the length of each source code string in the previous argument. In the previous code, we pass a value of `NULL`, which indicates that each source code string is terminated by a null character. If our source code strings were not null terminated then this argument must be a valid array. Note that once this function returns, the source code has been copied into OpenGL internal memory, so the memory used to store the source code can be freed.

The next step is to compile the source code for the shader. We do this by simply calling `glCompileShader`, and passing the handle to the shader that is to be compiled. Of course, depending on the correctness of the source code, the compilation may fail, so the next step is to check whether or not the compilation was successful.

We can query for the compilation status by calling `glGetShaderiv`, which is a function for querying the attributes of a shader object. In this case we are interested in the compilation status, so we use `GL_COMPILE_STATUS` as the second argument. The first argument is of course the handle to the shader object, and the third argument is a pointer to an integer where the status will be stored. The function provides a value of either `GL_TRUE` or `GL_FALSE` in the third argument indicating whether or not the compilation was successful.

If the compile status is `GL_FALSE`, then we can query for the shader log, which will provide additional details about the failure. We do so by first querying for the length of the log by calling `glGetShaderiv` again with a value of `GL_INFO_LOG_LENGTH`. This provides the length of the log in the variable `logLen`. Note that this includes the null termination character. We then allocate space for the log, and retrieve the log by calling `glGetShaderInfoLog`. The first parameter is the handle to the shader object, the second is the size of the character buffer for storing the log, the third argument is a pointer to an integer where the number of characters actually written (excluding the null terminator character) will be stored, and the fourth argument is a pointer to the character buffer for storing the log itself. Once the log is retrieved, we print it to `stderr` and free its memory space.

There's more...

The previous example only demonstrated compiling a vertex shader. There are several other types of shaders including fragment, geometry, and tessellation shaders. The technique for compiling is nearly identical for each shader type. The only significant difference is the argument to `glCreateShader`.

It is also important to note that shader compilation is only the first step. To create a working shader program, we often have at least two shaders to compile, and then the shaders must be linked together into a shader program object. We'll see the steps involved in linking in the next recipe.

Deleting a Shader Object

Shader objects can be deleted when no longer needed by calling `glDeleteShader`. This frees the memory used by the shader and invalidates its handle. Note that if a shader object is already attached to a program object (refer to the *Linking a shader program* recipe), it will not be immediately deleted, but flagged for deletion when it is detached from the program object.

See also

▶   The *Linking a shader program* recipe

Linking a shader program

Once we have compiled our shaders and before we can actually install them into the OpenGL pipeline, we need to link them together into a shader program. Among other things, the linking step involves making the connections between input variables from one shader to output variables of another, and making the connections between the input/output variables of a shader to appropriate locations in the OpenGL environment.

Linking involves steps that are similar to those involved in compiling a shader. We attach each shader object to a new shader program object and then tell the shader program object to link (making sure that the shader objects are compiled before linking).

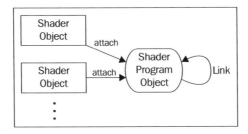

Getting ready

For this recipe, we'll assume that you've already compiled two shader objects whose handles are stored in the variables `vertShader` and `fragShader`.

For this and a few other recipes in this Chapter, we'll use the following source code for the fragment shader:

```
#version 430

in vec3 Color;

out vec4 FragColor;

void main() {
  FragColor = vec4(Color, 1.0);
}
```

For the vertex shader, we'll use the source code from the previous recipe, *Compiling a shader*.

How to do it...

In our OpenGL initialization function, and after the compilation of shader objects referred to by `vertShader` and `fragShader`, use the following steps:

1. Create the program object using the following code:

    ```
    GLuint programHandle = glCreateProgram();
    if( 0 == programHandle )
    {
      fprintf(stderr, "Error creating program object.\n");
      exit(1);
    }
    ```

2. Attach the shaders to the program object as follows:

    ```
    glAttachShader( programHandle, vertShader );
    glAttachShader( programHandle, fragShader );
    ```

3. Link the program:

    ```
    glLinkProgram( programHandle );
    ```

4. Verify the link status:

    ```
    GLint status;
    glGetProgramiv( programHandle, GL_LINK_STATUS, &status );
    if( GL_FALSE == status ) {

      fprintf( stderr, "Failed to link shader program!\n" );

      GLint logLen;
    ```

```
glGetProgramiv(programHandle, GL_INFO_LOG_LENGTH,
        &logLen);
if( logLen > 0 )
{
  char * log = new char[logLen];
  GLsizei written;
  glGetProgramInfoLog(programHandle, logLen, &written, log);
  fprintf(stderr, "Program log: \n%s", log);
  delete [] log;
}
}
```

5. If linking is successful, install the program into the OpenGL pipeline:

```
else
{
  glUseProgram( programHandle );
}
```

How it works...

We start by calling `glCreateProgram` to create an empty program object. This function returns a handle to the program object, which we store in a variable named `programHandle`. If an error occurs with program creation, the function will return 0. We check for that, and if it occurs, we print an error message and exit.

Next, we attach each shader to the program object using `glAttachShader`. The first argument is the handle to the program object, and the second is the handle to the shader object to be attached.

Then, we link the program by calling `glLinkProgram`, providing the handle to the program object as the only argument. As with compilation, we check for the success or failure of the link, with the subsequent query.

We check the status of the link by calling `glGetProgramiv`. Similar to `glGetShaderiv`, `glGetProgramiv` allows us to query various attributes of the shader program. In this case, we ask for the status of the link by providing `GL_LINK_STATUS` as the second argument. The status is returned in the location pointed to by the third argument, in this case named `status`.

The link status is either `GL_TRUE` or `GL_FALSE` indicating the success or failure of the link. If the value of status is `GL_FALSE`, we retrieve and display the program information log, which should contain additional information and error messages. The program log is retrieved by the call to `glGetProgramInfoLog`. The first argument is the handle to the program object, the second is the size of the buffer to contain the log, the third is a pointer to a `GLsizei` variable where the number of bytes written to the buffer will be stored (excluding the null terminator), and the fourth is a pointer to the buffer that will store the log. The buffer can be allocated based on the size returned by the call to `glGetProgramiv` with the parameter `GL_INFO_LOG_LENGTH`. The string that is provided in `log` will be properly null terminated.

Finally, if the link is successful, we install the program into the OpenGL pipeline by calling `glUseProgram`, providing the handle to the program as the argument.

With the simple fragment shader from this recipe and the vertex shader from the previous recipe compiled, linked, and installed into the OpenGL pipeline, we have a complete OpenGL pipeline and are ready to begin rendering. Drawing a triangle and supplying different values for the `Color` attribute yields an image of a multi-colored triangle where the vertices are red, green, and blue, and inside the triangle, the three colors are interpolated, causing a blending of colors throughout.

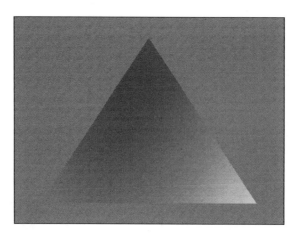

There's more...

You can use multiple shader programs within a single OpenGL program. They can be swapped in and out of the OpenGL pipeline by calling `glUseProgram` to select the desired program.

Deleting a Shader program

If a program is no longer needed, it can be deleted from OpenGL memory by calling `glDeleteProgram`, providing the program handle as the only argument. This invalidates the handle and frees the memory used by the program. Note that if the program object is currently in use, it will not be immediately deleted, but will be flagged for deletion when it is no longer in use.

Also, the deletion of a shader program detaches the shader objects that were attached to the program but does not delete them unless those shader objects have already been flagged for deletion by a previous call to `glDeleteShader`.

See also

▸ The *Compiling a shader* recipe

Sending data to a shader using vertex attributes and vertex buffer objects

The vertex shader is invoked once per vertex. Its main job is to process the data associated with the vertex, and pass it (and possibly other information) along to the next stage of the pipeline. In order to give our vertex shader something to work with, we must have some way of providing (per-vertex) input to the shader. Typically, this includes the vertex position, normal vector, and texture coordinates (among other things). In earlier versions of OpenGL (prior to 3.0), each piece of vertex information had a specific "channel" in the pipeline. It was provided to the shaders using functions such as `glVertex`, `glTexCoord`, and `glNormal` (or within client vertex arrays using `glVertexPointer`, `glTexCoordPointer`, or `glNormalPointer`). The shader would then access these values via built-in variables such as `gl_Vertex` and `gl_Normal`. This functionality was deprecated in OpenGL 3.0 and later removed. Instead, vertex information must now be provided using *generic vertex attributes*, usually in conjunction with (vertex) *buffer objects*. The programmer is now free to define an arbitrary set of per-vertex attributes to provide as input to the vertex shader. For example, in order to implement normal mapping, the programmer might decide that position, normal vector and tangent vector should be provided along with each vertex. With OpenGL 4, it's easy to define this as the set of input attributes. This gives us a great deal of flexibility to define our vertex information in any way that is appropriate for our application, but may require a bit of getting used to for those of us who are used to the old way of doing things.

In the vertex shader, the per-vertex input attributes are defined by using the GLSL qualifier `in`. For example, to define a 3-component vector input attribute named `VertexColor`, we use the following code:

```
in vec3 VertexColor;
```

Of course, the data for this attribute must be supplied by the OpenGL program. To do so, we make use of vertex buffer objects. The buffer object contains the values for the input attribute. In the main OpenGL program we make the connection between the buffer and the input attribute and define how to "step through" the data. Then, when rendering, OpenGL pulls data for the input attribute from the buffer for each invocation of the vertex shader.

For this recipe, we'll draw a single triangle. Our vertex attributes will be position and color. We'll use a fragment shader to blend the colors of each vertex across the triangle to produce an image similar to the one shown as follows. The vertices of the triangle are red, green, and blue, and the interior of the triangle has those three colors blended together. The colors may not be visible in the printed text, but the variation in the shade should indicate the blending.

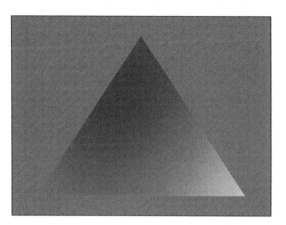

Getting ready

We'll start with an empty OpenGL program, and the following shaders:

The vertex shader (`basic.vert`):

```
#version 430

layout (location=0) in vec3 VertexPosition;
layout (location=1) in vec3 VertexColor;

out vec3 Color;

void main()
{
  Color = VertexColor;

  gl_Position = vec4(VertexPosition,1.0);
}
```

Attributes are the input variables to a vertex shader. In the previous code, there are two input attributes: `VertexPosition` and `VertexColor`. They are specified using the GLSL keyword `in`. Don't worry about the `layout` prefix, we'll discuss that later. Our main OpenGL program needs to supply the data for these two attributes for each vertex. We will do so by mapping our polygon data to these variables.

It also has one output variable named `Color`, which is sent to the fragment shader. In this case, `Color` is just an unchanged copy of `VertexColor`. Also, note that the attribute `VertexPosition` is simply expanded and passed along to the built-in output variable `gl_Position` for further processing.

The fragment shader (`basic.frag`):

```
#version 430

in vec3 Color;

out vec4 FragColor;

void main() {
   FragColor = vec4(Color, 1.0);
}
```

There is just one input variable for this shader, `Color`. This links to the corresponding output variable in the vertex shader, and will contain a value that has been interpolated across the triangle based on the values at the vertices. We simply expand and copy this color to the output variable `FragColor` (more about fragment shader output variables in later recipes).

Write code to compile and link these shaders into a shader program (see "Compiling a shader" and "Linking a shader program"). In the following code, I'll assume that the handle to the shader program is `programHandle`.

How to do it...

Use the following steps to set up your buffer objects and render the triangle:

1. Create a global (or private instance) variable to hold our handle to the vertex array object:

   ```
   GLuint vaoHandle;
   ```

2. Within the initialization function, we create and populate the vertex buffer objects for each attribute:

   ```
   float positionData[] = {
           -0.8f, -0.8f, 0.0f,
           0.8f, -0.8f, 0.0f,
           0.0f,  0.8f, 0.0f };
   float colorData[] = {
           1.0f, 0.0f, 0.0f,
           0.0f, 1.0f, 0.0f,
           0.0f, 0.0f, 1.0f };
   ```

```
// Create and populate the buffer objects
GLuint vboHandles[2];
glGenBuffers(2, vboHandles);
GLuint positionBufferHandle = vboHandles[0];
GLuint colorBufferHandle = vboHandles[1];

// Populate the position buffer
glBindBuffer(GL_ARRAY_BUFFER, positionBufferHandle);
glBufferData(GL_ARRAY_BUFFER, 9 * sizeof(float),
      positionData, GL_STATIC_DRAW);

// Populate the color buffer
glBindBuffer(GL_ARRAY_BUFFER, colorBufferHandle);
glBufferData(GL_ARRAY_BUFFER, 9 * sizeof(float), colorData,
      GL_STATIC_DRAW);
```

3. Create and define a vertex array object, which defines the relationship between the buffers and the input attributes. (See "There's more..." for an alternate way to do this that is valid for OpenGL 4.3 and later.)

```
// Create and set-up the vertex array object
glGenVertexArrays( 1, &vaoHandle );
glBindVertexArray(vaoHandle);

// Enable the vertex attribute arrays
glEnableVertexAttribArray(0);  // Vertex position
glEnableVertexAttribArray(1);  // Vertex color

// Map index 0 to the position buffer
glBindBuffer(GL_ARRAY_BUFFER, positionBufferHandle);
glVertexAttribPointer(0, 3, GL_FLOAT, GL_FALSE, 0, NULL);

// Map index 1 to the color buffer
glBindBuffer(GL_ARRAY_BUFFER, colorBufferHandle);
glVertexAttribPointer(1, 3, GL_FLOAT, GL_FALSE, 0, NULL);
```

4. In the render function, we bind to the vertex array object and call `glDrawArrays` to initiate rendering:

```
glBindVertexArray(vaoHandle);
glDrawArrays(GL_TRIANGLES, 0, 3 );
```

How it works...

Vertex attributes are the input variables to our vertex shader. In the given vertex shader, our two attributes are `VertexPosition` and `VertexColor`. The main OpenGL program refers to vertex attributes by associating each (active) input variable with a generic attribute index. These generic indices are simply integers between 0 and `GL_MAX_VERTEX_ATTRIBS` − 1. We can specify the relationship between these indices and the attributes using the `layout` qualifier. For example, in our vertex shader, we use the layout qualifier to assign `VertexPosition` to attribute index 0 and `VertexColor` to attribute index 1.

```
layout (location = 0) in vec3 VertexPosition;
layout (location = 1) in vec3 VertexColor;
```

We refer to the vertex attributes in our OpenGL code, by referring to the corresponding generic vertex attribute index.

It is not strictly necessary to explicitly specify the mappings between attribute variables and generic attribute indexes, because OpenGL will automatically map active vertex attributes to generic indexes when the program is linked. We could then query for the mappings and determine the indexes that correspond to the shader's input variables. It may be somewhat more clear however, to explicitly specify the mapping as we do in this example.

The first step involves setting up a pair of buffer objects to store our position and color data. As with most OpenGL objects, we start by creating the objects and acquiring handles to the two buffers by calling `glGenBuffers`. We then assign each handle to a separate descriptive variable to make the following code more clear.

For each buffer object, we first bind the buffer to the `GL_ARRAY_BUFFER` binding point by calling `glBindBuffer`. The first argument to `glBindBuffer` is the target binding point. In this case, since the data is essentially a generic array, we use `GL_ARRAY_BUFFER`. Examples of other kinds of targets (such as `GL_UNIFORM_BUFFER`, or `GL_ELEMENT_ARRAY_BUFFER`) will be seen in later examples. Once our buffer object is bound, we can populate the buffer with our vertex/color data by calling `glBufferData`. The second and third arguments to this function are the size of the array and a pointer to the array containing the data. Let's focus on the first and last arguments. The first argument indicates the target buffer object. The data provided in the third argument is copied into the buffer that is bound to this binding point. The last argument is one that gives OpenGL a hint about how the data will be used so that it can determine how best to manage the buffer internally. For full details about this argument, take a look into the OpenGL documentation. In our case, the data is specified once, will not be modified, and will be used many times for drawing operations, so this usage pattern best corresponds to the value `GL_STATIC_DRAW`.

Now that we have set up our buffer objects, we tie them together into a **Vertex Array Object** (**VAO**). The VAO contains information about the connections between the data in our buffers and the input vertex attributes. We create a VAO using the function `glGenVertexArrays`. This gives us a handle to our new object, which we store in the (global) variable `vaoHandle`. Then we enable the generic vertex attribute indexes 0 and 1 by calling `glEnableVertexAttribArray`. Doing so indicates that that the values for the attributes will be accessed and used for rendering.

The next step makes the connection between the buffer objects and the generic vertex attribute indexes.

```
// Map index 0 to the position buffer
glBindBuffer(GL_ARRAY_BUFFER, positionBufferHandle);
glVertexAttribPointer( 0, 3, GL_FLOAT, GL_FALSE, 0, NULL );
```

First we bind the buffer object to the `GL_ARRAY_BUFFER` binding point, then we call `glVertexAttribPointer`, which tells OpenGL which generic index that the data should be used with, the format of the data stored in the buffer object, and where it is located within the buffer object that is bound to the `GL_ARRAY_BUFFER` binding point. The first argument is the generic attribute index. The second is the number of components per vertex attribute (1, 2, 3, or 4). In this case, we are providing 3-dimensional data, so we want 3 components per vertex. The third argument is the data type of each component in the buffer. The fourth is a Boolean which specifies whether or not the data should be automatically normalized (mapped to a range of [-1, 1] for signed integral values or [0, 1] for unsigned integral values). The fifth argument is the stride, which indicates the byte offset between consecutive attributes. Since our data is tightly packed, we can use a value of zero. The last argument is a pointer, which is not treated as a pointer! Instead, its value is interpreted as a byte offset from the beginning of the buffer to the first attribute in the buffer. In this case, there is no additional data in either buffer before the first element, so we use a value of zero.

The `glVertexAttribPointer` function stores (in the VAO's state) a pointer to the buffer currently bound to the `GL_ARRAY_BUFFER` binding point. When another buffer is bound to that binding point, it does not change the value of the pointer.

The VAO stores all of the OpenGL state related to the relationship between buffer objects and the generic vertex attributes, as well as the information about the format of the data in the buffer objects. This allows us to quickly return all of this state when rendering. The VAO is an extremely important concept, but can be tricky to understand. It's important to remember that the VAO's state is primarily associated with the enabled attributes and their connection to buffer objects. It doesn't necessarily keep track of buffer bindings. For example, it doesn't remember what is bound to the `GL_ARRAY_BUFFER` binding point. We only bind to this point in order to set up the pointers via `glVertexAttribPointer`.

Once we have the VAO set up (a one-time operation), we can issue a draw command to render our image. In our render function, we clear the color buffer using `glClear`, bind to the vertex array object, and call `glDrawArrays` to draw our triangle. The function `glDrawArrays` initiates rendering of primitives by stepping through the buffers for each enabled attribute array, and passing the data down the pipeline to our vertex shader. The first argument is the render mode (in this case we are drawing triangles), the second is the starting index in the enabled arrays, and the third argument is the number of indices to be rendered (3 vertexes for a single triangle).

To summarize, we followed these steps:

1. Make sure to specify the generic vertex attribute indexes for each attribute in the vertex shader using the `layout` qualifier.

2. Create and populate the buffer objects for each attribute.

3. Create and define the vertex array object by calling `glVertexAttribPointer` while the appropriate buffer is bound.

4. When rendering, bind to the vertex array object and call `glDrawArrays`, or other appropriate rendering function (e.g. `glDrawElements`).

There's more...

In the following, we'll discuss some details, extensions, and alternatives to the previous technique.

Separate attribute format

With OpenGL 4.3, we have an alternate (arguably better) way of specifying the vertex array object state (attribute format, enabled attributes, and buffers). In the previous example, the `glVertexAttribPointer` function does two important things. First, it indirectly specifies which buffer contains the data for the attribute, which is the buffer currently bound (at the time of the call) to `GL_ARRAY_BUFFER`. Secondly, it specifies the format of that data (type, offset, stride, and so on). It is arguably clearer to separate these two concerns into their own functions. This is exactly what has been implemented in OpenGL 4.3. For example, to implement the same functionality as in step 3 of the previous *How to do it...* section, we would use the following code:

```
glGenVertexArrays(1, &vaoHandle);
glBindVertexArray(vaoHandle);
glEnableVertexArray(0);
glEnableVertexArray(1);

glBindVertexBuffer(0, positionBufferHandle, 0, sizeof(GLfloat)*3);
glBindVertexBuffer(1, colorBufferHandle, 0, sizeof(GLfloat)*3);
```

```
glVertexAttribFormat(0, 3, GL_FLOAT, GL_FALSE, 0);
glVertexAttribBinding(0, 0);
glVertexAttribFormat(1, 3, GL_FLOAT, GL_FALSE, 0);
glVertexAttribBinding(1, 1);
```

The first four lines of the previous code are exactly the same as in the first example. We create and bind to the VAO, then enable attributes 0 and 1. Next, we bind our two buffers to two different indexes within the vertex buffer binding point using `glBindVertexBuffer`. Note that we're no longer using `GL_ARRAY_BUFFER` binding point. Instead, we now have a new binding point specifically for vertex buffers. This binding point has several indexes (usually from 0 - 15), so we can bind multiple buffers to this point. The first argument to `glBindVertexBuffer` specifies the index within the vertex buffer binding point. Here, we bind our position buffer to index 0 and our color buffer to index 1.

 Note that the indexes within the vertex buffer binding point need not be the same as the attribute locations.

The other arguments to `glBindVertexBuffer` are as follows. The second argument is the buffer to be bound, the third is the offset from the beginning of the buffer to where the data begins, and the fourth is the stride, which is the distance between successive elements within the buffer. Unlike `glVertexAttribPointer`, we can't use a 0 value here for tightly packed data, because OpenGL can't determine the size of the data without more information, so we need to specify it explicitly here.

Next, we call `glVertexAttribFormat` to specify the format of the data for the attribute. Note that this time, this is decoupled from the buffer that stores the data. Instead, we're just specifying the format to expect for this attribute. The arguments are the same as the first four arguments to `glVertexAttribPointer`.

The function `glVertexAttribBinding` specifies the relationship between buffers that are bound to the vertex buffer binding point and attributes. The first argument is the attribute location, and the second is the index within the vertex buffer binding point. In this example, they are the same, but they need not be.

Also note that the buffer bindings of the vertex buffer binding point (specified by `glBindVertexBuffer`) *are* part of the VAO state, unlike the binding to `GL_ARRAY_BUFFER`, which is not.

This version is arguably more clear and easy to understand. It removes the confusing aspects of the "invisible" pointers that are managed in the VAO, and makes the relationship between attributes and buffers much more clear with `glVertexAttribBinding`. Additionally, it separates concerns that really need not be combined.

Fragment shader output

You may have noticed that I've neglected to say anything about the output variable `FragColor` in the fragment shader. This variable receives the final output color for each fragment (pixel). Like vertex input variables, this variable also needs to be associated with a proper location. Of course, we typically would like this to be linked to the back color buffer, which by default (in double buffered systems) is "color number" zero. (The relationship of the color numbers to render buffers can be changed by using `glDrawBuffers`). In this program, we are relying on the fact that the linker will automatically link our only fragment output variable to color number zero. To explicitly do so, we could (and probably should) have used a layout qualifier in the fragment shader:

```
layout (location = 0) out vec4 FragColor;
```

We are free to define multiple output variables for a fragment shader, thereby enabling us to render to multiple output buffers. This can be quite useful for specialized algorithms such as deferred rendering (see *Chapter 5, Image Processing and Screen Space Techniques*).

Specifying attribute indexes without using layout qualifiers

If you'd rather not clutter up your vertex shader code with the `layout` qualifiers (or you're using a version of OpenGL that doesn't support them), you can define the attribute indexes within the OpenGL program. We can do so by calling `glBindAttribLocation` just prior to linking the shader program. For example, we'd add the following code to the main OpenGL program just before the link step:

```
glBindAttribLocation(programHandle, 0, "VertexPosition");
glBindAttribLocation(programHandle, 1, "VertexColor");
```

This would indicate to the linker that `VertexPosition` should correspond to generic attribute index 0 and `VertexColor` to index 1.

Similarly, we can specify the color number for fragment shader output variables without using the layout qualifier. We do so by calling `glBindFragDataLocation` prior to linking the shader program:

```
glBindFragDataLocation(programHandle, 0, "FragColor");
```

This would tell the linker to bind the output variable `FragColor` to color number 0.

Using element arrays

It is often the case that we need to step through our vertex arrays in a non-linear fashion. In other words, we may want to "jump around" the data rather than just moving through it from beginning to end as we did in this example. For example, we might want to draw a cube where the vertex data consists of only eight positions (the corners of the cube). In order to draw the cube, we would need to draw 12 triangles (2 for each face), each of which consists of 3 vertices. All of the needed position data is in the original 8 positions, but to draw all the triangles, we'll need to jump around and use each position for at least three different triangles.

To jump around in our vertex arrays, we can make use of element arrays. The element array is another buffer that defines the indices used when stepping through the vertex arrays. For details on using element arrays, take a look at the function `glDrawElements` in the OpenGL documentation (`http://www.opengl.org/sdk/docs/man`).

Interleaved arrays

In this example, we used two buffers (one for color and one for position). Instead, we could have used just a single buffer and combined all of the data. In general, it is possible to combine the data for multiple attributes into a single buffer. The data for multiple attributes can be interleaved within an array, such that all of the data for a given vertex is grouped together within the buffer. Doing so just requires careful use of the `stride` argument to `glVertexAttribPointer` or `glBindVertexBuffer`. Take a look at the documentation for full details (`http://www.opengl.org/sdk/docs/man`).

The decision about when to use interleaved arrays and when to use separate arrays, is highly dependent on the situation. Interleaved arrays may bring better results due to the fact that data is accessed together and resides closer in memory (so-called locality of reference), resulting in better caching performance.

Getting a list of active vertex input attributes and locations

As covered in the previous recipe, the input variables within a vertex shader are linked to generic vertex attribute indices at the time the program is linked. If we need to specify the relationship, we can either use layout qualifiers within the shader, or we could call `glBindAttribLocation` before linking.

However, it may be preferable to let the linker create the mappings automatically and query for them after program linking is complete. In this recipe, we'll see a simple example that prints all the active attributes and their indices.

Getting ready

Start with an OpenGL program that compiles and links a shader pair. You could use the shaders from the previous recipe.

As in previous recipes, we'll assume that the handle to the shader program is stored in a variable named `programHandle`.

How to do it...

After linking and enabling the shader program, use the following code to display the list of active attributes:

1. Start by querying for the number of active attributes:

```
GLint numAttribs;
glGetProgramInterfaceiv(programHandle, GL_PROGRAM_INPUT,
        GL_ACTIVE_RESOURCES, &numAttribs);
```

2. Loop through each attribute and query for the length of the name, the type and the attribute location, and print the results to standard out:

```
GLenum properties[] = {GL_NAME_LENGTH, GL_TYPE,
        GL_LOCATION};

printf("Active attributes:\n");
for( int i = 0; i < numAttribs; ++i ) {
  GLint results[3];
  glGetProgramResourceiv(programHhandle, GL_PROGRAM_INPUT,
          i, 3, properties, 3, NULL, results);

  GLint nameBufSize = results[0] + 1;
  char * name = new char[nameBufSize];
  glGetProgramResourceName(programHandle,
      GL_PROGRAM_INPUT, i, nameBufSize, NULL, name);
  printf("%-5d %s (%s)\n", results[2],
      name, getTypeString(results[1]));
  delete [] name;
}
```

How it works...

In step 1, we query for the number of active attributes, by calling `glGetProgramInterfaceiv`. The first argument is the handle to the program object, and the second (GL_PROGRAM_INPUT) indicates that we are querying for information about the program input variables (the vertex attributes). The third argument (GL_ACTIVE_RESOURCES) indicates that we want the number of active resources. The result is stored in the location pointed to by the last argument numAttribs.

Now that we have the number of attributes, we query for information about each one. The indices of the attributes run from 0 to `numAttribs-1`. We loop over those indices and for each we call `glGetProgramResourceiv` to get the length of the name, the type and the location. We specify what information we would like to receive by means of an array of `GLenum` values called `properties`. The first argument is the handle to the program object, the second is the resource that we are querying (`GL_PROGRAM_INPUT`). The third is the index of the attribute, the fourth is the number of values in the `properties` array, which is the fifth argument. The `properties` array contains `GLenums`, which specify the specific properties we would like to receive. In this example, the array contains: `GL_NAME_LENGTH`, `GL_TYPE`, and `GL_LOCATION`, which indicates that we want the length of the attribute's name, the data type of the attribute and its location. The sixth argument is the size of the buffer that will receive the results; the seventh argument is a pointer to an integer that would receive the number of results that were written. If that argument is `NULL`, then no information is provided. Finally, the last argument is a pointer to a `GLint` array that will receive the results. Each item in the `properties` array corresponds to the same index in the `results` array.

Next, we retrieve the name of the attribute by allocating a buffer to store the name and calling `glGetProgramResourceName`. The `results` array contains the length of the name in the first element, so we allocate an array of that size with an extra character just for good measure. The OpenGL documentation says that the size returned from `glGetProgramResourceiv` includes the null terminator, but it doesn't hurt to make sure by making a bit of additional space. In my tests, I've found this to be necessary on the latest NVIDIA drivers.

Finally, we get the name by calling `glGetProgramResourceName`, and then print the information to the screen. We print the attribute's location, name and type. The location is available in the third element of the results array, and the type is in the second. Note the use of the function `getTypeString`. This is a simple custom function that just returns a string representation of the data type. The data type is represented by one of the OpenGL defined constants `GL_FLOAT`, `GL_FLOAT_VEC2`, `GL_FLOAT_VEC3`, and so on. The `getTypeString` function consists of just one big switch statement returning a human-readable string corresponding to the value of the parameter (see the source code for `glslprogram.cpp` in the example code for this book).

The output of the previous code looks like this when it is run on the shaders from the previous recipes:

```
Active attributes:
1       VertexColor (vec3)
0       VertexPosition (vec3)
```

There's more...

It should be noted that in order for a vertex shader input variable to be considered active, it must be used within the vertex shader. In other words, a variable is considered active if it is determined by the GLSL linker that it may be accessed during program execution. If a variable is declared within a shader, but not used, the previous code will not display the variable because it is not considered active and effectively ignored by OpenGL.

The previous code is only valid for OpenGL 4.3 and later. Alternatively, you can achieve similar results with the functions `glGetProgramiv`, `glGetActiveAttrib` and `glGetAttribLocation`.

See also

- ▶ The *Compiling a shader* recipe
- ▶ The *Linking a shader program* recipe
- ▶ The *Sending data to a shader using vertex attributes and vertex buffer objects* recipe

Sending data to a shader using uniform variables

Vertex attributes provide one avenue for providing input to shaders; a second technique is uniform variables. Uniform variables are intended to be used for data that may change relatively infrequently compared to per-vertex attributes. In fact, it is simply not possible to set per-vertex attributes with uniform variables. For example, uniform variables are well suited for the matrices used for modeling, viewing, and projective transformations.

Within a shader, uniform variables are read-only. Their values can only be changed from outside the shader, via the OpenGL API. However, they can be initialized within the shader by assigning to a constant value along with the declaration.

Uniform variables can appear in any shader within a shader program, and are always used as input variables. They can be declared in one or more shaders within a program, but if a variable with a given name is declared in more than one shader, its type must be the same in all shaders. In other words, the uniform variables are held in a shared uniform namespace for the entire shader program.

In this recipe, we'll draw the same triangle as in previous recipes in this chapter, however, this time, we'll rotate the triangle using a uniform matrix variable.

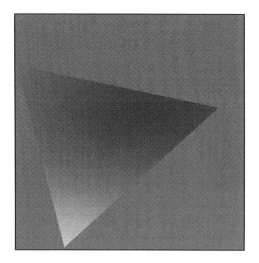

Getting ready

We'll use the following vertex shader:

```
#version 430

layout (location = 0) in vec3 VertexPosition;
layout (location = 1) in vec3 VertexColor;

out vec3 Color;

uniform mat4 RotationMatrix;

void main()
{
  Color = VertexColor;
  gl_Position = RotationMatrix * vec4(VertexPosition,1.0);
}
```

Note the variable RotationMatrix is declared using the uniform qualifier. We'll provide the data for this variable via the OpenGL program. The RotationMatrix is also used to transform VertexPosition before assigning it to the default output position variable gl_Position.

We'll use the same fragment shader as in previous recipes:

```
#version 430

in vec3 Color;

layout (location = 0) out vec4 FragColor;

void main() {
  FragColor = vec4(Color, 1.0);
}
```

Within the main OpenGL code, we determine the rotation matrix and send it to the shader's uniform variable. To create our rotation matrix, we'll use the GLM library (see the *Using the GLM for mathematics* recipe in this chapter). Within the main OpenGL code, add the following include statements:

```
#include <glm/glm.hpp>
using glm::mat4;
using glm::vec3;

#include <glm/gtc/matrix_transform.hpp>
```

We'll also assume that code has been written to compile and link the shaders, and to create the vertex array object for the color triangle. We'll assume that the handle to the vertex array object is `vaoHandle`, and the handle to the program object is `programHandle`.

How to do it...

Within the render method, use the following code:

```
glClear(GL_COLOR_BUFFER_BIT);

mat4 rotationMatrix = glm::rotate(mat4(1.0f), angle,
    vec3(0.0f,0.0f,1.0f));

GLuint location = glGetUniformLocation(programHandle,
    "RotationMatrix");

if( location >= 0 )
{
  glUniformMatrix4fv(location, 1, GL_FALSE,
      &rotationMatrix[0][0]);
}

glBindVertexArray(vaoHandle);
glDrawArrays(GL_TRIANGLES, 0, 3 );
```

How it works...

The steps involved with setting the value of a uniform variable include finding the location of the variable, then assigning a value to that location using one of the `glUniform` functions.

In this example, we start by clearing the color buffer, then creating a rotation matrix using GLM. Next, we query for the location of the uniform variable by calling `glGetUniformLocation`. This function takes the handle to the shader program object, and the name of the uniform variable and returns its location. If the uniform variable is not an active uniform variable, the function returns -1.

We then assign a value to the uniform variable's location using `glUniformMatrix4fv`. The first argument is the uniform variable's location. The second is the number of matrices that are being assigned (note that the uniform variable could be an array). The third is a Boolean value indicating whether or not the matrix should be transposed when loaded into the uniform variable. With GLM matrices, a transpose is not required, so we use `GL_FALSE` here. If you were implementing the matrix using an array, and the data was in row-major order, you might need to use `GL_TRUE` for this argument. The last argument is a pointer to the data for the uniform variable.

There's more...

Of course uniform variables can be any valid GLSL type including complex types such as arrays or structures. OpenGL provides a `glUniform` function with the usual suffixes, appropriate for each type. For example, to assign to a variable of type `vec3`, one would use `glUniform3f` or `glUniform3fv`.

For arrays, one can use the functions ending in "v" to initialize multiple values within the array. Note that if it is desired, one can query for the location of a particular element of the uniform array using the `[]` operator. For example, to query for the location of the second element of `MyArray`:

```
GLuint location =
    glGetUniformLocation( programHandle, "MyArray[1]" );
```

For structures, the members of the structure must be initialized individually. As with arrays, one can query for the location of a member of a structure using something like the following:

```
GLuint location =
    glGetUniformLocation( programHandle, "MyMatrices.Rotation" );
```

Where the structure variable is `MyMatrices` and the member of the structure is `Rotation`.

See also

▶ The *Compiling a shader* recipe

▶ The *Linking a shader program* recipe

▶ The *Sending data to a shader using vertex attributes and vertex buffer objects* recipe

Getting a list of active uniform variables

While it is a simple process to query for the location of an individual uniform variable, there may be instances where it can be useful to generate a list of all active uniform variables. For example, one might choose to create a set of variables to store the location of each uniform and assign their values after the program is linked. This would avoid the need to query for uniform locations when setting the value of the uniform variables, creating slightly more efficient code.

The process for listing uniform variables is very similar to the process for listing attributes (see the *Getting a list of active vertex input attributes and locations* recipe), so this recipe will refer the reader back to the previous recipe for detailed explanation.

Getting ready

Start with a basic OpenGL program that compiles and links a shader program. In the following, we'll assume that the handle to the program is in a variable named `programHandle`.

How to do it...

After linking and enabling the shader program, use the following code to display the list of active uniforms:

1. Start by querying for the number of active uniform variables:

```
GLint numUniforms = 0;
glGetProgramInterfaceiv( handle, GL_UNIFORM,
    GL_ACTIVE_RESOURCES, &numUniforms);
```

2. Loop through each uniform index and query for the length of the name, the type, the location and the block index:

```
GLenum properties[] = {GL_NAME_LENGTH, GL_TYPE,
    GL_LOCATION, GL_BLOCK_INDEX};

printf("Active uniforms:\n");
for( int i = 0; i < numUniforms; ++i ) {
  GLint results[4];
    glGetProgramResourceiv(handle, GL_UNIFORM, i, 4,
        properties, 4, NULL, results);
```

```
      if( results[3] != -1 )
            continue;          // Skip uniforms in blocks
      GLint nameBufSize = results[0] + 1;
      char * name = new char[nameBufSize];
      glGetProgramResourceName(handle, GL_UNIFORM, i,
            nameBufSize, NULL, name);
   printf("%-5d %s (%s)\n", results[2], name,
            getTypeString(results[1]));
      delete [] name;
   }
```

How it works...

The process is very similar to the process shown in the recipe *Getting a list of active vertex input attributes and locations*. I will focus on the main differences.

First and most obvious is that we use GL_UNIFORM instead of GL_PROGRAM_INPUT as the interface that we are querying in glGetProgramResourceiv and glGetProgramInterfaceiv. Second, we query for the block index (using GL_BLOCK_INDEX in the properties array). The reason for this is that some uniform variables are contained within a uniform block (see the recipe *Using uniform blocks and uniform buffer objects*). For this example, we only want information about uniforms that are not within blocks. The block index will be -1 if the uniform variable is not within a block, so we skip any uniform variables that do not have a block index of -1.

Again, we use the getTypeString function to convert the type value into a human-readable string (see example code).

When this is run on the shader program from the previous recipe, we see the following output:

```
Active uniforms:
0     RotationMatrix (mat4)
```

There's more...

As with vertex attributes, a uniform variable is not considered active unless it is determined by the GLSL linker that it will be used within the shader.

The previous code is only valid for OpenGL 4.3 and later. Alternatively, you can achieve similar results using the functions glGetProgramiv, glGetActiveUniform, glGetUniformLocation, and glGetActiveUniformName.

See also

▶ The *Sending data to a shader using uniform variables* recipe

Using uniform blocks and uniform buffer objects

If your program involves multiple shader programs that use the same uniform variables, one has to manage the variables separately for each program. Uniform locations are generated when a program is linked, so the locations of the uniforms may change from one program to the next. The data for those uniforms may have to be regenerated and applied to the new locations.

Uniform blocks were designed to ease the sharing of uniform data between programs. With uniform blocks, one can create a buffer object for storing the values of all the uniform variables, and bind the buffer to the uniform block. When changing programs, the same buffer object need only be re-bound to the corresponding block in the new program.

A uniform block is simply a group of uniform variables defined within a syntactical structure known as a uniform block. For example, in this recipe, we'll use the following uniform block:

```
uniform BlobSettings {
    vec4  InnerColor;
    vec4  OuterColor;
    float RadiusInner;
    float RadiusOuter;
};
```

This defines a block with the name `BlobSettings` that contains four uniform variables. With this type of block definition, the variables within the block are still part of the global scope and do not need to be qualified with the block name.

The buffer object used to store the data for the uniforms is often referred to as a *uniform buffer object*. We'll see that a uniform buffer object is simply just a buffer object that is bound to a certain location.

For this recipe, we'll use a simple example to demonstrate the use of uniform buffer objects and uniform blocks. We'll draw a quad (two triangles) with texture coordinates, and use our fragment shader to fill the quad with a fuzzy circle. The circle is a solid color in the center, but at its edge, it gradually fades to the background color, as shown in the following image:

Getting ready

Start with an OpenGL program that draws two triangles to form a quad. Provide the position at vertex attribute location 0, and the texture coordinate (0 to 1 in each direction) at vertex attribute location 1 (see the *Sending data to a shader using vertex attributes and vertex buffer objects* recipe).

We'll use the following vertex shader:

```
#version 430

layout (location = 0) in vec3 VertexPosition;
layout (location = 1) in vec3 VertexTexCoord;

out vec3 TexCoord;

void main()
{
  TexCoord = VertexTexCoord;
  gl_Position = vec4(VertexPosition,1.0);
}
```

The fragment shader contains the uniform block, and is responsible for drawing our fuzzy circle:

```
#version 430

in vec3 TexCoord;
layout (location = 0) out vec4 FragColor;

layout (binding = 0) uniform BlobSettings {
  vec4 InnerColor;
  vec4 OuterColor;
  float RadiusInner;
  float RadiusOuter;
};

void main() {
  float dx = TexCoord.x - 0.5;
  float dy = TexCoord.y - 0.5;
  float dist = sqrt(dx * dx + dy * dy);
  FragColor =
   mix( InnerColor, OuterColor,
      smoothstep( RadiusInner, RadiusOuter, dist ));
}
```

Note the uniform block named `BlobSettings`. The variables within this block define the parameters of our fuzzy circle. The variable `OuterColor` defines the color outside of the circle. `InnerColor` is the color inside of the circle. `RadiusInner` is the radius defining the part of the circle that is a solid color (inside the fuzzy edge), and the distance from the center of the circle to the inner edge of the fuzzy boundary. `RadiusOuter` is the outer edge of the fuzzy boundary of the circle (when the color is equal to `OuterColor`).

The code within the main function computes the distance of the texture coordinate to the center of the quad located at (0.5, 0.5). It then uses that distance to compute the color by using the `smoothstep` function. This function provides a value that smoothly varies between 0.0 and 1.0 when the value of the third argument is between the values of the first two arguments. Otherwise it returns 0.0 or 1.0 depending on whether `dist` is less than the first or greater than the second, respectively. The `mix` function is then used to linearly interpolate between `InnerColor` and `OuterColor` based on the value returned by the `smoothstep` function.

How to do it...

In the OpenGL program, after linking the shader program, use the following steps to assign data to the uniform block in the fragment shader:

1. Get the index of the uniform block using `glGetUniformBlockIndex`.

```
GLuint blockIndex = glGetUniformBlockIndex(programHandle,
    "BlobSettings");
```

2. Allocate space for the buffer to contain the data for the uniform block. We get the size using `glGetActiveUniformBlockiv`:

```
GLint blockSize;
glGetActiveUniformBlockiv(programHandle, blockIndex,
    GL_UNIFORM_BLOCK_DATA_SIZE, &blockSize);

GLubyte * blockBuffer;
blockBuffer = (GLubyte *) malloc(blockSize);
```

3. Query for the offset of each variable within the block. To do so, we first find the index of each variable within the block:

```
const GLchar *names[] = { "InnerColor", "OuterColor",
    "RadiusInner", "RadiusOuter" };
GLuint indices[4];
glGetUniformIndices(programHandle, 4, names, indices);

GLint offset[4];
glGetActiveUniformsiv(programHandle, 4, indices,
    GL_UNIFORM_OFFSET, offset);
```

4. Place the data into the buffer at the appropriate offsets:

```
// Store data within the buffer at the appropriate offsets
GLfloat outerColor[] = {0.0f, 0.0f, 0.0f, 0.0f};
GLfloat innerColor[] = {1.0f, 1.0f, 0.75f, 1.0f};
GLfloat innerRadius = 0.25f, outerRadius = 0.45f;

memcpy(blockBuffer + offset[0], innerColor,
        4 * sizeof(GLfloat));
memcpy(blockBuffer + offset[1], outerColor,
        4 * sizeof(GLfloat));
memcpy(blockBuffer + offset[2], &innerRadius,
        sizeof(GLfloat));
memcpy(blockBuffer + offset[3], &outerRadius,
        sizeof(GLfloat));
```

5. Create the buffer object and copy the data into it:

```
GLuint uboHandle;
glGenBuffers( 1, &uboHandle );
glBindBuffer( GL_UNIFORM_BUFFER, uboHandle );
glBufferData( GL_UNIFORM_BUFFER, blockSize, blockBuffer,
        GL_DYNAMIC_DRAW );
```

6. Bind the buffer object to the uniform buffer binding point at the index specified by the binding layout qualifier in the fragment shader (0):

```
glBindBufferBase(GL_UNIFORM_BUFFER, 0, uboHandle);
```

How it works...

Phew! This seems like a lot of work! However, the real advantage comes when using multiple programs where the same buffer object can be used for each program. Let's take a look at each step individually.

First we get the index of the uniform block by calling glGetUniformBlockIndex, then we query for the size of the block by calling glGetActiveUniformBlockiv. After getting the size, we allocate a temporary buffer named blockBuffer to hold the data for our block.

The layout of data within a uniform block is implementation dependent, and implementations may use different padding and/or byte alignment. So in order to accurately layout our data, we need to query for the offset of each variable within the block. This is done in two steps. First, we query for the index of each variable within the block by calling glGetUniformIndices. This accepts an array of variable names (third argument) and returns the indices of the variables in the array indices (fourth argument). Then we use the indices to query for the offsets by calling glGetActiveUniformsiv. When the fourth argument is GL_UNIFORM_OFFSET, this returns the offset of each variable in the array pointed to by the fifth argument. This function can also be used to query for the size and type, however, in this case we choose not to do so, to keep the code simple (albeit less general).

The next step involves filling our temporary buffer blockBuffer with the data for the uniforms at the appropriate offsets. Here we use the standard library function memcpy to accomplish this.

Now that the temporary buffer is populated with the data with the appropriate layout, we can create our buffer object and copy the data into the buffer object. We call glGenBuffers to generate a buffer handle, and then bind that buffer to the GL_UNIFORM_BUFFER binding point by calling glBindBuffer. The space is allocated within the buffer object and the data is copied when glBufferData is called. We use GL_DYNAMIC_DRAW as the usage hint here because uniform data may be changed somewhat often during rendering. Of course, this is entirely dependent on the situation.

Finally, we associate the buffer object with the uniform block by calling glBindBufferBase. This function binds to an index within a buffer binding point. Certain binding points are also so-called "indexed buffer targets". This means that the target is actually an array of targets, and glBindBufferBase allows us to bind to one index within the array. In this case, we bind it to the index that we specified in the layout qualifier in the fragment shader: layout (binding = 0) (see the "Getting ready..." section). These two indices must match.

You might be wondering why we use glBindBuffer and glBindBufferBase with GL_UNIFORM_BUFFER. Aren't these the same binding points used in two different contexts? The answer is that the GL_UNIFORM_BUFFER point can be used in each function with a slightly different meaning. With glBindBuffer, we bind to a point that can be used for filling or modifying a buffer, but can't be used as a source of data for the shader. When we use glBindBufferBase, we are binding to an index within a location that can be directly sourced by the shader. Granted, that's a bit confusing.

There's more...

If the data for a uniform block needs to be changed at some later time, one can call glBufferSubData to replace all or part of the data within the buffer. If you do so, don't forget to first bind the buffer to the generic binding point GL_UNIFORM_BUFFER.

Using an instance name with a uniform block

A uniform block can have an optional instance name. For example, with our BlobSettings block we could have used the instance name Blob, as shown here:

```
uniform BlobSettings {
  vec4 InnerColor;
  vec4 OuterColor;
  float RadiusInner;
  float RadiusOuter;
} Blob;
```

In this case, the variables within the block are placed within a namespace qualified by the instance name. Therefore our shader code needs to refer to them prefixed with the instance name. For example:

```
FragColor =
    mix( Blob.InnerColor, Blob.OuterColor,
        smoothstep( Blob.RadiusInner, Blob.RadiusOuter, dist )
    );
```

Additionally, we need to qualify the variable names (with the block name: `BlobSettings`) within the OpenGL code when querying for variable indices:

```
const GLchar *names[] = { "BlobSettings.InnerColor",
        "BlobSettings.OuterColor", "BlobSettings. RadiusInner",
        "BlobSettings.RadiusOuter" };
GLuint indices[4];
glGetUniformIndices(programHandle, 4, names, indices);
```

Using layout qualifiers with uniform blocks

Since the layout of the data within a uniform buffer object is implementation dependent, it required us to query for the variable offsets. However, one can avoid this by asking OpenGL to use the standard layout `std140`. This is accomplished by using a layout qualifier when declaring the uniform block. For example:

```
layout( std140 ) uniform BlobSettings {

};
```

The `std140` layout is described in detail within the OpenGL specification document (available at `http://www.opengl.org`).

Other options for the layout qualifier that apply to uniform block layouts include `packed` and `shared`. The `packed` qualifier simply states that the implementation is free to optimize memory in whatever way it finds necessary (based on variable usage or other criteria). With the `packed` qualifier, we still need to query for the offsets of each variable. The `shared` qualifier guarantees that the layout will be consistent between multiple programs and program stages provided that the uniform block declaration does not change. If you are planning to use the same buffer object between multiple programs and/or program stages, it is a good idea to use the `shared` option.

There are two other layout qualifiers that are worth mentioning: `row_major` and `column_major`. These define the ordering of data within the matrix type variables within the uniform block.

One can use multiple (non-conflicting) qualifiers for a block. For example, to define a block with both the `row_major` and `shared` qualifiers, we would use the following syntax:

```
layout ( row_major, shared ) uniform BlobSettings {

};
```

See also

▶ The *Sending data to a shader using uniform variables* recipe

Getting debug messages

Prior to recent versions of OpenGL, the traditional way to get debug information was to call `glGetError`. Unfortunately, that is an exceedingly tedious method for debugging a program. The `glGetError` function returns an error code if an error has occurred at some point previous to the time the function was called. This means that if we're chasing down a bug, we essentially need to call `glGetError` after every function call to an OpenGL function, or do a binary search-like process where we call it before and after a block of code, and then move the two calls closer to each other until we determine the source of the error. What a pain!

Thankfully, as of OpenGL 4.3, we now have support for a more modern method for debugging. Now we can register a debug callback function that will be executed whenever an error occurs, or other informational message is generated. Not only that, but we can send our own custom messages to be handled by the same callback, and we can filter the messages using a variety of criteria.

Getting ready

Create an OpenGL program with a debug context. While it is not strictly necessary to acquire a debug context, we might not get messages that are as informative as when we are using a debug context. To create an OpenGL context using GLFW with debugging enabled, use the following function call prior to creating the window.

```
glfwWindowHint(GLFW_OPENGL_DEBUG_CONTEXT, GL_TRUE);
```

An OpenGL debug context will have debug messages enabled by default. If, however, you need to enable debug messages explicitly, use the following call.

```
glEnable(GL_DEBUG_OUTPUT);
```

How to do it...

Use the following steps:

1. Create a callback function to receive the debug messages. The function must conform to a specific prototype described in the OpenGL documentation. For this example, we'll use the following one:

    ```
    void debugCallback(GLenum source, GLenum type, GLuint id,
            GLenum severity, GLsizei length,
            const GLchar * message, void * param) {

        // Convert GLenum parameters to strings


        printf("%s:%s[%s](%d): %s\n", sourceStr, typeStr,
            severityStr, id, message);
    }
    ```

2. Register our callback with OpenGL using `glDebugMessageCallback`:

    ```
    glDebugMessageCallback( debugCallback, NULL );
    ```

3. Enable all messages, all sources, all levels, and all IDs:

    ```
    glDebugMessageControl(GL_DONT_CARE, GL_DONT_CARE,
            GL_DONT_CARE, 0, NULL, GL_TRUE);
    ```

How it works...

The callback function `debugCallback` has several parameters, the most important of which is the debug message itself (the sixth parameter, `message`). For this example, we simply print the message to standard output, but we could send it to a log file or some other destination.

The first four parameters to `debugCallback` describe the source, type, id number, and severity of the message. The id number is an unsigned integer specific to the message. The possible values for the source, type and severity parameters are described in the following tables.

The source parameter can have any of the following values:

Source	Generated By
GL_DEBUG_SOURCE_API	Calls to the OpenGL API
GL_DEBUG_SOURCE_WINDOW_SYSTEM	Calls to a window system API
GL_DEBUG_SOURCE_THIRD_PARTY	An application associated with OpenGL
GL_DEBUG_SOURCE_APPLICATION	This application itself.
GL_DEBUG_SOURCE_OTHER	Some other source

The type parameter can have any of the following values:

Type	Description
GL_DEBUG_TYPE_ERROR	An error from the OpenGL API.
GL_DEBUG_TYPE_DEPRECATED_BEHAVIOR	Behavior that has been deprecated
GL_DEBUG_TYPE_UNDEFINED_BEHAVIOR	Undefined behaviour
GL_DEBUG_TYPE_PORTABILITIY	Some functionality is not portable.
GL_DEBUG_TYPE_PERFORMANCE	Possible performance issues
GL_DEBUG_TYPE_MARKER	An annotation
GL_DEBUG_TYPE_PUSH_GROUP	Messages related to debug group push.
GL_DEBUG_TYPE_POP_GROUP	Messages related to debug group pop.
GL_DEBUG_TYPE_OTHER	Other messages

The severity parameter can have the following values:

Severity	Meaning
GL_DEBUG_SEVERITY_HIGH	Errors or dangerous behaviour
GL_DEBUG_SEVERITY_MEDIUM	Major performance warnings, other warnings or use of deprecated functionality.
GL_DEBUG_SEVERITY_LOW	Redundant state changes, unimportant undefined behaviour.
GL_DEBUG_SEVERITY_NOTIFICATION	A notification, not an error or performance issue.

The length parameter is the length of the message string, excluding the null terminator. The last parameter param is a user-defined pointer. We can use this to point to some custom object that might be helpful to the callback function. For example, if we were logging the messages to a file, this could point to an object containing file I/O capabilities. This parameter can be set using the second parameter to glDebugMessageCallback (more on that in the following content).

Within debugCallback we convert each GLenum parameter into a string. Due to space constraints, I don't show all of that code here, but it can be found in the example code for this book. We then print all of the information to standard output.

The call to glDebugMessageCallback registers our callback function with the OpenGL debug system. The first parameter is a pointer to our callback function, and the second parameter (NULL in this example) can be a pointer to any object that we would like to pass into the callback. This pointer is passed as the last parameter with every call to debugCallback.

Finally, the call to `glDebugMessageControl` determines our message filters. This function can be used to selectively turn on or off any combination of message source, type, id, or severity. In this example, we turn everything on.

There's more...

OpenGL also provides support for stacks of named debug groups. Essentially what this means is that we can remember all of our debug message filter settings on a stack and return to them later after some changes have been made. This might be useful, for example, if there are sections of code where we have needs for filtering some kinds of messages and other sections where we want a different set of messages.

The functions involved are `glPushDebugGroup` and `glPopDebugGroup`. A call to `glPushDebugGroup` generates a debug message with type `GL_DEBUG_TYPE_PUSH_GROUP`, and retains the current state of our debug filters on a stack. We can then change our filters using `glDebugMessageControl`, and later return to the original state using `glPopDebugGroup`. Similarly, the function `glPopDebugGroup` generates a debug message with type `GL_DEBUG_TYPE_POP_GROUP`.

Building a C++ shader program class

If you are using C++, it can be very convenient to create classes to encapsulate some of the OpenGL objects. A prime example is the shader program object. In this recipe, we'll look at a design for a C++ class that can be used to manage a shader program.

Getting ready

There's not much to prepare for with this one, you just need a build environment that supports C++. Also, I'll assume that you are using GLM for matrix and vector support, if not just leave out the functions involving the GLM classes.

How to do it...

First, we'll use a custom exception class for errors that might occur during compilation or linking:

```
class GLSLProgramException : public std::runtime_error {
public:
  GLSLProgramException( const string & msg ) :
      std::runtime_error(msg) { }
};
```

We'll use an enum for the various shader types:

```
namespace GLSLShader {
  enum GLSLShaderType {
        VERTEX = GL_VERTEX_SHADER,
        FRAGMENT = GL_FRAGMENT_SHADER,
        GEOMETRY = GL_GEOMETRY_SHADER,
        TESS_CONTROL = GL_TESS_CONTROL_SHADER,
        TESS_EVALUATION = GL_TESS_EVALUATION_SHADER,
        COMPUTE = GL_COMPUTE_SHADER
  };
};
```

The program class itself has the following interface:

```
class GLSLProgram
{
private:
  int   handle;
  bool linked;
  std::map<string, int> uniformLocations;

  int  getUniformLocation(const char * name );

   // A few other helper functions

public:
  GLSLProgram();
  ~GLSLProgram();

  void compileShader( const char * filename )
      throw(GLSLProgramException);
  void compileShader( const char * filename,
      GLSLShader::GLSLShaderType type )
      throw(GLSLProgramException);
  void compileShader( const string & source,
      GLSLShader::GLSLShaderType type,
      const char * filename = NULL )
      throw(GLSLProgramException);
  void link()      throw(GLSLProgramException);
  void use()       throw(GLSLProgramException);
  void validate()  throw(GLSLProgramException);

  int    getHandle();
  bool   isLinked();
```

```
    void    bindAttribLocation( GLuint location,
        const char * name);
    void    bindFragDataLocation( GLuint location,
        const char * name );
    void    setUniform(const char *name, float x, float y,
        float z);
    void    setUniform(const char *name, const vec3 & v);
    void    setUniform(const char *name, const vec4 & v);
    void    setUniform(const char *name, const mat4 & m);
    void    setUniform(const char *name, const mat3 & m);
    void    setUniform(const char *name, float val );
    void    setUniform(const char *name, int val );
    void    setUniform(const char *name, bool val );

    void    printActiveUniforms();
    void    printActiveAttribs();
    void    printActiveUniformBlocks();
};
```

Code Download Tip

You can download the example code files for all Packt books you have purchased from your account at `http://www.packtpub.com`. If you purchased this book elsewhere, you can visit `http://www.packtpub.com/support` and register to have the files e-mailed directly to you.

Full source code for all of the recipes in this text is also available on GitHub at: `https://github.com/daw42/glslcookbook`.

The techniques involved in the implementation of these functions are covered in previous recipes in this chapter. Due to space limitations, I won't include the code here (it's available from this book's GitHub repository), but we'll discuss some of the design decisions in the next section.

How it works...

The state stored within a `GLSLProgram` object includes the handle to the OpenGL shader program object (`handle`), a Boolean variable indicating whether or not the program has been successfully linked (`linked`), and a `map` used to store `uniform` locations as they are discovered (`uniformLocations`).

The compileShader overloads will throw a GLSLProgramException if the compilation fails. The first version determines the type of shader based on the filename extension. In the second version, the caller provides the shader type, and the third version is used to compile a shader, taking the shader's source code from a string. The file name can be provided as a third argument in the case that the string was taken from a file, which is helpful for providing better error messages.

The GLSLProgramException's error message will contain the contents of the shader log or program log when an error occurs.

The private function getUniformLocation is used by the setUniform functions to find the location of a uniform variable. It checks the map uniformLocations first, and if the location is not found, queries OpenGL for the location, and stores the result in the map before returning. The fileExists function is used by compileShaderFromFile to check for file existence.

The constructor simply initializes linked to false and handle to zero. The variable handle will be initialized by calling glCreateProgram when the first shader is compiled.

The link function simply attempts to link the program by calling glLinkProgram. It then checks the link status, and if successful, sets the variable linked to true and returns true. Otherwise, it gets the program log (by calling glGetProgramInfoLog), stores the result in a GLSLProgramException and throws it.

The use function simply calls glUseProgram if the program has already been successfully linked, otherwise it does nothing.

The functions getHandle and isLinked are simply "getter" functions that return the handle to the OpenGL program object and the value of the linked variable.

The functions bindAttribLocation and bindFragDataLocation are wrappers around glBindAttribLocation and glBindFragDataLocation. Note that these functions should only be called prior to linking the program.

The setUniform overloaded functions are straightforward wrappers around the appropriate glUniform functions. Each of them calls getUniformLocation to query for the variable's location before calling the glUniform function.

Finally, the printActiveUniforms, printActiveUniformBlocks, and printActiveAttribs functions are useful for debugging purposes. They simply display a list of the active uniforms/attributes to standard output.

The following is a simple example of the use of the GLSLProgram class:

```
GLSLProgram prog;

try {
  prog.compileShader("myshader.vert");
  prog.compileShader("myshader.frag");
  prog.link();
  prog.validate();
  prog.use();
} catch( GLSLProgramException &e ) {
  cerr << e.what() << endl;
  exit(EXIT_FAILURE);
}


prog.printActiveUniforms();
prog.printActiveAttribs();

prog.setUniform("ModelViewMatrix", matrix);
prog.setUniform("LightPosition", 1.0f, 1.0f, 1.0f);
```

See also

▶ For full source code, check out the GitHub site for this book: http://github.com/daw42/glslcookbook

▶ All of the recipes in this chapter!

2
The Basics of GLSL Shaders

In this chapter, we will cover:

- ▶ Implementing diffuse, per-vertex shading with a single point light source
- ▶ Implementing per-vertex ambient, diffuse, and specular (ADS) shading
- ▶ Using functions in shaders
- ▶ Implementing two-sided shading
- ▶ Implementing flat shading
- ▶ Using subroutines to select shader functionality
- ▶ Discarding fragments to create a perforated look

Introduction

Shaders were first added into OpenGL in Version 2.0, introducing programmability into the formerly fixed-function OpenGL pipeline. Shaders give us the power to implement alternative rendering algorithms and a greater degree of flexibility in the implementation of those techniques. With shaders, we can run custom code directly on the GPU, providing us with the opportunity to leverage the high degree of parallelism available with modern GPUs.

Shaders are implemented using the **OpenGL Shading Language** (**GLSL**). The GLSL is syntactically similar to C, which should make it easier for experienced OpenGL programmers to learn. Due to the nature of this text, I won't present a thorough introduction to GLSL here. Instead, if you're new to GLSL, reading through these recipes should help you to learn the language by example. If you are already comfortable with GLSL, but don't have experience with Version 4.x, you'll see how to implement these techniques utilizing the newer API. However, before we jump into GLSL programming, let's take a quick look at how vertex and fragment shaders fit within the OpenGL pipeline.

Vertex and fragment shaders

In OpenGL Version 4.3, there are six shader stages/types: vertex, geometry, tessellation control, tessellation evaluation, fragment, and compute. In this chapter we'll focus only on the vertex and fragment stages. In *Chapter 6, Using Geometry and Tessellation Shaders*, I'll provide some recipes for working with the geometry and tessellation shaders, and in *Chapter 10, Using Compute Shaders*, I'll focus specifically on compute shaders.

Shaders replace parts of the OpenGL pipeline. More specifically, they make those parts of the pipeline programmable. The following block diagram shows a simplified view of the OpenGL pipeline with only the vertex and fragment shaders installed:

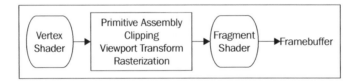

Vertex data is sent down the pipeline and arrives at the vertex shader via shader input variables. The vertex shader's input variables correspond to the vertex attributes (refer to the *Sending data to a shader using vertex attributes and vertex buffer objects* recipe in *Chapter 1, Getting Started with GLSL*). In general, a shader receives its input via programmer-defined input variables, and the data for those variables comes either from the main OpenGL application or previous pipeline stages (other shaders). For example, a fragment shader's input variables might be fed from the output variables of the vertex shader. Data can also be provided to any shader stage using uniform variables (refer to the *Sending data to a shader using uniform variables* recipe, in *Chapter 1, Getting Started with GLSL*). These are used for information that changes less often than vertex attributes (for example, matrices, light position, and other settings). The following figure shows a simplified view of the relationships between input and output variables when there are two shaders active (vertex and fragment):

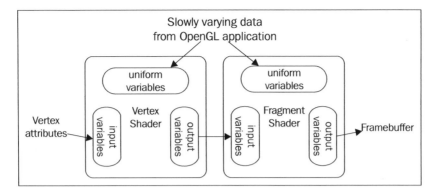

The vertex shader is executed once for each vertex, usually in parallel. The data corresponding to the position of the vertex must be transformed into clip coordinates and assigned to the output variable `gl_Position` before the vertex shader finishes execution. The vertex shader can send other information down the pipeline using shader output variables. For example, the vertex shader might also compute the color associated with the vertex. That color would be passed to later stages via an appropriate output variable.

Between the vertex and fragment shader, the vertices are assembled into primitives, clipping takes place, and the viewport transformation is applied (among other operations). The rasterization process then takes place and the polygon is filled (if necessary). The fragment shader is executed once for each fragment (pixel) of the polygon being rendered (typically in parallel). Data provided from the vertex shader is (by default) interpolated in a perspective correct manner, and provided to the fragment shader via shader input variables. The fragment shader determines the appropriate color for the pixel and sends it to the frame buffer using output variables. The depth information is handled automatically.

Replicating the old fixed functionality

Programmable shaders give us tremendous power and flexibility. However, in some cases we might just want to re-implement the basic shading techniques that were used in the default fixed-function pipeline, or perhaps use them as a basis for other shading techniques. Studying the basic shading algorithm of the old fixed-function pipeline can also be a good way to get started when learning about shader programming.

In this chapter, we'll look at the basic techniques for implementing shading similar to that of the old fixed-function pipeline. We'll cover the standard ambient, diffuse, and specular (ADS) shading algorithm, the implementation of two-sided rendering, and flat shading. Along the way, we'll also see some examples of other GLSL features such as functions, subroutines, and the `discard` keyword.

The algorithms presented within this chapter are largely unoptimized. I present them this way to avoid additional confusion for someone who is learning the techniques for the first time. We'll look at a few optimization techniques at the end of some recipes, and some more in the next chapter.

Implementing diffuse, per-vertex shading with a single point light source

One of the simplest shading techniques is to assume that the surface exhibits purely diffuse reflection. That is to say that the surface is one that appears to scatter light in all directions equally, regardless of direction. Incoming light strikes the surface and penetrates slightly before being re-radiated in all directions. Of course, the incoming light interacts with the surface before it is scattered, causing some wavelengths to be fully or partially absorbed and others to be scattered. A typical example of a diffuse surface is a surface that has been painted with a matte paint. The surface has a dull look with no shine at all.

The following screenshot shows a torus rendered with diffuse shading:

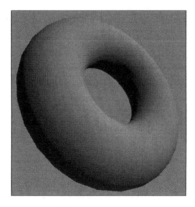

The mathematical model for diffuse reflection involves two vectors: the direction from the surface point to the light source (**s**), and the normal vector at the surface point (**n**). The vectors are represented in the following diagram:

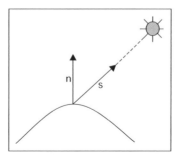

The amount of incoming light (or radiance) that reaches the surface is partially dependent on the orientation of the surface with respect to the light source. The physics of the situation tells us that the amount of radiation that reaches a point on a surface is maximal when the light arrives along the direction of the normal vector, and zero when the light is perpendicular to the normal. In between, it is proportional to the cosine of the angle between the direction towards the light source and the normal vector. So, since the dot product is proportional to the cosine of the angle between two vectors, we can express the amount of radiation striking the surface as the product of the light intensity and the dot product of **s** and **n**.

$$L_d \mathbf{s} \cdot \mathbf{n}$$

Where **L**$_d$ is the intensity of the light source, and the vectors **s** and **n** are assumed to be normalized.

 The dot product of two unit vectors is equal to the cosine of the angle between them.

As stated previously, some of the incoming light is absorbed before it is re-emitted. We can model this interaction by using a reflection coefficient (K_d), which represents the fraction of the incoming light that is scattered. This is sometimes referred to as the **diffuse reflectivity**, or the diffuse reflection coefficient. The diffuse reflectivity becomes a scaling factor for the incoming radiation, so the intensity of the outgoing light can be expressed as follows:

$$L = K_d L_d \mathbf{s} \cdot \mathbf{n}$$

Because this model depends only on the direction towards the light source and the normal to the surface, not on the direction towards the viewer, we have a model that represents uniform (omnidirectional) scattering.

In this recipe, we'll evaluate this equation at each vertex in the vertex shader and interpolate the resulting color across the face.

 In this and the following recipes, light intensities and material reflectivity coefficients are represented by 3-component (RGB) vectors. Therefore, the equations should be treated as component-wise operations, applied to each of the three components separately. Luckily, the GLSL will make this nearly transparent because the needed operators operate component-wise on vector variables.

Getting ready

Start with an OpenGL application that provides the vertex position in attribute location 0, and the vertex normal in attribute location 1 (refer to the *Sending data to a shader using vertex attributes and vertex buffer objects* recipe in *Chapter 1, Getting Started with GLSL*). The OpenGL application also should provide the standard transformation matrices (projection, modelview, and normal) via uniform variables.

The light position (in eye coordinates), Kd, and Ld should also be provided by the OpenGL application via uniform variables. Note that Kd and Ld are of type vec3. We can use vec3 to store an RGB color as well as a vector or point.

How to do it...

To create a shader pair that implements diffuse shading, use the following steps:

1. Use the following code for the vertex shader:

```
layout (location = 0) in vec3 VertexPosition;
layout (location = 1) in vec3 VertexNormal;

out vec3 LightIntensity;

uniform vec4 LightPosition;// Light position in eye coords.
uniform vec3 Kd;            // Diffuse reflectivity
uniform vec3 Ld;            // Light source intensity

uniform mat4 ModelViewMatrix;
uniform mat3 NormalMatrix;
uniform mat4 ProjectionMatrix;
uniform mat4 MVP;           // Projection * ModelView

void main()
{
    // Convert normal and position to eye coords
    vec3 tnorm = normalize( NormalMatrix * VertexNormal);
    vec4 eyeCoords = ModelViewMatrix *
                    vec4(VertexPosition,1.0));
    vec3 s = normalize(vec3(LightPosition - eyeCoords));

    // The diffuse shading equation
    LightIntensity = Ld * Kd * max( dot( s, tnorm ), 0.0 );

    // Convert position to clip coordinates and pass along
    gl_Position = MVP * vec4(VertexPosition,1.0);
}
```

2. Use the following code for the fragment shader:

```
in vec3 LightIntensity;

layout( location = 0 ) out vec4 FragColor;

void main() {
    FragColor = vec4(LightIntensity, 1.0);
}
```

3. Compile and link both shaders within the OpenGL application, and install the shader program prior to rendering. See *Chapter 1, Getting Started with GLSL*, for details about compiling, linking, and installing shaders.

How it works...

The vertex shader does all of the work in this example. The diffuse reflection is computed in eye coordinates by first transforming the normal vector using the normal matrix, normalizing, and storing the result in `tnorm`. Note that the normalization here may not be necessary if your normal vectors are already normalized and the normal matrix does not do any scaling.

> The normal matrix is typically the inverse transpose of the upper-left 3 x 3 portion of the model-view matrix. We use the inverse transpose because normal vectors transform differently than the vertex position. For a more thorough discussion of the normal matrix, and the reasons why, see any introductory computer graphics textbook (A good choice would be *Computer Graphics with OpenGL* by Hearn and Baker). If your model-view matrix does not include any non-uniform scalings, then one can use the upper-left 3 x 3 of the model-view matrix in place of the normal matrix to transform your normal vectors. However, if your model-view matrix does include (uniform) scalings, you'll still need to (re)normalize your normal vectors after transforming them.

The next step converts the vertex position to eye (camera) coordinates by transforming it via the model-view matrix. Then we compute the direction towards the light source by subtracting the vertex position from the light position and storing the result in `s`.

Next, we compute the scattered light intensity using the equation described previously and store the result in the output variable `LightIntensity`. Note the use of the `max` function here. If the dot product is less than zero, then the angle between the normal vector and the light direction is greater than 90 degrees. This means that the incoming light is coming from inside the surface. Since such a situation is not physically possible (for a closed mesh), we use a value of 0.0. However, you may decide that you want to properly light both sides of your surface, in which case the normal vector needs to be reversed for those situations where the light is striking the back side of the surface (refer to the *Implementing two-sided shading* recipe in this chapter).

Finally, we convert the vertex position to clip coordinates by multiplying with the model-view projection matrix, (which is: `projection * view * model`) and store the result in the built-in output variable `gl_Position`.

```
gl_Position = MVP * vec4(VertexPosition,1.0);
```

> The subsequent stage of the OpenGL pipeline expects that the vertex position will be provided in clip coordinates in the output variable `gl_Position`. This variable does not directly correspond to any input variable in the fragment shader, but is used by the OpenGL pipeline in the primitive assembly, clipping, and rasterization stages that follow the vertex shader. It is important that we always provide a valid value for this variable.

Since `LightIntensity` is an output variable from the vertex shader, its value is interpolated across the face and passed into the fragment shader. The fragment shader then simply assigns the value to the output fragment.

There's more...

Diffuse shading is a technique that models only a very limited range of surfaces. It is best used for surfaces that have a "matte" appearance. Additionally, with the technique used previously, the dark areas may look a bit too dark. In fact, those areas that are not directly illuminated are completely black. In real scenes, there is typically some light that has been reflected about the room that brightens these surfaces. In the following recipes, we'll look at ways to model more surface types, as well as provide some light for those dark parts of the surface.

See also

- ▶ The *Sending data to a shader using uniform variables* recipe in *Chapter 1, Getting Started with GLSL*
- ▶ The *Compiling a shader* recipe in *Chapter 1, Getting Started with GLSL*
- ▶ The *Linking a shader program* recipe in *Chapter 1, Getting Started with GLSL*
- ▶ The *Sending data to a shader using vertex attributes and vertex buffer objects* recipe in *Chapter 1, Getting Started with GLSL*

Implementing per-vertex ambient, diffuse, and specular (ADS) shading

The OpenGL fixed function pipeline implemented a default shading technique which is very similar to the one presented here. It models the light-surface interaction as a combination of three components: ambient, diffuse, and specular. The **ambient** component is intended to model light that has been reflected so many times that it appears to be emanating uniformly from all directions. The **diffuse** component was discussed in the previous recipe, and represents omnidirectional reflection. The **specular** component models the shininess of the surface and represents reflection around a preferred direction. Combining these three components together can model a nice (but limited) variety of surface types. This shading model is also sometimes called the **Phong reflection model** (or **Phong shading model**), after *Bui Tuong Phong*.

An example of a torus rendered with the ADS shading model is shown in the following screenshot:

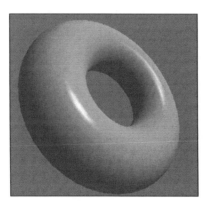

The ADS model is implemented as the sum of the three components: ambient, diffuse, and specular. The ambient component represents light that illuminates all surfaces equally and reflects equally in all directions. It is often used to help brighten some of the darker areas within a scene. Since it does not depend on the incoming or outgoing directions of the light, it can be modeled simply by multiplying the light source intensity (**L$_a$**) by the surface reflectivity (**K$_a$**).

$$I_a = L_a K_a$$

The diffuse component models a rough surface that scatters light in all directions (refer to the *Implementing diffuse, per-vertex shading with a single point light source* recipe in this chapter). The intensity of the outgoing light depends on the angle between the surface normal and the vector towards the light source.

$$I_d = L_d K_d (\mathbf{s} \cdot \mathbf{n})$$

The specular component is used for modeling the shininess of a surface. When a surface has a glossy shine to it, the light is reflected off of the surface in a mirror-like fashion. The reflected light is strongest in the direction of perfect (mirror-like) reflection. The physics of the situation tells us that for perfect reflection, the angle of incidence is the same as the angle of reflection and that the vectors are coplanar with the surface normal, as shown in the following diagram:

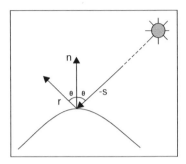

In the preceding diagram, **r** represents the vector of pure-reflection corresponding to the incoming light vector (**-s**), and **n** is the surface normal. We can compute **r** by using the following equation:

$$\mathbf{r} = -\mathbf{s} + 2(\mathbf{s} \cdot \mathbf{n})\mathbf{n}$$

To model specular reflection, we need to compute the following (normalized) vectors: the direction towards the light source (**s**), the vector of perfect reflection (**r**), the vector towards the viewer (**v**), and the surface normal (**n**). These vectors are represented in the following diagram:

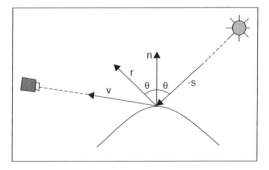

We would like the reflection to be maximal when the viewer is aligned with the vector **r**, and to fall off quickly as the viewer moves further away from alignment with **r**. This can be modeled using the cosine of the angle between **v** and **r** raised to some power (**f**).

$$I_s = L_s K_s (\mathbf{r} \cdot \mathbf{v})^f$$

(Recall that the dot product is proportional to the cosine of the angle between the vectors involved.) The larger the power, the faster the value drops towards zero as the angle between **v** and **r** increases. Again, similar to the other components, we also introduce a specular light intensity term (**L**$_s$) and reflectivity term (**K**$_s$).

The specular component creates **specular highlights** (bright spots) that are typical of glossy surfaces. The larger the power of **f** in the equation, the smaller the specular highlight and the shinier the surface appears. The value for **f** is typically chosen to be somewhere between 1 and 200.

Putting all of this together, we have the following shading equation:

$$I = I_a + I_d + I_s$$
$$= L_a K_a + L_d K_d (\mathbf{s} \cdot \mathbf{n}) + L_s K_s (\mathbf{r} \cdot \mathbf{v})^f$$

For more details about how this shading model was implemented in the fixed function pipeline, take a look at *Chapter 5, Image Processing and Screen Space Techniques*.

In the following code, we'll evaluate this equation in the vertex shader, and interpolate the color across the polygon.

Getting ready

In the OpenGL application, provide the vertex position in location 0 and the vertex normal in location 1. The light position and the other configurable terms for our lighting equation are uniform variables in the vertex shader and their values must be set from the OpenGL application.

How to do it...

To create a shader pair that implements ADS shading, use the following steps:

1. Use the following code for the vertex shader:

```glsl
layout (location = 0) in vec3 VertexPosition;
layout (location = 1) in vec3 VertexNormal;

out vec3 LightIntensity;

struct LightInfo {
    vec4 Position; // Light position in eye coords.
    vec3 La;       // Ambient light intensity
    vec3 Ld;       // Diffuse light intensity
    vec3 Ls;       // Specular light intensity
};
```

```glsl
uniform LightInfo Light;

struct MaterialInfo {
    vec3 Ka;            // Ambient reflectivity
    vec3 Kd;            // Diffuse reflectivity
    vec3 Ks;            // Specular reflectivity
    float Shininess;    // Specular shininess factor
};
uniform MaterialInfo Material;

uniform mat4 ModelViewMatrix;
uniform mat3 NormalMatrix;
uniform mat4 ProjectionMatrix;
uniform mat4 MVP;

void main()
{
    vec3 tnorm = normalize( NormalMatrix * VertexNormal);
    vec4 eyeCoords = ModelViewMatrix *
                    vec4(VertexPosition,1.0);
    vec3 s = normalize(vec3(Light.Position - eyeCoords));
    vec3 v = normalize(-eyeCoords.xyz);
    vec3 r = reflect( -s, tnorm );
    vec3 ambient = Light.La * Material.Ka;
    float sDotN = max( dot(s,tnorm), 0.0 );
    vec3 diffuse = Light.Ld * Material.Kd * sDotN;
    vec3 spec = vec3(0.0);
    if( sDotN > 0.0 )
        spec = Light.Ls * Material.Ks *
            pow(max( dot(r,v), 0.0 ), Material.Shininess);

    LightIntensity = ambient + diffuse + spec;
    gl_Position = MVP * vec4(VertexPosition,1.0);
}
```

2. Use the following code for the fragment shader:

```glsl
in vec3 LightIntensity;

layout( location = 0 ) out vec4 FragColor;

void main() {
    FragColor = vec4(LightIntensity, 1.0);
}
```

3. Compile and link both shaders within the OpenGL application, and install the shader program prior to rendering.

How it works...

The vertex shader computes the shading equation in eye coordinates. It begins by transforming the vertex normal into eye coordinates and normalizing, then storing the result in `tnorm`. The vertex position is then transformed into eye coordinates and stored in `eyeCoords`.

Next, we compute the normalized direction towards the light source (`s`). This is done by subtracting the vertex position in eye coordinates from the light position and normalizing the result.

The direction towards the viewer (`v`) is the negation of the position (normalized) because in eye coordinates the viewer is at the origin.

We compute the direction of pure reflection by calling the GLSL built-in function `reflect`, which reflects the first argument about the second. We don't need to normalize the result because the two vectors involved are already normalized.

The ambient component is computed and stored in the variable `ambient`. The dot product of `s` and `n` is computed next. As in the preceding recipe, we use the built-in function `max` to limit the range of values to between one and zero. The result is stored in the variable named `sDotN`, and is used to compute the diffuse component. The resulting value for the diffuse component is stored in the variable `diffuse`. Before computing the specular component, we check the value of `sDotN`. If `sDotN` is zero, then there is no light reaching the surface, so there is no point in computing the specular component, as its value must be zero. Otherwise, if `sDotN` is greater than zero, we compute the specular component using the equation presented earlier. Again, we use the built-in function `max` to limit the range of values of the dot product to between one and zero, and the function `pow` raises the dot product to the power of the `Shininess` exponent (corresponding to **f** in our lighting equation).

If we did not check `sDotN` before computing the specular component, it is possible that some specular highlights could appear on faces that are facing away from the light source. This is clearly a non-realistic and undesirable result. Some people solve this problem by multiplying the specular component by the diffuse component, which would decrease the specular component substantially and alter its color. The solution presented here avoids this, at the cost of a branch statement (the `if` statement). (Branch statements can have a significant impact on performance.)

The sum of the three components is then stored in the output variable `LightIntensity`. This value will be associated with the vertex and passed down the pipeline. Before reaching the fragment shader, its value will be interpolated in a perspective correct manner across the face of the polygon.

Finally, the vertex shader transforms the position into clip coordinates, and assigns the result to the built-in output variable `gl_Position` (refer to the *Implementing diffuse, per-vertex shading with a single point light source* recipe in this chapter).

The fragment shader simply applies the interpolated value of `LightIntensity` to the output fragment by storing it in the shader output variable `FragColor`.

There's more...

This version of the ADS (Ambient, Diffuse, and Specular) reflection model is by no means optimal. There are several improvements that could be made. For example, the computation of the vector of pure reflection can be avoided via the use of the so-called "halfway vector". This is discussed in the *Using the halfway vector for improved performance* recipe in *Chapter 3, Lighting, Shading, and Optimization*.

Using a non-local viewer

We can avoid the extra normalization needed to compute the vector towards the viewer (v), by using a so-called **non-local viewer**. Instead of computing the direction towards the origin, we simply use the constant vector (0, 0, 1) for all vertices. This is similar to assuming that the viewer is located infinitely far away in the z direction. Of course, it is not accurate, but in practice the visual results are very similar, often visually indistinguishable, saving us normalization.

In the old fixed-function pipeline, the non-local viewer was the default, and could be adjusted (turned on or off) using the function `glLightModel`.

Per-vertex versus per-fragment

Since the shading equation is computed within the vertex shader, we refer to this as **per-vertex shading**. One of the disadvantages of this is that specular highlights can be warped or lost, due to the fact that the shading equation is not evaluated at each point across the face. For example, a specular highlight that should appear in the middle of a polygon might not appear at all when per-vertex shading is used, because of the fact that the shading equation is only computed at the vertices where the specular component is near zero. In the *Using per-fragment shading for improved realism* recipe of *Chapter 3, Lighting, Shading, and Optimization*, we'll look at the changes needed to move the shading computation into the fragment shader, producing more realistic results.

Directional lights

We can also avoid the need to compute a light direction (s), for each vertex if we assume a directional light. A **directional light source** is one that can be thought of as located infinitely far away in a given direction. Instead of computing the direction towards the source for each vertex, a constant vector is used, which represents the direction towards the remote light source. We'll look at an example of this in the *Shading with a directional light source* recipe of *Chapter 3, Lighting, Shading, and Optimization*.

Light attenuation with distance

You might think that this shading model is missing one important component. It doesn't take into account the effect of the distance to the light source. In fact, it is known that the intensity of radiation from a source falls off in proportion to the inverse square of the distance from the source. So why not include this in our model?

It would be fairly simple to do so, however, the visual results are often less than appealing. It tends to exaggerate the distance effects and create unrealistic looking images. Remember, our equation is just an approximation of the physics involved and is not a truly realistic model, so it is not surprising that adding a term based on a strict physical law produces unrealistic results.

In the OpenGL fixed-function pipeline, it was possible to turn on distance attenuation using the `glLight` function. If desired, it would be straightforward to add a few uniform variables to our shader to produce the same effect.

See also

- The *Shading with a directional light source* recipe in *Chapter 3, Lighting, Shading, and Optimization*
- The *Using per-fragment shading for improved realism* recipe in *Chapter 3, Lighting, Shading, and Optimization*
- The *Using the halfway vector for improved performance* recipe in *Chapter 3, Lighting, Shading, and Optimization*

Using functions in shaders

The GLSL supports functions that are syntactically similar to C functions. However, the calling conventions are somewhat different. In the following example, we'll revisit the ADS shader using functions to help provide abstractions for the major steps.

Getting ready

As with previous recipes, provide the vertex position at attribute location 0 and the vertex normal at attribute location 1. Uniform variables for all of the ADS coefficients should be set from the OpenGL side, as well as the light position and the standard matrices.

How to do it...

To implement ADS shading using functions, use the following code:

1. Use the following vertex shader:

```glsl
layout (location = 0) in vec3 VertexPosition;
layout (location = 1) in vec3 VertexNormal;

out vec3 LightIntensity;

struct LightInfo {
    vec4 Position; // Light position in eye coords.
    vec3 La;       // Ambient light intensity
    vec3 Ld;       // Diffuse light intensity
    vec3 Ls;       // Specular light intensity
};
uniform LightInfo Light;

struct MaterialInfo {
    vec3 Ka;            // Ambient reflectivity
    vec3 Kd;            // Diffuse reflectivity
    vec3 Ks;            // Specular reflectivity
    float Shininess;    // Specular shininess factor
};
uniform MaterialInfo Material;

uniform mat4 ModelViewMatrix;
uniform mat3 NormalMatrix;
uniform mat4 ProjectionMatrix;
uniform mat4 MVP;

void getEyeSpace( out vec3 norm, out vec4 position )
{
    norm = normalize( NormalMatrix * VertexNormal);
    position = ModelViewMatrix * vec4(VertexPosition,1.0);
}

vec3 phongModel( vec4 position, vec3 norm )
{
    vec3 s = normalize(vec3(Light.Position - position));
    vec3 v = normalize(-position.xyz);
    vec3 r = reflect( -s, norm );
    vec3 ambient = Light.La * Material.Ka;
    float sDotN = max( dot(s,norm), 0.0 );
    vec3 diffuse = Light.Ld * Material.Kd * sDotN;
    vec3 spec = vec3(0.0);
```

```
        if ( sDotN > 0.0 )
            spec = Light.Ls * Material.Ks *
                pow ( max ( dot (r,v), 0.0 ), Material.Shininess );

        return ambient + diffuse + spec;
    }

void main ()
{
    vec3 eyeNorm;
    vec4 eyePosition;

    // Get the position and normal in eye space
    getEyeSpace (eyeNorm, eyePosition);

    // Evaluate the lighting equation.
    LightIntensity = phongModel ( eyePosition, eyeNorm );

    gl_Position = MVP * vec4 (VertexPosition,1.0);
}
```

2. Use the following fragment shader:

```
in vec3 LightIntensity;


layout ( location = 0 ) out vec4 FragColor;


void main () {
    FragColor = vec4 (LightIntensity, 1.0);
}
```

3. Compile and link both shaders within the OpenGL application, and install the shader program prior to rendering.

How it works...

In GLSL functions, the evaluation strategy is "call by value-return" (also called "call by copy-restore" or "call by value-result"). Parameter variables can be qualified with in, out, or inout. Arguments corresponding to input parameters (those qualified with in or inout) are copied into the parameter variable at call time, and output parameters (those qualified with out or inout) are copied back to the corresponding argument before the function returns. If a parameter variable does not have any of the three qualifiers, the default qualifier is in.

We've created two functions in the vertex shader. The first, named `getEyeSpace`, transforms the vertex position and vertex normal into eye space, and returns them via output parameters. In the `main` function, we create two uninitialized variables (`eyeNorm` and `eyePosition`) to store the results, and then call the function with the variables as the function's arguments. The function stores the results into the parameter variables (`norm` and `position`) which are copied into the arguments before the function returns.

The second function, `phongModel`, uses only input parameters. The function receives the eye-space position and normal, and computes the result of the ADS shading equation. The result is returned by the function and stored in the shader output variable `LightIntensity`.

There's more...

Since it makes no sense to read from an output parameter variable, output parameters should only be written to within the function. Their value is undefined.

Within a function, writing to an input-only parameter (qualified with `in`) is allowed. The function's copy of the argument is modified, and changes are not reflected in the argument.

The const qualifier

The additional qualifier `const` can be used with input-only parameters (not with `out` or `inout`). This qualifier makes the input parameter read-only, so it cannot be written to within the function.

Function overloading

Functions can be overloaded by creating multiple functions with the same name, but with different number and/or type of parameters. As with many languages, two overloaded functions may not differ in return type only.

Passing arrays or structures to a function

It should be noted that when passing arrays or structures to functions, they are passed by value. If a large array or structure is passed, it can incur a large copy operation which may not be desired. It would be a better choice to declare these variables in the global scope.

See also

▶   The *Implementing per-vertex ambient, diffuse, and specular (ADS) shading* recipe

Implementing two-sided shading

When rendering a mesh that is completely closed, the back faces of polygons are hidden. However, if a mesh contains holes, it might be the case that the back faces would become visible. In this case, the polygons may be shaded incorrectly due to the fact that the normal vector is pointing in the wrong direction. To properly shade those back faces, one needs to invert the normal vector and compute the lighting equations based on the inverted normal.

The following screenshot shows a teapot with the lid removed. On the left, the ADS lighting model is used. On the right, the ADS model is augmented with the two-sided rendering technique discussed in this recipe.

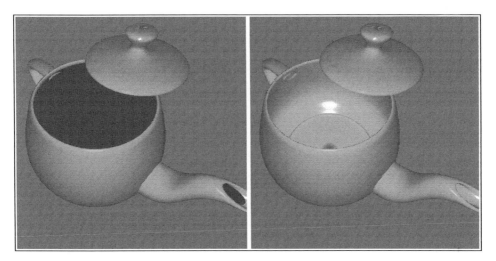

In this recipe, we'll look at an example that uses the ADS model discussed in the previous recipes, augmented with the ability to correctly shade back faces.

Getting ready

The vertex position should be provided in attribute location 0 and the vertex normal in attribute location 1. As in previous examples, the lighting parameters must be provided to the shader via uniform variables.

How to do it...

To implement a shader pair that uses the ADS shading model with two-sided lighting, use the following steps:

1. Use the following code for the vertex shader:

```glsl
layout (location = 0) in vec3 VertexPosition;
layout (location = 1) in vec3 VertexNormal;

out vec3 FrontColor;
out vec3 BackColor;

struct LightInfo {
    vec4 Position; // Light position in eye coords.
    vec3 La;       // Ambient light intensity
    vec3 Ld;       // Diffuse light intensity
    vec3 Ls;       // Specular light intensity
};
uniform LightInfo Light;

struct MaterialInfo {
    vec3 Ka;            // Ambient reflectivity
    vec3 Kd;            // Diffuse reflectivity
    vec3 Ks;            // Specular reflectivity
    float Shininess;    // Specular shininess factor
};
uniform MaterialInfo Material;

uniform mat4 ModelViewMatrix;
uniform mat3 NormalMatrix;
uniform mat4 ProjectionMatrix;
uniform mat4 MVP;

vec3 phongModel( vec4 position, vec3 normal ) {
    // The ADS shading calculations go here ("Implementing
    // per-vertex ambient, diffuse, and specular (ADS)
    // shading")
    ...
}

void main()
{
    vec3 tnorm = normalize( NormalMatrix * VertexNormal);
    vec4 eyeCoords = ModelViewMatrix *
                        vec4(VertexPosition,1.0);
```

```
        FrontColor = phongModel( eyeCoords, tnorm );
        BackColor = phongModel( eyeCoords, -tnorm );

        gl_Position = MVP * vec4(VertexPosition,1.0);
    }
```

2. Use the following for the fragment shader:

```
in vec3 FrontColor;
in vec3 BackColor;

layout( location = 0 ) out vec4 FragColor;

void main() {
    if( gl_FrontFacing ) {
        FragColor = vec4(FrontColor, 1.0);
    } else {
        FragColor = vec4(BackColor, 1.0);
    }
}
```

3. Compile and link both shaders within the OpenGL application, and install the shader program prior to rendering.

How it works...

In the vertex shader, we compute the lighting equation using both the vertex normal and the inverted version, and pass each resultant color to the fragment shader. The fragment shader chooses and applies the appropriate color depending on the orientation of the face.

The vertex shader is a slightly modified version of the vertex shader presented in the *Implementing per-vertex ambient, diffuse, and specular (ADS) shading* recipe of this chapter. The evaluation of the shading model is placed within a function named phongModel. The function is called twice, first using the normal vector (transformed into eye coordinates), and second using the inverted normal vector. The combined results are stored in FrontColor and BackColor, respectively.

 Note that there are a few aspects of the shading model that are independent of the orientation of the normal vector (such as the ambient component). One could optimize this code by rewriting it so that the redundant calculations are only done once. However, in this recipe we compute the entire shading model twice in the interest of making things clear and readable.

In the fragment shader, we determine which color to apply based on the value of the built-in variable `gl_FrontFacing`. This is a `bool` value that indicates whether the fragment is part of a front or back facing polygon. Note that this determination is based on the **winding** of the polygon, and not the normal vector. (A polygon is said to have counter-clockwise winding if the vertices are specified in counter-clockwise order as viewed from the front side of the polygon.) By default when rendering, if the order of the vertices appear on the screen in a counter-clockwise order, it indicates a front facing polygon, however, we can change this by calling `glFrontFace` from the OpenGL program.

There's more...

In the vertex shader we determine the front side of the polygon by the direction of the normal vector, and in the fragment shader, the determination is based on the polygon's winding. For this to work properly, the normal vector must be defined appropriately for the face determined by the setting of `glFrontFace`.

Using two-sided rendering for debugging

It can sometimes be useful to visually determine which faces are front facing and which are back facing. For example, when working with arbitrary meshes, polygons may not be specified using the appropriate winding. As another example, when developing a mesh procedurally, it can sometimes be helpful to determine which faces are oriented in the proper direction in order to help with debugging. We can easily tweak our fragment shader to help us solve these kinds of problems by mixing a solid color with all back (or front) faces. For example, we could change the `else` clause within our fragment shader to the following:

```
FragColor = mix( vec4(BackColor,1.0),
                 vec4(1.0,0.0,0.0,1.0), 0.7 );
```

This would mix a solid red color with all back faces, helping them to stand out, as shown in the following screenshot. In the screenshot, back faces are mixed with 70 percent red as shown in the preceding code.

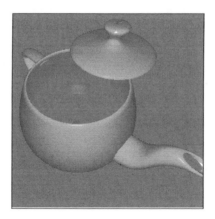

▶ The *Implementing per-vertex ambient, diffuse, and specular (ADS) shading* recipe

Implementing flat shading

Per-vertex shading involves computation of the shading model at each vertex and associating the result (a color) with that vertex. The colors are then interpolated across the face of the polygon to produce a smooth shading effect. This is also referred to as **Gouraud shading**. In earlier versions of OpenGL, this per-vertex shading with color interpolation was the default shading technique.

It is sometimes desirable to use a single color for each polygon so that there is no variation of color across the face of the polygon, causing each polygon to have a flat appearance. This can be useful in situations where the shape of the object warrants such a technique, perhaps because the faces really are intended to look flat, or to help visualize the locations of the polygons in a complex mesh. Using a single color for each polygon is commonly called **flat shading**.

The following screenshot shows a mesh rendered with the ADS shading model. On the left, Gouraud shading is used. On the right, flat shading is used.

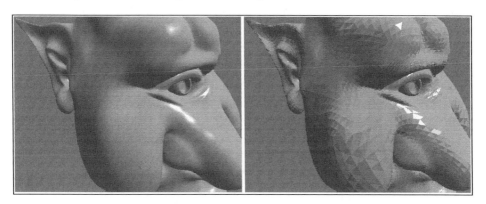

In earlier versions of OpenGL, flat shading was enabled by calling the function `glShadeModel` with the argument `GL_FLAT`. In which case, the computed color of the last vertex of each polygon was used across the entire face.

In OpenGL 4, flat shading is facilitated by the interpolation qualifiers available for shader input/output variables.

How to do it...

To modify the ADS shading model to implement flat shading, use the following steps:

1. Use the same vertex shader as in the ADS example provided earlier. Change the output variable LightIntensity as follows:

    ```
    layout (location = 0) in vec3 VertexPosition;
    layout (location = 1) in vec3 VertexNormal;

    flat out vec3 LightIntensity;

    // the rest is identical to the ADS shader...
    ```

2. Use the following code for the fragment shader:

    ```
    flat in vec3 LightIntensity;

    layout ( location = 0 ) out vec4 FragColor;

    void main() {
        FragColor = vec4(LightIntensity, 1.0);
    }
    ```

3. Compile and link both shaders within the OpenGL application, and install the shader program prior to rendering.

How it works...

Flat shading is enabled by qualifying the vertex output variable (and its corresponding fragment input variable) with the `flat` qualifier. This qualifier indicates that no interpolation of the value is to be done before it reaches the fragment shader. The value presented to the fragment shader will be the one corresponding to the result of the invocation of the vertex shader for either the first or last vertex of the polygon. This vertex is called the **provoking vertex**, and can be configured using the OpenGL function `glProvokingVertex`. For example, the call:

```
glProvokingVertex(GL_FIRST_VERTEX_CONVENTION);
```

This indicates that the first vertex should be used as the value for the flat shaded variable. The argument `GL_LAST_VERTEX_CONVENTION` indicates that the last vertex should be used.

See also

▶   The *Implementing per-vertex ambient, diffuse, and specular (ADS) shading* recipe

Using subroutines to select shader functionality

In GLSL, a subroutine is a mechanism for binding a function call to one of a set of possible function definitions based on the value of a variable. In many ways it is similar to function pointers in C. A uniform variable serves as the pointer and is used to invoke the function. The value of this variable can be set from the OpenGL side, thereby binding it to one of a few possible definitions. The subroutine's function definitions need not have the same name, but must have the same number and type of parameters and the same return type.

Subroutines therefore provide a way to select alternate implementations at runtime without swapping shader programs and/or recompiling, or using the `if` statements along with a uniform variable. For example, a single shader could be written to provide several shading algorithms intended for use on different objects within the scene. When rendering the scene, rather than swapping shader programs (or using a conditional statement), we can simply change the subroutine's uniform variable to choose the appropriate shading algorithm as each object is rendered.

 Since performance is crucial in shader programs, avoiding a conditional statement or a shader swap can be very valuable. With subroutines, we can implement the functionality of a conditional statement or shader swap without the computational overhead.

In this example, we'll demonstrate the use of subroutines by rendering a teapot twice. The first teapot will be rendered with the full ADS shading model described earlier. The second teapot will be rendered with diffuse shading only. A subroutine uniform will be used to choose between the two shading techniques.

In the following screenshot, we see an example of a rendering that was created using subroutines. The teapot on the left is rendered with the full ADS shading model, and the teapot on the right is rendered with diffuse shading only. A subroutine is used to switch between shader functionality.

Getting ready

As with previous recipes, provide the vertex position at attribute location 0 and the vertex normal at attribute location 1. Uniform variables for all of the ADS coefficients should be set from the OpenGL side, as well as the light position and the standard matrices.

We'll assume that, in the OpenGL application, the variable `programHandle` contains the handle to the shader program object.

How to do it...

To create a shader program that uses a subroutine to switch between pure-diffuse and ADS shading, use the following steps:

1. Use the following code for the vertex shader:

    ```glsl
    subroutine vec3 shadeModelType( vec4 position, vec3 normal);
    subroutine uniform shadeModelType shadeModel;

    layout (location = 0) in vec3 VertexPosition;
    layout (location = 1) in vec3 VertexNormal;

    out vec3 LightIntensity;

    struct LightInfo {
        vec4 Position; // Light position in eye coords.
        vec3 La;       // Ambient light intensity
        vec3 Ld;       // Diffuse light intensity
        vec3 Ls;       // Specular light intensity
    };
    uniform LightInfo Light;

    struct MaterialInfo {
        vec3 Ka;            // Ambient reflectivity
        vec3 Kd;            // Diffuse reflectivity
        vec3 Ks;            // Specular reflectivity
        float Shininess;    // Specular shininess factor
    };
    uniform MaterialInfo Material;

    uniform mat4 ModelViewMatrix;
    uniform mat3 NormalMatrix;
    uniform mat4 ProjectionMatrix;
    uniform mat4 MVP;
    ```

```
void getEyeSpace( out vec3 norm, out vec4 position )
{
    norm = normalize( NormalMatrix * VertexNormal);
    position = ModelViewMatrix * vec4(VertexPosition,1.0);
}

subroutine( shadeModelType )
vec3 phongModel( vec4 position, vec3 norm )
{
    // The ADS shading calculations go here (see: "Using
    // functions in shaders," and "Implementing
    // per-vertex ambient, diffuse, and specular (ADS)
    // shading")
    ...
}

subroutine( shadeModelType )
vec3 diffuseOnly( vec4 position, vec3 norm )
{
    vec3 s = normalize( vec3(Light.Position - position) );
    return
        Light.Ld * Material.Kd * max( dot(s, norm), 0.0 );
}

void main()
{
    vec3 eyeNorm;
    vec4 eyePosition;

    // Get the position and normal in eye space
    getEyeSpace(eyeNorm, eyePosition);

    // Evaluate the shading equation, calling one of
    // the functions: diffuseOnly or phongModel.
    LightIntensity = shadeModel(eyePosition, eyeNorm);

    gl_Position = MVP * vec4(VertexPosition,1.0);
}
```

2. Use the following code for the fragment shader:

```
in vec3 LightIntensity;

layout( location = 0 ) out vec4 FragColor;

void main() {
    FragColor = vec4(LightIntensity, 1.0);
}
```

3. In the OpenGL application, compile and link the previous shaders into a shader program, and install the program into the OpenGL pipeline.

4. Within the render function of the OpenGL application, use the following code:

```
GLuint adsIndex =
    glGetSubroutineIndex(programHandle,
                        GL_VERTEX_SHADER,"phongModel");
GLuint diffuseIndex =
    glGetSubroutineIndex(programHandle,
                        GL_VERTEX_SHADER, "diffuseOnly");

glUniformSubroutinesuiv( GL_VERTEX_SHADER, 1, &adsIndex);
... // Render the left teapot

glUniformSubroutinesuiv( GL_VERTEX_SHADER, 1, &diffuseIndex);
... // Render the right teapot
```

How it works...

In this example, the subroutine is defined within the vertex shader. The first step involves declaring the subroutine type:

```
subroutine vec3 shadeModelType( vec4 position, vec3 normal);
```

This defines a new subroutine type with the name shadeModelType. The syntax is very similar to a function prototype, in that it defines a name, a parameter list, and a return type. As with function prototypes, the parameter names are optional.

After creating the new subroutine type, we declare a uniform variable of that type named shadeModel:

```
subroutine uniform shadeModelType shadeModel;
```

This variable serves as our function pointer and will be assigned to one of the two possible functions in the OpenGL application.

We declare two functions to be part of the subroutine by prefixing their definition with the subroutine qualifier:

```
subroutine ( shadeModelType )
```

This indicates that the function matches the subroutine type, and therefore its header must match the one in the subroutine type definition. We use this prefix for the definition of the functions phongModel and diffuseOnly. The diffuseOnly function computes the diffuse shading equation, and the phongModel function computes the complete ADS shading equation.

We call one of the two subroutine functions by utilizing the subroutine uniform `shadeModel` within the main function:

```
LightIntensity = shadeModel( eyePosition, eyeNorm );
```

Again, this call will be bound to one of the two functions depending on the value of the subroutine uniform `shadeModel`, which we will set within the OpenGL application.

Within the render function of the OpenGL application, we assign a value to the subroutine uniform with the following two steps. First, we query for the index of each subroutine function using `glGetSubroutineIndex`. The first argument is the program handle. The second is the shader stage. In this case, the subroutine is defined within the vertex shader, so we use `GL_VERTEX_SHADER` here. The third argument is the name of the subroutine. We query for each function individually and store the indexes in the variables `adsIndex` and `diffuseIndex`.

Second, we select the appropriate subroutine function, To do so we need to set the value of the subroutine uniform `shadeModel` by calling `glUniformSubroutinesuiv`. This function is designed for setting multiple subroutine uniforms at once. In our case, of course, we are setting only a single uniform. The first argument is the shader stage (`GL_VERTEX_SHADER`), the second is the number of uniforms being set, and the third is a pointer to an array of subroutine function indexes. Since we are setting a single uniform, we simply provide the address of the `GLuint` variable containing the index, rather than a true array of values. Of course, we would use an array if multiple uniforms were being set. In general, the array of values provided as the third argument is assigned to subroutine uniform variables in the following way. The *i*th element of the array is assigned to the subroutine uniform variable with index *i*. Since we have provided only a single value, we are setting the subroutine uniform at index zero.

You may be wondering, "How do we know that our subroutine uniform is located at index zero? We didn't query for the index before calling `glUniformSubroutinesuiv`!" The reason that this code works is that we are relying on the fact that OpenGL will always number the indexes of the subroutines consecutively starting at zero. If we had multiple subroutine uniforms, we could (and should) query for their indexes using `glGetSubroutineUniformLocation`, and then order our array appropriately.

> `glUniformSubroutinesuiv` requires us to set all subroutine uniform variables at once, in a single call. This is so that they can be validated by OpenGL in a single burst.

There's more...

Unfortunately, subroutine bindings get reset when a shader program is unbound (switched out) from the pipeline, by calling `glUseProgram` or other technique. This requires us to call `glUniformSubroutinsuiv` each time that we activate a shader program.

A subroutine function defined in a shader can match more than one subroutine type. The subroutine qualifier can contain a comma-separated list of subroutine types. For example, if a subroutine matched the types `type1` and `type2`, we could use the following qualifier:

```
subroutine ( type1, type2 )
```

This would allow us to use subroutine uniforms of differing types to refer to the same subroutine function.

See also

▶ The *Implementing per-vertex ambient, diffuse, and specular (ADS) shading* recipe

▶ The *Implementing diffuse, per-vertex shading with a single point light source* recipe

Discarding fragments to create a perforated look

Fragment shaders can make use of the `discard` keyword to "throw away" fragments. Use of this keyword causes the fragment shader to stop execution, without writing anything (including depth) to the output buffer. This provides a way to create holes in polygons without using blending. In fact, since fragments are completely discarded, there is no dependence on the order in which objects are drawn, saving us the trouble of doing any depth sorting that might have been necessary if blending was used.

In this recipe, we'll draw a teapot, and use the `discard` keyword to remove fragments selectively, based on texture coordinates. The result will look like the following diagram:

Getting ready

The vertex position, normal, and texture coordinates must be provided to the vertex shader from the OpenGL application. The position should be provided at location 0, the normal at location 1, and the texture coordinates at location 2. As in the previous examples, the lighting parameters must be set from the OpenGL application via the appropriate uniform variables.

How to do it...

To create a shader program that discards fragments based on a square lattice (as in the preceding screenshot), use the following code:

1. Use the following code for the vertex shader:

```
layout (location = 0) in vec3 VertexPosition;
layout (location = 1) in vec3 VertexNormal;
layout (location = 2) in vec2 VertexTexCoord;

out vec3 FrontColor;
out vec3 BackColor;
out vec2 TexCoord;

struct LightInfo {
    vec4 Position; // Light position in eye coords.
    vec3 La;       // Ambient light intensity
    vec3 Ld;       // Diffuse light intensity
    vec3 Ls;       // Specular light intensity
};
uniform LightInfo Light;

struct MaterialInfo {
    vec3 Ka;            // Ambient reflectivity
    vec3 Kd;            // Diffuse reflectivity
    vec3 Ks;            // Specular reflectivity
    float Shininess;    // Specular shininess factor
};

uniform MaterialInfo Material;

uniform mat4 ModelViewMatrix;
uniform mat3 NormalMatrix;
uniform mat4 ProjectionMatrix;
uniform mat4 MVP;

void getEyeSpace( out vec3 norm, out vec4 position )
{
```

```
        norm = normalize( NormalMatrix * VertexNormal);
        position = ModelViewMatrix * vec4(VertexPosition,1.0);
    }

    vec3 phongModel( vec4 position, vec3 norm )
    {
        // The ADS shading calculation (see: "Implementing
        // per-vertex ambient, diffuse, and specular (ADS)
        // shading")
        ...
    }

    void main()
    {
        vec3 eyeNorm;
        vec4 eyePosition;

        TexCoord = VertexTexCoord;

        // Get the position and normal in eye space
        getEyeSpace(eyeNorm, eyePosition);

        FrontColor = phongModel( eyePosition, eyeNorm );
        BackColor = phongModel( eyePosition, -eyeNorm );

        gl_Position = MVP * vec4(VertexPosition,1.0);
    }
```

2. Use the following code for the fragment shader:

```
    in vec3 FrontColor;
    in vec3 BackColor;
    in vec2 TexCoord;

    layout( location = 0 ) out vec4 FragColor;

    void main() {
        const float scale = 15.0;

        bvec2 toDiscard = greaterThan( fract(TexCoord * scale),
                                       vec2(0.2,0.2) );

        if( all(toDiscard) )
            discard;

        if( gl_FrontFacing )
```

```
        FragColor = vec4(FrontColor, 1.0);
    else
        FragColor = vec4(BackColor, 1.0);
}
```

3. Compile and link both shaders within the OpenGL application, and install the shader program prior to rendering.

How it works...

Since we will be discarding some parts of the teapot, we will be able to see through the teapot to the other side. This will cause the back sides of some polygons to become visible. Therefore, we need to compute the lighting equation appropriately for both sides of each face. We'll use the same technique presented earlier in the two-sided shading recipe.

The vertex shader is essentially the same as in the two-sided shading recipe, with the main difference being the addition of the texture coordinate. The differences are highlighted in the previous listing. To manage the texture coordinate, we have an additional input variable, `VertexTexCoord`, that corresponds to attribute location 2. The value of this input variable is passed directly on to the fragment shader unchanged via the output variable `TexCoord`. The ADS shading model is calculated twice, once using the given normal vector, storing the result in `FrontColor`, and again using the reversed normal, storing that result in `BackColor`.

In the fragment shader, we calculate whether or not the fragment should be discarded based on a simple technique designed to produce the lattice-like pattern shown in the preceding screenshot. We first scale the texture coordinate by the arbitrary scaling factor `scale`. This corresponds to the number of lattice rectangles per unit (scaled) texture coordinate. We then compute the fractional part of each component of the scaled texture coordinate using the built-in function `fract`. Each component is compared to 0.2 using the built-in function `greaterThan`, and the result is stored in the `bool` vector `toDiscard`. The `greaterThan` function compares the two vectors component-wise, and stores the Boolean results in the corresponding components of the return value.

If both components of the vector `toDiscard` are true, then the fragment lies within the inside of each lattice frame, and therefore we wish to discard this fragment. We can use the built-in function `all` to help with this check. The function `all` will return true if all of the components of the parameter vector are true. If the function returns true, we execute the `discard` statement to reject the fragment.

In the else branch, we color the fragment based on the orientation of the polygon, as in the *Implementing two-sided shading* recipe presented earlier.

See also

▸ The *Implementing two-sided shading* recipe

3
Lighting, Shading, and Optimization

In this chapter, we will cover:

- ▶ Shading with multiple positional lights
- ▶ Shading with a directional light source
- ▶ Using per-fragment shading for improved realism
- ▶ Using the halfway vector for improved performance
- ▶ Simulating a spotlight
- ▶ Creating a cartoon shading effect
- ▶ Simulating fog
- ▶ Configuring the depth test

Introduction

In *Chapter 2, The Basics of GLSL Shaders*, we covered a number of techniques for implementing some of the shading effects that were produced by the former fixed-function pipeline. We also looked at some basic features of GLSL such as functions and subroutines. In this chapter, we'll move beyond the shading model introduced in *Chapter 2, The Basics of GLSL Shaders*, and see how to produce shading effects such as spotlights, fog, and cartoon style shading. We'll cover how to use multiple light sources, and how to improve the realism of the results with a technique called per-fragment shading.

We'll also see techniques for improving the efficiency of the shading calculations by using the so-called "halfway vector" and directional light sources.

Finally, we'll cover how to fine-tune the depth test by configuring the early depth test optimization.

Shading with multiple positional lights

When shading with multiple light sources, we need to evaluate the shading equation for each light and sum the results to determine the total light intensity reflected by a surface location. The natural choice is to create uniform arrays to store the position and intensity of each light. We'll use an array of structures so that we can store the values for multiple lights within a single uniform variable.

The following figure shows a "pig" mesh rendered with five light sources of different colors. Note the multiple specular highlights.

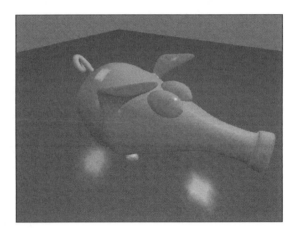

Getting ready

Set up your OpenGL program with the vertex position in attribute location zero, and the normal in location one.

How to do it...

To create a shader program that renders using the ADS (Phong) shading model with multiple light sources, use the following steps:

1. Use the following vertex shader:

    ```
    layout (location = 0) in vec3 VertexPosition;
    layout (location = 1) in vec3 VertexNormal;
    ```

```glsl
out vec3 Color;

struct LightInfo {
  vec4 Position;  // Light position in eye coords.
  vec3 Intensity; // Light intensity
};
uniform LightInfo lights[5];

// Material parameters
uniform vec3 Kd;           // Diffuse reflectivity
uniform vec3 Ka;           // Ambient reflectivity
uniform vec3 Ks;           // Specular reflectivity
uniform float Shininess;   // Specular shininess factor

uniform mat4 ModelViewMatrix;
uniform mat3 NormalMatrix;
uniform mat4 MVP;

vec3 ads( int lightIndex, vec4 position, vec3 norm )
{
  vec3 s = normalize( vec3(lights[lightIndex].Position -
                           position) );
  vec3 v = normalize(vec3(-position));
  vec3 r = reflect( -s, norm );
  vec3 I = lights[lightIndex].Intensity;
  return
       I * ( Ka +
       Kd * max( dot(s, norm), 0.0 ) +
       Ks * pow( max( dot(r,v), 0.0 ), Shininess ) );
}
void main()
{
  vec3 eyeNorm = normalize( NormalMatrix * VertexNormal);
  vec4 eyePosition = ModelViewMatrix *
                     vec4(VertexPosition,1.0);

  // Evaluate the lighting equation for each light
  Color = vec3(0.0);
  for( int i = 0; i < 5; i++ )
    Color += ads( i, eyePosition, eyeNorm );

  gl_Position = MVP * vec4(VertexPosition,1.0);
}
```

2. Use the following simple fragment shader:

```
in vec3 Color;

layout ( location = 0 ) out vec4 FragColor;

void main() {
   FragColor = vec4(Color, 1.0);
}
```

3. In the OpenGL application, set the values for the `lights` array in the vertex shader. For each light, use something similar to the following code. This example uses the C++ shader program class (`prog` is a `GLSLProgram` object).

```
prog.setUniform("lights[0].Intensity",
                vec3(0.0f,0.8f,0.8f) );
prog.setUniform("lights[0].Position", position );
```

Update the array index as appropriate for each light.

How it works...

Within the vertex shader, the lighting parameters are stored in the uniform array lights. Each element of the array is a struct of type `LightInfo`. This example uses five lights. The light intensity is stored in the `Intensity` field, and the position in eye coordinates is stored in the `Position` field.

The rest of the uniform variables are essentially the same as in the ADS (ambient, diffuse, and specular) shader presented in *Chapter 2, The Basics of GLSL Shaders*.

The `ads` function is responsible for computing the shading equation for a given light source. The index of the light is provided as the first parameter `lightIndex`. The equation is computed based on the values in the `lights` array at that index.

In the `main` function, a `for` loop is used to compute the shading equation for each light, and the results are summed into the shader output variable `Color`.

The fragment shader simply applies the interpolated color to the fragment.

See also

▶ The *Implementing per-vertex ambient, diffuse, and specular (ADS) shading* recipe in *Chapter 2, The Basics of GLSL shaders*

▶ The *Shading with a directional light source* recipe

Shading with a directional light source

A core component of a shading equation is the vector that points from the surface location towards the light source (s in previous examples). For lights that are extremely far away, there is very little variation in this vector over the surface of an object. In fact, for very distant light sources, the vector is essentially the same for all points on a surface. (Another way of thinking about this is that the light rays are nearly parallel.) Such a model would be appropriate for a distant, but powerful, light source such as the sun. Such a light source is commonly called a **directional light source** because it does not have a specific position, only a direction.

 Of course, we are ignoring the fact that, in reality, the intensity of the light decreases with the square of the distance from the source. However, it is not uncommon to ignore this aspect for directional light sources.

If we are using a directional light source, the direction towards the source is the same for all points in the scene. Therefore, we can increase the efficiency of our shading calculations because we no longer need to recompute the direction towards the light source for each location on the surface.

Of course, there is a visual difference between a positional light source and a directional one. The following figures show a torus rendered with a positional light (left) and a directional light (right). In the left figure, the light is located somewhat close to the torus. The directional light covers more of the surface of the torus due to the fact that all of the rays are parallel.

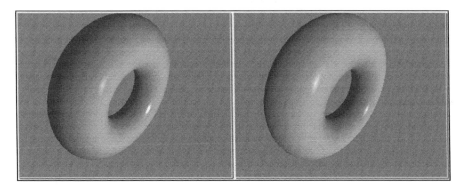

In previous versions of OpenGL, the fourth component of the light position was used to determine whether or not a light was considered directional. A zero in the fourth component indicated that the light source was directional and the position was to be treated as a direction towards the source (a vector). Otherwise, the position was treated as the actual location of the light source. In this example, we'll emulate the same functionality.

Getting ready

Set up your OpenGL program with the vertex position in attribute location zero, and the vertex normal in location one.

How to do it...

To create a shader program that implements ADS shading using a directional light source, use the following code:

1. Use the following vertex shader:

    ```
    layout (location = 0) in vec3 VertexPosition;
    layout (location = 1) in vec3 VertexNormal;

    out vec3 Color;

    uniform vec4 LightPosition;
    uniform vec3 LightIntensity;

    uniform vec3 Kd;            // Diffuse reflectivity
    uniform vec3 Ka;            // Ambient reflectivity
    uniform vec3 Ks;            // Specular reflectivity
    uniform float Shininess;    // Specular shininess factor

    uniform mat4 ModelViewMatrix;
    uniform mat3 NormalMatrix;
    uniform mat4 ProjectionMatrix;
    uniform mat4 MVP;

    vec3 ads( vec4 position, vec3 norm )
    {
      vec3 s;
      if( LightPosition.w == 0.0 )
        s = normalize(vec3(LightPosition));
      else
        s = normalize(vec3(LightPosition - position));
      vec3 v = normalize(vec3(-position));
      vec3 r = reflect( -s, norm );
      return
        LightIntensity * ( Ka +
                       Kd * max( dot(s, norm), 0.0 ) +
                       Ks * pow( max( dot(r,v), 0.0 ),
                        Shininess ) );
    }
    ```

```
void main()
{
  vec3 eyeNorm = normalize( NormalMatrix * VertexNormal);
  vec4 eyePosition = ModelViewMatrix *
                        vec4(VertexPosition,1.0);

  // Evaluate the lighting equation
  Color = ads( eyePosition, eyeNorm );
  gl_Position = MVP * vec4(VertexPosition,1.0);
}
```

2. Use the same simple fragment shader from the previous recipe:

```
in vec3 Color;

layout( location = 0 ) out vec4 FragColor;

void main() {
  FragColor = vec4(Color, 1.0);
}
```

How it works...

Within the vertex shader, the fourth coordinate of the uniform variable LightPosition is used to determine whether or not the light is to be treated as a directional light. Inside the ads function, which is responsible for computing the shading equation, the value of the vector s is determined based on whether or not the fourth coordinate of LightPosition is zero. If the value is zero, LightPosition is normalized and used as the direction towards the light source. Otherwise, LightPosition is treated as a location in eye coordinates, and we compute the direction towards the light source by subtracting the vertex position from LightPosition and normalizing the result.

There's more...

There is a slight efficiency gain when using directional lights due to the fact that there is no need to recompute the light direction for each vertex. This saves a subtraction operation, which is a small gain, but could accumulate when there are several lights, or when the lighting is computed per-fragment.

See also

▶ The *Implementing per-vertex ambient, diffuse, and specular (ADS) shading* recipe in Chapter 2, *The Basics of GLSL Shaders*.

▶ The *Using per-fragment shading for improved realism* recipe

Using per-fragment shading for improved realism

When the shading equation is evaluated within the vertex shader (as we have done in previous recipes), we end up with a color associated with each vertex. That color is then interpolated across the face, and the fragment shader assigns that interpolated color to the output fragment. As mentioned previously (the *Implementing flat shading* recipe in *Chapter 2, The Basics of GLSL Shaders*), this technique is often called **Gouraud shading**. Gouraud shading (like all shading techniques) is an approximation, and can lead to some less than desirable results when; for example, the reflection characteristics at the vertices have little resemblance to those in the center of the polygon. For example, a bright specular highlight may reside in the center of a polygon, but not at its vertices. Simply evaluating the shading equation at the vertices would prevent the specular highlight from appearing in the rendered result. Other undesirable artifacts, such as edges of polygons, may also appear when Gouraud shading is used, due to the fact that color interpolation is less physically accurate.

To improve the accuracy of our results, we can move the computation of the shading equation from the vertex shader to the fragment shader. Instead of interpolating color across the polygon, we interpolate the position and normal vector, and use these values to evaluate the shading equation at each fragment. This technique is often called **Phong shading** or **Phong interpolation**. The results from Phong shading are much more accurate and provide more pleasing results, but some undesirable artifacts may still appear.

The following figure shows the difference between Gouraud and Phong shading. The scene on the left is rendered with Gouraud (per-vertex) shading, and on the right is the same scene rendered using Phong (per-fragment) shading. Underneath the teapot is a partial plane, drawn with a single quad. Note the difference in the specular highlight on the teapot, as well as the variation in the color of the plane beneath the teapot.

In this example, we'll implement Phong shading by passing the position and normal from the vertex shader to the fragment shader, and then evaluate the ADS shading model within the fragment shader.

Getting ready

Set up your OpenGL program with the vertex position in attribute location zero, and the normal in location one. Your OpenGL application must also provide the values for the uniform variables Ka, Kd, Ks, Shininess, LightPosition, and LightIntensity, the first four of which are the standard material properties (reflectivities) of the ADS shading model. The latter two are the position of the light in eye coordinates, and the intensity of the light source, respectively. Finally, the OpenGL application must also provide the values for the uniforms ModelViewMatrix, NormalMatrix, ProjectionMatrix, and MVP.

How to do it...

To create a shader program that can be used for implementing per-fragment (or Phong) shading using the ADS shading model, use the following steps:

1. Use the following code for the vertex shader:

```
layout (location = 0) in vec3 VertexPosition;
layout (location = 1) in vec3 VertexNormal;

out vec3 Position;
out vec3 Normal;

uniform mat4 ModelViewMatrix;
uniform mat3 NormalMatrix;
uniform mat4 ProjectionMatrix;
uniform mat4 MVP;

void main()
{
    Normal = normalize( NormalMatrix * VertexNormal);
    Position = vec3( ModelViewMatrix *
                    vec4(VertexPosition,1.0) );
    gl_Position = MVP * vec4(VertexPosition,1.0);
}
```

2. Use the following code for the fragment shader:

```
in vec3 Position;
in vec3 Normal;

uniform vec4 LightPosition;
uniform vec3 LightIntensity;
uniform vec3 Kd;            // Diffuse reflectivity
uniform vec3 Ka;            // Ambient reflectivity
uniform vec3 Ks;            // Specular reflectivity
uniform float Shininess;    // Specular shininess factor
```

```
layout( location = 0 ) out vec4 FragColor;

vec3 ads( )
{
  vec3 n = normalize( Normal );
  vec3 s = normalize( vec3(LightPosition) - Position );
  vec3 v = normalize(vec3(-Position));
  vec3 r = reflect( -s, n );
  return
    LightIntensity *
      ( Ka +
      Kd * max( dot(s, n), 0.0 ) +
      Ks * pow( max( dot(r,v), 0.0 ), Shininess ) );
}

void main() {
  FragColor = vec4(ads(), 1.0);
}
```

How it works...

The vertex shader has two output variables: `Position` and `Normal`. In the `main` function, we convert the vertex normal to eye coordinates by transforming with the normal matrix, and then store the converted value in `Normal`. Similarly, the vertex position is converted to eye coordinates by transforming it by the model-view matrix, and the converted value is stored in `Position`.

The values of `Position` and `Normal` are automatically interpolated and provided to the fragment shader via the corresponding input variables. The fragment shader then computes the standard ADS shading equation using the values provided. The result is then stored in the output variable, `FragColor`.

There's more...

Evaluating the shading equation within the fragment shader produces more accurate renderings. However, the price we pay is in the evaluation of the shading model for each pixel of the polygon, rather than at each vertex. The good news is that with modern graphics cards, there may be enough processing power to evaluate all of the fragments for a polygon in parallel. This can essentially provide nearly equivalent performance for either per-fragment or per-vertex shading.

See also

▶ The *Implementing per-vertex ambient, diffuse, and specular (ADS) shading* recipe in Chapter 2, *The Basics of GLSL Shaders*

Using the halfway vector for improved performance

As covered in the *Implementing per-vertex ambient, diffuse, and specular (ADS) shading* recipe in *Chapter 2, The Basics of GLSL Shaders*, the specular term in the ADS shading equation involves the dot product of the vector of pure reflection (**r**), and the direction towards the viewer (**v**).

$$I_s = L_s K_s (\mathbf{r} \cdot \mathbf{v})^f$$

In order to evaluate the above equation, we need to find the vector of pure reflection (**r**), which is the reflection of the vector towards the light source (**s**) about the normal vector (**n**).

$$\mathbf{r} = -\mathbf{s} + 2(\mathbf{s} \cdot \mathbf{n})\mathbf{n}$$

 This equation is implemented by the GLSL function: `reflect`.

The above equation requires a dot product, an addition, and a couple of multiplication operations. We can gain a slight improvement in the efficiency of the specular calculation by making use of the following observation. When **v** is aligned with **r**, the normal vector (**n**) must be halfway between **v** and **s**.

Let's define the halfway vector (**h**) as the vector that is halfway between **v** and **s**, where h is normalized after the addition:

$$\mathbf{h} = \mathbf{v} + \mathbf{s}$$

The following diagram shows the relative positions of the halfway vector and the others:

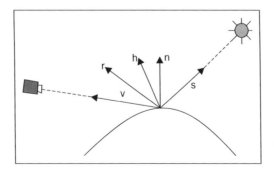

We can then replace the dot product in the equation for the specular component, with the dot product of **h** and **n**.

$$I_s = L_s K_s (\mathbf{h} \cdot \mathbf{n})^f$$

Computing **h** requires fewer operations than it takes to compute **r**, so we should expect some efficiency gain by using the halfway vector. The angle between the halfway vector and the normal vector is proportional to the angle between the vector of pure reflection (**r**) and the vector towards the viewer (**v**) when all vectors are coplanar. Therefore, we expect that the visual results will be similar, although not exactly the same.

Getting ready

Start by utilizing the same shader program that was presented in the recipe, *Using per-fragment shading for improved realism*, and set up your OpenGL program as described there.

How to do it...

Using the same shader pair as in the recipe, *Using per-fragment shading for improved realism*, replace the ads function in the fragment shader with the following code:

```
vec3 ads( )
{
    vec3 n = normalize( Normal );
    vec3 s = normalize( vec3 (LightPosition) - Position );
    vec3 v = normalize (vec3 (-Position));
    vec3 h = normalize( v + s );

    return
        LightIntensity *
            (Ka +
            Kd * max( dot (s, Normal), 0.0 ) +
            Ks * pow (max (dot (h,n),0.0), Shininess ) );
}
```

How it works...

We compute the halfway vector by summing the direction towards the viewer (v), and the direction towards the light source (s), and normalizing the result. The value for the halfway vector is then stored in h.

The specular calculation is then modified to use the dot product between h and the normal vector (`Normal`). The rest of the calculation is unchanged.

There's more...

The halfway vector provides a slight improvement in the efficiency of our specular calculation, and the visual results are quite similar. The following figure shows the teapot rendered using the halfway vector (right), versus the same rendering using the equation provided in the *Implementing per-vertex ambient, diffuse, and specular (ADS) shading* recipe in *Chapter 2, The Basics of GLSL Shaders* (left). The halfway vector produces a larger specular highlight, but the visual impact is not substantially different. If desired, we could compensate for the difference in the size of the specular highlight by increasing the value of the exponent `Shininess`.

See also

▶ The *Using per-fragment shading for improved realism* recipe

Simulating a spotlight

The fixed function pipeline had the ability to define light sources as spotlights. In such a configuration, the light source was considered to be one that only radiated light within a cone, the apex of which was located at the light source. Additionally, the light was attenuated so that it was maximal along the axis of the cone and decreased towards the outside edges. This allowed us to create light sources that had a similar visual effect to a real spotlight.

The following figure shows a teapot and a torus rendered with a single spotlight. Note the slight decrease in the intensity of the spotlight from the center towards the outside edge.

In this recipe, we'll use a shader to implement a spotlight effect similar to that produced by the fixed-function pipeline.

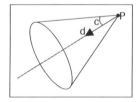

The spotlight's cone is defined by a spotlight direction (**d** in the preceding figure), a cutoff angle (**c** in the preceding figure), and a position (**P** in the preceding figure). The intensity of the spotlight is considered to be strongest along the axis of the cone, and decreases as you move towards the edges.

Getting ready

Start with the same vertex shader from the recipe, *Using per-fragment shading for improved realism*. Your OpenGL program must set the values for all uniform variables defined in that vertex shader as well as the fragment shader shown below.

How to do it...

To create a shader program that uses the ADS shading model with a spotlight, use the following code for the fragment shader:

```glsl
in vec3 Position;
in vec3 Normal;

struct SpotLightInfo {
  vec4 position;  // Position in eye coords.
  vec3 intensity; // Amb., Diff., and Specular intensity
  vec3 direction; // Normalized direction of the spotlight
  float exponent; // Angular attenuation exponent
  float cutoff;   // Cutoff angle (between 0 and 90)
};
uniform SpotLightInfo Spot;

uniform vec3 Kd;            // Diffuse reflectivity
uniform vec3 Ka;            // Ambient reflectivity
uniform vec3 Ks;            // Specular reflectivity
uniform float Shininess;    // Specular shininess factor

layout( location = 0 ) out vec4 FragColor;

vec3 adsWithSpotlight( )
{
  vec3 s = normalize( vec3( Spot.position) - Position );
  float angle = acos( dot(-s, Spot.direction) );
  float cutoff = radians( clamp( Spot.cutoff, 0.0, 90.0 ) );
  vec3 ambient = Spot.intensity * Ka;

  if( angle < cutoff ) {
    float spotFactor = pow( dot(-s, Spot.direction),
                            Spot.exponent );
  vec3 v = normalize(vec3(-Position));
  vec3 h = normalize( v + s );
  return
    ambient +
    spotFactor * Spot.intensity * (
      Kd * max( dot(s, Normal), 0.0 ) +
      Ks * pow(max(dot(h,Normal), 0.0),Shininess));
  } else {
    return ambient;
    }
}

void main() {
  FragColor = vec4(adsWithSpotlight(), 1.0);
}
```

How it works...

The structure `SpotLightInfo` defines all of the configuration options for the spotlight. We declare a single uniform variable named `Spot` to store the data for our spotlight. The `position` field defines the location of the spotlight in eye coordinates. The `intensity` field is the intensity (ambient, diffuse, and specular) of the spotlight. If desired, you could break this into three variables. The `direction` field will contain the direction that the spotlight is pointing, which defines the center axis of the spotlight's cone. This vector should be specified in eye coordinates. Within the OpenGL program it should be transformed by the normal matrix in the same way that normal vectors would be transformed. We could do so within the shader; however, within the shader, the normal matrix would be specified for the object being rendered. This may not be the appropriate transform for the spotlight's direction.

The `exponent` field defines the exponent that is used when calculating the angular attenuation of the spotlight. The intensity of the spotlight is decreased in proportion to the cosine of the angle between the vector from the light to the surface location (the negation of the variable s) and the direction of the spotlight. That cosine term is then raised to the power of the variable exponent. The larger the value of this variable, the faster the intensity of the spotlight is decreased. This is quite similar to the exponent in the specular shading term.

The `cutoff` field defines the angle between the central axis and the outer edge of the spotlight's cone of light. We specify this angle in degrees, and clamp its value between 0 and 90.

The function, `adsWithSpotlight`, computes the standard ambient, diffuse, and specular (ADS) shading equation, using a spotlight as the light source. The first line computes the vector from the surface location to the spotlight's position (s). Next, the spotlight's direction is normalized and stored within `spotDir`. The angle between `spotDir` and the negation of s is then computed and stored in the variable `angle`. The `cutoff` variable stores the value of `Spot.cutoff` after it has been clamped between 0 and 90, and converted from degrees to radians. Next, the ambient lighting component is computed and stored in the `ambient` variable.

We then compare the value of the `angle` variable with that of the `cutoff` variable. If `angle` is less than `cutoff`, then the surface point is within the spotlight's cone. Otherwise the surface point only receives ambient light, so we return only the ambient component.

If `angle` is less than `cutoff`, we compute the `spotFactor` variable by raising the dot product of −s and `spotDir` to the power of `Spot.exponent`. The value of `spotFactor` is used to scale the intensity of the light so that the light is maximal in the center of the cone, and decreases as you move towards the edges. Finally, the ADS shading equation is computed as usual, but the diffuse and specular terms are scaled by `spotFactor`.

See also

- ▶ The *Using per-fragment shading for improved realism* recipe
- ▶ The *Implementing per-vertex ambient, diffuse, and specular shading (ADS)* recipe in Chapter 2, *The Basics of GLSL Shaders*

Creating a cartoon shading effect

Toon shading (also called **Celshading**) is a non-photorealistic technique that is intended to mimic the style of shading often used in hand-drawn animation. There are many different techniques that are used to produce this effect. In this recipe, we'll use a very simple technique that involves a slight modification to the ambient and diffuse shading model.

The basic effect is to have large areas of constant color with sharp transitions between them. This simulates the way that an artist might shade an object using strokes of a pen or brush. The following figure shows an example of a teapot and torus rendered with toon shading.

The technique presented here involves computing only the ambient and diffuse components of the typical ADS shading model, and quantizing the cosine term of the diffuse component. In other words, the value of the dot product normally used in the diffuse term is restricted to a fixed number of possible values. The following table illustrates the concept for four levels:

Cosine of the Angle between s and n	Value used
Between 1 and 0.75	0.75
Between 0.75 and 0.5	0.5
Between 0.5 and 0.25	0.25
Between 0.25 and 0.0	0.0

In the preceding table, **s** is the vector towards the light source and **n** is the normal vector at the surface. By restricting the value of the cosine term in this way, the shading displays strong discontinuities from one level to another (see the preceding figure), simulating the pen strokes of hand-drawn cel animation.

Getting ready

Start with the same vertex shader from the *Using per-fragment shading for improved realism* recipe. Your OpenGL program must set the values for all uniform variables defined in that vertex shader as well as the fragment shader code described below.

How to do it...

To create a shader program that produces a toon shading effect, use the following fragment shader:

```
in vec3 Position;
in vec3 Normal;

struct LightInfo {
  vec4 position;
  vec3 intensity;
};
uniform LightInfo Light;

uniform vec3 Kd;           // Diffuse reflectivity
uniform vec3 Ka;           // Ambient reflectivity

const int levels = 3;
const float scaleFactor = 1.0 / levels;
layout( location = 0 ) out vec4 FragColor;
vec3 toonShade( )
{
  vec3 s = normalize( Light.position.xyz - Position.xyz );
  float cosine = max( 0.0, dot( s, Normal ) );
  vec3 diffuse = Kd * floor( cosine * levels ) *
                 scaleFactor;

  return Light.intensity * (Ka + diffuse);
}

void main() {
  FragColor = vec4(toonShade(), 1.0);
}
```

How it works...

The constant variable, `levels`, defines how many distinct values will be used in the diffuse calculation. This could also be defined as a uniform variable to allow for configuration from the main OpenGL application. We will use this variable to quantize the value of the cosine term in the diffuse calculation.

The `toonShade` function is the most significant part of this shader. We start by computing `s`, the vector towards the light source. Next, we compute the cosine term of the diffuse component by evaluating the dot product of `s` and `Normal`. The next line quantizes that value in the following way. Since the two vectors are normalized, and we have removed negative values with the max function, we are sure that the value of cosine is between zero and one. By multiplying this value by levels and taking the floor, the result will be an integer between 0 and levels -1. When we divide that value by levels (by multiplying by `scaleFactor`), we scale these integral values to be between zero and one again. The result is a value that can be one of `levels` possible values spaced between zero and one. This result is then multiplied by `Kd`, the diffuse reflectivity term.

Finally, we combine the diffuse and ambient components together to get the final color for the fragment.

There's more...

When quantizing the cosine term, we could have used `ceil` instead of `floor`. Doing so would have simply shifted each of the possible values up by one level. This would make the levels of shading slightly brighter.

The typical cartoon style seen in most cel animation includes black outlines around the silhouettes and along other edges of a shape. The shading model presented here does not produce those black outlines. There are several techniques for producing them, and we'll look at one later on in this book.

See also

- ▶ The *Using per-fragment shading for improved realism* recipe
- ▶ The *Implementing per-vertex ambient, diffuse, and specular (ADS) shading* recipe in *Chapter 2, The Basics of GLSL Shaders*
- ▶ The *Drawing silhouette lines using the geometry shader* recipe in *Chapter 6, Using Geometry and Tessellation Shaders*

Simulating fog

A simple fog effect can be achieved by mixing the color of each fragment with a constant fog color. The amount of influence of the fog color is determined by the distance from the camera. We could use either a linear relationship between the distance and the amount of fog color, or we could use a non-linear relationship such as an exponential one.

The following figure shows four teapots rendered with a fog effect produced by mixing the fog color in a linear relationship with distance.

To define this linear relationship we can use the following equation:

$$f = \frac{d_{\max} - |z|}{d_{\max} - d_{\min}}$$

In the preceding equation, $d_{\min}$ is the distance from the eye where the fog is minimal (no fog contribution), and $d_{\max}$ is the distance where the fog color obscures all other colors in the scene. The variable z represents the distance from the eye. The value f is the fog factor. A fog factor of zero represents 100 percent fog, and a factor of one represents no fog. Since fog typically looks thickest at large distances, the fog factor is minimal when $|z|$ is equal to $d_{\max}$, and maximal when $|z|$ is equal to $d_{\min}$.

Since the fog is applied by the fragment shader, the effect will only be visible on the objects that are rendered. It will not appear on any "empty" space in the scene (the background). To help make the fog effect consistent, you should use a background color that matches the maximum fog color.

Getting ready

Start with the same vertex shader from the *Using per-fragment shading for improved realism* recipe. Your OpenGL program must set the values for all uniform variables defined in that vertex shader as well as the fragment shader shown in the following section.

How to do it...

To create a shader that produces a fog-like effect, use the following code for the fragment shader:

```
in vec3 Position;
in vec3 Normal;

struc tLightInfo {
  vec4 position;
  vec3 intensity;
};
uniform LightInfo Light;

struct FogInfo {
  float maxDist;
  float minDist;
  vec3 color;
};
uniform FogInfo Fog;

uniform vec3 Kd;          // Diffuse reflectivity
uniform vec3 Ka;          // Ambient reflectivity
uniform vec3 Ks;          // Specular reflectivity
uniform float Shininess;  // Specular shininess factor

layout( location = 0 ) out vec4 FragColor;

vec3 ads( )
{
    // … The ADS shading algorithm
}

void main() {
  float dist = abs( Position.z );
  float fogFactor = (Fog.maxDist - dist) /
                    (Fog.maxDist - Fog.minDist);
  fogFactor = clamp( fogFactor, 0.0, 1.0 );
  vec3 shadeColor = ads();
  vec3 color = mix( Fog.color, shadeColor, fogFactor );

  FragColor = vec4(color, 1.0);
}
```

How it works...

In this shader, the `ads` function is exactly the same as the one used in the recipe *Using the halfway vector for improved performance*. The part of this shader that deals with the fog effect lies within the `main` function.

The uniform variable `Fog` contains the parameters that define the extent and color of the fog. The `minDist` field is the distance from the eye to the fog's starting point, and `maxDist` is the distance to the point where the fog is maximal. The `color` field is the color of the fog.

The `dist` variable is used to store the distance from the surface point to the eye position. The `z` coordinate of the position is used as an estimate of the actual distance. The `fogFactor` variable is computed using the preceding equation. Since `dist` may not be between `minDist` and `maxDist`, we clamp the value of `fogFactor` to be between zero and one.

We then call the `ads` function to evaluate the basic ADS shading model. The result of this is stored in the `shadeColor` variable.

Finally, we mix `shadeColor` and `Fog.color` together based on the value of `fogFactor`, and the result is used as the fragment color.

There's more...

In this recipe, we used a linear relationship between the amount of fog color and the distance from the eye. Another choice would be to use an exponential relationship. For example, the following equation could be used:

$$f = e^{-d|z|}$$

In the above equation, **d** represents the density of the fog. Larger values would create "thicker" fog. We could also square the exponent to create a slightly different relationship (a faster increase in the fog with distance).

$$f = e^{-(dz)^2}$$

Computing distance from the eye

In the above code, we used the absolute value of the z coordinate as the distance from the camera. This may cause the fog to look a bit unrealistic in certain situations. To compute a more precise distance, we could replace the line:

```
float dist = abs( Position.z );
```

with the following:

```
float dist = length( Position.xyz );
```

Of course, the latter version requires a square root, and therefore would be a bit slower in practice.

See also

▶ The *Using per-fragment shading for improved realism* recipe

▶ The *Implementing per-vertex ambient, diffuse, and specular (ADS) shading* recipe in *Chapter 2, The Basics of GLSL Shaders*

Configuring the depth test

GLSL 4 provides the ability to configure how the depth test is performed. This gives us additional control over how and when fragments are tested against the depth buffer.

Many OpenGL implementations automatically provide an optimization known as the early depth test or early fragment test. With this optimization, the depth test is performed before the fragment shader is executed. Since fragments that fail the depth test will not appear on the screen (or the framebuffer), there is no point in executing the fragment shader at all for those fragments and we can save some time by avoiding the execution.

The OpenGL specification, however, states that the depth test is performed *after* the fragment shader. This means that if an implementation wishes to use the early depth test optimization, it must be careful. The implementation must make sure that if anything within the fragment shader might change the results of the depth test, then it should avoid using the early depth test.

For example, a fragment shader can change the depth of a fragment by writing to the output variable, `gl_FragDepth`. If it does so, then the early depth test cannot be performed because, of course, the final depth of the fragment is not known prior to the execution of the fragment shader. However, the GLSL provides ways to notify the pipeline roughly how the depth will be modified, so that the implementation may determine when it might be ok to use the early depth test.

Another possibility is that the fragment shader might conditionally discard the fragment using the `discard` keyword. If there is any possibility that the fragment may be discarded, some implementations may not perform the early depth test.

There are also certain situations where we want to rely on the early depth test. For example, if the fragment shader writes to memory other than the framebuffer (with image load/store, shader storage buffers, or other incoherent memory writing), we might not want the fragment shader to execute for fragments that fail the depth test. This would help us to avoid writing data for fragments that fail. The GLSL provides a technique for forcing the early depth test optimization.

How to do it...

To ask the OpenGL pipeline to always perform the early depth test optimization, use the following layout qualifier in your fragment shader:

```
layout(early_fragment_tests) in;
```

If your fragment shader will modify the fragment's depth, but you still would like to take advantage of the early depth test when possible, use the following layout qualifier in a declaration of `gl_FragDepth` within your fragment shader:

```
layout (depth_*) out float gl_FragDepth;
```

Where, `depth_*` is one of the following: `depth_any`, `depth_greater`, `depth_less`, or `depth_unchanged`.

How it works...

The following statement forces the OpenGL implementation to always perform the early depth test:

```
layout(early_fragment_tests) in;
```

We must keep in mind that if we attempt to modify the depth anywhere within the shader by writing to `gl_FragDepth`, the value that is written will be ignored.

If your fragment shader needs to modify the depth value, then we can't force early fragment tests. However, we can help the pipeline to determine when it can still apply the early test. We do so by using one of the layout qualifiers for `gl_FragDepth` as shown above. This places some limits on how the value will be modified. The OpenGL implementation can then determine if the fragment shader can be skipped. If it can be determined that the depth will not be changed in such a way that it would cause the result of the test to change, the implementation can still use the optimization.

The layout qualifier for the output variable `gl_FragDepth` tells the OpenGL implementation specifically how the depth might change within the fragment shader. The qualifier `depth_any` indicates that it could change in any way. This is the default.

The other qualifiers describe how the value may change with respect to `gl_FragCoord.z`.

  ▸   `depth_greater`: This fragment shader promises to only increase the depth.

  ▸   `depth_less`: This fragment shader promises to only decrease the depth.

  ▸   `depth_unchanged`: This fragment shader promises not to change the depth. If it writes to `gl_FragDepth`, the value will be equal to `gl_FragCoord.z`.

If you use one of these qualifiers, but then go on to modify the depth in an incompatible way, the results are undefined. For example, if you declare gl_FragDepth with depth_greater, but decrease the depth of the fragment, the code will compile and execute, but you shouldn't expect to see accurate results.

 If your fragment shader writes to gl_FragDepth, then it must be sure to write a value in all circumstances. In other words, it must write a value no matter which branches are taken within the code.

See also

▶ The *Implementing order-independent transparency* recipe in *Chapter 5, Image Processing and Screen Space Techniques*

4

Using Textures

In this chapter, we will cover:

- ▶ Applying a 2D texture
- ▶ Applying multiple textures
- ▶ Using alpha maps to discard pixels
- ▶ Using normal maps
- ▶ Simulating reflection with cube maps
- ▶ Simulating refraction with cube maps
- ▶ Applying a projected texture
- ▶ Rendering to a texture
- ▶ Using sampler objects

Introduction

Textures are an important and fundamental aspect of real-time rendering in general, and OpenGL in particular. The use of textures within a shader opens up a huge range of possibilities. Beyond just using textures as sources of color information, they can be used for things like depth information, shading parameters, displacement maps, normal vectors, or other vertex data. The list is virtually endless. Textures are among the most widely used tools for advanced effects in OpenGL programs, and that isn't likely to change anytime soon.

In OpenGL 4, we now have the ability to read and write to memory via buffer textures, shader storage buffer objects, and image textures (image load/store). This further muddies the waters of what exactly defines a texture. In general, we might just think of it as a buffer of data that may or may not contain an image.

OpenGL 4.2 introduced **immutable storage textures**. Despite what the term may imply, immutable storage textures are not textures that can't change. Instead, the term *immutable* refers to the fact that, once the texture is allocated, the *storage* cannot be changed. That is, the size, format, and number of layers are fixed, but the texture content itself can be modified. The word immutable refers to the allocation of the memory, not the contents of the memory. Immutable storage textures are preferable in the vast majority of cases because of the fact that many run-time (draw-time) consistency checks can be avoided, and you include a certain degree of "type safety," since we can't accidentally change the allocation of a texture. Throughout this book, we'll use immutable storage textures exclusively.

 Immutable storage textures are allocated using the `glTexStorage*` functions. If you're experienced with textures, you might be accustomed to using `glTexImage*` functions, which are still supported, but create mutable storage textures.

In this chapter, we'll look at some basic and advanced texturing techniques. We'll start with the basics, just applying color textures, and move on to using textures as normal maps and environment maps. With environment maps, we can simulate things like reflection and refraction. We'll see an example of projecting a texture onto objects in a scene similar to the way that a slide projector projects an image. Finally, we'll wrap up with an example of rendering directly to a texture(using **framebuffer objects** (**FBO**s) and then applying that texture to an object.

Applying a 2D texture

In GLSL, applying a texture to a surface involves accessing texture memory to retrieve a color associated with a texture coordinate, and then applying that color to the output fragment. The application of the color to the output fragment could involve mixing the color with the color produced by a shading model, simply applying the color directly, using the color in the reflection model, or some other mixing process. In GLSL, textures are accessed via **sampler** variables. A sampler variable is a "handle" to a texture unit. It is typically declared as a uniform variable within the shader and initialized within the main OpenGL application to point to the appropriate texture unit.

In this recipe, we'll look at a simple example involving the application of a 2D texture to a surface as shown in the following image. We'll use the texture color to scale the color provided by the **ambient, diffuse, and specular** (**ADS**) reflection model. The following image shows the results of a brick texture applied to a cube. The texture is shown on the right and the rendered result is on the left.

Getting ready

Set up your OpenGL application to provide the vertex position in attribute location 0, the vertex normal in attribute location 1, and the texture coordinate in attribute location 2. The parameters for the ADS reflection model are declared again as uniform variables within the shader, and must be initialized from the OpenGL program. Make the handle to the shader available in a variable named `programHandle`.

How to do it...

To render a simple shape with a 2D texture, use the following steps:

1. In your initialization of the OpenGL application, use the following code to load the texture. (The following makes use of a simple TGA image loader, provided with the sample code.)

```
GLint width, height;
GLubyte * data = TGAIO::read("brick1.tga", width, height);

// Copy file to OpenGL
glActiveTexture(GL_TEXTURE0);
GLuint tid;
glGenTextures(1, &tid);
glBindTexture(GL_TEXTURE_2D, tid);
glTexStorage2D(GL_TEXTURE_2D, 1, GL_RGBA8, w, h);
glTexSubImage2D(GL_TEXTURE_2D, 0, 0, 0, width, height,
                GL_RGBA, GL_UNSIGNED_BYTE, data);
glTexParameteri(GL_TEXTURE_2D, GL_TEXTURE_MAG_FILTER,
                GL_LINEAR);
glTexParameteri(GL_TEXTURE_2D, GL_TEXTURE_MIN_FILTER,
                GL_LINEAR);
```

```
      delete [] data;

      // Set the Tex1 sampler uniform to refer to texture unit 0
      int loc = glGetUniformLocation(programHandle, "Tex1");
      if( loc >= 0 )
        glUniform1i(loc, 0);
```

2. Use the following code for the vertex shader:

```
      layout (location = 0) in vec3 VertexPosition;
      layout (location = 1) in vec3 VertexNormal;
      layout (location = 2) in vec2 VertexTexCoord;

      out vec3 Position;
      out vec3 Normal;
      out vec2 TexCoord;

      uniform mat4 ModelViewMatrix;
      uniform mat3 NormalMatrix;
      uniform mat4 ProjectionMatrix;
      uniform mat4 MVP;

      void main()
      {
        TexCoord = VertexTexCoord;
        Normal = normalize( NormalMatrix * VertexNormal);
        Position = vec3( ModelViewMatrix *
                        vec4(VertexPosition,1.0) );

        gl_Position = MVP * vec4(VertexPosition,1.0);
      }
```

3. Use the following code for the fragment shader:

```
      in vec3 Position;
      in vec3 Normal;
      in vec2 TexCoord;

      uniform sampler2D Tex1;

      struct LightInfo {
        vec4 Position;  // Light position in eye coords.
        vec3 Intensity; // A,D,S intensity
      };
```

```
uniform LightInfo Light;

struct MaterialInfo {
  vec3 Ka;              // Ambient reflectivity
  vec3 Kd;              // Diffuse reflectivity
  vec3 Ks;              // Specular reflectivity
  float Shininess;      // Specular shininess factor
};
uniform MaterialInfo Material;

layout( location = 0 ) out vec4 FragColor;

void phongModel( vec3 pos, vec3 norm,
    out vec3 ambAndDiff, out vec3 spec ) {
      // Compute the ADS shading model here, return ambient
      // and diffuse color in ambAndDiff, and return specular
      // color in spec

}
void main() {
  vec3 ambAndDiff, spec;
  vec4 texColor = texture( Tex1, TexCoord );
  phongModel(Position, Normal, ambAndDiff, spec);
  FragColor = vec4(ambAndDiff, 1.0) * texColor +
              vec4(spec, 1.0);
}
```

How it works...

The first code segment demonstrates the steps needed to load the texture from a file, copy the texture data to OpenGL memory, and initialize the sampler variable within the GLSL program. The first step, loading the texture image file, is accomplished via a simple TGA image loader that is provided along with the example code (TGAIO::read()). It reads the image data from a file in the TGA format, and stores the data into an array of unsigned bytes in RGBA order. The width and height of the image are returned via the last two parameters. We keep a pointer to the image data, simply named data.

The TGA format is simple and easy to understand, it is free of any encumbering patents, and supports true color images with an alpha channel. This makes it a very convenient format for texture reading/writing. If your images are not in that format, just grab a copy of ImageMagick and convert. However, the TGA format is not very memory efficient. If you want to load images stored in other formats, there are a variety of other options. For example, check out ResIL (`http://resil.sourceforge.net/`), or Freeimage (`http://freeimage.sourceforge.net/`).

Experienced OpenGL programmers should be familiar with the next part of the code. First, we call `glActiveTexture` to set the current active texture unit to `GL_TEXTURE0` (the first texture unit, also called a texture *channel*). The subsequent texture state calls will be effective on texture unit zero. The next two lines involve creating a new texture object by calling `glGenTextures`.. The handle for the new texture object is stored in the variable `tid`. Then, we call `glBindTexture` to bind the new texture object to the `GL_TEXTURE_2D` target. Once the texture is bound to that target, we allocate immutable storage for the texture with `glTexStorage2D`. After that, we copy the data for that texture into the texture object using `glTexSubImage2D`. The last argument to this function is a pointer to the raw data for the image.

The next steps involve setting the magnification and minimization filters for the texture object using `glTexParameteri`. For this example, we'll use `GL_LINEAR`.

The texture filter setting determines whether any interpolation will be done prior to returning the color from the texture. This setting can have a strong effect on the quality of the results. In this example, `GL_LINEAR` indicates that it will return a weighted average of the four texels that are nearest to the texture coordinates. For details on the other filtering options, see the OpenGL documentation for `glTexParameteri`: `http://www.opengl.org/wiki/GLAPI/glTexParameter`.

Next, we delete the texture data pointed to by `data`. There's no need to hang on to this, because it was copied into texture memory via `glTexSubImage2D`.

Finally, we set the uniform variable `Tex1` in the GLSL program to zero. This is our sampler variable. Note that it is declared within the fragment shader with type `sampler2D`. Setting its value to zero indicates to the OpenGL system that the variable should refer to texture unit zero (the same one selected previously with `glActiveTexture`).

The vertex shader is very similar to the one used in previous examples except for the addition of the texture coordinate input variable `VertexTexCoord`, which is bound to attribute location 2. Its value is simply passed along to the fragment shader by assigning it to the shader output variable `TexCoord`.

The fragment shader is also very similar to those used in the recipes of previous chapters. The important parts for the purpose of this recipe involve the variable `Tex1`. `Tex1` is a `sampler2D` variable that was assigned by the OpenGL program to refer to texture unit zero. In the main function, we use that variable along with the texture coordinate (`TexCoord`) to access the texture. We do so by calling the built-in function `texture`. This is a general purpose function, used to access a texture. The first parameter is a sampler variable indicating which texture unit is to be accessed, and the second parameter is the texture coordinate used to access the texture. The return value is a `vec4` containing the color obtained by the texture access (stored in `texColor`), which in this case is an interpolated value with the four nearest texture values (texels).

Next, the shading model is evaluated by calling `phongModel` and the results are returned in the parameters `ambAndDiff` and `spec`. The variable `ambAndDiff` contains only the ambient and diffuse components of the shading model. A color texture is often only intended to affect the diffuse component of the shading model and not the specular. So we multiply the texture color by the ambient and diffuse components and then add the specular. The final sum is then applied to the output fragment `FragColor`.

There's more...

There are several choices that could be made when deciding how to combine the texture color with other colors associated with the fragment. In this example, we decided to multiply the colors, but one could have chosen to use the texture color directly, or to mix them in some way based on the alpha value.

Another choice would be to use the texture value as the value of the diffuse and/or specular reflectivity coefficient(s) in the Phong reflection model. The choice is up to you!

Specifying the sampler binding within GLSL

As of OpenGL 4.2, we now have the ability to specify the default value of the sampler's binding (the value of the sampler uniform) within GLSL. In the previous example, we of set the value of the uniform variable from the OpenGL side using the following code:

```
int loc = glGetUniformLocation(programHandle, "Tex1");
if( loc >= 0 )
  glUniform1i(loc, 0);
```

Instead, if we're using OpenGL 4.2, we can specify the default value within the shader, using the layout qualifier as shown in the following statement:

```
layout (binding=0) uniform sampler2D Tex1;
```

Thus simplifying the code on the OpenGL side, and making one less thing we need to worry about. The example code that accompanies this book uses this technique to specify the value of `Tex1`, so take a look there for a more complete example. We'll also use this layout qualifier in the following recipes.

See also

▸ For more information about sending data to a shader via vertex attributes refer the *Sending data to a shader using vertex attributes and vertex buffer objects* recipe in *Chapter 1, Getting Started with GLSL*

▸ *The Using per-fragment shading for improved realism* recipe in *Chapter 3, Lighting, Shading and Optimization*

Applying multiple textures

The application of multiple textures to a surface can be used to create a wide variety of effects. The base layer texture might represent the "clean" surface and the second layer could provide additional detail such as shadow, blemishes, roughness, or damage. In many games, so-called light maps are applied as an additional texture layer to provide the information about light exposure, effectively producing shadows and shading without the need to explicitly calculate the reflection model. These kinds of textures are sometimes referred to as "prebaked" lighting.

In this recipe, we'll demonstrate this multiple texture technique by applying two layers of texture. The base layer will be a fully opaque brick image, and the second layer will be one that is partially transparent. The non-transparent parts look like moss that has grown on the bricks beneath.

The following image shows an example of multiple textures. The textures on the left are applied to the cube on the right. The base layer is the brick texture, and the moss texture is applied on top. The transparent parts of the moss texture reveal the brick texture underneath.

Getting ready

Set up your OpenGL application to provide the vertex position in attribute location 0, the vertex normal in attribute location 1, and the texture coordinate in attribute location 2. The parameters for the Phong reflection model are declared as uniform variables within the shader and must be initialized from the OpenGL program.

How to do it...

To render objects with multiple textures, use the following steps:

1. In the initialization section of your OpenGL program, load the two images into texture memory in the same way as indicated in the previous recipe *Applying a 2D texture*. Make sure that the brick texture is loaded into texture unit 0 and the moss texture is in texture unit 1. Use the following code to do this:

```
GLuint texIDs[2];
GLint w, h;
glGenTextures(2, texIDs);

// Load brick texture file
GLubyte * brickImg = TGAIO::read("brick1.tga", w, h);

// Copy brick texture to OpenGL
glActiveTexture(GL_TEXTURE0);
glBindTexture(GL_TEXTURE_2D, texIDs[0]);
glTexStorage2D(GL_TEXTURE_2D, 1, GL_RGBA8, w, h);
glTexSubImage2D(GL_TEXTURE_2D, 0, 0, 0, w, h, GL_RGBA,
                GL_UNSIGNED_BYTE, brickImg);
glTexParameteri(GL_TEXTURE_2D, GL_TEXTURE_MAG_FILTER,
                GL_LINEAR);
glTexParameteri(GL_TEXTURE_2D, GL_TEXTURE_MIN_FILTER,
                GL_LINEAR);
delete [] brickImg;


// Load moss texture file
GLubyte * mossImg = TGAIO::read("moss.tga", w, h);

// Copy moss texture to OpenGL
glActiveTexture(GL_TEXTURE1);
glBindTexture(GL_TEXTURE_2D, texIDs[1]);
glTexStorage2D(GL_TEXTURE_2D, 1, GL_RGBA8, w, h);
glTexSubImage2D(GL_TEXTURE_2D, 0, 0, 0, w, h, GL_RGBA,
                GL_UNSIGNED_BYTE, mossImg);
```

```
glTexParameteri(GL_TEXTURE_2D, GL_TEXTURE_MAG_FILTER,
                GL_LINEAR);
glTexParameteri(GL_TEXTURE_2D, GL_TEXTURE_MIN_FILTER,
                GL_LINEAR);

delete [] mossImg;
```

2. Use the vertex shader from the previous recipe *Applying a 2D texture*.

3. Starting with the fragment shader from the recipe *Applying a 2D texture*, replace the declaration of the sampler variable `Tex1` with the following code:

    ```
    layout (binding=0) uniform sampler2D BrickTex;
    layout (binding=1) uniform sampler2D MossTex;
    ```

4. Replace the main function in the fragment shader with the following code:

    ```
    void main() {
      vec3 ambAndDiff, spec;
      vec4 brickTexColor = texture( BrickTex, TexCoord );
      vec4 mossTexColor = texture( MossTex, TexCoord );
      phongModel(Position, Normal, ambAndDiff, spec);
      vec3 texColor = mix(brickTexColor, mossTexColor,
                          mossTexColor.a);
      FragColor = vec4(ambAndDiff, 1.0) * texColor +
                  vec4(spec,1.0);
    }
    ```

How it works...

The preceding code that loads the two textures into the OpenGL program is very similar to the code from the previous recipe *Applying a 2D texture*. The main difference is that we load each texture into a different texture unit. When loading the brick texture, we set the OpenGL state such that the active texture unit is unit zero.

```
glActiveTexture(GL_TEXTURE0);
```

And when loading the second texture, we set the OpenGL state to texture unit one.

```
glActiveTexture(GL_TEXTURE1);
```

In step 3, we specify the texture binding for each sampler variable using the layout qualifier, corresponding to the appropriate texture unit.

Within the fragment shader, we access the two textures using the corresponding uniform variables, and store the results in `brickTexColor` and `mossTexColor`. The two colors are blended together using the built-in function `mix`. The third parameter to the `mix` function is the percentage used when mixing the two colors. The alpha value of the moss texture is used for that parameter. This causes the result to be a linear interpolation of the two colors based on the value of the alpha in the moss texture. For those familiar with OpenGL blending functions, this is the same as the following blending function:

```
glBlendFunc( GL_SRC_ALPHA, GL_ONE_MINUS_SRC_ALPHA );
```

In this case, the moss color would be the source color, and the brick color would be the destination color.

Finally, we multiply the result of the `mix` function by the ambient and diffuse components of the Phong reflection model, add the specular component, and apply the result to the fragment.

There's more...

In this example, we mixed the two texture colors together using the alpha value of the second texture. This is just one of many options for mixing the texture colors. There are a number of different choices here, and your choice will be dependent on the kind of texture data available and the desired effect.

A popular technique is to use an additional vertex attribute to augment the amount of blending between the textures. This additional vertex attribute would allow us to vary the blending factor throughout a model. For example, we could vary the amount of moss that grows on a surface by defining another vertex attribute, which would control the amount of blending between the moss texture and the base texture. A value of zero might correspond to zero moss, up to a value of one that would enable blending based on the texture's alpha value alone.

See also

▶ The *Applying a 2D texture* recipe

Using alpha maps to discard pixels

To create the effect of an object that has holes, we could use a texture with an appropriate alpha channel that contains information about the transparent parts of the object. However, that requires us to make sure to make the depth buffer read-only, and render all of our polygons from back to front in order to avoid blending problems. We would need to sort our polygons based on the camera position and then render them in the correct order. What a pain!

With GLSL shaders, we can avoid all of this by using the `discard` keyword to completely discard fragments when the alpha value of the texture map is below a certain value. By completely discarding the fragments, there's no need to modify the depth buffer because when discarded, they aren't evaluated against the depth buffer at all. We don't need to depth-sort our polygons because there is no blending.

The following image on the right shows the teapot with fragments discarded based upon the texture on the left. The fragment shader discards fragments that correspond to texels that have an alpha value below a certain threshold.

If we create a texture map that has an alpha channel, we can use the value of the alpha channel to determine whether or not the fragment should be discarded. If the alpha value is below a certain value, then the pixel is discarded.

As this will allow the viewer to see within the object, possibly making some back faces visible, we'll need to use two-sided lighting when rendering the object.

Getting ready

1. Start with the same shader pair and set up from the previous recipe, *Applying multiple textures*.

2. Load the base texture for the object into texture unit 0, and your alpha map into texture unit 1.

How to do it...

To discard fragments based on alpha data from a texture, use the following steps:

1. Use the same vertex and fragment shaders from the recipe *Applying multiple textures*. However, make the following modifications to the fragment shader.

2. Replace the `sampler2D` uniform variables with the following:

```
layout(binding=0) uniform sampler2D BaseTex;
layout(binding=1) uniform sampler2D AlphaTex;
```

3. Replace the contents of the `main` function with the following code:

```
void main() {
  vec4 baseColor = texture( BaseTex, TexCoord );
  vec4 alphaMap  = texture( AlphaTex, TexCoord );

  if(alphaMap.a < 0.15 )
    discard;
  else {
    if( gl_FrontFacing ) {
      FragColor = vec4(phongModel(Position,Normal),1.0 ) *
                baseColor;
    } else {
      FragColor = vec4(phongModel(Position,-Normal),1.0) *
                baseColor;
    }
  }
}
```

How it works...

Within the `main` function of the fragment shader, we access the base color texture, and store the result in `baseColor`. We access the alpha map texture and store the result in `alphaMap`. If the alpha component of `alphaMap` is less than a certain value (0.15 in this example), then we discard the fragment using the `discard` keyword.

Otherwise, we compute the Phong lighting model using the normal vector oriented appropriately, depending on whether or not the fragment is a front facing fragment. The result of the Phong model is multiplied by the base color from `BaseTex`.

There's more...

This technique is fairly simple and straightforward, and is a nice alternative to traditional blending techniques. It is a great way to make holes in objects or to present the appearance of decay. If your alpha map has a gradual change in the alpha throughout the map, (for example, an alpha map where the alpha values make a smoothly varying height field) then it can be used to animate the decay of an object. We could vary the alpha threshold (0.15 in the preceding example) from 0.0 to 1.0 to create an animated effect of the object gradually decaying away to nothing.

See also

▸   The *Applying multiple textures* recipe

Using normal maps

Normal mapping is a technique for "faking" variations in a surface that doesn't really exist in the geometry of the surface. It is useful for producing surfaces that have bumps, dents, roughness, or wrinkles without actually providing enough position information (vertices) to fully define those deformations. The underlying surface is actually smooth, but is made to appear rough by varying the normal vectors using a texture (the normal map). The technique is closely related to bump mapping or displacement mapping. With normal maps, we modify the normal vectors based on information that is stored in a texture. This creates the appearance of a bumpy surface without actually providing the geometry of the bumps.

A normal map is a texture in which the data stored within the texture is interpreted as normal vectors instead of colors. The normal vectors are typically encoded into the RGB information of the normal map such that the red channel contains the x coordinate, the green channel contains the y, and the blue channel contains the z coordinate. The normal map can then be used as a "texture" in the sense that the texture values affect the normal vector used in the reflection model rather than the color of the surface. This can be used to make a surface look like it contains variations (bumps or wrinkles) that do not actually exist in the geometry of the mesh.

The following images show an ogre mesh (courtesy of Keenan Crane) with and without a normal map. The upper-left corner shows the base color texture for the ogre. In this example, we use this texture as the diffuse reflectivity in the Phong reflection model. The upper right shows the ogre with the color texture and default normal vectors. The bottom left is the normal map texture. The bottom right shows the ogre with the color texture and normal map. Note the additional detail in the wrinkles provided by the normal map.

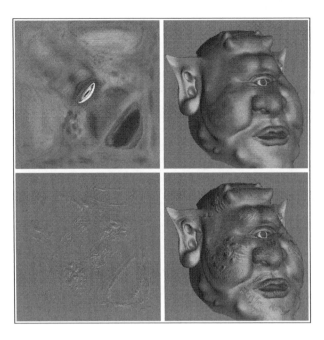

A normal map can be produced in a number of ways. Many 3D modeling programs such as Maya, Blender, or 3D Studio Max can generate normal maps. Normal maps can also be generated directly from grayscale hightmap textures. There is a NVIDIA plugin for Adobe Photoshop that provides this functionality (see http://developer.nvidia.com/object/photoshop_dds_plugins.html).

Normal maps are interpreted as vectors in a **tangent space** (also called the **object local coordinate system**). In the tangent coordinate system, the origin is located at the surface point and the normal to the surface is aligned with the z axis (0, 0, 1). Therefore, the x and y axes are at a tangent to the surface. The following image shows an example of the tangent frames at two different positions on a surface.

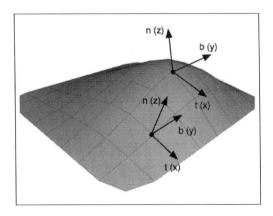

The advantage of using such a coordinate system lies in the fact that the normal vectors stored within the normal map can be treated as perturbations to the true normal, and are independent of the object coordinate system. This saves us the need to transform the normals, add the perturbed normal, and renormalize. Instead, we can use the value in the normal map directly in the reflection model without any modification.

To make all of this work, we need to evaluate the reflection model in tangent space. In order to do so, we transform the vectors used in our reflection model into tangent space in the vertex shader, and then pass them along to the fragment shader where the reflection model will be evaluated. To define a transformation from the camera (eye) coordinate system to the tangent space coordinate system, we need three normalized, co-orthogonal vectors (defined in eye coordinates) that define the tangent space system. The z axis is defined by the normal vector (n), the x axis is defined by a vector called the *tangent vector* (t), and the y axis is often called the *binormal vector* (b). A point P, defined in eye coordinates, could then be transformed into tangent space by multiplying by the following matrix:

$$\begin{bmatrix} S_x \\ S_y \\ S_z \end{bmatrix} = \begin{bmatrix} t_x & t_y & t_z \\ b_x & b_y & b_z \\ n_x & n_y & n_z \end{bmatrix} \begin{bmatrix} P_x \\ P_y \\ P_z \end{bmatrix}$$

In the preceding equation, S is the point in tangent space and P is the point in eye coordinates. In order to apply this transformation within the vertex shader, the OpenGL program must provide at least two of the three vectors that define the object local system along with the vertex position. The usual situation is to provide the normal vector (n) and the tangent vector (t). If the tangent vector is provided, the binormal vector can be computed as the cross product of the tangent and normal vectors.

Tangent vectors are sometimes included as additional data in mesh data structures. If the tangent data is not available, we can approximate the tangent vectors by deriving them from the variation of the texture coordinates across the surface (see *Computing Tangent Space Basis Vectors for an Arbitrary Mesh*, Eric Lengyel, Terathon Software 3D Graphics Library, 2001, at http://www.terathon.com/code/tangent.html).

One must take care that the tangent vectors are consistently defined across the surface. In other words, the direction of the tangent vectors should not vary greatly from one vertex to its neighboring vertex. Otherwise, it can lead to ugly shading artifacts.

In the following example, we'll read the vertex position, normal vector, tangent vector, and texture coordinate in the vertex shader. We'll transform the position, normal, and tangent to eye space, and then compute the binormal vector (in eye space). Next, we'll compute the viewing direction (v) and the direction towards the light source (s) in eye space, and then transform them to tangent space. We'll pass the tangent space v and s vectors and the (unchanged) texture coordinate to the fragment shader, where we'll evaluate the Phong reflection model, using the tangent space vectors and the normal vector retrieved from the normal map.

Getting ready

Set up your OpenGL program to provide the position in attribute location 0, the normal in attribute location 1, the texture coordinate in location 2, and the tangent vector in location 3. For this example, the fourth coordinate of the tangent vector should contain the "handedness" of the tangent coordinate system (either -1 or +1). This value will be multiplied by the result of the cross product.

Load the normal map into texture unit one and the color texture into texture unit zero.

How to do it...

To render an image using normal mapping, use the following shaders:

1. Use the following code for the vertex shader:

```
layout (location = 0) in vec3 VertexPosition;
layout (location = 1) in vec3 VertexNormal;
layout (location = 2) in vec2 VertexTexCoord;
layout (location = 3) in vec4 VertexTangent;

struct LightInfo {
  vec4 Position;  // Light position in eye coords.
  vec3 Intensity; // A,D,S intensity
};
uniform LightInfo Light;

out vec3 LightDir;
out vec2 TexCoord;
out vec3 ViewDir;

uniform mat4 ModelViewMatrix;
uniform mat3 NormalMatrix;
uniform mat4 ProjectionMatrix;
uniform mat4 MVP;

void main()
{
  // Transform normal and tangent to eye space
  vec3 norm = normalize(NormalMatrix * VertexNormal);
  vec3 tang = normalize(NormalMatrix *
                        vec3(VertexTangent));
  // Compute the binormal
  vec3 binormal = normalize( cross( norm, tang ) ) *
```

```
        VertexTangent.w;
        // Matrix for transformation to tangent space
        mat3 toObjectLocal = mat3 (
        tang.x, binormal.x, norm.x,
        tang.y, binormal.y, norm.y,
        tang.z, binormal.z, norm.z ) ;
        // Get the position in eye coordinates
        vec3 pos = vec3 ( ModelViewMatrix *
                        vec4 (VertexPosition, 1.0) );

        // Transform light dir. and view dir. to tangent space
        LightDir = normalize ( toObjectLocal *
                            (Light.Position.xyz - pos) );
        ViewDir = toObjectLocal * normalize (-pos);

        // Pass along the texture coordinate
        TexCoord = VertexTexCoord;

        gl_Position = MVP * vec4 (VertexPosition, 1.0);
}
```

2. Use the following code for the fragment shader:

```
in vec3 LightDir;
in vec2 TexCoord;
in vec3 ViewDir;

layout (binding=0) uniform sampler2D ColorTex;
layout (binding=1) uniform sampler2D NormalMapTex;

struct LightInfo {
  vec4 Position;  // Light position in eye coords.
  vec3 Intensity; // A,D,S intensity
};
uniform LightInfo Light;

struct MaterialInfo {
  vec3 Ka;                // Ambient reflectivity
  vec3 Ks;                // Specular reflectivity
  float Shininess;     // Specular shininess factor
};
uniform MaterialInfo Material;

layout ( location = 0 ) out vec4 FragColor;
```

```glsl
vec3 phongModel( vec3 norm, vec3 diffR ) {
  vec3 r = reflect( -LightDir, norm );
  vec3 ambient = Light.Intensity * Material.Ka;
  float sDotN = max( dot(LightDir, norm), 0.0 );
  vec3 diffuse = Light.Intensity * diffR * sDotN;

  vec3 spec = vec3(0.0);
  if( sDotN > 0.0 )
       spec = Light.Intensity * Material.Ks *
              pow( max( dot(r,ViewDir), 0.0 ),
                  Material.Shininess );

  return ambient + diffuse + spec;
}

void main() {
  // Lookup the normal from the normal map
  vec4 normal = 2.0 * texture( NormalMapTex, TexCoord ) -
                  1.0;

  // The color texture is used as the diff. reflectivity
  vec4 texColor = texture( ColorTex, TexCoord );

  FragColor = vec4( phongModel(normal.xyz, texColor.rgb),
                  1.0 );
}
```

How it works...

The vertex shader starts by transforming the vertex normal and the tangent vectors into eye coordinates by multiplying by the normal matrix (and renormalizing). The binormal vector is then computed as the cross product of the normal and tangent vectors. The result is multiplied by the w coordinate of the vertex tangent vector, which determines the handedness of the tangent space coordinate system. Its value will be either -1 or +1.

Next, we create the transformation matrix used to convert from eye coordinates to tangent space and store the matrix in toObjectLocal. The position is converted to eye space and stored in pos, and we compute the light direction by subtracting pos from the light position. The result is multiplied by toObjectLocal to convert it into tangent space, and the final result is normalized and stored in the output variable LightDir. This value is the direction to the light source in tangent space, and will be used by the fragment shader in the Phong reflection model.

Similarly, the view direction is computed and converted to tangent space by normalizing `-pos` and multiplying by `toObjectLocal`. The result is stored in the output variable `ViewDir`.

The texture coordinate is passed to the fragment shader unchanged by just assigning it to the output variable `TexCoord`.

In the fragment shader, the tangent space values for the light direction and view direction are received in the variables `LightDir` and `ViewDir`. The `phongModel` function is slightly modified from what has been used in previous recipes. The first parameter is the normal vector, and the second is the diffuse reflectivity coefficient. The value for this will be taken from the color texture. The function computes the Phong reflection model with the parameter `diffR`, used as the diffuse reflectivity, and uses `LightDir` and `ViewDir` for the light and view directions rather than computing them.

In the main function, the normal vector is retrieved from the normal map texture and stored in the variable `normal`. Since textures store values that range from zero to one, and normal vectors should have components that range from -1 to +1, we need to re-scale the value to that range. We do so by multiplying the value by 2.0, and then subtracting 1.0.

The color texture is then accessed to retrieve the color to be used as the diffuse reflectivity coefficient, and the result is stored in `texColor`. Finally, the `phongModel` function is called, and is provided `normal` and `texColor`. The `phongModel` function evaluates the Phong reflection model using `LightDir`, `ViewDir`, and `norm`, all of which are defined in tangent space. The result is applied to the output fragment by assigning it to `FragColor`.

See also

- ▸ The *Applying multiple textures* recipe
- ▸ The *Implementing per-vertex ambient, diffuse, and specular (ADS) shading* recipe in Chapter 2, *The Basics of GLSL Shaders*

Simulating reflection with cube maps

Textures can be used to simulate a surface that has a component which is purely reflective (a mirror-like surface such as chrome). In order to do so, we need a texture that is representative of the environment surrounding the reflective object. This texture could then be mapped onto the surface of the object in a way that represents how it would look when reflected off of the surface. This general technique is known as **environment mapping**. In general, environment mapping involves creating a texture that is representative of the environment and mapping it onto the surface of an object. It is typically used to simulate the effects of reflection or refraction.

A **cube map** is one of the more common varieties of textures used in environment mapping. A cube map is a set of six separate images that represent the environment projected onto each of the six faces of a cube. The six images represent a view of the environment from the point of view of a viewer located at the center of the cube. An example of a cube map is shown in the following image. The images are laid out as if the cube was "unfolded" and laid flat. The four images across the middle would make up the sides of the cube, and the top and bottom images correspond to the top and bottom of the cube.

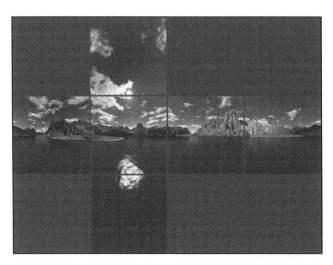

OpenGL provides built-in support for cube map textures (using the GL_TEXTURE_CUBE_MAP target). The texture is accessed using a 3-dimensional texture coordinate (s, t, r). The texture coordinate is interpreted as a direction vector from the center of the cube. The line defined by the vector and the center of the cube is extended to intersect one of the faces of the cube. The image that corresponds to that face is then accessed at the location of the intersection.

Truth be told, the conversion between the 3-dimensional texture coordinate used to access the cube map, and the 2-dimensional texture coordinate used to access the individual face image is somewhat complicated. It can be non-intuitive and confusing. A very good explanation can be found on NVIDIA's developer website: http://developer.nvidia.com/content/cube-map-ogl-tutorial. However, the good news is that if you are careful to orient your textures correctly within the cube map, the details of the conversion can be ignored, and the texture coordinate can be visualized as a 3-dimensional vector as described previously.

In this example, we'll demonstrate using a cube map to simulate a reflective surface. We'll also use the cube map to draw the environment around the reflective object (sometimes called a **skybox**).

Getting ready

Prepare the six images of the cube map. In this example, the images will have the following naming convention. There is a base name (stored in variable `baseFileName`) followed by an underscore, followed by one of the six possible suffixes (`posx`, `negx`, `posy`, `negy`, `posz`, or `negz`), followed by the file extension (`.tga`). The suffixes `posx`, `posy`, and so on, indicate the axis that goes through the center of the face (positive x, positive y, and so on).

Make sure that they are all square images (preferably with dimensions that are a power of 2), and that they are all the same size. You will need to orient them appropriately for the way that OpenGL accesses them. As mentioned previously, this can be a bit tricky. One way to do this is to load the textures in their default orientation and draw the sky box (more on how to do that follows). Then re-orient the textures (by trial and error) until they line up correctly. Alternatively, take a close look at the conversion described in the NVIDIA link mentioned in the previous tip and determine the proper orientation based on the texture coordinate conversions.

Set up your OpenGL program to provide the vertex position in attribute location 0, and the vertex normal in attribute location 1.

This vertex shader requires the modeling matrix (the matrix that converts from object coordinates to world coordinates) to be separated from the model-view matrix and provided to the shader as a separate uniform. Your OpenGL program should provide the modeling matrix in the uniform variable `ModelMatrix`.

The vertex shader also requires the location of the camera in world coordinates. Make sure that your OpenGL program sets the uniform `WorldCameraPosition` to the appropriate value.

How to do it...

To render an image with reflection based on a cube map, and also render the cube map itself, carry out the following steps:

1. Load the six images of the cube map into a single texture target using the following code within the main OpenGL program:

    ```
    glActiveTexture(GL_TEXTURE0);

    GLuint texID;
    glGenTextures(1, &texID);
    glBindTexture(GL_TEXTURE_CUBE_MAP, texID);

    const char * suffixes[] = { "posx", "negx", "posy",
                                "negy", "posz", "negz" };
    GLuint targets[] = {
       GL_TEXTURE_CUBE_MAP_POSITIVE_X,
       GL_TEXTURE_CUBE_MAP_NEGATIVE_X,
    ```

```
    GL_TEXTURE_CUBE_MAP_POSITIVE_Y,
    GL_TEXTURE_CUBE_MAP_NEGATIVE_Y,
    GL_TEXTURE_CUBE_MAP_POSITIVE_Z,
    GL_TEXTURE_CUBE_MAP_NEGATIVE_Z
};
GLint w,h;
glTexStorage2D(GL_TEXTURE_CUBE_MAP, 1, GL_RGBA8, 256, 256);
for( int i = 0; i < 6; i++ ) {
    string texName = string(baseFileName) +
                     "_" + suffixes[i] + ".tga";
    GLubyte *data = TGAIO::read(texName.c_str(), w, h);
    glTexSubImage2D(targets[i], 0, 0, 0, w, h,
                    GL_RGBA, GL_UNSIGNED_BYTE, data);
    delete [] data;
}


// Typical cube map settings
glTexParameteri(GL_TEXTURE_CUBE_MAP, GL_TEXTURE_MAG_FILTER,
                GL_LINEAR);
glTexParameteri(GL_TEXTURE_CUBE_MAP, GL_TEXTURE_MIN_FILTER,
                GL_LINEAR);
glTexParameteri(GL_TEXTURE_CUBE_MAP, GL_TEXTURE_WRAP_S,
                GL_CLAMP_TO_EDGE);
glTexParameteri(GL_TEXTURE_CUBE_MAP, GL_TEXTURE_WRAP_T,
                GL_CLAMP_TO_EDGE);
glTexParameteri(GL_TEXTURE_CUBE_MAP, GL_TEXTURE_WRAP_R,
                GL_CLAMP_TO_EDGE);
```

2. Use the following code for the vertex shader:

```
layout (location = 0) in vec3 VertexPosition;
layout (location = 1) in vec3 VertexNormal;
layout (location = 2) in vec2 VertexTexCoord;

out vec3 ReflectDir;  // The direction of the reflected ray
uniform bool DrawSkyBox;  // Are we drawing the sky box?
uniform vec3 WorldCameraPosition;
uniform mat4 ModelViewMatrix;
uniform mat4 ModelMatrix;
uniform mat3 NormalMatrix;
uniform mat4 ProjectionMatrix;
uniform mat4 MVP;
```

```
      void main()
      {
        if( DrawSkyBox ) {
          ReflectDir = VertexPosition;
        } else {

            // Compute the reflected direction in world coords.
          vec3 worldPos = vec3( ModelMatrix *
                                    vec4(VertexPosition,1.0) );
          vec3 worldNorm = vec3(ModelMatrix *
                                    vec4(VertexNormal, 0.0));
          vec3 worldView = normalize( WorldCameraPosition -
                                        worldPos );

          ReflectDir = reflect(-worldView, worldNorm );
        }

        gl_Position = MVP * vec4(VertexPosition,1.0);
      }
```

3. Use the following code for the fragment shader:

```
      in vec3 ReflectDir;    // The direction of the reflected ray

      // The cube map
      layout(binding=0) uniform samplerCube CubeMapTex;

      uniform bool DrawSkyBox;      // Are we drawing the sky box?
      uniform float ReflectFactor;// Amount of reflection
      uniform vec4 MaterialColor; // Color of the object's "Tint"

      layout( location = 0 ) out vec4 FragColor;

      void main() {
        // Access the cube map texture
        vec4 cubeMapColor = texture(CubeMapTex,ReflectDir);
        if( DrawSkyBox )
          FragColor = cubeMapColor;
        else
          FragColor = mix(MaterialColor, CubeMapColor, ReflectFactor);

      }
```

4. In the render portion of the OpenGL program, set the uniform `DrawSkyBox` to true, and then draw a cube surrounding the entire scene, centered at the origin. This will become the sky box. Following that, set `DrawSkyBox` to false, and draw the object(s) within the scene.

How it works...

In OpenGL, a cube map texture is actually six separate images. To fully initialize a cube map texture, we need to bind to the cube map texture, and then load each image individually into the six "slots" within that texture. In the preceding code (within the main OpenGL application), we start by binding to texture unit zero with `glActiveTexture`. Then we create a new texture object by calling `glGenTextures`, and store its handle within the variable `texID`, and then bind that texture object to the `GL_TEXTURE_CUBE_MAP` target using `glBindTexture`. The following loop loads each texture file, and copies the texture data into OpenGL memory using `glTexSubImage2D`. Note that the first argument to this function is the texture target, which corresponds to `GL_TEXTURE_CUBE_MAP_POSITIVE_X`, `GL_TEXTURE_CUBE_MAP_NEGATIVE_X`, and so on. After the loop is finished, the cube map texture should be fully initialized with the six images.

Following this, we set up the cube map texture environment. We use linear filtering, and we also set the texture wrap mode to `GL_CLAMP_TO_EDGE` for all three of the texture coordinate's components. This tends to work the best, avoiding the possibility of a border color appearing between the cube edges.

Within the vertex shader, the main goal is to compute the direction of reflection and pass that to the fragment shader to be used to access the cube map. The output variable `ReflectDir` will store this result. If we are not drawing the sky box (the value of `DrawSkyBox` is `false`), then we can compute the reflected direction (in world coordinates) by reflecting the vector towards the viewer about the normal vector.

> We choose to compute the reflection direction in world coordinates because, if we were to use eye coordinates, the reflection would not change as the camera moved within the scene.

In the `else` branch within the main function, we start by converting the position to world coordinates and storing in `worldPos`. We then do the same for the normal, storing the result in `worldNorm`. Note that the `ModelMatrix` is used to transform the vertex normal. It is important when doing this to use a value of 0.0 for the fourth coordinate of the normal, to avoid the translation component of the model matrix affecting the normal. Also, the model matrix must not contain any non-uniform scaling component; otherwise the normal vector will be transformed incorrectly.

The direction towards the viewer is computed in world coordinates and stored in `worldView`.

Finally, we reflect `worldView` about the normal and store the result in the output variable `ReflectDir`. The fragment shader will use this direction to access the cube map texture and apply the corresponding color to the fragment. One can think of this as a light ray that begins at the viewer's eye, strikes the surface, reflects off of the surface, and hits the cube map. The color that the ray "sees" when it strikes the cube map is the color that we need for the object.

If we are drawing the sky box, (`DrawSkyBox` is `true`), then we use the vertex position as the reflection direction. Why? Well, when the sky box is rendered, we want the location on the sky box to correspond to the equivalent location in the cube map (the sky box is really just a rendering of the cube map). In the fragment shader, `ReflectDir` will be used as the texture coordinate to access the cube map. Therefore, if we want to access a position on the cube map corresponding to a location on a cube centered at the origin, we need a vector that points at that location. The vector we need is the position of that point minus the origin (which is (0,0,0)). Hence, we just need the position of the vertex.

Sky boxes are often rendered with the viewer at the center of the sky box and the sky box moving along with the viewer (so the viewer is always at the center of the sky box). We have not done so in this example; however, we could do so by transforming the sky box using the rotational component of the view matrix (not the translational).

Within the fragment shader, we simply use the value of `ReflectDir` to access the cube map texture.

```
vec4 cubeMapColor = texture(CubeMapTex, ReflectDir)
```

If we are drawing the sky box, we simply use the color unchanged. However, if we are not drawing the sky box, then we'll mix the sky box color with some material color. This allows us to provide some slight "tint" to the object. The amount of tint is adjusted by the variable `ReflectFactor`. A value of 1.0 would correspond to zero tint (all reflection), and a value of 0.0 corresponds to no reflection. The following images show the teapot rendered with different values of `ReflectFactor`. The teapot on the left uses a reflection factor of 0.5, the one on the right uses a value of 0.85. The base material color is grey. (Cube map used is an image of St. Peter's Basilica, Rome. ©Paul Debevec.)

There's more...

There are two important points to keep in mind about this technique. First, the objects will only reflect the environment map. They will not reflect the image of any other objects within the scene. In order to do so, we would need to generate an environment map from the point of view of each object by rendering the scene six times with the view point located at the center of the object and the view direction in each of the six coordinate directions. Then we could use the appropriate environment map for the appropriate object's reflections. Of course, if any of the objects were to move relative to one another, we'd need to regenerate the environment maps. All of this effort may be prohibitive in an interactive application.

The second point involves the reflections that appear on moving objects. In these shaders, we compute the reflection direction and treat it as a vector emanating from the center of the environment map. This means that regardless of where the object is located, the reflections will appear as if the object is in the center of the environment. In other words, the environment is treated as if it were "infinitely" far away. *Chapter 19* of the book *GPU Gems*, by Randima Fernando, Addison-Wesley Professional, 2009 has an excellent discussion of this issue and provides some possible solutions for localizing the reflections.

See also

▶   The *Applying a 2D texture* recipe

Simulating refraction with cube maps

Objects that are transparent cause the light rays that pass through them to bend slightly at the interface between the object and the surrounding environment. This effect is called **refraction**. When rendering transparent objects, we simulate that effect by using an environment map, and mapping the environment onto the object is such a way as to mimic the way that light would pass through the object. In other words, we can trace the rays from the viewer, through the object (bending in the process), and along to the environment. Then we can use that ray intersection as the color for the object.

As in the previous recipe, we'll do this using a cube map for the environment. We'll trace rays from the viewer position, through the object, and finally intersect with the cube map.

The process of refraction is described by **Snell's law**, which defines the relationship between the angle of incidence and the angle of refraction.

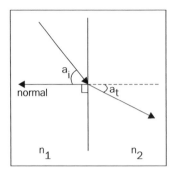

Snell's law describes the angle of incidence (a_i) as the angle between the incoming light ray and the normal to the surface, and the angle of refraction (a_t) as the angle between the transmitted ray and the extended normal. The material through which the incident light ray travels and the material containing the transmitted light ray are each described by an index of refraction (n_1 and n_2 in the figure). The ratio between the two indices of refraction defines the amount that the light ray will be bent at the interface.

Starting with Snell's law, and with a bit of mathematical effort, we can derive a formula for the transmitted vector, given the ratio of the indices of refraction, the normal vector, and the incoming vector.

$$\frac{\sin a_i}{\sin a_t} = \frac{n_2}{n_1}$$

However, there's no real need to do so, because GLSL provides a built-in function for computing this transmitted vector called `refract`. We'll make use of that function within this example.

It is usually the case that for transparent objects, not all of the light is transmitted through the surface. Some of the light is reflected. In this example, we'll model that in a very simple way, and at the end of this recipe we'll discuss a more accurate representation.

Getting ready

Set up your OpenGL program to provide the vertex position in attribute location 0 and the vertex normal in attribute location 1. As with the previous recipe, we'll need to provide the model matrix in the uniform variable `ModelMatrix`.

Load the cube map using the technique shown in the previous recipe. Place it in texture unit zero.

Set the uniform variable `WorldCameraPosition` to the location of your viewer in world coordinates. Set the value of the uniform variable `Material.Eta` to the ratio between the index of refraction of the environment n1 and the index of refraction of the material n2 (n1/n2). Set the value of the uniform `Material.ReflectionFactor` to the fraction of light that is reflected at the interface (a small value is probably what you want).

As with the preceding example, if you want to draw the environment, set the uniform variable `DrawSkyBox` to `true`, then draw a large cube surrounding the scene, and then set `DrawSkyBox` to `false`.

How to do it...

To render an object with reflection and refraction as well as the cube map itself, carry out the following steps:

1. Use the following code within the vertex shader:

```
layout (location = 0) in vec3 VertexPosition;
layout (location = 1) in vec3 VertexNormal;

out vec3 ReflectDir;  // Reflected direction
out vec3 RefractDir;  // Transmitted direction

struct MaterialInfo {
    float Eta;          // Ratio of indices of refraction
    float ReflectionFactor; // Percentage of reflected light
};
uniform MaterialInfo Material;

uniform bool DrawSkyBox;

uniform vec3 WorldCameraPosition;
uniform mat4 ModelViewMatrix;
uniform mat4 ModelMatrix;
uniform mat3 NormalMatrix;
uniform mat4 ProjectionMatrix;
uniform mat4 MVP;

void main()
{
    if( DrawSkyBox ) {
        ReflectDir = VertexPosition;
    } else {
        vec3 worldPos = vec3( ModelMatrix *
```

```
                                       vec4(VertexPosition,1.0) );
                vec3 worldNorm = vec3(ModelMatrix *
                                       vec4(VertexNormal, 0.0));
                vec3 worldView = normalize( WorldCameraPosition -
                                              worldPos );

                ReflectDir = reflect(-worldView, worldNorm );
                RefractDir = refract(-worldView, worldNorm,
                                      Material.Eta );
        }
        gl_Position = MVP * vec4(VertexPosition,1.0);
    }
```

2. Use the following code within the fragment shader:

```
in vec3 ReflectDir;
in vec3 RefractDir;

layout(binding=0) uniform samplerCube CubeMapTex;
uniform bool DrawSkyBox;
struct MaterialInfo {
   float Eta;   // Ratio of indices of refraction
   float ReflectionFactor; // Percentage of reflected light
};
uniform MaterialInfo Material;

layout( location = 0 ) out vec4 FragColor;

void main() {
    // Access the cube map texture
    vec4 reflectColor = texture(CubeMapTex, ReflectDir);
    vec4 refractColor = texture(CubeMapTex, RefractDir);

    if( DrawSkyBox )
        FragColor = reflectColor;
    else
        FragColor = mix(refractColor, reflectColor,
                        Material.ReflectionFactor);
}
```

3. In the render portion of the OpenGL program, set the uniform `DrawSkyBox` to `true`, and then draw a cube surrounding the entire scene, centered at the origin. This will become the sky box. Following that, set `DrawSkyBox` to `false`, and draw the object(s) within the scene.

How it works...

Both shaders are quite similar to the shaders in the previous recipe.

The vertex shader computes the position, normal, and view direction in world coordinates (`worldPos`, `worldNorm`, and `worldView`). They are then used to compute the reflected direction using the `reflect` function, and the result is stored in the output variable `ReflectDir`. The transmitted direction is computed using the built-in function `refract` (which requires the ratio of the indices of refraction `Material.Eta`). This function makes use of Snell's law to compute the direction of the transmitted vector which is then stored in the output variable `RefractDir`.

In the fragment shader, we use the two vectors `ReflectDir` and `RefractDir` to access the cube map texture. The color retrieved by the reflected ray is stored in `reflectColor` and the color retrieved by the transmitted ray is stored in `refractColor`. We then mix those two colors together based on the value of `Material.ReflectionFactor`. The result is a mixture between the color of the reflected ray and the color of the transmitted ray.

The following image shows the teapot rendered with 10% reflection and 90% refraction. (Cubemap © Paul Debevec.)

There's more...

This technique has the same drawbacks that were discussed in the *There's more...* section of the preceding recipe, *Simulating reflection with cube maps*.

Like most real-time techniques, this is a simplification of the real physics of the situation. There are a number of things about the technique that could be improved to provide more realistic looking results.

The Fresnel equations

The amount of reflected light actually depends on the angle of incidence of the incoming light. For example, when looking at the surface of a lake from the shore, much of the light is reflected and it is easy to see reflections of the surrounding environment on the surface. However, when floating on a boat on the surface of the lake and looking straight down, there is less reflection and it is easier to see what lies below the surface. This effect is described by the Fresnel equations (after Augustin-Jean Fresnel).

The Fresnel equations describe the amount of light that is reflected as a function of the angle of incidence, the polarization of the light, and the ratio of the indices of refraction. If we ignore the polarization, it is easy to incorporate the Fresnel equations into the preceding shaders. A very good explanation of this can be found in the book *The OpenGL Shading Language, 3rd Edition*, Randi J Rost, Addison-Wesley Professional, 2009.

Chromatic aberration

White light is of course composed of many different individual wavelengths (or colors). The amount that a light ray is refracted is actually wavelength dependent. This causes the effect where a spectrum of colors can be observed at the interface between materials. The most well-known example of this is the rainbow that is produced by a prism.

We can model this effect by using slightly different values of `Eta` for the red, green, and blue components of the light ray. We would store three different values for `Eta`, compute three different reflection directions (red, green, and blue), and use those three directions to look up colors in the cube map. We take the red component from the first color, the green component from the second, and the blue component for the third, and combine the three components together to create the final color for the fragment.

Refracting through both sides of the object

It is important to note that we have simplified things by only modeling the interaction of the light with one of the boundaries of the object. In reality the light would be bent once when entering the transparent object, and again when leaving the other side. However, this simplification generally does not result in unrealistic looking results. As is often the case in real-time graphics, we are more interested in a result that looks good than one that models the physics accurately.

See also

 ▸   The *Simulating reflection with cube maps* recipe

Applying a projected texture

We can apply a texture to the objects in a scene as if the texture was a projection from a hypothetical "slide projector" located somewhere within the scene. This technique is often called **projective texture mapping** and produces a very nice effect.

The following images show an example of projective texture mapping. The flower texture on the left (Stan Shebs via Wikimedia Commons) is projected onto the teapot and plane beneath.

To project a texture onto a surface, all we need to do is determine the texture coordinates based on the relative position of the surface location and the source of the projection (the "slide projector"). An easy way to do this is to think of the projector as a camera located somewhere within the scene. In the same way that we would define an OpenGL camera, we define a coordinate system centered at the projector's location, and a **view matrix (V)** that converts coordinates to the projector's coordinate system. Next, we'll define a perspective **projection matrix (P)** that converts the view frustum (in the projector's coordinate system) into a cubic volume of size 2, centered at the origin. Putting these two things together, and adding an additional matrix for rescaling and translating the volume to a volume of size one (shifted so that the volume is centered at (0.5, 0.5, 0.5), we have the following transformation matrix:

$$\mathbf{M} = \begin{bmatrix} 0.5 & 0 & 0 & 0.5 \\ 0 & 0.5 & 0 & 0.5 \\ 0 & 0 & 0.5 & 0.5 \\ 0 & 0 & 0 & 1 \end{bmatrix} \mathbf{PV}$$

The goal here is basically to convert the view frustum to a range between 0 and 1 in x and y. The preceding matrix can be used to do just that! It will convert world coordinates that lie within the view frustum of the projector to a range between 0 and 1 (homogeneous), which can then be used to access the texture. Note that the coordinates are homogeneous and need to be divided by the w coordinate before they can be used as a real position.

> For more details on the mathematics of this technique, take a look at the following white paper, written by Cass Everitt from NVIDIA:
>
> `http://developer.nvidia.com/content/projective-texture-mapping`

In this example, we'll apply a single texture to a scene using projective texture mapping.

Getting ready

Set up your OpenGL application to provide the vertex position in attribute location 0 and the normal in attribute location 1. The OpenGL application must also provide the material and lighting properties for the Phong reflection model (see the fragment shader given in the following section). Make sure to provide the model matrix (for converting to world coordinates) in the uniform variable `ModelMatrix`.

How to do it...

To apply a projected texture to a scene, use the following steps:

1. In the OpenGL application, load the texture into texture unit zero. While the texture object is bound to the `GL_TEXTURE_2D` target, use the following code to set the texture's settings:

```
glTexParameteri(GL_TEXTURE_2D, GL_TEXTURE_MAG_FILTER,
                GL_LINEAR);
glTexParameteri(GL_TEXTURE_2D, GL_TEXTURE_MIN_FILTER,
                GL_LINEAR);
glTexParameteri(GL_TEXTURE_2D, GL_TEXTURE_WRAP_S,
                GL_CLAMP_TO_BORDER);
glTexParameteri(GL_TEXTURE_2D, GL_TEXTURE_WRAP_T,
                GL_CLAMP_TO_BORDER);
```

2. Also within the OpenGL application, set up your transformation matrix for the "slide projector", and assign it to the uniform `ProjectorMatrix`. Use the following code to do this. Note that this code makes use of the GLM libraries discussed in *Chapter 1, Getting Started with GLSL*.

```
vec3 projPos = vec3(2.0f,5.0f,5.0f);
vec3 projAt = vec3(-2.0f,-4.0f,0.0f);
vec3 projUp = vec3(0.0f,1.0f,0.0f);

mat4 projView = glm::lookAt(projPos, projAt, projUp);
mat4 projProj = glm::perspective(30.0f, 1.0f, 0.2f,
                                 1000.0f);
```

```
mat4 projScaleTrans = glm::translate(vec3(0.5f)) *
                      glm::scale(vec3(0.5f));

mat4 m = projScaleTrans * projProj * projView;

// Set the uniform variable
int loc =
  glGetUniformLocation(progHandle,"ProjectorMatrix");
glUniformMatrix4fv(loc, 1, GL_FALSE, &m[0][0]);
```

3. Use the following code for the vertex shader:

```
layout (location = 0) in vec3 VertexPosition;
layout (location = 1) in vec3 VertexNormal;

out vec3 EyeNormal;        // Normal in eye coordinates
out vec4 EyePosition;      // Position in eye coordinates
out vec4 ProjTexCoord;

uniform mat4 ProjectorMatrix;
uniform vec3 WorldCameraPosition;
uniform mat4 ModelViewMatrix;
uniform mat4 ModelMatrix;
uniform mat3 NormalMatrix;
uniform mat4 ProjectionMatrix;
uniform mat4 MVP;

void main()
{
  vec4 pos4 = vec4(VertexPosition,1.0);

  EyeNormal = normalize(NormalMatrix * VertexNormal);
  EyePosition = ModelViewMatrix * pos4;
  ProjTexCoord = ProjectorMatrix * (ModelMatrix * pos4);
  gl_Position = MVP * pos4;
}
```

4. Use the following code for the fragment shader:

```
in vec3 EyeNormal;        // Normal in eye coordinates
in vec4 EyePosition;      // Position in eye coordinates
in vec4 ProjTexCoord;

layout(binding=0) uniform sampler2D ProjectorTex;
```

```
struct MaterialInfo {
  vec3 Kd;
  vec3 Ks;
  vec3 Ka;
  float Shininess;
};
uniform MaterialInfo Material;

struct LightInfo {
  vec3 Intensity;
  vec4 Position;    // Light position in eye coordinates
};
uniform LightInfo Light;

layout( location = 0 ) out vec4 FragColor;

vec3 phongModel( vec3 pos, vec3 norm ) {
  vec3 s = normalize(vec3(Light.Position) - pos);
  vec3 v = normalize(-pos.xyz);
  vec3 r = reflect( -s, norm );
  vec3 ambient = Light.Intensity * Material.Ka;
  float sDotN = max( dot(s,norm), 0.0 );
  vec3 diffuse = Light.Intensity * Material.Kd * sDotN;
  vec3 spec = vec3(0.0);
  if( sDotN > 0.0 )
    spec = Light.Intensity * Material.Ks *
          pow( max( dot(r,v), 0.0 ), Material.Shininess);

  return ambient + diffuse + spec;
}

void main() {
  vec3 color = phongModel(vec3(EyePosition), EyeNormal);

  vec4 projTexColor = vec4(0.0);
  if( ProjTexCoord.z > 0.0 )
    projTexColor = textureProj(ProjectorTex,ProjTexCoord);

  FragColor = vec4(color,1.0) + projTexColor * 0.5;
}
```

How it works...

When loading the texture into the OpenGL application, we make sure to set the wrap mode for the s and t directions to GL_CLAMP_TO_BORDER. We do this because if the texture coordinates are outside of the range of zero to one, we do not want any contribution from the projected texture. With this mode, using the default border color, the texture will return (0,0,0,0) when the texture coordinates are outside of the range between 0 and 1 inclusive.

The transformation matrix for the slide projector is set up in the OpenGL application. We start by using the GLM function glm::lookAt to produce a view matrix for the projector. In this example, we locate the projector at (5, 5, 5), looking towards the point (-2, -4,0), with an "up vector" of (0, 1, 0). This function works in a similar way to the gluLookAt function. It returns a matrix for converting to the coordinate system located at (5, 5, 5), and oriented based on the second and third arguments.

Next, we create the projection matrix using glm::perspective, and the scale/translate matrix M (shown in the introduction to this recipe). These two matrices are stored in projProj and projScaleTrans respectively. The final matrix is the product of projScaleTrans, projProj, and projView, which is stored in m and assigned to the uniform variable ProjectorTex.

In the vertex shader, we have three output variables EyeNormal, EyePosition, and ProjTexCoord. The first two are the vertex normal and vertex position in eye coordinates. We transform the input variables appropriately, and assign the results to the output variables within the main function.

We compute ProjTexCoord by first transforming the position to world coordinates (by multiplying by ModelMatrix), and then applying the projector's transformation.

In the fragment shader, within the main function, we start by computing the Phong reflection model and storing the result in the variable color. The next step is to look up the color from the texture. First, however, we check the z coordinate of ProjTexCoord. If this is negative then the location is behind the projector, so we avoid doing the texture lookup. Otherwise we use textureProj to look up the texture value and store it in projTexColor.

The function textureProj is designed for accessing textures with coordinates that have been projected. It will divide the coordinates of the second argument by its last coordinate before accessing the texture. In our case, that is exactly what we want. We mentioned earlier that after transforming by the projector's matrix we will be left with homogeneous coordinates, so we need to divide by the w coordinate before accessing the texture. The textureProj function will do exactly that for us.

Finally, we add the projected texture's color to the base color from the Phong model. We scale the projected texture color slightly so that it is not overwhelming.

There's more...

There's one big drawback to the technique presented here. There is no support for shadows yet, so the projected texture will shine right through any objects in the scene and appear on objects that are behind them (with respect to the projector). In later recipes, we will look at some examples of techniques for handling shadows that could help to solve this problem.

See also

▶ The *Implementing per-vertex ambient, diffuse, and specular (ADS) shading* recipe in Chapter 2, *The Basics of GLSL Shaders*

▶ The *Applying a 2D texture* recipe

Rendering to a texture

Sometimes it makes sense to generate textures "on the fly" during the execution of the program. The texture could be a pattern that is generated from some internal algorithm (a so-called **procedural texture**), or it could be that the texture is meant to represent another portion of the scene. An example of the latter case might be a video screen where one can see another part of the "world", perhaps via a security camera in another room. The video screen could be constantly updated as objects move around in the other room, by re-rendering the view from the security camera to the texture that is applied to the video screen!

In the following image, the texture appearing on the cube was generated by rendering a teapot to an internal texture and then applying that texture to the faces of the cube.

In recent versions of OpenGL, rendering directly to textures has been greatly simplified with the introduction of **framebuffer objects** (**FBOs**). We can create a separate rendering target buffer (the FBO), attach our texture to that FBO, and render to the FBO in exactly the same way that we would render to the default framebuffer. All that is required is to swap in the FBO, and swap it out when we are done.

Basically, the process involves the following steps when rendering:

1. Bind to the FBO.
2. Render the texture.
3. Unbind from the FBO (back to the default framebuffer).
4. Render the scene using the texture.

There's actually not much that we need to do on the GLSL side in order to use this kind of texture. In fact, the shaders will see it as any other texture. However, there are some important points that we'll talk about regarding fragment output variables.

In this example, we'll cover the steps needed to create the FBO and its backing texture, and how to set up a shader to work with the texture.

Getting ready

For this example, we'll use the shaders from the previous recipe *Applying a 2D texture*, with some minor changes. Set up your OpenGL program as described in that recipe. The only change that we'll make to the shaders is changing the name of the `sampler2D` variable from `Tex1` to `Texture`.

How to do it...

To render to a texture and then apply that texture to a scene in a second pass, use the following steps:

1. Within the main OpenGL program, use the following code to set up the framebuffer object:

```
GLuint fboHandle;   // The handle to the FBO

// Generate and bind the framebuffer
glGenFramebuffers(1, &fboHandle);
glBindFramebuffer(GL_FRAMEBUFFER, fboHandle);

// Create the texture object
GLuint renderTex;
glGenTextures(1, &renderTex);
glActiveTexture(GL_TEXTURE0);   // Use texture unit 0
glBindTexture(GL_TEXTURE_2D, renderTex);
```

```
glTexStorage2D(GL_TEXTURE_2D, 1, GL_RGBA8, 512, 512);
glTexParameteri(GL_TEXTURE_2D, GL_TEXTURE_MIN_FILTER,
                GL_LINEAR);
glTexParameteri(GL_TEXTURE_2D, GL_TEXTURE_MAG_FILTER,
                GL_LINEAR);

// Bind the texture to the FBO
glFramebufferTexture2D(GL_FRAMEBUFFER,GL_COLOR_ATTACHMENT0,
                GL_TEXTURE_2D, renderTex, 0);

// Create the depth buffer
GLuint depthBuf;
glGenRenderbuffers(1, &depthBuf);
glBindRenderbuffer(GL_RENDERBUFFER, depthBuf);
glRenderbufferStorage(GL_RENDERBUFFER, GL_DEPTH_COMPONENT,
                512, 512);

// Bind the depth buffer to the FBO
glFramebufferRenderbuffer(GL_FRAMEBUFFER,
                GL_DEPTH_ATTACHMENT,
                GL_RENDERBUFFER, depthBuf);

// Set the target for the fragment shader outputs
GLenum drawBufs[] = {GL_COLOR_ATTACHMENT0};
glDrawBuffers(1, drawBufs);

// Unbind the framebuffer, and revert to default
glBindFramebuffer(GL_FRAMEBUFFER, 0);
```

2. Use the following code to create a simple 1 x 1 texture that can be used as a "non-texture texture". Note that we place this one in texture unit 1:

```
// One pixel white texture
GLuint whiteTexHandle;
GLubyte whiteTex[] = { 255, 255, 255, 255 };
glActiveTexture(GL_TEXTURE1);
glGenTextures(1, &whiteTexHandle);
glBindTexture(GL_TEXTURE_2D,whiteTexHandle);
glTexStorage2D(GL_TEXTURE_2D, 1, GL_RGBA8, 1, 1);
glTexSubImage2D(GL_TEXTURE_2D,0,0,0,1,1,GL_RGBA,
                GL_UNSIGNED_BYTE,whiteTex);
```

3. In your render function within the OpenGL program, use the following code, or something similar:

```
// Bind to texture's FBO
glBindFramebuffer(GL_FRAMEBUFFER, fboHandle);
glViewport(0,0,512,512);  // Viewport for the texture
```

```
// Use the "white" texture here
int loc = glGetUniformLocation(programHandle, "Texture");
glUniform1i(loc, 1);

// Setup the projection matrix and view matrix
// for the scene to be rendered to the texture here.
// (Don't forget to match aspect ratio of the viewport.)


renderTextureScene();

// Unbind texture's FBO (back to default FB)
glBindFramebuffer(GL_FRAMEBUFFER, 0);
glViewport(0,0,width,height);   // Viewport for main window

// Use the texture that is associated with the FBO
int loc = glGetUniformLocation(programHandle, "Texture");
glUniform1i(loc, 0);

// Reset projection and view matrices here


renderScene();
```

How it works...

Let's start by looking at the code for creating the framebuffer object (the preceding step 1). Our FBO will be 512 pixels square because we intend to use it as a texture. We begin by generating the FBO using `glGenFramebuffers` and binding the framebuffer to the `GL_FRAMEBUFFER` target with `glBindFramebuffer`. Next, we create the texture object to which we will be rendering, and use `glActiveTexture` to select texture unit zero. The rest is very similar to creating any other texture. We allocate space for the texture using `glTexStorage2D`. We don't need to copy any data into that space (using `glTexSubImage2D`), because we'll be writing to that memory later when rendering to the FBO.

Next, we link the texture to the FBO by calling the function `glFramebufferTexture2D`. This function attaches a texture object to an attachment point in the currently bound framebuffer object. The first argument (`GL_FRAMEBUFFER`) indicates that the texture is to be attached to the FBO currently bound to the `GL_FRAMEBUFFER` target. The second argument is the attachment point. Framebuffer objects have several attachment points for color buffers, one for the depth buffer, and a few others. This allows us to have several color buffers to target from our fragment shaders. We'll see more about this later. We use `GL_COLOR_ATTACHMENT0` to indicate that this texture is linked to color attachment 0 of the FBO. The third argument (`GL_TEXTURE_2D`) is the texture target, and the fourth (`renderTex`) is the handle to our texture. The last argument (`0`) is the mip-map level of the texture that is being attached to the FBO. In this case, we only have a single level, so we use a value of zero.

As we want to render to the FBO with depth testing, we need to also attach a depth buffer. The next few lines of code create the depth buffer. The function `glGenRenderbuffer` creates a `renderbuffer` object, and `glRenderbufferStorage` allocates space for the `renderbuffer`. The second argument to `glRenderbufferStorage` indicates the internal format for the buffer, and as we are using this as a depth buffer, we use the special format `GL_DEPTH_COMPONENT`.

Next, the depth buffer is attached to the `GL_DEPTH_ATTACHMENT` attachment point of the FBO using `glFramebufferRenderbuffer`.

The shader's output variables are assigned to the attachments of the FBO using `glDrawBuffers`. The second argument to `glDrawBuffers` is an array indicating the FBO buffers to be associated with the output variables. The *i*th element of the array corresponds to the fragment shader output variable at location i. In our case, we only have one shader output variable (`FragColor`) at location zero. This statement associates that output variable with `GL_COLOR_ATTACHMENT0`.

The last statement in step 1 unbinds the FBO to revert back to the default framebuffer.

Step 2 creates a 1 x 1 white texture in texture unit one. We use this texture when rendering the texture so that we don't need to change anything about our shader. As our shader multiplies the texture color by the result of the Phong reflection model, this texture will effectively work as a "non-texture" because multiplying will not change the color. When rendering the texture, we want to use this "non-texture", but when rendering the scene, we'll use the texture attached to the FBO.

This use of a 1 x 1 texture is certainly not necessary in general. We use it here just so that we can draw to the FBO without a texture being applied to the scene. If you have a texture that should be applied, then that would be more appropriate here.

In step 3 (within the render function), we bind to the FBO, use the "non-texture" in unit one, and render the texture. Note that we need to be careful to set up the viewport (`glViewport`), and the view and projection matrices appropriately for our FBO. As our FBO is 512 x 512, we use `glViewport(0,0,512,512)`. Similar changes should be made to the view and projection matrices to match the aspect ratio of the viewport and set up the scene to be rendered to the FBO.

Once we've rendered to the texture, we unbind from the FBO, reset the viewport, and the view and projection matrices, use the FBO's texture (texture unit 0), and draw the scene!

There's more...

As FBOs have multiple color attachment points, we can have several output targets from our fragment shaders. Note that so far, all of our fragment shaders have only had a single output variable assigned to location zero. Hence, we set up our FBO so that its texture corresponds to color attachment zero. In later chapters, we'll look at examples where we use more than one of these attachments for things like deferred shading.

See also

▸ The *Applying a 2D texture* recipe

Using sampler objects

Sampler objects were introduced in OpenGL 3.3, and provide a convenient way to specify the sampling parameters for a GLSL sampler variable. The traditional way to specify the parameters for a texture is to specify them using `glTexParameter`, typically at the time that the texture is defined. The parameters define the sampling state (sampling mode, wrapping and clamping rules, and so on.) for the associated texture. This essentially combines the texture and its sampling state into a single object. If we wanted to sample from a single texture in more than one way (with and without linear filtering for example), we'd have two choices. We would either need to modify the texture's sampling state, or use two copies of the same texture.

In addition, we might want to use the same set of texture sampling parameters for multiple textures. With what we've seen up until now, there's no easy way to do that. With sampler objects we can specify the parameters once, and share them among several texture objects.

Sampler objects separate the sampling state from the texture object. We can create sampler objects that define a particular sampling state and apply that to multiple textures or bind different sampler objects to the same texture. A single sampler object can be bound to multiple textures, which allows us to define a particular sampling state once and share it among several texture objects.

Sampler objects are defined on the OpenGL side (not in GLSL), which makes it effectively transparent to the GLSL.

In this recipe, we'll define two sampler objects and apply them to a single texture. The following image shows the result. The same texture is applied to the two planes. On the left, we use a sampler object set up for nearest-neighbor filtering, and on the right we use the same texture with a sampler object set up for linear filtering.

Getting ready

Will start with the same shaders used in the recipe *Applying a 2D texture*. The shader code will not change at all, but we'll use sampler objects to change the state of the sampler variable `Tex1`.

How to do it...

To set up the texture object and the sampler objects, use the following steps.

1. Create and fill the texture object in the usual way, but this time, we won't set any sampling state using `glTexParameter`.

   ```
   GLuint texID;
   glGenTextures(1, &texID);
   glBindTexture(GL_TEXTURE_2D, texID);
   glTexStorage2D(GL_TEXTURE_2D, 1, GL_RGBA8, w, h);
   glTexSubImage2D(GL_TEXTURE_2D, 0, 0, 0, w, h, GL_RGBA,
       GL_UNSIGNED_BYTE, data);
   ```

2. Bind the texture to texture unit 0, which is the unit that is used by the shader.

   ```
   glActiveTexture(GL_TEXTURE0);
   glBindTexture(GL_TEXTURE_2D, texID);
   ```

3. Next, we create two sampler objects and assign their IDs to separate variables for clarity:

```
GLuint samplers[2];
glGenSamplers(2, samplers);
linearSampler = samplers[0];
nearestSampler = samplers[1];
```

4. Set up `linearSampler` for linear interpolation:

```
glSamplerParameteri(linearSampler, GL_TEXTURE_MAG_FILTER,
                    GL_LINEAR);
glSamplerParameteri(linearSampler, GL_TEXTURE_MIN_FILTER,
                    GL_LINEAR);
```

5. Set up `nearestSampler` for nearest-neighbor sampling:

```
glSamplerParameteri(nearestSampler, GL_TEXTURE_MAG_FILTER,
                    GL_NEAREST);
glSamplerParameteri(nearestSampler, GL_TEXTURE_MIN_FILTER,
                    GL_NEAREST);
```

6. When rendering, we bind to each sampler object when needed:

```
glBindSampler(0, nearestSampler);
// Render objects that use nearest-neighbor sampling
glBindSampler(0, linearSampler);
// Render objects that use linear sampling
```

How it works...

Sampler objects are simple to use, and make it easy to switch between different sampling parameters for the same texture, or use the same sampling parameters for different textures. In steps 1 and 2, we create a texture and bind it to texture unit 0. Normally, we would set the sampling parameters here using `glTexParameteri`, but in this case, we'll set them in the sampler objects using `glSamplerParameter`. In step 3, we create the sampler objects and assign their IDs to some variables. In steps 4 and 5, we set up the appropriate sampling parameters using `glSamplerParameter`. This function is almost exactly the same as `glTexParameter` except the first argument is the ID of the sampler object instead of the texture target. This defines the sampling state for each of the two sampler objects (linear for `linearSampler` and nearest for `nearestSampler`).

Finally, we use the sampler objects by binding them to the appropriate texture unit using `glBindSampler` just prior to rendering. In step 6 we bind `nearestSampler` to texture unit 0 first, render some objects, bind `linearSampler` to texture unit 0, and render some more objects. The result here is that the same texture uses different sampling parameters by binding different sampler objects to the texture unit during rendering.

See also

▶ The *Applying a 2D texture* recipe

5
Image Processing and Screen Space Techniques

In this chapter, we will cover:

- ▶ Applying an edge detection filter
- ▶ Applying a Gaussian blur filter
- ▶ Implementing HDR shading with tone mapping
- ▶ Creating a bloom effect
- ▶ Using gamma correction to improve image quality
- ▶ Using multisample anti-aliasing
- ▶ Using deferred shading
- ▶ Implementing order-independent transparency

Introduction

In this chapter, we will focus on techniques that work directly with the pixels in a framebuffer. These techniques typically involve multiple passes. An initial pass produces the pixel data and subsequent passes apply effects or further process those pixels. To implement this we make use of the ability provided in OpenGL for rendering directly to a texture or set of textures (refer to the *Rendering to a texture* recipe in *Chapter 4, Using Textures*).

The ability to render to a texture, combined with the power of the fragment shader, opens up a huge range of possibilities. We can implement image processing techniques such as brightness, contrast, saturation, and sharpness by applying an additional process in the fragment shader prior to output. We can apply **convolution** filters such as edge detection, smoothing (blur), or sharpening. We'll take a closer look at convolution filters in the recipe on edge detection.

A related set of techniques involves rendering additional information to textures beyond the traditional color information and then, in a subsequent pass, further processing that information to produce the final rendered image. These techniques fall under the general category that is often called **deferred shading**.

In this chapter, we'll look at some examples of each of the preceding techniques. We'll start off with examples of convolution filters for edge detection, blur, and bloom. Then we'll move on to the important topics of gamma correction and multisample anti-aliasing. Finally, we'll finish with a full example of deferred shading.

Most of the recipes in this chapter involve multiple passes. In order to apply a filter that operates on the pixels of the final rendered image, we start by rendering the scene to an intermediate buffer (a texture). Then, in a final pass, we render the texture to the screen by drawing a single full-screen quad, applying the filter in the process. You'll see several variations on this theme in the following recipes.

Applying an edge detection filter

Edge detection is an image processing technique that identifies regions where there is a significant change in the brightness of the image. It provides a way to detect the boundaries of objects and changes in the topology of the surface. It has applications in the field of computer vision, image processing, image analysis, and image pattern recognition. It can also be used to create some visually interesting effects. For example, it can make a 3D scene look similar to a 2D pencil sketch as shown in the following image. To create this image, a teapot, and torus were rendered normally, and then an edge detection filter was applied in a second pass.

The edge detection filter that we'll use here involves the use of a convolution filter, or convolution kernel (also called a filter kernel). A convolution filter is a matrix that defines how to transform a pixel by replacing it with the sum of the products between the values of nearby pixels and a set of pre-determined weights. As a simple example, consider the following convolution filter:

10	11	12	13	14
1 17	**0** 18	**1** 19	20	21
0 24	**2** 25	**0** 26	27	28
1 31	**0** 32	**1** 33	34	35
38	39	40	41	42

The 3 x 3 filter is shaded in gray superimposed over a hypothetical grid of pixels. The bold faced numbers represent the values of the filter kernel (weights), and the non-bold faced values are the pixel values. The values of the pixels could represent gray-scale intensity or the value of one of the RGB components. Applying the filter to the center pixel in the gray area involves multiplying the corresponding cells together and summing the results. The result would be the new value for the center pixel (25). In this case, the value would be (17 + 19 + 2 * 25 + 31 + 33) or 150.

Of course, in order to apply a convolution filter, we need access to the pixels of the original image and a separate buffer to store the results of the filter. We'll achieve this here by using a two-pass algorithm. In the first pass, we'll render the image to a texture; and then in the second pass, we'll apply the filter by reading from the texture and send the filtered results to the screen.

One of the simplest, convolution-based techniques for edge detection is the so-called **Sobel operator**. The Sobel operator is designed to approximate the gradient of the image intensity at each pixel. It does so by applying two 3 x 3 filters. The results of the two are the vertical and horizontal components of the gradient. We can then use the magnitude of the gradient as our edge trigger. When the magnitude of the gradient is above a certain threshold, then we assume that the pixel is on an edge.

The 3 x 3 filter kernels used by the Sobel operator are shown in the following equation:

$$\mathbf{S}_x = \begin{bmatrix} -1 & 0 & 1 \\ -2 & 0 & 2 \\ -1 & 0 & 1 \end{bmatrix} \quad \mathbf{S}_y = \begin{bmatrix} -1 & -2 & -1 \\ 0 & 0 & 0 \\ 1 & 2 & 1 \end{bmatrix}$$

If the result of applying Sx is sx and the result of applying Sy is sy, then an approximation of the magnitude of the gradient is given by the following equation:

$$g = \sqrt{s_x^2 + s_y^2}$$

If the value of g is above a certain threshold, we consider the pixel to be an edge pixel, and we highlight it in the resulting image.

In this example, we'll implement this filter as the second pass of a two-pass algorithm. In the first pass, we'll render the scene using an appropriate lighting model, but we'll send the result to a texture. In the second pass, we'll render the entire texture as a screen-filling quad, and apply the filter to the texture.

Getting ready

Set up a framebuffer object (refer to the *Rendering to a texture* recipe in *Chapter 4, Using Textures*) that has the same dimensions as the main window. Connect the first color attachment of the FBO to a texture object in texture unit zero. During the first pass, we'll render directly to this texture. Make sure that the mag and min filters for this texture are set to GL_NEAREST. We don't want any interpolation for this algorithm.

Provide vertex information in vertex attribute zero, normals in vertex attribute one, and texture coordinates in vertex attribute two.

The following uniform variables need to be set from the OpenGL application:

- ▶ Width: This is used to set the width of the screen window in pixels
- ▶ Height: This is used to set the height of the screen window in pixels
- ▶ EdgeThreshold: This is the minimum value of g squared required to be considered "on an edge"
- ▶ RenderTex: This is the texture associated with the FBO

Any other uniforms associated with the shading model should also be set from the OpenGL application.

How to do it...

To create a shader program that applies the Sobel edge detection filter, use the following steps:

1. Use the following code for the vertex shader:

```
layout (location = 0) in vec3 VertexPosition;
layout (location = 1) in vec3 VertexNormal;

out vec3 Position;
out vec3 Normal;
uniform mat4 ModelViewMatrix;
uniform mat3 NormalMatrix;
uniform mat4 ProjectionMatrix;
uniform mat4 MVP;

void main()
{
    Normal = normalize( NormalMatrix * VertexNormal);
    Position = vec3( ModelViewMatrix *
                    vec4(VertexPosition,1.0) );

    gl_Position = MVP * vec4(VertexPosition,1.0);
}
```

2. Use the following code for the fragment shader:

```
in vec3 Position;
in vec3 Normal;

// The texture containing the results of the first pass
layout( binding=0 ) uniform sampler2D RenderTex;

uniform float EdgeThreshold;   // The squared threshold

// This subroutine is used for selecting the functionality
// of pass1 and pass2.
subroutine vec4 RenderPassType();
subroutine uniform RenderPassType RenderPass;

// Other uniform variables for the Phong reflection model
// can be placed here...

layout( location = 0 ) out vec4 FragColor;
const vec3 lum = vec3(0.2126, 0.7152, 0.0722);
```

```
vec3 phongModel( vec3 pos, vec3 norm )
{
    // The code for the basic ADS shading model goes here...
}


// Approximates the brightness of a RGB value.
float luminance( vec3 color ) {
  return dot(lum, color);

}
subroutine (RenderPassType)
vec4 pass1()
{
  return vec4(phongModel( Position, Normal ),1.0);
}
subroutine( RenderPassType )
vec4 pass2()
{
  ivec2 pix = ivec2(gl_FragCoord.xy);
  float s00 = luminance(
              texelFetchOffset(RenderTex, pix, 0,
                              ivec2(-1,1)).rgb);
  float s10 = luminance(
              texelFetchOffset(RenderTex, pix, 0,
                              ivec2(-1,0)).rgb);
  float s20 = luminance(
              texelFetchOffset(RenderTex, pix, 0,
                              ivec2(-1,-1)).rgb);
  float s01 = luminance(
              texelFetchOffset(RenderTex, pix, 0,
                              ivec2(0,1)).rgb);
  float s21 = luminance(
              texelFetchOffset(RenderTex, pix, 0,
                              ivec2(0,-1)).rgb);
  float s02 = luminance(
              texelFetchOffset(RenderTex, pix, 0,
                              ivec2(1,1)).rgb);
  float s12 = luminance(
              texelFetchOffset(RenderTex, pix, 0,
                              ivec2(1,0)).rgb);
  float s22 = luminance(
              texelFetchOffset(RenderTex, pix, 0,
                              ivec2(1,-1)).rgb);
```

```
    float sx = s00 + 2 * s10 + s20 - (s02 + 2 * s12 + s22);
    float sy = s00 + 2 * s01 + s02 - (s20 + 2 * s21 + s22);

    float g = sx * sx + sy * sy;

    if( g > EdgeThreshold ) return vec4(1.0);
    else return vec4(0.0,0.0,0.0,1.0);
}

void main()
{
    // This will call either pass1() or pass2()
    FragColor = RenderPass();
}
```

In the render function of your OpenGL application, follow these steps for pass #1:

1. Select the framebuffer object (FBO), and clear the color/depth buffers.

2. Select the `pass1` subroutine function (refer to the *Using subroutines to select shader functionality* recipe in *Chapter 2, The Basics of GLSL Shaders*).

3. Set up the model, view, and projection matrices, and draw the scene.

For pass #2, carry out the following steps:

1. Deselect the FBO (revert to the default framebuffer), and clear the color/depth buffers.

2. Select the `pass2` subroutine function.

3. Set the model, view, and projection matrices to the identity matrix.

4. Draw a single quad (or two triangles) that fills the screen (-1 to +1 in x and y), with texture coordinates that range from 0 to 1 in each dimension.

How it works...

The first pass renders all of the scene's geometry sending the output to a texture. We select the subroutine function `pass1`, which simply computes and applies the Phong reflection model (refer to the *Implementing per-vertex ambient, diffuse, and specular (ADS) shading* recipe in *Chapter 2, The Basics of GLSL Shaders*).

In the second pass, we select the subroutine function `pass2`, and render only a single quad that covers the entire screen. The purpose of this is to invoke the fragment shader once for every pixel in the image. In the `pass2` function, we retrieve the values of the eight neighboring pixels of the texture containing the results from the first pass, and compute their brightness by calling the `luminance` function. The horizontal and vertical Sobel filters are then applied and the results are stored in `sx` and `sy`.

The `luminance` function determines the brightness of an RGB value by computing a weighted sum of the intensities. The weights are from the ITU-R Recommendation Rec. 709. For more details on this, see the Wikipedia entry for "luma".

We then compute the squared value of the magnitude of the gradient (in order to avoid the square root) and store the result in `g`. If the value of `g` is greater than `EdgeThreshold`, we consider the pixel to be on an edge, and we output a white pixel. Otherwise, we output a solid black pixel.

There's more...

The Sobel operator is somewhat crude, and tends to be sensitive to high frequency variations in the intensity. A quick look at Wikipedia will guide you to a number of other edge detection techniques that may be more accurate. It is also possible to reduce the amount of high frequency variation by adding a "blur pass" between the render and edge detection passes. The "blur pass" will smooth out the high frequency fluctuations and may improve the results of the edge detection pass.

Optimization techniques

The technique discussed here requires eight texture fetches. Texture accesses can be somewhat slow, and reducing the number of accesses can result in substantial speed improvements. *Chapter 24* of *GPU Gems: Programming Techniques, Tips and Tricks for Real-Time Graphics*, edited by Randima Fernando (Addison-Wesley Professional 2004), has an excellent discussion of ways to reduce the number of texture fetches in a filter operation by making use of so-called "helper" textures.

See also

▶ D. Ziou and S. Tabbone (*1998*), *Edge detection techniques: An overview, International Journal of Computer Vision, Vol 24, Issue 3*

▶ *Frei-Chen edge detector*: `http://rastergrid.com/blog/2011/01/frei-chen-edge-detector/`

▶ The *Using subroutines to select shader functionality* recipe in *Chapter 2, The Basics of GLSL Shaders*

▶ The *Rendering to a texture* recipe in *Chapter 4, Using Textures*

▶ The *Implementing per-vertex ambient, diffuse, and specular (ADS) shading* recipe in *Chapter 2, The Basics of GLSL Shaders*

Applying a Gaussian blur filter

A blur filter can be useful in many different situations where the goal is to reduce the amount of noise in the image. As mentioned in the previous recipe, applying a blur filter prior to the edge detection pass may improve the results by reducing the amount of high frequency fluctuation across the image. The basic idea of any blur filter is to mix the color of a pixel with that of nearby pixels using a weighted sum. The weights typically decrease with the distance from the pixel (in 2D screen space) so that pixels that are far away contribute less than those closer to the pixel being blurred.

A **Gaussian blur** uses the 2-dimensional Gaussian function to weight the contributions of the nearby pixels.

$$G(x, y) = \frac{1}{2\pi\sigma^2} e^{-\frac{x^2+y^2}{2\sigma^2}}$$

The sigma squared term is the **variance** of the Gaussian, and determines the width of the Gaussian curve. The Gaussian function is maximum at (0,0), which corresponds to the location of the pixel being blurred and its value decreases as x or y increases. The following graph shows the two-dimensional Gaussian function with a sigma squared value of 4.0:

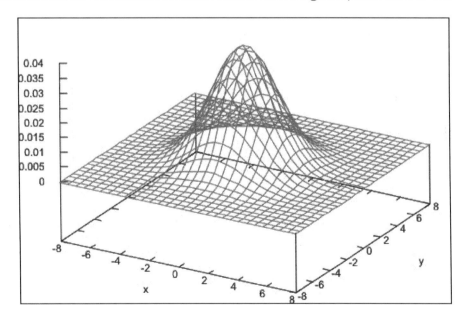

The following images show a portion of an image before (left) and after (right) the Gaussian blur operation:

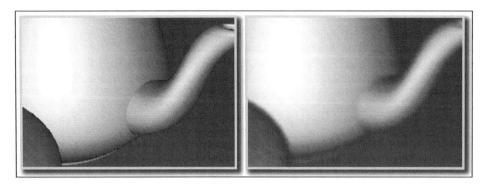

To apply a Gaussian blur, for each pixel, we need to compute the weighted sum of all pixels in the image scaled by the value of the Gaussian function at that pixel (where the x and y coordinates of each pixel are based on an origin located at the pixel being blurred). The result of that sum is the new value for the pixel. However, there are two problems with the algorithm so far:

> ▶ As this is a $O(n^2)$ process (where n is the number of pixels in the image), it is likely to be too slow for real-time use

> ▶ The weights must sum to one in order to avoid changing the overall brightness of the image

As we sampled the Gaussian function at discrete locations, and didn't sum over the entire (infinite) bounds of the function, the weights almost certainly do not sum to one.

We can deal with both of the preceding problems by limiting the number of pixels that we blur with a given pixel (instead of the entire image), and by normalizing the values of the Gaussian function. In this example, we'll use a 9 x 9 Gaussian blur filter. That is, we'll only compute the contributions of the 81 pixels in the neighborhood of the pixel being blurred.

Such a technique would require 81 texture fetches in the fragment shader, which is executed once for each pixel. The total number of texture fetches for an image of size 800 x 600 would be 800 * 600 * 81 = 38,880,000. This seems like a lot, doesn't it? The good news is that we can substantially reduce the number of texture fetches by doing the Gaussian blur in two passes.

The two-dimensional Gaussian function is actually just the product of two one-dimensional Gaussians:

$$G(x, y) = G(x)G(y)$$

Where the one-dimensional Gaussian function is given by the following equation:

$$G(x) = \frac{1}{\sqrt{2\pi\sigma^2}} e^{-\frac{x^2}{2\sigma^2}}$$

So if C_{ij} is the color of the pixel at pixel location (i, j), the sum that we need to compute is given by the following equation:

$$C_{lm} \leftarrow \sum_{i=-4}^{4} \sum_{j=-4}^{4} G(i,j) C_{l+i\ m+j}$$

This can be re-written using the fact that the two-dimensional Gaussian is a product of two one-dimensional Gaussians:

$$C_{lm} \leftarrow \sum_{i=-4}^{4} G(i) \sum_{j=-4}^{4} G(j) C_{l+i\ m+j}$$

This implies that we can compute the Gaussian blur in two passes. In the first pass, we can compute the sum over j (the vertical sum) in the preceding equation and store the results in a temporary texture. In the second pass, we compute the sum over i (the horizontal sum) using the results from the previous pass.

Now, before we look at the code, there is one important point that has to be addressed. As we mentioned previously, the Gaussian weights must sum to one in order to be a true weighted average. Therefore, we need to normalize our Gaussian weights as in the following equation:

$$C_{lm} \leftarrow \sum_{i=-4}^{4} \frac{G(i)}{k} \sum_{j=-4}^{4} \frac{G(j)}{k} C_{l+i\ m+j}$$

The value of k in the preceding equation is just the sum of the raw Gaussian weights.

$$k = \sum_{i=-4}^{4} G(i)$$

Phew! We've reduced the $O(n_2)$ problem to one that is O(n). OK, with that, let's move on to the code.

We'll implement this technique using three passes and two textures. In the first pass, we'll render the entire scene to a texture. Then, in the second pass, we'll apply the first (vertical) sum to the texture from the first pass and store the results in another texture. Finally, in the third pass, we'll apply the horizontal sum to the texture from the second pass, and send the results to the default framebuffer.

Getting ready

Set up two framebuffer objects (refer to the *Rendering to a texture* recipe in *Chapter 4, Using Textures*), and two corresponding textures. The first FBO should have a depth buffer because it will be used for the first pass. The second FBO need not have a depth buffer because, in the second and third passes, we'll only render a single screen-filling quad in order to execute the fragment shader once for each pixel.

As with the previous recipe, we'll use a subroutine to select the functionality of each pass. The OpenGL program should also set the following uniform variables:

- ▶ `Width`: This is used to set the width of the screen in pixels
- ▶ `Height`: This is used to set the height of the screen in pixels
- ▶ `Weight []`: This is the array of normalized Gaussian weights
- ▶ `Texture0`: This is to set this to texture unit zero
- ▶ `PixOffset []`: This is the array of offsets from the pixel being blurred

How to do it...

To create a shader program that implements Gaussian blur, use the following code:

1. Use the same vertex shader as was used in the previous recipe *Applying an edge detection filter*.

2. Use the following code for the fragment shader:

```
in vec3 Position;   // Vertex position
in vec3 Normal;     // Vertex normal
layout (binding=0) uniform sampler2D Texture0;

subroutine vec4 RenderPassType();
subroutine uniform RenderPassType RenderPass;

// Other uniform variables for the Phong reflection model
// can be placed here…
layout ( location = 0 ) out vec4 FragColor;

uniform int PixOffset[5] = int[](0,1,2,3,4);
uniform float Weight[5];
```

```glsl
vec3 phongModel( vec3 pos, vec3 norm )
{
    // The code for the Phong reflection model goes here...
}

subroutine (RenderPassType)
vec4 pass1()
{
  return vec4(phongModel( Position, Normal ),1.0);
}

subroutine ( RenderPassType )
vec4 pass2()
{
  ivec2 pix = ivec2(gl_FragCoord.xy);
  vec4 sum = texelFetch(Texture0, pix, 0) * Weight[0];
  for( int i = 1; i < 5; i++ )
  {
    sum += texelFetchOffset( Texture0, pix, 0,
              ivec2(0,PixOffset[i])) * Weight[i];
    sum += texelFetchOffset( Texture0, pix, 0,
              ivec2(0,-PixOffset[i])) * Weight[i];
  }
  return sum;
}

subroutine ( RenderPassType )
vec4 pass3()
{
  ivec2 pix = ivec2(gl_FragCoord.xy);
  vec4 sum = texelFetch(Texture0, pix, 0) * Weight[0];
  for( int i = 1; i < 5; i++ )
  {
    sum += texelFetchOffset( Texture0, pix, 0,
              ivec2(PixOffset[i],0)) * Weight[i];
    sum += texelFetchOffset( Texture0, pix, 0,
              ivec2(-PixOffset[i],0)) * Weight[i];
  }
  return sum;
}

void main()
{
  // This will call either pass1(), pass2(), or pass3()
  FragColor = RenderPass();
}
```

3. In the OpenGL application, compute the Gaussian weights for the offsets found in the uniform variable `PixOffset`, and store the results in the array `Weight`. You could use the following code to do so:

```
char uniName[20];
float weights[5], sum, sigma2 = 4.0f;

// Compute and sum the weights
weights[0] = gauss(0,sigma2); // The 1-D Gaussian function
sum = weights[0];
for( int i = 1; i < 5; i++ ) {
  weights[i] = gauss(i, sigma2);
  sum += 2 * weights[i];
}

// Normalize the weights and set the uniform
for( int i = 0; i < 5; i++ ) {
  snprintf(uniName, 20, "Weight[%d]", i);
  prog.setUniform(uniName, weights[i] / sum);
}
```

In the main render function, implement the following steps for pass #1:

1. Select the render framebuffer, enable the depth test, and clear the color/depth buffers.
2. Select the `pass1` subroutine function.
3. Draw the scene.

Use the following steps for pass #2:

1. Select the intermediate framebuffer, disable the depth test, and clear the color buffer.
2. Select the `pass2` subroutine function.
3. Set the view, projection, and model matrices to the identity matrix.
4. Bind the texture from pass #1 to texture unit zero.
5. Draw a full-screen quad.

Use the following steps for pass #3:

1. Deselect the framebuffer (revert to the default), and clear the color buffer.
2. Select the `pass3` subroutine function.
3. Bind the texture from pass #2 to texture unit zero.
4. Draw a full-screen quad.

How it works...

In the preceding code for computing the Gaussian weights (code segment 3), the function named `gauss` computes the one-dimensional Gaussian function where the first argument is the value for x and the second argument is sigma squared. Note that we only need to compute the positive offsets because the Gaussian is symmetric about zero. As we are only computing the positive offsets, we need to carefully compute the sum of the weights. We double all of the non-zero values because they will be used twice (for the positive and negative offset).

The first pass (subroutine function `pass1`) renders the scene to a texture using the Phong reflection model (refer to the *Implementing per-vertex ambient, diffuse, and specular (ADS) shading* recipe in *Chapter 2, The Basics of GLSL Shaders*).

The second pass (subroutine function `pass2`) applies the weighted vertical sum of the Gaussian blur operation, and stores the results in yet another texture. We read pixels from the texture created in the first pass, offset in the vertical direction by the amounts in the `PixOffset` array. We sum using weights from the `Weight` array. (The `dy` term is the height of a texel in texture coordinates.) We sum in both directions at the same time, a distance of four pixels in each vertical direction.

The third pass (subroutine `pass3`) is very similar to the second pass. We accumulate the weighted, horizontal sum using the texture from the second pass. By doing so, we are incorporating the sums produced in the second pass into our overall weighted sum as described earlier. Thereby, we are creating a sum over a 9 x 9 pixel area around the destination pixel. For this pass, the output color goes to the default framebuffer to make up the final result.

There's more...

We can further optimize the preceding technique to reduce the number of texture accesses by half. If we make clever use of the automatic linear interpolation that takes place when accessing a texture (when `GL_LINEAR` is the mag/min mode), we can actually get information about two texels with one texture access! A great blog post by Daniel Rákos describes the technique in detail (visit `http://rastergrid.com/blog/2010/09/efficient-gaussian-blur-with-linear-sampling/`).

Of course, we can also adapt the preceding technique to blur a larger range of texels by increasing the size of the arrays `Weight` and `PixOffset` and re-computing the weights, and/or we could use different values of `sigma2` to vary the shape of the Gaussian.

See also

▸ Bilateral filtering: `http://people.csail.mit.edu/sparis/bf_course/`

▸ The *Rendering to a texture* recipe in *Chapter 4, Using Textures*

▸ The *Applying an edge detection filter* recipe

▸ The *Using subroutines to select shader functionality* recipe in *Chapter 2, The Basics of GLSL Shaders*

Implementing HDR lighting with tone mapping

When rendering for most output devices (monitors or televisions), the device only supports a typical color precision of 8 bits per color component, or 24 bits per pixel. Therefore, for a given color component, we're limited to a range of intensities between 0 and 255. Internally, OpenGL uses floating-point values for color intensities, providing a wide range of both values and precision. These are eventually converted to 8 bit values by mapping the floating-point range [0.0, 1.0] to the range of an unsigned byte [0, 255] before rendering.

Real scenes, however, have a much wider range of luminance. For example, light sources that are visible in a scene, or direct reflections of them, can be hundreds to thousands of times brighter than the objects that are illuminated by the source. When we're working with 8 bits per channel, or the floating-point range [0.0, -1.0], we can't represent this range of intensities. If we decide to use a larger range of floating point values, we can do a better job of internally representing these intensities, but in the end, we still need to compress down to the 8-bit range.

The process of computing the lighting/shading using a larger dynamic range is often referred to as **High Dynamic Range rendering** (**HDR rendering**). Photographers are very familiar with this concept. When a photographer wants to capture a larger range of intensities than would normally be possible in a single exposure, he/she might take several images with different exposures to capture a wider range of values. This concept, called **High Dynamic Range imaging** (**HDR imaging**), is very similar in nature to the concept of HDR rendering. A post-processing pipeline that includes HDR is now considered a fundamentally essential part of any game engine.

Tone mapping is the process of taking a wide dynamic range of values and compressing them into a smaller range that is appropriate for the output device. In computer graphics, generally, tone mapping is about mapping to the 8-bit range from some arbitrary range of values. The goal is to maintain the dark and light parts of the image so that both are visible, and neither is completely "washed out".

For example, a scene that includes a bright light source might cause our shading model to produce intensities that are greater than 1.0. If we were to simply send that to the output device, anything greater than 1.0 would be clamped to 255, and would appear white. The result might be an image that is mostly white, similar to a photograph that is over exposed. Or, if we were to linearly compress the intensities to the [0, 255] range, the darker parts might be too dark, or completely invisible. With tone mapping, we want to maintain the brightness of the light source, and also maintain detail in the darker areas.

 This description just scratches the surface when it comes to tone mapping and HDR rendering/imaging. For more details, I recommend the book *High Dynamic Range Imaging* by Reinhard et al.

The mathematical function used to map from one dynamic range to a smaller range is called the **Tone Mapping Operator** (**TMO**). These generally come in two "flavors", local operators and global operators. A local operator determines the new value for a given pixel by using its current value and perhaps the value of some nearby pixels. A global operator needs some information about the entire image, in order to do its work. For example, it might need to have the overall average luminance of all pixels in the image. Other global operators use a histogram of luminance values over the entire image to help fine-tune the mapping.

In this recipe, we'll use a simple global operator that is described in the book *Real Time Rendering*. This operator uses the log-average luminance of all pixels in the image. The log-average is determined by taking the logarithm of the luminance and averaging those values, then converting back, as shown in the following equation:

$$\bar{L}_w = \exp\left(\frac{1}{N}\sum_{x,y}\ln(0.0001 + L_w(x,y))\right)$$

$L_w(x, y)$ is the luminance of the pixel at (x, y). The 0.0001 term is included in order to avoid taking the logarithm of zero for black pixels. This log-average is then used as part of the tone mapping operator shown as follows:.

$$L(x,y) = \frac{a}{\bar{L}_w}L_w(x,y)$$

The *a* term in this equation is the key. It acts in a similar way to the exposure level in a camera. The typical values for *a* range from 0.18 to 0.72. Since this tone mapping operator compresses the dark and light values a bit too much, we'll use a modification of the previous equation that doesn't compress the dark values as much, and includes a maximum luminance (L_{white}), a configurable value that helps to reduce some of the extremely bright pixels.

$$L_d(x, y) = \frac{L(x, y) \left(1 + \frac{L(x,y)}{L_{white}^2}\right)}{1 + L(x, y)}$$

This is the tone mapping operator that we'll use in this example. We'll render the scene to a high-resolution buffer, compute the log-average luminance, and then apply the previous tone-mapping operator in a second pass.

However, there's one more detail that we need to deal with before we can start implementing. The previous equations all deal with luminance. Starting with an RGB value, we can compute its luminance, but once we modify the luminance, how do we modify the RGB components to reflect the new luminance, but without changing the hue (or **chromaticity**)?

The chromaticity is the perceived color, independent of the brightness of that color. For example, grey and white are two brightness levels for the same color.

The solution involves switching color spaces. If we convert the scene to a color space that separates out the luminance from the chromaticity, then we can change the luminance value independently. The **CIE XYZ** color space has just what we need. The CIE XYZ color space was designed so that the Y component describes the luminance of the color, and the chromaticity can be determined by two derived parameters (x and y). The derived color space is called the **CIE xyY** space, and is exactly what we're looking for. The Y component contains the luminance and the x and y components contain the chromaticity. By converting to the CIE xyY space, we've factored out the luminance from the chromaticity allowing us to change the luminance without affecting the perceived color.

So the process involves converting from RGB to CIE XYZ, then converting to CIE xyY, modifying the luminance and reversing the process to get back to RGB. To convert from RGB to CIE XYZ (and vice-versa) can be described as a transformation matrix (refer to the code or the *See also* section for the matrix).

The conversion from XYZ to xyY involves the following:

$$x = \frac{X}{X + Y + Z} \quad y = \frac{Y}{X + Y + Z}$$

Finally, converting from xyY back to XYZ is done using the following equations:

$$X = \frac{Y}{y}x \quad Z = \frac{Y}{y}(1 - x - y)$$

The following images show an example of the results of this tone mapping operator. The left image shows the scene rendered without any tone mapping. The shading was deliberately calculated with a wide dynamic range using three strong light sources. The scene appears "blown out" because any values that are greater than 1.0 simply get clamped to the maximum intensity. The image on the right uses the same scene and the same shading, but with the previous tone mapping operator applied. Note the recovery of the specular highlights from the "blown-out" areas on the sphere and teapot.

Getting ready

The steps involved are the following:

1. Render the scene to a high-resolution texture.
2. Compute the log-average luminance (on the CPU).
3. Render a screen-filling quad to execute the fragment shader for each screen pixel. In the fragment shader, read from the texture created in step 1, apply the tone mapping operator, and send the results to the screen.

To get set up, create a high-res texture (using `GL_RGB32F` or similar format) attached to a framebuffer with a depth attachment. Set up your fragment shader with a subroutine for each pass. The vertex shader can simply pass through the position and normal in eye coordinates.

How to do it...

To implement HDR tone mapping, we'll use the following steps:

1. In the first pass we want to just render the scene to the high-resolution texture. Bind to the framebuffer that has the texture attached and render the scene normally. Apply whatever shading equation strikes your fancy.

2. Compute the log average luminance of the pixels in the texture. To do so, we'll pull the data from the texture and loop through the pixels on the CPU side. We do this on the CPU for simplicity, a GPU implementation, perhaps with a compute shader, would be faster.

```
GLfloat *texData = new GLfloat[width*height*3];
glActiveTexture(GL_TEXTURE0);
glBindTexture(GL_TEXTURE_2D, hdrTex);
glGetTexImage(GL_TEXTURE_2D, 0, GL_RGB, GL_FLOAT, texData);
float sum = 0.0f;
int size = width*height;
for( int i = 0; i < size; i++ ) {
  float lum = computeLuminance(
         texData[i*3+0], texData[i*3+1], texData[i*3+2]));
  sum += logf( lum + 0.00001f );
}
delete [] texData;
float logAve = expf( sum / size );
```

3. Set the `AveLum` uniform variable using `logAve`. Switch back to the default frame buffer, and draw a screen-filling quad. In the fragment shader, apply the tone mapping operator to the values from the texture produced in step 1.

```
// Retrieve high-res color from texture
vec4 color = texture( HdrTex, TexCoord );

// Convert to XYZ
vec3 xyzCol = rgb2xyz * vec3(color);

// Convert to xyY
float xyzSum = xyzCol.x + xyzCol.y + xyzCol.z;
vec3 xyYCol = vec3(0.0);
if( xyzSum > 0.0 )   // Avoid divide by zero
   xyYCol = vec3( xyzCol.x / xyzSum,
                  xyzCol.y / xyzSum, xyzCol.y);

// Apply the tone mapping operation to the luminance
//   (xyYCol.z or xyzCol.y)
float L = (Exposure * xyYCol.z) / AveLum;
```

```
L = (L * ( 1 + L / (White * White) )) / ( 1 + L );

// Using the new luminance, convert back to XYZ
if( xyYCol.y > 0.0 ) {
  xyzCol.x = (L * xyYCol.x) / (xyYCol.y);
  xyzCol.y = L;
  xyzCol.z = (L * (1 - xyYCol.x - xyYCol.y))/xyYCol.y;
}

// Convert back to RGB and send to output buffer
FragColor = vec4( xyz2rgb * xyzCol, 1.0);
```

How it works...

In the first step, we render the scene to an HDR texture. In step 2, we compute the log-average luminance by retrieving the pixels from the texture and doing the computation on the CPU (OpenGL side).

In step 3, we render a single screen-filling quad to execute the fragment shader for each screen pixel. In the fragment shader, we retrieve the HDR value from the texture and apply the tone-mapping operator. There are two "tunable" variables in this calculation. The variable `Exposure` corresponds to the *a* term in the tone mapping operator, and the variable `White` corresponds to L_{white}. For the previous image, we used values of 0.35 and 0.928 respectively.

There's more...

Tone mapping is not an exact science. Often, it is a process of experimenting with the parameters until you find something that works well and looks good.

We could improve the efficiency of the previous technique by implementing step 2 on the GPU using compute shaders (refer to *Chapter 10, Using Compute Shaders*) or some other clever technique. For example, we could write the logarithms to a texture, then iteratively downsample the full frame to a 1 x 1 texture. The final result would be available in that single pixel. However, with the flexibility of the compute shader, we could optimize this process even more.

See also

▶ Bruce Justin Lindbloom has provided a useful web resource for conversion between color spaces. It includes among other things the transformation matrices needed to convert from RGB to XYZ. Visit: `http://www.brucelindbloom.com/index.html?Eqn_XYZ_to_RGB.html`.

▶ The *Rendering to a texture* recipe in *Chapter 4, Using Textures*.

Creating a bloom effect

A **bloom** is a visual effect where the bright parts of an image seem to have fringes that extend beyond the boundaries into the darker parts of the image. This effect has its basis in the way that cameras and the human visual system perceive areas of high contrast. Sources of bright light "bleed" into other areas of the image due to the so-called **Airy disc**, which is a diffraction pattern produced by light that passes through an aperture.

The following image shows a bloom effect in the animated film Elephant's Dream (© 2006, Blender Foundation / Netherlands Media Art Institute / www.elephantsdream.org). The bright white color from the light behind the door "bleeds" into the darker parts of the image.

Producing such an effect within an artificial CG rendering requires determining which parts of the image are bright enough, extracting those parts, blurring, and re-combining with the original image. Typically, the bloom effect is associated with HDR (High Dynamic Range) rendering. With HDR rendering, we can represent a larger range of intensities for each pixel (without quantizing artifacts). The bloom effect is more accurate when used in conjunction with HDR rendering due to the fact that a wider range of brightness values can be represented.

Despite the fact that HDR produces higher quality results, it is still possible to produce a bloom effect when using standard (non-HDR) color values. The result may not be as effective, but the principles involved are similar for either situation.

In the following example, we'll implement a bloom effect using five passes, consisting of four major steps:

1. In the first pass, we will render the scene to an HDR texture.

2. The second pass will extract the parts of the image that are brighter than a certain threshold value. We'll refer to this as the **bright-pass filter**. We'll also downsample to a lower resolution buffer when applying this filter. We do so because we will gain additional blurring of the image when we read back from this buffer using a linear sampler.

3. The third and fourth passes will apply the Gaussian blur to the bright parts (refer to the *Applying a Gaussian blur filter* recipe in this chapter).

4. In the fifth pass, we'll apply tone mapping and add the tone-mapped result to the blurred bright-pass filter results.

The following diagram summarizes the process. The upper-left shows the scene rendered to an HDR buffer, with some of the colors out of gamut, causing much of the image to be "blown-out". The bright-pass filter produces a smaller (about a quarter or an eighth of the original size) image with only pixels that correspond to a luminance that is above a threshold. The pixels are shown as white because they have values that are greater than one in this example. A two-pass Gaussian blur is applied to the downsampled image, and tone mapping is applied to the original image. The final image is produced by combining the tone-mapped image with the blurred bright-pass filter image. When sampling the latter, we use a linear filter to get additional blurring. The final result is shown at the bottom. Note the bloom on the bright highlights on the sphere and the back wall.

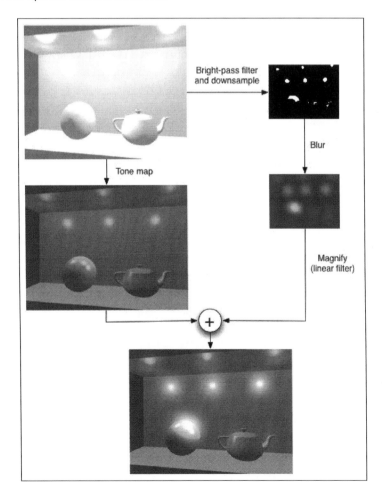

Getting ready

For this recipe, we'll need two framebuffer objects, each associated with a texture. The first will be used for the original HDR render, the second will be used for the two passes of the Gaussian blur operation. In the fragment shader, we'll access the original render via the variable `HdrTex`, and the two stages of the Gaussian blur will be accessed via `BlurTex`.

The uniform variable `LumThresh` is the minimum luminance value used in the second pass. Any pixels greater than that value will be extracted and blurred in the following passes.

Use a vertex shader that passes through the position and normal in eye coordinates.

How to do it...

To generate a bloom effect, use the following steps:

1. In the first pass, render the scene to the framebuffer with a high-res backing texture.

2. In the second pass, switch to a framebuffer containing a high-res texture that is smaller than the size of the full render. In the example code, we use a texture that is one-eighth the size. Draw a full screen quad to initiate the fragment shader for each pixel, and in the fragment shader sample from the high-res texture, and write only those values that are larger than `LumThresh`. Otherwise, color the pixel black.

   ```
   vec4 val = texture(HdrTex, TexCoord);
   if( luminance(val.rgb) > LumThresh )
       FragColor = val;
   else
       FragColor = vec4(0.0);
   ```

3. In the third and fourth passes, apply the Gaussian blur to the results of the second pass. This can be done with a single framebuffer and two textures. "Ping-pong" between them, reading from one and writing to the other. For details, refer to the *Applying a Gaussian blur filter* recipe in this chapter.

4. In the fifth and final pass, switch to linear filtering from the texture that was produced in the fourth pass. Switch to the default frame buffer (the screen). Apply the tone-mapping operator from the *Implementing HDR lighting with tone mapping* recipe to the original image texture (`HdrTex`), and combine the results with the blurred texture from step 3. The linear filtering and magnification should provide an additional blur.

   ```
   // Retrieve high-res color from texture
   vec4 color = texture( HdrTex, TexCoord );

   // Apply tone mapping to color, result is toneMapColor
   ...
   ```

```
///////// Combine with blurred texture //////////
vec4 blurTex = texture(BlurTex1, TexCoord);

FragColor = toneMapColor + blurTex;
```

How it works...

Due to space constraints, I haven't show the entire fragment shader code here. The code is available from the GitHub repository. The fragment shader is implemented with five subroutine methods, one for each pass. The first pass renders the scene normally to the HDR texture. During this pass, the active framebuffer object (FBO) is the one associated with the texture corresponding to HdrTex, so output is sent directly to that texture.

The second pass reads from HdrTex, and writes out only pixels that have a luminance above the threshold value LumThresh. The value is (0,0,0,0) for pixels that have a brightness (luma) value below LumThresh. The output goes to the second framebuffer, which contains a much smaller texture (one-eighth the size of the original).

The third and fourth passes apply the basic Gaussian blur operation (refer to the *Applying a Gaussian blur filter* recipe in this chapter). In these passes, we "ping-pong" between BlurTex1 and BlurTex2, so we must be careful to swap the appropriate texture into the framebuffer.

In the fifth pass, we switch back to the default framebuffer, and read from HdrTex and BlurTex1. BlurTex1 contains the final blurred result from step four, and HdrTex contains the original render. We apply tone mapping to the results of HdrTex and add to BlurTex1. When pulling from BlurTex1, we are applying a linear filter, gaining additional blurring.

There's more...

Note that we applied the tone-mapping operator to the original rendered image, but not to the blurred bright-pass filter image. One could choose apply the TMO to the blurred image as well, but in practice, it is often not necessary.

We should keep in mind that the bloom effect can also be visually distracting if it is overused. A little goes a long way.

See also

- ▶ *HDR meets Black&White 2* by Francesco Caruzzi in *Shader X6*
- ▶ The *Rendering to a texture* in recipe in *Chapter 4, Using Textures*
- ▶ The *Applying an edge detection filter* recipe
- ▶ The *Using subroutines to select shader functionality* recipe in *Chapter 2, The Basics of GLSL Shaders*

Using gamma correction to improve image quality

It is common for many books about OpenGL and 3D graphics to somewhat neglect the subject of gamma correction. Lighting and shading calculations are performed, and the results are sent directly to the output buffer without modification. However, when we do this, we may produce results that don't quite end up looking the way we might expect they should. This may be due to the fact that computer monitors (both the old CRT and the newer LCD) have a non-linear response to pixel intensity. For example, without gamma correction, a grayscale value of 0.5 will not appear half as bright as a value of 1.0. Instead, it will appear to be darker than it should.

The lower curve in the following graph shows the response curves of a typical monitor (gamma of 2.2). The x axis is the intensity, and the y axis is the perceived intensity. The dashed line represents a linear set of intensities. The upper curve represents gamma correction applied to linear values. The lower curve represents the response of a typical monitor. A grayscale value of 0.5 would appear to have a value of 0.218 on a screen that had a similar response curve.

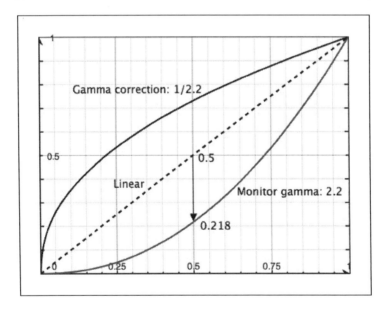

The non-linear response of a typical monitor can usually be modeled using a simple power function. The perceived intensity (P) is proportional to the pixel intensity (I) raised to a power that is usually called "gamma".

$$P = I^{\gamma}$$

Depending on the display device, the value of gamma is usually somewhere between 2.0 and 2.4. Some kind of monitor calibration is often needed to determine a precise value.

In order to compensate for this non-linear response, we can apply **gamma correction** before sending our results to the output framebuffer. Gamma correction involves raising the pixel intensities to a power that will compensate for the monitor's non-linear response to achieve a perceived result that appears linear. Raising the linear-space values to the power of 1/gamma will do the trick.

$$I = \left(I^{\frac{1}{\gamma}} \right)^{\gamma}$$

When rendering, we can do all of our lighting and shading computations ignoring the fact that the monitor's response curve is non-linear. This is sometimes referred to as "working in linear space". When the final result is to be written to the output framebuffer, we can apply the gamma correction by raising the pixel to the power of 1/gamma just before writing. This is an important step that will help to improve the look of the rendered result.

As an example, consider the following images. The image on the left is the mesh rendered without any consideration of gamma at all. The reflection model is computed and the results are directly sent to the framebuffer. On the right is the same mesh with gamma correction applied to the color just prior to output.

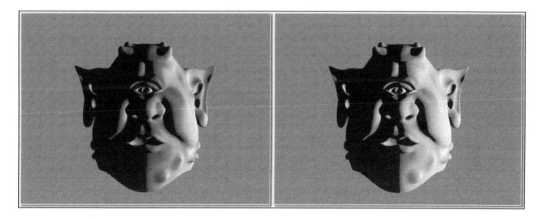

The obvious difference is that the left image appears much darker than the image on the right. However, the more important distinction is the variations from light to dark across the face. While the transition at the shadow terminator seems stronger than before, the variations within the lighted areas are less extreme.

Applying gamma correction is an important technique, and can be effective in improving the results of a lighting model.

How to do it...

Adding gamma correction to an OpenGL program can be as simple as carrying out the following steps:

1. Set up a uniform variable named `Gamma` and set it to an appropriate value for your system.

2. Use the following code or something similar in a fragment shader:

```
vec3 color = lightingModel( ... );
FragColor = vec4( pow( color, vec3(1.0/Gamma) ), 1.0 );
```

If your shader involves texture data, care must be taken to make sure that the texture data is not already gamma-corrected so that you don't apply gamma correction twice (refer to the *There's more...* section of this recipe).

How it works...

The color determined by the lighting/shading model is computed and stored in the variable `color`. We think of this as computing the color in "linear space". There is no consideration of the monitor's response during the calculation of the shading model (assuming that we don't access any texture data that might already be gamma-corrected).

To apply the correction, in the fragment shader, we raise the color of the pixel to the power of 1.0 / `Gamma`, and apply the result to the output variable `FragColor`. Of course, the inverse of `Gamma` could be computed outside the fragment shader to avoid the division operation.

We do not apply the gamma correction to the alpha component because it is typically not desired.

There's more...

The application of gamma correction is a good idea in general; however, some care must be taken to make sure that computations are done within the correct "space". For example, textures could be photographs or images produced by other imaging applications that apply gamma correction before storing the data within the image file. Therefore, if we use a texture in our application as a part of the lighting model and then apply gamma correction, we will be effectively applying gamma correction twice to the data from the texture. Instead, we need to be careful to "decode" the texture data, by raising to the power of gamma prior to using the texture data in our lighting model.

There is a very detailed discussion about these and other issues surrounding gamma correction in *Chapter 24, The Importance of Being Linear* in the book *GPU Gems 3*, edited by Hubert Nguyen (Addison-Wesley Professional 2007), and this is highly recommended supplemental reading.

Using multisample anti-aliasing

Anti-aliasing is the technique of removing or reducing the visual impact of **aliasing artifacts** that are present whenever high-resolution or continuous information, is presented at a lower resolution. In real-time graphics, aliasing often reveals itself in the jagged appearance of polygon edges, or the visual distortion of textures that have a high degree of variation.

The following images show an example of aliasing artifacts at the edge of an object. On the left, we see that the edge appears jagged. This occurs because each pixel is determined to lie either completely inside the polygon, or completely outside it. If the pixel is determined to be inside, it is shaded, otherwise it is not. Of course, this is not entirely accurate. Some pixels lie directly on the edge of the polygon. Some of the screen area that the pixel encompasses actually lies within the polygon and some lies outside. Better results could be achieved if we were to modify the shading of a pixel based upon the amount of the pixel's area that lies within the polygon. The result could be a mixture of the shaded surface's color with the color outside the polygon, where the area that is covered by the pixel determines the proportions. You might be thinking that this sounds like it would be prohibitively expensive to do. That may be true; however, we can approximate the results by using multiple **samples** per pixel.

Multisample anti-aliasing involves evaluating multiple samples per pixel and combining the results of those samples to determine the final value for the pixel. The samples are located at various points within the pixel's extent. Most of these samples will fall inside the polygon; but for pixels near a polygon's edge, some will fall outside. The fragment shader will typically execute only once for each pixel as usual. For example, with 4x multisample anti-aliasing (MSAA), rasterization happens at four times the frequency. For each pixel, the fragment shader is executed once and the result is scaled based on how many of the four samples fall within the polygon.

The following image on the right shows the results when multisample anti-aliasing is used. The inset image is a zoomed portion of the inside edge of a torus. On the left, the torus is rendered without MSAA. The right-hand image shows the results with MSAA enabled:

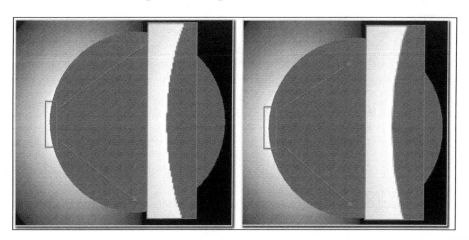

OpenGL has supported multisampling for some time now, and it is nearly transparent to use. It is simply a matter of turning it on or off. It works by using additional buffers to store the subpixel samples as they are processed. Then the samples are combined together to produce a final color for the fragment. Nearly all of this is automatic, and there is little that a programmer can do to fine-tune the results. However, at the end of this recipe, we'll discuss the interpolation qualifiers that can affect the results.

In this recipe, we'll see the code needed to enable multisample anti-aliasing in an OpenGL application.

Getting ready

The technique for enabling multisampling is unfortunately dependent on the window system API. In this example, we'll demonstrate how it is done using GLFW. The steps will be similar in GLUT or other APIs that support OpenGL.

How to do it...

To make sure that the multisample buffers are created and available, use the following steps:

1. When creating your OpenGL window, you need to select an OpenGL context that supports MSAA. The following is how one would do so in GLFW:

    ```
    glfwWindowHint(GLFW_SAMPLES, 8);
    … // Other settings
    window = glfwCreateWindow( WIN_WIDTH, WIN_HEIGHT,
                          "Window title", NULL, NULL );
    ```

2. To determine whether multisample buffers are available and how many samples per-pixel are actually being used, you can use the following code (or something similar):

    ```
    GLint bufs, samples;
    glGetIntegerv(GL_SAMPLE_BUFFERS, &bufs);
    glGetIntegerv(GL_SAMPLES, &samples);
    printf("MSAA: buffers = %d samples = %d\n", bufs, samples);
    ```

3. To enable multisampling, use the following:

    ```
    glEnable(GL_MULTISAMPLE);
    ```

4. To disable multisampling, use the following:

    ```
    glDisable(GL_MULTISAMPLE);
    ```

How it works...

As just mentioned, the technique for creating an OpenGL context with multisample buffers is dependent on the API used for interacting with the window system. The preceding example demonstrates how it might be done using GLFW. Once the OpenGL context is created, it is easy to enable multisampling by simply using the `glEnable` call shown in the preceding example.

Stay tuned, because in the next section, I'll discuss a subtle issue surrounding interpolation of shader variables when multisample anti-aliasing is enabled.

There's more...

There are two interpolation qualifiers within the GLSL that allow the programmer to fine-tune some aspects of multisampling. They are: `sample` and `centroid`.

Before we can get into how `sample` and `centroid` work, we need a bit of background. Let's consider the way that polygon edges are handled without multisampling. A fragment is determined to be inside or outside of a polygon by determining where the center of that pixel lies. If the center is within the polygon, the pixel is shaded, otherwise it is not. The following image represents this behavior. It shows pixels near a polygon edge without MSAA. The line represents the edge of the polygon. Gray pixels are considered to be inside the polygon. White pixels are outside and are not shaded. The dots represent the pixel centers.

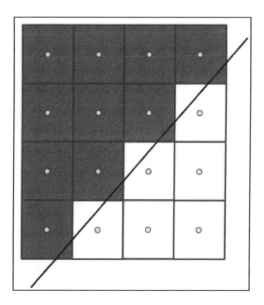

The values for the interpolated variables (the fragment shader's input variables) are interpolated with respect to the center of each fragment, which will always be inside the polygon.

When multisample anti-aliasing is enabled, multiple samples are computed per fragment at various locations within the fragment's extent. If any of those samples lie within the polygon, then the shader is executed at least once for that pixel (but not necessarily for each sample). As a visual example, the following image represents pixels near a polygon's edge. The dots represent the samples. The dark samples lie within the polygon and the white samples lie outside the polygon. If any sample lies within the polygon, the fragment shader is executed (usually only once) for that pixel. Note that for some pixels, the pixel centers lie outside the polygon. So with MSAA, the fragment shader may execute slightly more often near the edges of polygons.

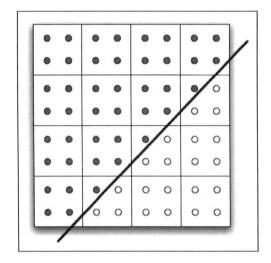

Now, here's the important point. The values of the fragment shader's input variables are normally interpolated to the center of the pixel rather than to the location of any particular sample. In other words, the value that is used by the fragment shader is determined by interpolating to the location of the fragment's center, which may lie outside the polygon! If we are relying on the fact that the fragment shader's input variables are interpolated strictly between their values at the vertices (and not outside that range) then this might lead to unexpected results.

As an example, consider the following portion of a fragment shader:

```
in vec2 TexCoord;

layout( location = 0 ) out vec4 FragColor;

void main()
{
  vec3 yellow = vec3(1.0,1.0,0.0);
  vec3 color = vec3(0.0);    // black
  if( TexCoord.s > 1.0 )
    color = yellow;
  FragColor = vec4( color , 1.0 );
}
```

This shader is designed to color the polygon black unless the s component of the texture coordinate is greater than one. In that case, the fragment gets a yellow color. If we render a square with texture coordinates that range from zero to one in each direction, we may get the results shown in the following image on the left. The images show the enlarged edge of a polygon where the s texture coordinate is about 1.0. Both images were rendered using the preceding shader. The right-hand image was created using the centroid qualifier (more on this later in this chapter).

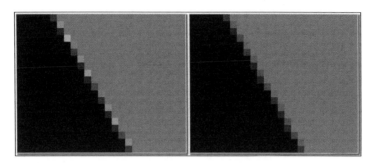

The left image shows that some pixels along the edge have a lighter color (yellow if the image is in full color). This is due to the fact that the texture coordinate is interpolated to the pixel's center, rather than to any particular sample's location. Some of the fragments along the edge have a center that lies outside of the polygon, and therefore end up with a texture coordinate that is greater than one!

We can ask OpenGL to instead compute the value for the input variable by interpolating to some location that is not only within the pixel, but also within the polygon. We can do so by using the centroid qualifier as shown in the following code:

```
centroid in vec2 TexCoord;
```

(The qualifier needs to also be included with the corresponding output variable in the vertex shader.) When centroid is used with the preceding shader, we get the preceding image shown on the right.

 In general, we should use centroid or sample when we know that the interpolation of the input variables should not extend beyond the values of those variables at the vertices.

The sample qualifier forces OpenGL to interpolate the shader's input variables to the actual location of the sample itself.

```
sample in vec2 TexCoord;
```

This, of course, requires that the fragment shader be executed once for each sample. This will produce the most accurate results, but the performance hit may not be worthwhile, especially if the visual results produced by centroid (or without the default) are good enough.

Using deferred shading

Deferred shading is a technique that involves postponing (or "deferring") the lighting/shading step to a second pass. We do this (among other reasons) in order to avoid shading a pixel more than once. The basic idea is as follows:

1. In the first pass, we render the scene, but instead of evaluating the reflection model to determine a fragment color, we simply store all of the geometry information (position, normal, texture coordinate, reflectivity, and so on) in an intermediate set of buffers, collectively called the **g-buffer** (g for geometry).

2. In the second pass, we simply read from the g-buffer, evaluate the reflection model, and produce a final color for each pixel.

When deferred shading is used, we avoid evaluating the reflection model for a fragment that will not end up being visible. For example, consider a pixel located in an area where two polygons overlap. The fragment shader may be executed once for each polygon that covers that pixel; however, the resulting color of only one of the two executions will end up being the final color for that pixel (assuming that blending is not enabled). The cycles spent in evaluating the reflection model for one of the two fragments are effectively wasted. With deferred shading, the evaluation of the reflection model is postponed until all the geometry has been processed, and the visible geometry is known at each pixel location. Hence, the reflection model is evaluated only once for each pixel on the screen. This allows us to do lighting in a more efficient fashion. For example, we could use even hundreds of light sources because we are only evaluating the lighting once per screen pixel.

Deferred shading is fairly simple to understand and work with. It can therefore help with the implementation of complex lighting/reflection models.

In this recipe, we'll go through a simple example of deferred shading. We'll store the following information in our g-buffer: the position, normal, and diffuse color (the diffuse reflectivity). In the second pass, we'll simply evaluate the diffuse lighting model using the data stored in the g-buffer.

This recipe is meant to be a starting point for deferred shading. If we were to use deferred shading in a more substantial (real-world) application, we'd probably need more components in our g-buffer. It should be straightforward to extend this example to use more complex lighting/shading models.

Getting ready

The g-buffer will contain three textures for storing the position, normal, and diffuse color. There are three uniform variables that correspond to these three textures: `PositionTex`, `NormalTex`, and `ColorTex`; these textures should be assigned to texture units 0, 1, and 2, respectively. Likewise, the vertex shader assumes that position information is provided in vertex attribute 0, the normal is provided in attribute 1, and the texture coordinate in attribute 2.

The fragment shader has several uniform variables related to light and material properties that must be set from the OpenGL program. Specifically, the structures `Light` and `Material` apply to the shading model used here.

You'll need a variable named `deferredFBO` (type `GLuint`) to store the handle to the FBO.

How to do it...

To create a shader program that implements deferred shading (with diffuse shading only), use the following code:

1. To create the framebuffer object that contains our g-buffer use the following code (or something similar):

```
void createGBufTex(GLenum texUnit, GLenum format,
                   GLuint &texid ) {
    glActiveTexture(texUnit);
    glGenTextures(1, &texid);
    glBindTexture(GL_TEXTURE_2D, texid);
    glTexStorage2D(GL_TEXTURE_2D,1,format,width,height);
    glTexParameteri(GL_TEXTURE_2D, GL_TEXTURE_MIN_FILTER,
                    GL_NEAREST);
    glTexParameteri(GL_TEXTURE_2D, GL_TEXTURE_MAG_FILTER,
                    GL_NEAREST);
}
...
GLuint depthBuf, posTex, normTex, colorTex;

// Create and bind the FBO
glGenFramebuffers(1, &deferredFBO);
glBindFramebuffer(GL_FRAMEBUFFER, deferredFBO);

// The depth buffer
glGenRenderbuffers(1, &depthBuf);
glBindRenderbuffer(GL_RENDERBUFFER, depthBuf);
glRenderbufferStorage(GL_RENDERBUFFER, GL_DEPTH_COMPONENT,
                      width, height);
```

```
    // The position, normal and color buffers
    createGBufTex(GL_TEXTURE0, GL_RGB32F, posTex);   // Position
    createGBufTex(GL_TEXTURE1, GL_RGB32F, normTex);  // Normal
    createGBufTex(GL_TEXTURE2, GL_RGB8, colorTex);   // Color

    // Attach the images to the framebuffer
    glFramebufferRenderbuffer(GL_FRAMEBUFFER,
            GL_DEPTH_ATTACHMENT, GL_RENDERBUFFER, depthBuf);
    glFramebufferTexture2D(GL_FRAMEBUFFER,
            GL_COLOR_ATTACHMENT0, GL_TEXTURE_2D, posTex, 0);
    glFramebufferTexture2D(GL_FRAMEBUFFER,
            GL_COLOR_ATTACHMENT1, GL_TEXTURE_2D, normTex, 0);
    glFramebufferTexture2D(GL_FRAMEBUFFER,
            GL_COLOR_ATTACHMENT2, GL_TEXTURE_2D, colorTex, 0);

    GLenumdrawBuffers[] = {GL_NONE, GL_COLOR_ATTACHMENT0,
            GL_COLOR_ATTACHMENT1,GL_COLOR_ATTACHMENT2};
    glDrawBuffers(4, drawBuffers);
```

2. Use the following code for the vertex shader:

```
    layout( location = 0 ) in vec3 VertexPosition;
    layout( location = 1 ) in vec3 VertexNormal;
    layout( location = 2 ) in vec2 VertexTexCoord;

    out vec3 Position;
    out vec3 Normal;
    out vec2 TexCoord;

    uniform mat4 ModelViewMatrix;
    uniform mat3 NormalMatrix;
    uniform mat4 ProjectionMatrix;
    uniform mat4 MVP;
    void main()
    {
        Normal = normalize( NormalMatrix * VertexNormal);
        Position = vec3( ModelViewMatrix *
                        vec4(VertexPosition,1.0) );
        TexCoord = VertexTexCoord;
        gl_Position = MVP * vec4(VertexPosition,1.0);
    }
```

3. Use the following code for the fragment shader:

```
    struct LightInfo {
      vec4 Position;  // Light position in eye coords.
      vec3 Intensity; // Diffuse intensity
    };
```

```glsl
uniform LightInfo Light;
struct MaterialInfo {
  vec3 Kd;                 // Diffuse reflectivity
};
uniform MaterialInfo Material;

subroutine void RenderPassType();
subroutine uniform RenderPassType RenderPass;

// The g-buffer textures
layout(binding = 0) uniform sampler2D PositionTex;
layout(binding = 1) uniform sampler2D NormalTex;
layout(binding = 2) uniform sampler2D ColorTex;
in vec3 Position;
in vec3 Normal;
in vec2 TexCoord;

layout (location = 0) out vec4 FragColor;
layout (location = 1) out vec3 PositionData;
layout (location = 2) out vec3 NormalData;
layout (location = 3) out vec3 ColorData;

vec3 diffuseModel( vec3 pos, vec3 norm, vec3 diff )
{
  vec3 s = normalize(vec3(Light.Position) - pos);
  float sDotN = max( dot(s,norm), 0.0 );
  vec3 diffuse = Light.Intensity * diff * sDotN;

  return diffuse;
}

subroutine (RenderPassType)
void pass1()
{
    // Store position, norm, and diffuse color in g-buffer
    PositionData = Position;
    NormalData = Normal;
    ColorData = Material.Kd;
}

subroutine(RenderPassType)
void pass2()
{
    // Retrieve position, normal and color information from
    // the g-buffer textures
    vec3 pos = vec3( texture( PositionTex, TexCoord ) );
```

```
        vec3 norm = vec3( texture( NormalTex, TexCoord ) );
        vec3 diffColor = vec3( texture(ColorTex, TexCoord) );

        FragColor=vec4(diffuseModel(pos,norm,diffColor), 1.0);
    }

    void main() {
        // This will call either pass1 or pass2
        RenderPass();
    }
```

In the render function of the OpenGL application, use the following steps for pass #1:

1. Bind to the framebuffer object `deferredFBO`.
2. Clear the color/depth buffers, select the `pass1` subroutine function, and enable the depth test (if necessary).
3. Render the scene normally.

Use the following steps for pass #2:

1. Revert to the default FBO (bind to framebuffer 0).
2. Clear the color buffer, select the `pass2` subroutine function, and disable the depth test (if desired).
3. Render a screen-filling quad (or two triangles) with texture coordinates that range from zero to one in each direction.

How it works...

When setting up the framebuffer object (FBO) for the g-buffer, we use textures with internal format `GL_RGB32F` for the position and normal components. As we are storing geometry information, rather than simply color information, there is a need to use a higher resolution (that is more bits per pixel). The buffer for the diffuse reflectivity just uses `GL_RGB8` since we don't need the extra resolution for these values.

The three textures are then attached to the framebuffer at color attachments 0, 1, and 2 using `glFramebufferTexture2D`. They are then connected to the fragment shader's output variables with the call to `glDrawBuffers`.

```
    glDrawBuffers(4, drawBuffers);
```

The array `drawBuffers` indicates the relationship between the framebuffer's components and the fragment shader's output variable locations. The *i*th item in the array corresponds to the *i*th output variable location. This call sets color attachments 0, 1, and 2 to output variable locations 1, 2, and 3, respectively. (Note that the fragment shader's corresponding variables are `PositionData`, `NormalData`, and `ColorData`.)

The vertex shader is a basic "pass-through" shader. It just converts the position and normal to eye (camera) coordinates and passes them along to the fragment shader. The texture coordinate is passed through unchanged.

> During pass 2, it is not strictly necessary to convert and pass through the normal and position, as they will not be used in the fragment shader at all. However, to keep things simple, I did not include this optimization. It would be a simple matter to add a subroutine to the vertex shader in order to "switch off" the conversion during pass 2. (Of course, we need to set `gl_Position` regardless.)

In the fragment shader, the functionality depends on the value of the subroutine variable `RenderPass`. It will either call `pass1` or `pass2`, depending on its value. In the `pass1` function, we store the values of `Position`, `Normal`, and `Material.Kd` in the appropriate output variables, effectively storing them in the textures that we just talked about.

In the `pass2` function, the values of the position, normal, and color are retrieved from the textures, and used to evaluate the diffuse lighting model. The result is then stored in the output variable `FragColor`. In this pass, `FragColor` should be bound to the default framebuffer, so the results of this pass will appear on the screen.

There's more...

In the graphics community, the relative advantages and disadvantages of deferred shading are a source of much debate. Deferred shading is not ideal for all situations. It depends greatly on the specific requirements of your application, and one needs to carefully evaluate the benefits and drawbacks before deciding whether or not to use deferred shading.

Multi-sample anti-aliasing with deferred shading is possible in recent versions of OpenGL by making use of `GL_TEXTURE_2D_MULTISAMPLE`.

Another consideration is that deferred shading can't do blending/transparency very well. In fact, blending is impossible with the basic implementation we saw some time ago. Additional buffers with depth-peeling can help by storing additional layered geometry information in the g-buffer.

One notable advantage of deferred shading is that one can retain the depth information from the first pass and access it as a texture during the shading pass. Having access to the entire depth buffer as a texture can enable algorithms such as depth of field (depth blur), screen space ambient occlusion, volumetric particles, and other similar techniques.

For much more information about deferred shading, refer to *Chapter 9* in *GPU Gems 2* edited by Matt Pharr and Randima Fernando (Addison-Wesley Professional 2005) and *Chapter 19* of *GPU Gems 3* edited by Hubert Nguyen (Addison-Wesley Professional 2007). Both combined, provide an excellent discussion of the benefits and drawbacks of deferred shading, and how to make the decision of whether or not to use it in your application.

See also

▸   The *Rendering to a texture* recipe in *Chapter 4, Using Textures*

Implementing order-independent transparency

Transparency can be a difficult effect to do accurately in pipeline architectures like OpenGL. The general technique is to draw opaque objects first, with the depth buffer enabled, then to make the depth buffer read-only (using glDepthMask), disable the depth test, and draw the transparent geometry. However, care must be taken to ensure that the transparent geometry is drawn from "back to front". That is, objects farther from the viewer should be drawn before the objects that are closer. This requires some sort of depth-sorting to take place prior to rendering.

The following images show an example of a block of small, semi-transparent spheres with some semi-transparent cubes placed evenly within them. On the right-hand side, the objects are rendered in an arbitrary order, using standard OpenGL blending. The result looks incorrect because objects are blended in an improper order. The cubes, which were drawn last, appear to be on top of the spheres, and the spheres look "jumbled", especially in the middle of the block. On the left, the scene is drawn using proper ordering, so objects appear to be oriented correctly with respect to depth, and the overall look is more realistic looking.

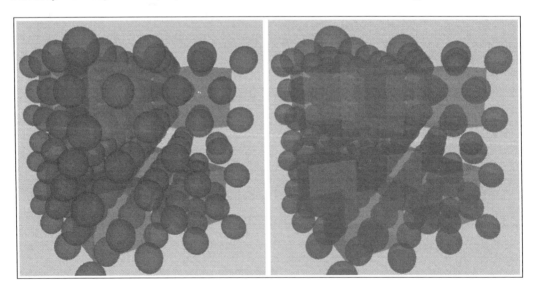

Order Independent Transparency (**OIT**) means that we can draw objects in any order, and still get accurate results. Depth sorting is done at some other level, perhaps within the fragment shader, so that the programmer need not sort objects before rendering. There are a variety of techniques for doing this; one of the most common technique is to keep a list of colors for each pixel, sort them by depth, and then blend them together in the fragment shader. In this recipe we'll use this technique to implement OIT making use of some of the newest features in OpenGL 4.3.

Shader storage buffer objects (**SSBO**) and **image load/store** are some of the newest features in OpenGL, introduced in 4.3 and 4.2, respectively. They allow arbitrary read/write access to data from within a shader. Prior to this, shaders were very limited in terms of what data they could access. They could read from a variety of locations (textures, uniforms, and so on), but writing was very limited. Shaders could only write to controlled, isolated locations such as fragment shader outputs and transform feedback buffers. This was for very good reason. Since shaders can execute in parallel and in a seemingly arbitrary order, it is very difficult to ensure that data is consistent between instantiations of a shader. Data written by one shader instance might not be visible to another shader instance whether or not that instance is executed after the other. Despite this, there are good reasons for wanting to read and write to shared locations. With the advent of SSBOs and image load/store, that capability is now available to us. We can create buffers and textures (called images) with read/write access to any shader instance. This is especially important for compute shaders, the subject of *Chapter 10, Using Compute Shaders*. However, this power comes at a price. The programmer must now be very careful to avoid the types of memory consistency errors that come along with writing to memory that is shared among parallel threads. Additionally, the programmer must be aware of the performance issues that come with synchronization between shader invocations.

> For a more thorough discussion of the issues involved with memory consistency and shaders, refer to *Chapter 11*, of The OpenGL Programming Guide, 8th Edition. That chapter also includes another similar implementation of OIT.

In this recipe, we'll use SSBOs and image load/store to implement order-independent transparency. We'll use two passes. In the first pass, we'll render the scene geometry and store a linked list of fragments for each pixel. After the first pass, each pixel will have a corresponding linked list containing all fragments that were written to that pixel including their depth and color. In the second pass, we'll draw a full-screen quad to invoke the fragment shader for each pixel. In the fragment shader, we'll extract the linked list for the pixel, sort the fragments by depth (largest to smallest), and blend the colors in that order. The final color will then be sent to the output device.

That's the basic idea, so let's dig into the details. We'll need three memory objects that are shared among the fragment shader instances.

1. **An atomic counter:** This is just an unsigned integer that we'll use to keep track of the size of our linked list buffer. Think of this as the index of the first unused slot in the buffer.

2. **A head-pointer texture that corresponds to the size of the screen**: The texture will store a single unsigned integer in each texel. The value is the index of the head of the linked list for the corresponding pixel.

3. **A buffer containing all of our linked lists:** Each item in the buffer will correspond to a fragment, and contains a struct with the color and depth of the fragment as well as an integer, which is the index of the next fragment in the linked list.

In order to understand how all of this works together, let's consider a simple example. Suppose that our screen is 3 pixels wide and 3 pixels high. We'll have a head pointer texture that is the same dimensions, and we'll initialize all of the texels to a special value that indicates the end of the linked list (an empty list). In the following diagram, that value is shown as an 'x', but in practice, we'll use `0xffffffff`. The initial value of the counter is zero, and the linked list buffer is allocated to a certain size, but treated as empty initially. The initial state of our memory looks like the following diagram:

Now suppose that a fragment is rendered at the position (0,1) with a depth of 0.75. The fragment shader will take the following steps:

1. Increment the atomic counter. The new value will be 1, but we'll use the previous value (0) as the index for our new node in the linked list.

2. Update the head pointer texture at (0,1) with the previous value of the counter (0). This is the index of the new head of the linked list at that pixel. Hold on to the previous value that was stored there (x), we'll need that in the next step.

3. Add a new value into the linked list buffer at the location corresponding to the previous value of the counter (0). Store here the color of the fragment and its depth. Store in the "next" component the previous value of the head pointer texture at (0,1) that we held on to in step 2. In this case, it is the special value indicating the end of the list.

After processing this fragment, the memory layout looks like the following:

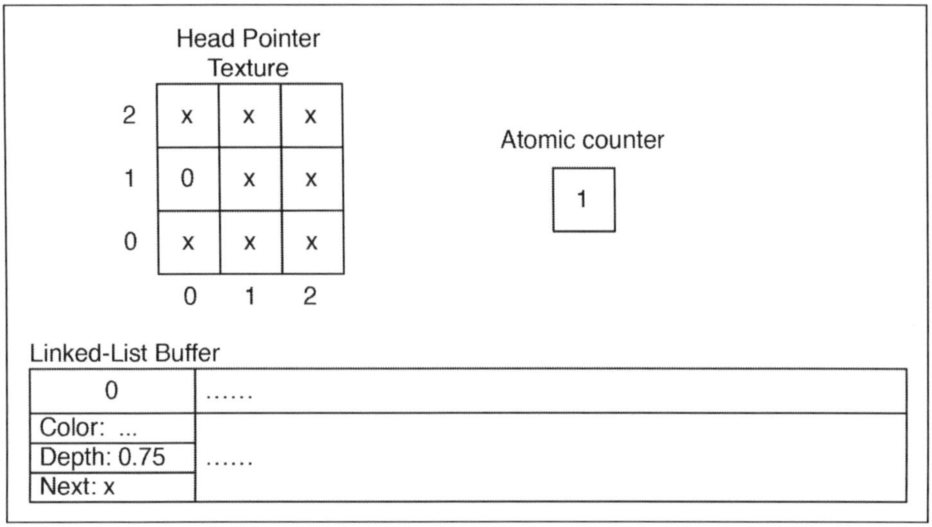

Now, suppose another fragment is rendered at (0,1), with a depth of 0.5. The fragment shader will execute the same steps as the previous ones, resulting in the following memory layout:

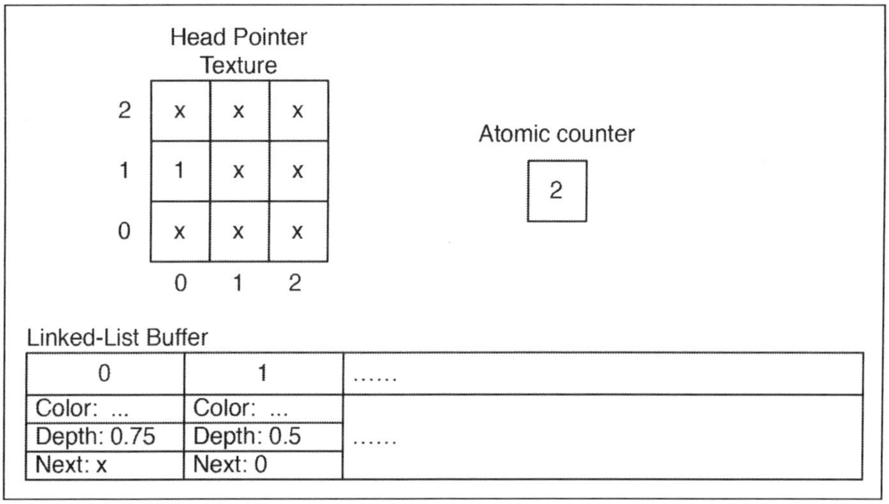

We now have a 2-element linked list starting at index 1 and ending at index 0. Suppose, now that we have three more fragments in the following order: a fragment at (1,1) with a depth of 0.2, a fragment at (0,1) with a depth of 0.3, and a fragment at (1,1) with a depth of 0.4. Following the same steps for each fragment, we get the following result:

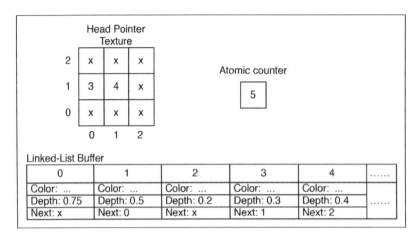

The linked list at (0,1) consists of fragments{3, 1, 0} and the linked list at (1,1) contains fragments {4, 2}.

Now, we must keep in mind that due to the highly parallel nature of GPUs, fragments can be rendered in virtually any order. For example, fragments from two different polygons might proceed through the pipeline in the opposite order as to when the draw instructions for polygons were issued. As a programmer, we must not expect any specific ordering of fragments. Indeed, instructions from separate instances of the fragment shader may interleave in arbitrary ways. The only thing that we can be sure of is that the statements within a particular instance of the shader will execute in order. Therefore, we need to convince ourselves that any interleaving of the previous three steps will still result in a consistent state. For example, suppose instance one executes steps 1 and 2, then another instance (another fragment, perhaps at the same fragment coordinates) executes steps 1, 2, and 3, before the first instance executes step 3. Will the result still be consistent? I think you can convince yourself that it will be, even though the linked list will be broken for a short time during the process. Try working through other interleavings and convince yourself that we're OK.

 Not only can statements within separate instances of a shader interleave with each other, but the subinstructions that make up the statements can interleave. (For example, the subinstructions for an increment operation consist of a load, increment, and a store.) What's more, they could actually execute at exactly the same time. Consequently, if we aren't careful, nasty memory consistency issues can crop up. To help avoid this, we need to make careful use of the GLSL support for atomic operations.

Recent versions of OpenGL (4.2 and 4.3) have introduced the tools that we need to make this algorithm possible. OpenGL 4.2 introduced atomic counters and the ability to read and write to arbitrary locations within a texture (called image load/store). OpenGL 4.3 introduced shader storage buffer objects. We'll make use of all three of these features in this example, as well as the various atomic operations and memory barriers that go along with them.

Getting ready

There's a bunch of setup needed here, so I'll go into a bit of detail with some code segments. First, we'll set up a buffer for our atomic counter:

```
GLuint counterBuffer;
glGenBuffers(1, &counterBuffer);
glBindBufferBase(GL_ATOMIC_COUNTER_BUFFER, 0, counterBuffer);
glBufferData(GL_ATOMIC_COUNTER_BUFFER, sizeof(GLuint), NULL,
            GL_DYNAMIC_DRAW);
```

Next, we create a buffer for our linked list storage:

```
GLuint llBuf;
glGenBuffers(1, &llBuf);
glBindBufferBase(GL_SHADER_STORAGE_BUFFER, 0, llBuf);
glBufferData(GL_SHADER_STORAGE_BUFFER, maxNodes * nodeSize, NULL,
            GL_DYNAMIC_DRAW);
```

> `nodeSize` in the previous code is the size of a `struct NodeType` used in the fragment shader (in the later part of code). This is computed based on the `std430` layout. For details on the `std430` layout, see the OpenGL specification document. For this example, `nodeSize` is `5 * sizeof(GLfloat) + sizeof(GLuint)`.

We also need to create a texture to hold the list head pointers. We'll use 32-bit unsigned integers, and bind it to image unit 0:

```
glGenTextures(1, &headPtrTex);
glBindTexture(GL_TEXTURE_2D, headPtrTex);
glTexStorage2D(GL_TEXTURE_2D, 1, GL_R32UI, width, height);
glBindImageTexture(0, headPtrTex, 0, GL_FALSE, 0, GL_READ_WRITE,
                  GL_R32UI);
```

After we render each frame, we need to clear the texture by setting all texels to a value of `0xffffffff`. To help with that, we'll create a buffer of the same size as the texture, with each value set to our "clear value":

```
vector<GLuint> headPtrClear(width * height, 0xffffffff);
GLuint clearBuf;
```

```
glGenBuffers(1, &clearBuf);
glBindBuffer(GL_PIXEL_UNPACK_BUFFER, clearBuf);
glBufferData(GL_PIXEL_UNPACK_BUFFER,
             headPtrClear.size()*sizeof(GLuint),
             &headPtrClear[0], GL_STATIC_COPY);
```

That's all the buffers we'll need. Note the fact that we've bound the head pointer texture to image unit 0, the atomic counter buffer to index 0 of the GL_ATOMIC_COUNTER_BUFFER binding point (glBindBufferBase), and the linked list storage buffer to index 0 of the GL_SHADER_STORAGE_BUFFER binding point. We'll refer back to that later.

Use a pass-through vertex shader that sends the position and normal along in eye coordinates.

How to do it...

With all of the buffers set up, we need two render passes. Before the first pass, we want to clear our buffers to default values (that is, empty lists), and to reset our atomic counter buffer to zero.

```
glBindBuffer(GL_PIXEL_UNPACK_BUFFER, clearBuf);
glBindTexture(GL_TEXTURE_2D, headPtrTex);
glTexSubImage2D(GL_TEXTURE_2D, 0, 0, 0, width, height,
                GL_RED_INTEGER, GL_UNSIGNED_INT, NULL);
GLuint zero = 0;
glBindBufferBase(GL_ATOMIC_COUNTER_BUFFER, 0, counterBuffer);
glBufferSubData(GL_ATOMIC_COUNTER_BUFFER, sizeof(GLuint), &zero);
```

In the first pass, we'll render the full scene geometry. Generally, we should render all the opaque geometry first, and store the results in a texture. However, we'll skip that step for this example to keep things simple and focused. Instead, we'll render only transparent geometry. When rendering the transparent geometry, we need to make sure to put the depth buffer in read-only mode (use glDepthMask). In the fragment shader, we add each fragment to the appropriate linked list.

```
layout (early_fragment_tests) in;

#define MAX_FRAGMENTS 75

in vec3 Position;
in vec3 Normal;

struct NodeType {
  vec4 color;
  float depth;
  uint next;
};
```

```
layout(binding=0, r32ui) uniform uimage2D headPointers;
layout(binding=0, offset=0) uniform atomic_uint
                                        nextNodeCounter;
layout(binding=0, std430) buffer linkedLists {
  NodeType nodes[];
};
uniform uint MaxNodes;

subroutine void RenderPassType();
subroutine uniform RenderPassType RenderPass;

...

subroutine(RenderPassType)
void pass1()
{
  // Get the index of the next empty slot in the buffer
  uint nodeIdx = atomicCounterIncrement(nextNodeCounter);

  // Is there space left in the buffer?
  if( nodeIdx < MaxNodes ) {
    // Update the head pointer image
    uint prevHead = imageAtomicExchange(headPointers,
                          ivec2(gl_FragCoord.xy), nodeIdx);

    // Set the color and depth of this new node to the color
    // and depth of the fragment.  The next pointer points to the
    // previous head of the list.
    nodes[nodeIdx].color = vec4(shadeFragment(), Kd.a);
    nodes[nodeIdx].depth = gl_FragCoord.z;
    nodes[nodeIdx].next = prevHead;
  }
}
```

Before rendering the second pass, we need to be sure that all of the data has been written to our buffers. In order to ensure that is indeed the case, we can use a memory barrier.

```
glMemoryBarrier( GL_ALL_BARRIER_BITS );
```

In the second pass, we don't render the scene geometry, just a single, screen-filling quad in order to invoke the fragment shader for each screen pixel. In the fragment shader, we start by copying the linked list for the fragment into a temporary array.

```
struct NodeType frags[MAX_FRAGMENTS];
int count = 0;
```

```
// Get the index of the head of the list
uint n = imageLoad(headPointers, ivec2(gl_FragCoord.xy)).r;

// Copy the linked list for this fragment into an array
while( n != 0xffffffff && count < MAX_FRAGMENTS) {
  frags[count] = nodes[n];
  n = frags[count].next;
  count++;
}
```

Then, we sort the fragments using insertion sort:

```
// Sort the array by depth (largest to smallest).
for( uint i = 1; i < count; i++ )
{
  struct NodeType toInsert = frags[i];
  uint j = i;
  while( j > 0 && toInsert.depth > frags[j-1].depth ) {
    frags[j] = frags[j-1];
    j--;
  }
  frags[j] = toInsert;
}
```

Finally, we blend the fragments "manually", and send the result to the output variable:

```
// Traverse the array, and blend the colors.
vec4 color = vec4(0.5, 0.5, 0.5, 1.0);   // Background color
for( int i = 0; i < count; i++ ) {
  color = mix( color, frags[i].color, frags[i].color.a);
}

// Output the final color
FragColor = color;
```

How it works...

To clear our buffers, prior to the first pass, we bind `clearBuf` to the GL_PIXEL_UNPACK_ BUFFER binding point, and call `glTexSubImage2D` to copy data from `clearBuf` to the the head pointer texture. Note that when a non-zero buffer is bound to GL_PIXEL_UNPACK_ BUFFER, `glTexSubImage2D` treats the last parameter as an offset into the buffer that is bound there. Therefore, this will initiate a copy from `clearBuf` into `headPtrTex`. Clearing the atomic counter is straightforward, but the use of `glBindBufferBase` may be a bit confusing. If there can be several buffers bound to the binding point (at different indices), then how does `glBufferSubData` know which buffer to target? It turns out that when we bind a buffer using `glBindBufferBase`, it is also bound to the "generic" binding point as well.

In the fragment shader during the first pass, we start with the layout specification enabling the early fragment test optimization.

```
layout (early_fragment_tests) in;
```

This is important because if any fragments are obscured by the opaque geometry, we don't want to add them to a linked list. If the early fragment test optimization is not enabled, the fragment shader may be executed for fragments that will fail the depth test, and hence will get added to the linked list. The previous statement ensures that the fragment shader will not execute for those fragments.

The definition of `struct NodeType` specifies the type of data that is stored in our linked list buffer. We need to store color, depth, and a pointer to the next node in the linked list.

The next three statements declare the objects related to our linked list storage. The first, `headPointers`, is the image object that stores the locations of the heads of each linked list. The layout qualifier indicates that it is located at image unit 0 (refer to the *Getting ready* section of this recipe), and the data type is `r32ui` (red, 32-bit, unsigned integer). The second object is our atomic counter `nextNodeCounter`. The layout qualifier indicates the index within the `GL_ATOMIC_COUTER_BUFFER` binding point (refer to the *Getting ready* section of this recipe), and the offset within the buffer at that location. Since we only have a single value in the buffer, the offset is 0, but in general, you might have several atomic counters located within a single buffer. Third is our linked-list storage buffer `linkedLists`. This is a shader storage buffer object. The organization of the data within the object is defined within the curly braces here. In this case, we just have an array of `NodeType` structures. The bounds of the array can be left undefined, the size being limited by the underlying buffer object that we created. The layout qualifiers define the binding and memory layout. The first, binding, indicates that the buffer is located at index 0 within the `GL_SHADER_STORAGE_BUFFER` binding point. The second, `std430`, indicates how memory is organized within the buffer. This is mainly important when we want to read the data back from the OpenGL side. As mentioned previously, this is documented in the OpenGL specification document.

The first step in the fragment shader during the first pass is to increment our atomic counter using `atomicCounterIncrement`. This will increment the counter in such a way that there is no possibility of memory consistency issues if another shader instance is attempting to increment the counter at the same time.

An atomic operation is one that is isolated from other threads and can be considered to be a single, uninterruptable operation. Other threads cannot interleave with an atomic operation. It is always a good idea to use atomic operations when writing to shared data within a shader.

The return value of `atomicCounterIncrement` is the previous value of the counter. It is the next unused location in our linked list buffer. We'll use this value as the location where we'll store this fragment, so we store it in a variable named `nodeIdx`. It will also become the new head of the linked list, so the next step is to update the value in the `headPointers` image at this pixel's location `gl_FragCoord.xy`. We do so using another atomic operation: `imageAtomicExchange`. This replaces the value within the image at the location specified by the second parameter with the value of the third parameter. The return value is the previous value of the image at that location. This is the previous head of our linked list. We hold on to this value in `prevHead`, because we want to link our new head to that node, thereby restoring the consistency of the linked list with our new node at the head.

Finally, we update the node at `nodeIdx` with the color and depth of the fragment, and set the `next` value to the previous head of the list (`prevHead`). This completes the insertion of this fragment into the linked list at the head of the list.

After the first pass is complete, we need to make sure that all changes are written to our shader storage buffer and image object before proceeding. The only way to guarantee this is to use a memory barrier. The call to `glMemoryBarrier` will take care of this for us. The parameter to `glMemoryBarrier` is the type of barrier. We can "fine tune" the type of barrier to specifically target the kind of data that we want to read. However, just to be safe, and for simplicity, we'll use `GL_ALL_BARRIER_BITS`, which ensures that all possible data has been written.

In the second pass, we start by copying the linked list for the fragment into a temporary array. We start by getting the location of the head of the list from the `headPointers` image using `imageLoad`. Then we traverse the linked list with the `while` loop, copying the data into the array frags.

Next, we sort the array by depth from largest to smallest, using the insertion sort algorithm. Insertion sort works well on small arrays, so should be a fairly efficient choice here.

Finally, we combine all the fragments in order, using the `mix` function to blend them together based on the value of the alpha channel. The final result is stored in the output variable `FragColor`.

There's more...

As mentioned previously, we've skipped anything that deals with opaque geometry. In general, one would probably want to render any opaque geometry first, with the depth buffer enabled, and store the rendered fragments in a texture. Then, when rendering the transparent geometry, one would disable writing to the depth buffer, and build the linked list as shown previously. Finally, you could use the value of the opaque texture as the background color when blending the linked lists.

This is the first example in this book that makes use of reading and writing from/to arbitrary (shared) storage from a shader. This capability, only recently introduced, has given us much more flexibility, but that comes at a price. As indicated previously, we have to be very careful to avoid memory consistency and coherence issues. The tools to do so include atomic operations and memory barriers, and this example has just scratched the surface. There's much more to come in *Chapter 10, Using Compute Shaders* when we look at compute shaders, and I recommend you read through the memory chapter in the *OpenGL Programming Guide* for much more detail than I can provide here.

See also

- *Chapter 10, Using Compute Shaders*
- *OpenGL Development Cookbook* by Muhammad Mobeen Movania has several recipes in *Chapter 6, GPU-based Alpha Blending and Global Illumination*.

6
Using Geometry and Tessellation Shaders

In this chapter, we will cover:

- ▶ Point sprites with the geometry shader
- ▶ Drawing a wireframe on top of a shaded mesh
- ▶ Drawing silhouette lines using the geometry shader
- ▶ Tessellating a curve
- ▶ Tessellating a 2D quad
- ▶ Tessellating a 3D surface
- ▶ Tessellating based on depth

Introduction

Tessellation and geometry shaders are relatively new additions to the OpenGL pipeline, and provide programmers with additional ways to modify geometry as it progresses through the shader pipeline. Geometry shaders can be used to add, modify, or delete geometry, and tessellation shaders can be configured to automatically generate geometry at various levels of detail and to facilitate interpolation based on arbitrary input (patches).

In this chapter, we'll look at several examples of geometry and tessellation shaders in various contexts. However, before we get into the recipes, let's investigate how all of this fits together.

The shader pipeline extended

The following diagram shows a simplified view of the shader pipeline when the shader program includes geometry and tessellation shaders:

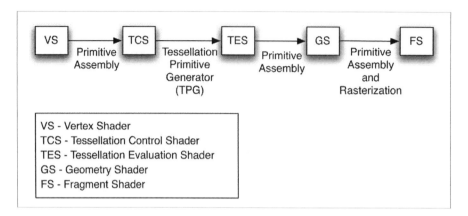

The tessellation portion of the shader pipeline includes two stages: the **tessellation control shader (TCS)**, and the **tessellation evaluation shader (TES)**. The geometry shader follows the tessellation stages and precedes the fragment shader. The tessellation shader and geometry shader are optional; however, when a shader program includes a tessellation or geometry shader, a vertex shader must be included.

Other than the preceding requirement, all shaders are optional. However, when a shader program does not include a vertex or fragment shader, the results are undefined. When using a geometry shader, there is no requirement that you also include a tessellation shader and vice versa. It is rare to have a shader program that does not include at least a fragment shader and a vertex shader.

The geometry shader

The **geometry shader (GS)** is designed to execute once for each primitive. It has access to all of the vertices of the primitive, as well as the values of any input variables associated with each vertex. In other words, if a previous stage (such as the vertex shader) provides an output variable, the geometry shader has access to the value of that variable for all vertices in the primitive. As a result, the input variables within the geometry shader are always arrays.

The geometry shader can output zero, one, or more primitives. Those primitives need not be of the same kind that were received by the geometry shader. However, the GS can only output one primitive type. For example, a GS could receive a triangle, and output several line segments as a line strip. Or a GS could receive a triangle and output zero or many triangles as a triangle strip.

This enables the GS to act in many different ways. A GS could be responsible for culling (removing) geometry based on some criteria, such as visibility based on occlusions. It could generate additional geometry to augment the shape of the object being rendered. The GS could simply compute additional information about the primitive and pass the primitive along unchanged. Or the GS could produce primitives that are entirely different from the input geometry.

The functionality of the GS is centered around the two built-in functions, `EmitVertex` and `EndPrimitive`. These two functions allow the GS to send multiple vertices and primitives down the pipeline. The GS defines the output variables for a particular vertex, and then calls `EmitVertex`. After that, the GS can proceed to re-define the output variables for the next vertex, call `EmitVertex` again, and so on. After emitting all of the vertices for the primitive, the GS can call `EndPrimitive` to let the OpenGL system know that all the vertices of the primitive have been emitted. The `EndPrimitive` function is implicitly called when the GS finishes execution. If a GS does not call `EmitVertex` at all, then the input primitive is effectively dropped (it is not rendered).

In the following recipes, we'll examine a few examples of the geometry shader. In the *Point sprites with the geometry shader* recipe, we'll see an example where the input primitive type is entirely different than the output type. In the *Drawing a wireframe on top of a shaded mesh* recipe, we'll pass the geometry along unchanged, but also produce some additional information about the primitive to help in drawing wireframe lines. In the *Drawing silhouette lines using the geometry shader* recipe, we'll see an example where the GS passes along the input primitive, but generates additional primitives as well.

The tessellation shaders

When the tessellation shaders are active, we can only render one kind of primitive: the patch (`GL_PATCHES`). Rendering any other kind of primitive (such as triangles, or lines) while a tessellation shader is active is an error. The **patch primitive** is an arbitrary "chunk" of geometry (or any information) that is completely defined by the programmer. It has no geometrical interpretation beyond how it is interpreted within the TCS and TES. The number of vertices within the patch primitive is also configurable. The maximum number of vertices per patch is implementation dependent, and can be queried via the following command:

```
glGetIntegerv(GL_MAX_PATCH_VERTICES, &maxVerts);
```

We can define the number of vertices per patch with the following function:

```
glPatchParameteri( GL_PATCH_VERTICES, numPatchVerts );
```

A very common application of this is when the patch primitive consists of a set of control points that define an interpolated surface or curve (such as a Bezier curve or surface). However, there is no reason why the information within the patch primitive couldn't be used for other purposes.

The patch primitive is never actually rendered, instead, it is used as additional information for the TCS and TES. The primitives that actually make their way further down the pipeline are created by the **tessellation primitive generator (TPG)**, which lies between the TCS and the TES. Think of the tessellation primitive generator as a configurable engine that produces primitives based on a set of standard tessellation algorithms. The TCS and the TES have access to the entire input patch, but have fundamentally different responsibilities. The TCS is responsible for setting up the TPG, defining how the primitives should be generated by the TPG (how many and what algorithm to use), and producing per-vertex output attributes. The TES has the job of determining the position (and any other information) of each vertex of the primitives that are produced by the TPG. For example, the TCS might tell the TPG to generate a line strip consisting of 100 line segments, and the TES is responsible for determining the position of each vertex of those 100 line segments. The TES would likely make use of the information within the entire patch primitive in order to do so.

The TCS is executed once for each vertex in the output patch (specified in the TCS code). It can compute additional information about the patch and pass it along to the TES using output variables. However, the most important task of the TCS is to tell the TPG how many primitives it should produce. It does this by defining tessellation levels via the `gl_TessLevelInner` and `gl_TessLevelOuter` arrays. These arrays define the granularity of the tessellation produced by the TPG.

The TPG generates primitives based on a particular algorithm (quads, isolines, or triangles). Each algorithm produces primitives in a slightly different fashion, and we will see examples of isolines and quads in the recipes in this chapter. Each vertex of the generated primitives is associated with a position in parameter space (u, v, w). Each coordinate of this position is a number that can range from zero to one. This coordinate can be used for evaluating the location of the vertex, often by interpolation of the patch primitive's vertices. The primitive generation algorithms produce vertices (and the associated parametric coordinates) in a slightly different fashion. The tessellation algorithms for quads and isolines make use of only the first two parametric coordinates: u and v. The following diagram illustrates the process for an input and output patch consisting of four vertices. In the diagram, the TPG uses the quad tessellation algorithm with inner and outer tessellation levels set at four.

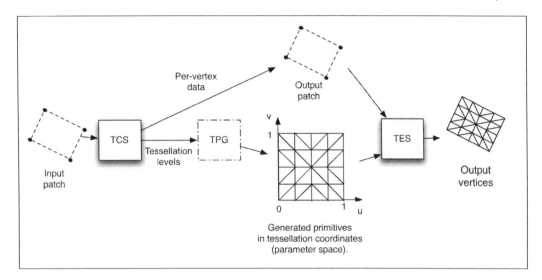

The number of vertices in the input patch need not be the same as the number of vertices in the output patch, although that will be the case in all of the examples in this chapter.

The TES is executed once for each parameter-space vertex that is generated by the TPG. Somewhat strangely, the TES is actually the shader that defines the algorithm used by the TPG. It does so via its input layout qualifier. As stated above, its main responsibility is to determine the position of the vertex (possibly along with other information, such as normal vector and texture coordinate). Typically, the TES uses the parametric coordinate (u,v) provided by the TPG along with the positions of all of the input patch vertices to do so. For example, when drawing a curve, the patch might consist of four vertices, which are the control points for the curve. The TPG would then generate 101 vertices to create a line strip (if the tessellation level was set to 100), and each vertex might have a **u** coordinate that ranged appropriately between zero and one. The TES would then use that **u** coordinate along with the positions of the four patch vertices to determine the position of the vertex associated with the shader's execution.

If all of this seems confusing, start with the *Tessellating a curve* recipe, and work your way through the following recipes.

In the *Tessellating a curve* recipe, we'll go through a basic example where we use tessellation shaders to draw a Bezier curve with four control points. In the *Tessellating a 2D quad* recipe, we'll try to understand how the quad tessellation algorithm works by rendering a simple quad and visualizing the triangles produced by the TPG. In the *Tessellating a 3D surface* recipe, we'll use quad tessellation to render a 3D Bezier surface. Finally, in the *Tessellating based on depth* recipe, we'll see how the tessellation shaders make it easy to implement **level-of-detail** (**LOD**) algorithms.

Point sprites with the geometry shader

Point sprites are simple quads (usually texture mapped) that are aligned such that they are always facing the camera. They are very useful for particle systems in 3D (refer to *Chapter 9, Particles Systems and Animation*) or 2D games. The point sprites are specified by the OpenGL application as single point primitives, via the `GL_POINTS` rendering mode. This simplifies the process, because the quad itself and the texture coordinates for the quad are determined automatically. The OpenGL side of the application can effectively treat them as point primitives, avoiding the need to compute the positions of the quad vertices.

The following screenshot shows a group of point sprites. Each sprite is rendered as a point primitive. The quad and texture coordinates are generated automatically (within the geometry shader) and aligned to face the camera.

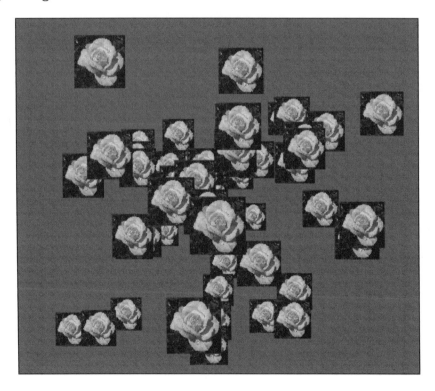

OpenGL already has built-in support for point sprites in the `GL_POINTS` rendering mode. When rendering point primitives using this mode, the points are rendered as screen-space squares that have a diameter (side length) as defined by the `glPointSize` function. In addition, OpenGL will automatically generate texture coordinates for the fragments of the square. These coordinates run from zero to one in each direction (left-to-right for s, bottom-to-top for t), and are accessible in the fragment shader via the `gl_PointCoord` built-in variable.

There are various ways to fine-tune the rendering of point sprites within OpenGL. One can define the origin of the automatically generated texture coordinates using the `glPointParameter` functions. The same set of functions also can be used to tweak the way that OpenGL defines the alpha value for points when multisampling is enabled.

The built-in support for point sprites does not allow the programmer to rotate the screen-space squares, or define them as different shapes such as rectangles or triangles. However, one can achieve similar effects with creative use of textures and transformations of the texture coordinates. For example, we could transform the texture coordinates using a rotation matrix to create the look of a rotating object even though the geometry itself is not actually rotating. In addition, the size of the point sprite is a screen-space size. In other words, the point size must be adjusted with the depth of the point sprite if we want to get a perspective effect (sprites get smaller with distance).

If these (and possibly other) issues make the default support for point sprites too limiting, we can use the geometry shader to generate our point sprites. In fact, this technique is a good example of using the geometry shader to generate different kinds of primitives than it receives. The basic idea here is that the geometry shader will receive point primitives (in camera coordinates) and will output a quad centered at the point and aligned so that it is facing the camera. The geometry shader will also automatically generate texture coordinates for the quad.

If desired, we could generate other shapes such as hexagons, or we could rotate the quads before they are output from the geometry shader. The possibilities are endless. Implementing the primitive generation within the geometry shader gives us a great deal of flexibility, but possibly at the cost of some efficiency. The default OpenGL support for point sprites is highly optimized and is likely to be faster in general.

Before jumping directly into the code, let's take a look at some of the mathematics. In the geometry shader, we'll need to generate the vertices of a quad that is centered at a point and aligned with the camera's coordinate system (eye coordinates). Given the point location (P) in camera coordinates, we can generate the vertices of the corners of the quad by simply translating P in a plane parallel to the x-y plane of the camera's coordinate system as shown in the following figure:

$$A = P + \left(-\frac{w}{2}, -\frac{w}{2}, 0\right)$$

$$B = P + \left(-\frac{w}{2}, \frac{w}{2}, 0\right)$$

$$C = P + \left(\frac{w}{2}, \frac{w}{2}, 0\right)$$

$$D = P + \left(\frac{w}{2}, -\frac{w}{2}, 0\right)$$

The geometry shader will receive the point location in camera coordinates, and output the quad as a triangle strip with texture coordinates. The fragment shader will then just apply the texture to the quad.

Getting ready

For this example, we'll need to render a number of point primitives. The positions can be sent via attribute location 0. There's no need to provide normal vectors or texture coordinates for this one.

The following uniform variables are defined within the shaders, and need to be set within the OpenGL program:

- `Size2`: This should be half the width of the sprite's square
- `SpriteTex`: This is the texture unit containing the point sprite texture

As usual, uniforms for the standard transformation matrices are also defined within the shaders, and need to be set within the OpenGL program.

How to do it...

To create a shader program that can be used to render point primitives as quads, use the following steps:

1. Use the following code for the vertex shader:

```
layout (location = 0) in vec3 VertexPosition;

uniform mat4 ModelViewMatrix;
uniform mat3 NormalMatrix;
uniform mat4 ProjectionMatrix;

void main()
{
    gl_Position = ModelViewMatrix *
                  vec4(VertexPosition,1.0);
}
```

2. Use the following code for the geometry shader:

```
layout( points ) in;
layout( triangle_strip, max_vertices = 4 ) out;

uniform float Size2;    // Half the width of the quad
```

```
uniform mat4 ProjectionMatrix;

out vec2 TexCoord;

void main()
{
    mat4 m = ProjectionMatrix;   // Reassign for brevity

    gl_Position = m * (vec4(-Size2,-Size2,0.0,0.0) +
                        gl_in[0].gl_Position);
    TexCoord = vec2(0.0,0.0);
    EmitVertex();

    gl_Position = m * (vec4(Size2,-Size2,0.0,0.0) +
                        gl_in[0].gl_Position);
    TexCoord = vec2(1.0,0.0);
    EmitVertex();

    gl_Position = m * (vec4(-Size2,Size2,0.0,0.0) +
                        gl_in[0].gl_Position);
    TexCoord = vec2(0.0,1.0);
    EmitVertex();

    gl_Position = m * (vec4(Size2,Size2,0.0,0.0) +
                        gl_in[0].gl_Position);
    TexCoord = vec2(1.0,1.0);
    EmitVertex();

    EndPrimitive();
}
```

3. Use the following code for the fragment shader:

```
in vec2 TexCoord;   // From the geometry shader

uniform sampler2D SpriteTex;

layout( location = 0 ) out vec4 FragColor;

void main()
{
    FragColor = texture(SpriteTex, TexCoord);
}
```

4. Within the OpenGL render function, render a set of point primitives.

How it works...

The vertex shader is almost as simple as it can get. It converts the point's position to camera coordinates by multiplying by the model-view matrix, and assigns the result to the built-in output variable `gl_Position`.

In the geometry shader, we start by defining the kind of primitive that this geometry shader expects to receive. The first layout statement indicates that this geometry shader will receive point primitives.

```
layout( points ) in;
```

The next layout statement indicates the kind of primitives produced by this geometry shader, and the maximum number of vertices that will be output.

```
layout( triangle_strip, max_vertices = 4 ) out;
```

In this case, we want to produce a single quad for each point received, so we indicate that the output will be a triangle strip with a maximum of four vertices.

The input primitive is available to the geometry shader via the built-in input variable `gl_in`. Note that it is an array of structures. You might be wondering why this is an array since a point primitive is only defined by a single position. Well, in general the geometry shader can receive triangles, lines, or points (and possibly adjacency information). So, the number of values available may be more than one. If the input were triangles, the geometry shader would have access to three input values (associated with each vertex). In fact, it could have access to as many as six values when `triangles_adjacency` is used (more on that in a later recipe).

The `gl_in` variable is an array of structs. Each struct contains the following fields: `gl_Position`, `gl_PointSize`, and `gl_ClipDistance[]`. In this example, we are only interested in `gl_Position`. However, the others can be set in the vertex shader to provide additional information to the geometry shader.

Within the `main` function of the geometry shader, we produce the quad (as a triangle strip) in the following way. For each vertex of the triangle strip we execute the following steps:

1. Compute the attributes for the vertex (in this case the position and texture coordinate), and assign their values to the appropriate output variables (`gl_Position` and `TexCoord`). Note that the position is also transformed by the projection matrix. We do this because the variable `gl_Position` must be provided in clip coordinates to later stages of the pipeline.

2. Emit the vertex (send it down the pipeline) by calling the built-in function `EmitVertex()`.

Once we have emitted all vertices for the output primitive, we call `EndPrimitive()` to finalize the primitive and send it along.

 It is not strictly necessary to call `EndPrimitive()` in this case because it is implicitly called when the geometry shader finishes. However, like closing files, it is good practice to do so anyway.

The fragment shader is also very simple. It just applies the texture to the fragment using the (interpolated) texture coordinate provided by the geometry shader.

There's more...

This example is fairly straightforward and is intended as a gentle introduction to geometry shaders. We could expand on this by allowing the quad to rotate or to be oriented in different directions. We could also use the texture to discard fragments (in the fragment shader) in order to create point sprites of arbitrary shapes. The power of the geometry shader opens up plenty of possibilities!

Drawing a wireframe on top of a shaded mesh

The preceding recipe demonstrated the use of a geometry shader to produce a different variety of primitive than it received. Geometry shaders can also be used to provide additional information to later stages. They are quite well suited to do so because they have access to all of the vertices of the primitive at once, and can do computations based on the entire primitive rather than a single vertex.

This example involves a geometry shader that does not modify the triangle at all. It essentially passes the primitive along unchanged. However, it computes additional information about the triangle that will be used by the fragment shader to highlight the edges of the polygon. The basic idea here is to draw the edges of each polygon directly on top of the shaded mesh.

The following figure shows an example of this technique. The mesh edges are drawn on top of the shaded surface by using information computed within the geometry shader.

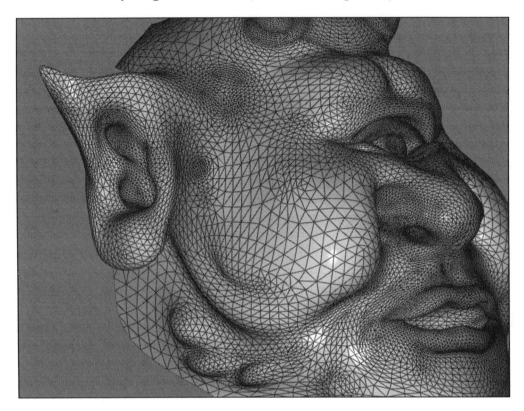

There are many techniques for producing wireframe structures on top of shaded surfaces. This technique comes from an NVIDIA whitepaper published in 2007. We make use of the geometry shader to produce the wireframe and shaded surface in a single pass. We also provide some simple anti-aliasing of the mesh lines that are produced, and the results are quite nice (refer to the preceding figure).

To render the wireframe on top of the shaded mesh, we'll compute the distance from each fragment to the nearest triangle edge. When the fragment is within a certain distance from the edge, it will be shaded and mixed with the edge color. Otherwise, the fragment will be shaded normally.

To compute the distance from a fragment to the edge, we use the following technique. In the geometry shader, we compute the minimum distance from each vertex to the opposite edge (also called the **triangle altitude**). In the following figure, the desired distances are **ha**, **hb**, and **hc**.

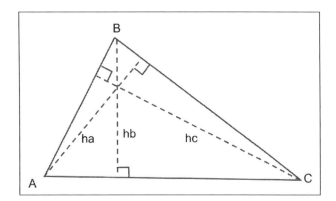

We can compute these altitudes using the interior angles of the triangle, which can be determined using the law of cosines. For example, to find **ha**, we use the interior angle at vertex **C** (**β**).

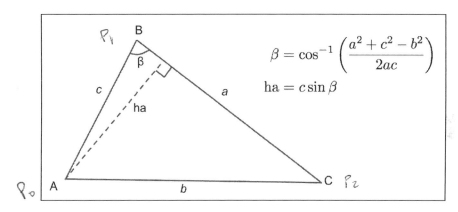

$$\beta = \cos^{-1}\left(\frac{a^2 + c^2 - b^2}{2ac}\right)$$

$$ha = c\sin\beta$$

The other altitudes can be computed in a similar way. (Note that **β** could be greater than 90 degrees, in which case, we would want the sine of 180-β. However, the sine of 180-β is the same as the sine of β.)

Once we have computed these triangle altitudes, we can create an output vector (an "edge-distance" vector) within the geometry shader for interpolation across the triangle. The components of this vector represent the distances from the fragment to each edge of the triangle. The x component represents the distance from edge **a**, the y component is the distance from edge **b**, and the z component is the distance from edge **c**. If we assign the correct values to these components at the vertices, the hardware will automatically interpolate them for us to provide the appropriate distances at each fragment. At vertex **A** the value of this vector should be (**ha**, 0, 0) because the vertex **A** is at a distance of ha from edge **a** and directly on edges **b** and **c**. Similarly, the value for vertex **B** is (0, **hb**, 0) and for vertex C is (0, 0, **hc**). When these three values are interpolated across the triangle, we should have the distance from the fragment to each of the three edges.

We will calculate all of this in screen space. That is, we'll transform the vertices to screen space within the geometry shader before computing the altitudes. Since we are working in screen space, there's no need (and it would be incorrect) to interpolate the values in a perspective correct manner. So we need to be careful to tell the hardware to interpolate linearly.

Within the fragment shader, all we need to do is find the minimum of the three distances, and if that distance is less than the line width, we mix the fragment color with the line color. However, we'd also like to apply a bit of anti-aliasing while we're at it. To do so, we'll fade the edge of the line using the GLSL `smoothstep` function.

We'll scale the intensity of the line in a two-pixel range around the edge of the line. Pixels that are at a distance of one or less from the true edge of the line get 100 percent of the line color, and pixels that are at a distance of one or more from the edge of the line get zero percent of the line color. In between, we'll use the `smoothstep` function to create a smooth transition. Of course, the edge of the line itself is a configurable distance (we'll call it `Line.Width`) from the edge of the polygon.

Getting ready

The typical setup is needed for this example. The vertex position and normal should be provided in attributes zero and one respectively, and you need to provide the appropriate parameters for your shading model. As usual, the standard matrices are defined as uniform variables and should be set within the OpenGL application. However, note that this time we also need the viewport matrix (uniform variable `ViewportMatrix`) in order to transform into screen space.

There are a few uniforms related to the mesh lines that need to be set:

▸ `Line.Width`: This should be half the width of the mesh lines
▸ `Line.Color`: This is the color of the mesh lines

How to do it...

To create a shader program that utilizes the geometry shader to produce a wireframe on top of a shaded surface, use the following steps:

1. Use the following code for the vertex shader:

```
layout (location = 0 ) in vec3 VertexPosition;
layout (location = 1 ) in vec3 VertexNormal;

out vec3 VNormal;
out vec3 VPosition;

uniform mat4 ModelViewMatrix;
uniform mat3 NormalMatrix;
uniform mat4 ProjectionMatrix;
uniform mat4 MVP;

void main()
{
    VNormal = normalize( NormalMatrix * VertexNormal);
    VPosition = vec3(ModelViewMatrix *
                        vec4(VertexPosition,1.0));
    gl_Position = MVP * vec4(VertexPosition,1.0);
}
```

2. Use the following code for the geometry shader:

```
layout( triangles ) in;
layout( triangle_strip, max_vertices = 3 ) out;

out vec3 GNormal;
out vec3 GPosition;
noperspective out vec3 GEdgeDistance;

in vec3 VNormal[];
in vec3 VPosition[];

uniform mat4 ViewportMatrix;  // Viewport matrix

void main()
{
    // Transform each vertex into viewport space
    vec3 p0 = vec3(ViewportMatrix * (gl_in[0].gl_Position /
                            gl_in[0].gl_Position.w));
    vec3 p1 = vec3(ViewportMatrix * (gl_in[1].gl_Position /
                            gl_in[1].gl_Position.w));
```

```
        vec3 p2 = vec3(ViewportMatrix * (gl_in[2].gl_Position /
                               gl_in[2].gl_Position.w));

        // Find the altitudes (ha, hb and hc)
        float a = length(p1 - p2);
        float b = length(p2 - p0);
        float c = length(p1 - p0);
        float alpha = acos( (b*b + c*c - a*a) / (2.0*b*c) );
        float beta = acos( (a*a + c*c - b*b) / (2.0*a*c) );
        float ha = abs( c * sin( beta ) );
        float hb = abs( c * sin( alpha ) );
        float hc = abs( b * sin( alpha ) );

        // Send the triangle along with the edge distances
        GEdgeDistance = vec3( ha, 0, 0 );
        GNormal = VNormal[0];
        GPosition = VPosition[0];
        gl_Position = gl_in[0].gl_Position;
        EmitVertex();

        GEdgeDistance = vec3( 0, hb, 0 );
        GNormal = VNormal[1];
        GPosition = VPosition[1];
        gl_Position = gl_in[1].gl_Position;
        EmitVertex();

        GEdgeDistance = vec3( 0, 0, hc );
        GNormal = VNormal[2];
        GPosition = VPosition[2];
        gl_Position = gl_in[2].gl_Position;
        EmitVertex();

        EndPrimitive();
    }
```

3. Use the following code for the fragment shader:

```
    // *** Insert appropriate uniforms for the Phong model ***

    // The mesh line settings
    uniform struct LineInfo {
       float Width;
       vec4 Color;
    } Line;

    in vec3 GPosition;
```

```
in vec3 GNormal;
noperspective in vec3 GEdgeDistance;

layout( location = 0 ) out vec4 FragColor;
vec3 phongModel( vec3 pos, vec3 norm )
{
    // *** Phong model evaluation code goes here ***
}

void main() {

    // The shaded surface color.
    vec4 color=vec4(phongModel(GPosition, GNormal), 1.0);

    // Find the smallest distance
    float d = min( GEdgeDistance.x, GEdgeDistance.y );
    d = min( d, GEdgeDistance.z );

    // Determine the mix factor with the line color
    float mixVal = smoothstep( Line.Width - 1,
                               Line.Width + 1, d );

    // Mix the surface color with the line color
    FragColor = mix( Line.Color, color, mixVal );
}
```

How it works...

The vertex shader is pretty simple. It passes the normal and position along to the geometry shader after converting them into camera coordinates. The built-in variable gl_Position gets the position in clip coordinates. We'll use this value in the geometry shader to determine the screen space coordinates.

In the geometry shader, we begin by defining the input and output primitive types for this shader.

```
layout( triangles ) in;
layout( triangle_strip, max_vertices = 3 ) out;
```

We don't actually change anything about the geometry of the triangle, so the input and output types are essentially the same. We will output exactly the same triangle that was received as input.

The output variables for the geometry shader are `GNormal`, `GPosition`, and `GEdgeDistance`. The first two are simply the values of the normal and position in camera coordinates, passed through unchanged. The third is the vector that will store the distance to each edge of the triangle (described previously). Note that it is defined with the `noperspective` qualifier.

```
noperspective out vec3 GEdgeDistance;
```

The `noperspective` qualifier indicates that the values are to be interpolated linearly, instead of the default perspective correct interpolation. As mentioned previously, these distances are in screen space, so it would be incorrect to interpolate them in a non-linear fashion.

Within the `main` function, we start by transforming the position of each of the three vertices of the triangle from clip coordinates to screen space coordinates by multiplying with the viewport matrix. (Note that it is also necessary to divide by the w coordinate as the clip coordinates are homogeneous and may need to be converted back to true Cartesian coordinates.)

Next, we compute the three altitudes `ha`, `hb`, and `hc` using the law of cosines as described earlier.

Once we have the three altitudes, we set `GEdgeDistance` appropriately for the first vertex; pass along `GNormal`, `GPosition`, and `gl_Position` unchanged; and emit the first vertex by calling `EmitVertex()`. This finishes the vertex and emits the vertex position and all of the per-vertex output variables. We then proceed similarly for the other two vertices of the triangle, finishing the polygon by calling `EndPrimitive()`.

In the fragment shader, we start by evaluating the basic shading model and storing the resulting color in `color`. At this stage in the pipeline, the three components of the `GEdgeDistance` variable should contain the distance from this fragment to each of the three edges of the triangle. We are interested in the minimum distance, so we find the minimum of the three components and store that in the `d` variable. The `smoothstep` function is then used to determine how much to mix the line color with the shaded color (`mixVal`).

```
float mixVal = smoothstep( Line.Width - 1,
                           Line.Width + 1, d );
```

If the distance is less than `Line.Width - 1`, then `smoothstep` will return a value of `0`, and if it is greater than `Line.Width + 1`, it will return `1`. For values of d that are in between the two, we'll get a smooth transition. This gives us a value of `0` when inside the line, a value of `1` when outside the line, and in a two pixel area around the edge, we'll get a smooth variation between 0 and 1. Therefore, we can use the result directly to mix the color with the line color.

Finally, the fragment color is determined by mixing the shaded color with the line color using `mixVal` as the interpolation parameter.

There's more...

This technique produces very nice looking results and has relatively few drawbacks. It is a good example of how geometry shaders can be useful for tasks other than modification of the actual geometry. In this case, we used the geometry shader simply to compute additional information about the primitive as it was being sent down the pipeline.

This shader can be dropped in and applied to any mesh without any modification to the OpenGL side of the application. It can be useful when debugging mesh issues or when implementing a mesh modeling program.

Other common techniques for accomplishing this effect typically involve rendering the shaded object and wireframe in two passes with a polygon offset (via the `glPolygonOffset` function) applied to avoid the "z-fighting", which takes place between the wireframe and the shaded surface beneath. This technique is not always effective because the modified depth values might not always be correct, or as desired, and it can be difficult to find the "sweet-spot" for the polygon offset value. For a good survey of techniques, refer to *Section 11.4.2 in Real Time Rendering, third edition*, by *T Akenine-Moller, E Haines*, and *N Hoffman, AK Peters, 2008*.

See also...

- ▶ This technique was originally published in an NVIDIA whitepaper in 2007 (*Solid Wireframe, NVIDIA Whitepaper WP-03014-001_v01* available at `developer. nvidia.com`). The whitepaper was listed as a Direct3D example, but of course our implementation here is provided in OpenGL.

- ▶ The *Creating shadows using shadow volumes and the geometry shader* recipe in *Chapter 7, Shadows*.

- ▶ The *Implementing per-vertex ambient, diffuse, and specular (ADS) shading* recipe in *Chapter 2, The Basics of GLSL Shaders*.

Drawing silhouette lines using the geometry shader

When a cartoon or hand-drawn effect is desired, we often want to draw black outlines around the edges of a model and along ridges or creases (silhouette lines). In this recipe, we'll discuss one technique for doing this using the geometry shader, to produce the additional geometry for the silhouette lines. The geometry shader will approximate these lines by generating small, skinny quads aligned with the edges that make up the silhouette of the object.

The following figure shows the ogre mesh with black silhouette lines generated by the geometry shader. The lines are made up of small quads that are aligned with certain mesh edges.

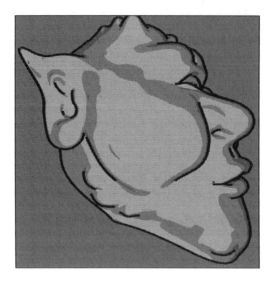

The technique shown in this recipe is based on a technique published in a recent blog post by *Philip Rideout* (`prideout.net/blog/?p=54`). His implementation uses two passes (base geometry and silhouette), and includes many optimizations, such as anti-aliasing and custom depth testing (with g-buffers). To keep things simple, as our main goal is to demonstrate the features of the geometry shader, we'll implement the technique using a single pass without anti-aliasing or custom depth testing. If you are interested in adding these additional features, refer to Philip's excellent blog posting.

One of the most important features of the geometry shader is that it allows us to provide additional vertex information beyond just the primitive being rendered. When geometry shaders were introduced into OpenGL, several additional primitive rendering modes were also introduced. These "adjacency" modes allow additional vertex data to be associated with each primitive. Typically, this additional information is related to the nearby primitives within a mesh, but there is no requirement that this be the case (we could actually use the additional information for other purposes if desired). The following list includes the adjacency modes along with a short description:

- ▶ GL_LINES_ADJACENCY: This mode defines lines with adjacent vertices (four vertices per line segment)
- ▶ GL_LINE_STRIP_ADJACENCY: This mode defines a line strip with adjacent vertices (for n lines, there are n+3 vertices)
- ▶ GL_TRIANGLES_ADJACENCY: This mode defines triangles along with vertices of adjacent triangles (six vertices per primitive)
- ▶ GL_TRIANGLE_STRIP_ADJACENCY: This mode defines a triangle strip along with vertices of adjacent triangles (for n triangles, there are 2(n+2) vertices provided)

For full details on each of these modes, check out the official OpenGL documentation. In this recipe, we'll use the GL_TRIANGLES_ADJACENCY mode to provide information about adjacent triangles in our mesh. With this mode, we provide six vertices per primitive. The following diagram illustrates the locations of these vertices:

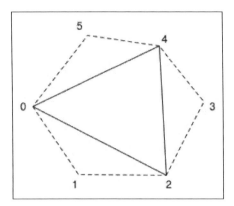

In the preceding diagram, the solid line represents the triangle itself, and the dotted lines represent adjacent triangles. The first, third, and fifth vertices (**0**, **2**, and **4**) make up the triangle itself. The second, fourth, and sixth are vertices that make up the adjacent triangles.

Mesh data is not usually provided in this form, so we need to preprocess our mesh to include the additional vertex information. Typically, this only means expanding the element index array by a factor of two. The position, normal, and texture coordinate arrays can remain unchanged.

When a mesh is rendered with adjacency information, the geometry shader has access to all six vertices associated with a particular triangle. We can then use the adjacent triangles to determine whether or not a triangle edge is part of the silhouette of the object. The basic assumption is that an edge is a silhouette edge if the triangle is front facing and the corresponding adjacent triangle is not front facing.

We can determine whether or not a triangle is front facing within the geometry shader by computing the triangle's normal vector (using a cross product). If we are working within eye coordinates (or clip coordinates), the z coordinate of the normal vector will be positive for front facing triangles. Therefore, we only need to compute the z coordinate of the normal vector, which should save a few cycles. For a triangle with vertices A, B, and C, the z coordinate of the normal vector is given by the following equation:

$$n_z = (A_x B_y - B_x A_y) + (B_x C_y - C_x B_y) + (C_x A_y - A_x C_y)$$

Once we determine which edges are silhouette edges, the geometry shader will produce additional skinny quads aligned with the silhouette edge. These quads, taken together, will make up the desired dark lines (refer to the preceding figure). After generating all the silhouette quads, the geometry shader will output the original triangle.

In order to render the mesh in a single pass with appropriate shading for the base mesh, and no shading for the silhouette lines, we'll use an additional output variable. This variable will let the fragment shader know when we are rendering the base mesh and when we are rendering the silhouette edge.

Getting ready

Set up your mesh data so that adjacency information is included. As just mentioned, this probably requires expanding the element index array to include the additional information. This can be done by passing through your mesh and looking for shared edges. Due to space limitations, we won't go through the details here, but the blog post mentioned some time back has some information about how this might be done. Also, the source code for this example contains a simple (albeit not very efficient) technique.

The important uniform variables for this example are as follows:

- `EdgeWidth`: This is the width of the silhouette edge in clip (normalized device) coordinates

- `PctExtend`: This is a percentage to extend the quads beyond the edge

- `LineColor`: This is the color of the silhouette edge lines

As usual, there are also the appropriate uniforms for the shading model, and the standard matrices.

How to do it...

To create a shader program that utilizes the geometry shader to render silhouette edges, use the following steps:

1. Use the following code for the vertex shader:

```
layout (location = 0 ) in vec3 VertexPosition;
layout (location = 1 ) in vec3 VertexNormal;

out vec3 VNormal;
out vec3 VPosition;

uniform mat4 ModelViewMatrix;
uniform mat3 NormalMatrix;
uniform mat4 ProjectionMatrix;
uniform mat4 MVP;
void main()
{
    VNormal = normalize( NormalMatrix * VertexNormal);
```

```
            VPosition = vec3(ModelViewMatrix *
                         vec4(VertexPosition,1.0));
            gl_Position = MVP * vec4(VertexPosition,1.0);
        }
```

2. Use the following code for the geometry shader:

```
layout( triangles_adjacency ) in;
layout( triangle_strip, max_vertices = 15 ) out;

out vec3 GNormal;
out vec3 GPosition;

// Which output primitives are silhouette edges
flat out bool GIsEdge;

in vec3 VNormal[];   // Normal in camera coords.
in vec3 VPosition[]; // Position in camera coords.

uniform float EdgeWidth;  // Width of sil. edge in clip cds.
uniform float PctExtend;  // Percentage to extend quad

bool isFrontFacing( vec3 a, vec3 b, vec3 c )
{
    return ((a.x * b.y - b.x * a.y) +
            (b.x * c.y - c.x * b.y) +
            (c.x * a.y - a.x * c.y)) > 0;
}
void emitEdgeQuad( vec3 e0, vec3 e1 )
{
    vec2 ext = PctExtend * (e1.xy - e0.xy);
    vec2 v = normalize(e1.xy - e0.xy);
    vec2 n = vec2(-v.y, v.x) * EdgeWidth;

    // Emit the quad
    GIsEdge = true;   // This is part of the sil. edge

    gl_Position = vec4( e0.xy - ext, e0.z, 1.0 );
    EmitVertex();
    gl_Position = vec4( e0.xy - n - ext, e0.z, 1.0 );
    EmitVertex();
    gl_Position = vec4( e1.xy + ext, e1.z, 1.0 );
    EmitVertex();
    gl_Position = vec4( e1.xy - n + ext, e1.z, 1.0 );
    EmitVertex();
```

```
        EndPrimitive();
    }

    void main()
    {
        vec3 p0 = gl_in[0].gl_Position.xyz /
                  gl_in[0].gl_Position.w;
        vec3 p1 = gl_in[1].gl_Position.xyz /
                  gl_in[1].gl_Position.w;
        vec3 p2 = gl_in[2].gl_Position.xyz /
                  gl_in[2].gl_Position.w;
        vec3 p3 = gl_in[3].gl_Position.xyz /
                  gl_in[3].gl_Position.w;
        vec3 p4 = gl_in[4].gl_Position.xyz /
                  gl_in[4].gl_Position.w;
        vec3 p5 = gl_in[5].gl_Position.xyz /
                  gl_in[5].gl_Position.w;

        if( isFrontFacing(p0, p2, p4) ) {
            if( ! isFrontFacing(p0,p1,p2) )
                    emitEdgeQuad(p0,p2);
            if( ! isFrontFacing(p2,p3,p4) )
                    emitEdgeQuad(p2,p4);
            if( ! isFrontFacing(p4,p5,p0) )
                    emitEdgeQuad(p4,p0);
        }

        // Output the original triangle
        GIsEdge = false; // Triangle is not part of an edge.

        GNormal = VNormal[0];
        GPosition = VPosition[0];
        gl_Position = gl_in[0].gl_Position;
        EmitVertex();
        GNormal = VNormal[2];
        GPosition = VPosition[2];
        gl_Position = gl_in[2].gl_Position;
        EmitVertex();

        GNormal = VNormal[4];
        GPosition = VPosition[4];
        gl_Position = gl_in[4].gl_Position;
        EmitVertex();

        EndPrimitive();
    }
```

3. Use the following code for the fragment shader:

```
//*** Light and material uniforms go here ****

uniform vec4 LineColor;   // The sil. edge color

in vec3 GPosition;   // Position in camera coords
in vec3 GNormal;      // Normal in camera coords.

flat in bool GIsEdge; // Whether or not we're drawing an edge

layout( location = 0 ) out vec4 FragColor;

vec3 toonShade( )
{
   // *** toon shading algorithm from Chapter 3 ***
}

void main()
{
    // If we're drawing an edge, use constant color,
    // otherwise, shade the poly.
    if( GIsEdge ) {
        FragColor = LineColor;
    } else {
        FragColor = vec4( toonShade(), 1.0 );
    }

}
```

How it works...

The vertex shader is a simple "pass-through" shader. It converts the vertex position and normal to camera coordinates and sends them along, via `VPosition` and `VNormal`. These will be used for shading within the fragment shader and will be passed along (or ignored) by the geometry shader. The position is also converted to clip coordinates (or normalized device coordinates) by transforming with the model-view projection matrix, and it is then assigned to the built-in `gl_Position`.

The geometry shader begins by defining the input and output primitive types using the layout directive.

```
layout( triangles_adjacency ) in;
layout( triangle_strip, max_vertices = 15 ) out;
```

This indicates that the input primitive type is triangles with adjacency information, and the output type is triangle strips. This geometry shader will produce a single triangle (the original triangle) and at most one quad for each edge. This corresponds to a maximum of 15 vertices that could be produced, and we indicate that maximum within the output layout directive.

The output variable `GIsEdge` is used to indicate to the fragment shader whether or not the polygon is an edge quad. The fragment shader will use this value to determine whether or not to shade the polygon. There is no need to interpolate the value and since it is a Boolean, interpolation doesn't quite make sense, so we use the `flat` qualifier.

The first few lines within the `main` function take the position for each of the six vertices (in clip coordinates) and divides it by the fourth coordinate in order to convert from its homogeneous representation to the true Cartesian value. This is necessary if we are using a perspective projection, but is not necessary for orthographic projections.

Next, we determine whether the main triangle (defined by points 0, 2, and 4) is front facing. The function `isFrontFacing`, returns whether or not the triangle defined by its three parameters is front facing using the equation described previously. If the main triangle is front facing, then we will emit a silhouette edge quad only if the adjacent triangle is not front facing.

The function `emitEdgeQuad` produces a quad that is aligned with an edge defined by the points `e0` and `e1`. It begins by computing `ext`, which is the vector from `e0` to `e1`, scaled by `PctExtend` (in order to slightly lengthen the edge quad). We lengthen the edge quad in order to cover gaps that may appear between quads (we'll discuss this further in *There's more…*).

Note also that we drop the z coordinate here. As the points are defined in clip coordinates, and we are going to produce a quad that is aligned with the x-y plane (facing the camera), we want to compute the positions of the vertices by translating within the x-y plane. Therefore we can ignore the z coordinate for now. We'll use its value unchanged in the final position of each vertex.

Next, the variable `v` is assigned to the normalized vector from `e0` to `e1`. The variable `n` gets a vector that is perpendicular to `v` (in 2D this can be achieved by swapping the x and y coordinates and negating the new x coordinate). This is just a counter-clockwise 90 degree rotation in 2D. We scale the vector `n` by `EdgeWidth` because we want the length of the vector to be the same as the width of the quad. The two vectors `ext` and `n` will be used to determine the vertices of the quad as shown in the following figure:

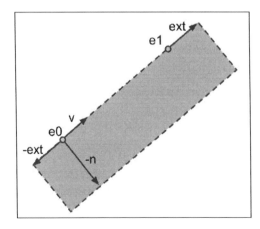

The four corners of the quad are given by: **e0 – ext**, **e0 – n – ext**, **e1 + ext**, and **e1 –n + ext**. The z coordinate for the lower two vertices is the same as the z coordinate for **e0**, and the z coordinate for the upper two vertices is the z coordinate for **e1**.

We then finish up the emitEdgeQuad function by setting GIsEdge to true in order to let the fragment shader know that we are rendering a silhouette edge, and then emitting the four vertices of the quad. The function ends with a call to EndPrimitive to terminate the processing of the triangle strip for the quad.

Back within the main function, after producing the silhouette edges, we proceed by emitting the original triangle unchanged. VNormal, VPosition, and gl_Position for vertices 0, 2, and 4 are passed along without any modification to the fragment shader. Each vertex is emitted with a call to EmitVertex, and the primitive is completed with EndPrimitive.

Within the fragment shader we either shade the fragment (using the toon shading algorithm), or simply give the fragment a constant color. The GIsEdge input variable will indicate which option to choose. If GIsEdge is true, then we are rendering a silhouette edge so the fragment is given the line color. Otherwise, we are rendering a mesh polygon, so we shade the fragment using the toon shading technique from *Chapter 3, Lighting, Shading Effects, and Optimizations*.

There's more...

One of the problems with the preceding technique is that "feathering" can occur due to the gaps between consecutive edge quads.

The preceding figure shows the feathering of a silhouette edge. The gaps between the polygons can be filled with triangles, but in our example, we simply extend the length of each quad to fill in the gap. This can, of course, cause artifacts if the quads are extended too far, but in practice they haven't been very distracting in my experience.

A second issue is related to depth testing. If an edge polygon extends into another area of the mesh, it can be clipped due to the depth test. The following is an example:

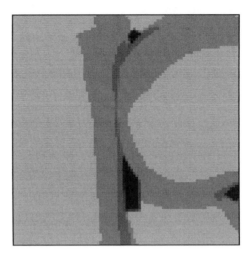

The edge polygon should extend vertically throughout the middle of the preceding figure, but is clipped because it falls behind the part of the mesh that is nearby. This issue can be solved by using custom depth testing when rendering the silhouette edges. Refer to the blog post mentioned earlier for details on this technique. It may also be possible to turn depth testing off when rendering the edges, being careful not to render any edges from the opposite side of the model.

See also

- A whitepaper on using the geometry shader for fur and fins: `http://developer.download.nvidia.com/whitepapers/2007/SDK10/FurShellsAndFins.pdf`

- The *Creating shadows using shadow volumes and the geometry shader* recipe in *Chapter 7, Shadows*

- The *Creating a cartoon shading effect* recipe in *Chapter 3, Lighting, Shading, and Optimization*

Tessellating a curve

In this recipe, we'll take a look at the basics of tessellation shaders by drawing a **cubic Bezier curve**. A Bezier curve is a parametric curve defined by four control points. The control points define the overall shape of the curve. The first and last of the four points define the start and end of the curve, and the middle points guide the shape of the curve, but do not necessarily lie directly on the curve itself. The curve is defined by interpolating the four control points using a set of **blending functions**. The blending functions define how much each control point contributes to the curve for a given position along the curve. For Bezier curves, the blending functions are known as the **Bernstein polynomials**.

$$B_i^n(t) = \binom{n}{i}(1-t)^{n-i}t^i$$

In the preceding equation, the first term is the binomial coefficient function (shown in the following equation), **n** is the degree of the polynomial, **i** is the polynomial number, and **t** is the parametric parameter.

$$\binom{n}{i} = \frac{n!}{i!(n-i)!}$$

The general parametric form for the Bezier curve is then given as a sum of the products of the Bernstein polynomials with the control points (**P**$_i$).

$$P(t) = \sum_{i=0}^{n} B_i^n(t)P_i$$

In this example, we will draw a cubic Bezier curve, which involves four control points (n = 3).

$$P(t) = B_0^3(t)P_0 + B_1^3(t)P_1 + B_2^3(t)P_2 + B_3^3(t)P_3$$

And the cubic Bernstein polynomials are:

$$B_0^3(t) = (1-t)^3$$
$$B_1^3(t) = 3(1-t)^2t$$
$$B_2^3(t) = 3(1-t)t^2$$
$$B_3^3(t) = t^3$$

As stated in the introduction of this chapter, the tessellation functionality within OpenGL involves two shader stages. They are the tessellation control shader (TCS) and the tessellation evaluation shader (TES). In this example, we'll define the number of line segments for our Bezier curve within the TCS (by defining the outer tessellation levels), and evaluate the Bezier curve at each particular vertex location within the TES. The following screenshot shows the output of this example for three different tessellation levels. The left figure uses three line segments (level 3), the middle uses level 5, and the right-hand figure is created with tessellation level 30. The small squares are the control points.

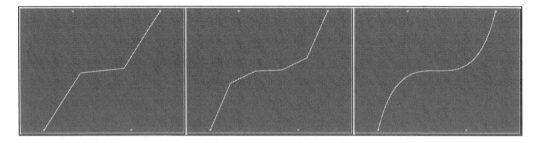

The control points for the Bezier curve are sent down the pipeline as a patch primitive consisting of four vertices. A patch primitive is a programmer-defined primitive type. Basically, it is a set of vertices that can be used for anything that the programmer chooses. The TCS is executed once for each vertex within the patch, and the TES is executed, a variable number of times, depending on the number of vertices produced by the TPG. The final output of the tessellation stages is a set of primitives. In our case, it will be a line strip.

Part of the job for the TCS is to define the tessellation level. In very rough terms, the tessellation level is related to the number of vertices that will be generated. In our case, the TCS will be generating a line strip, so the tessellation level is the number of line segments in the line strip. Each vertex that is generated for this line strip will be associated with a tessellation coordinate that will vary between zero and one. We'll refer to this as the u coordinate, and it will correspond to the parametric parameter t in the preceding Bezier curve equation.

What we've looked at so far is not, in fact, the whole story. Actually, the TCS will trigger a generation of a set of line strips called isolines. Each vertex in this set of isolines will have a u and a v coordinate. The u coordinate will vary from zero to one along a given isoline, and v will be constant for each isoline. The number of distinct values of u and v is associated with two separate tessellation levels, the so-called "outer" levels. For this example, however, we'll only generate a single line strip, so the second tessellation level (for v) will always be one.

Within the TES, the main task is to determine the position of the vertex associated with this execution of the shader. We have access to the u and v coordinates associated with the vertex, and we also have (read-only) access to all of the vertices of the patch. We can then determine the appropriate position for the vertex by using the parametric equation described above, with u as the parametric coordinate (t in the preceding equation).

Getting ready

The following are the important uniform variables for this example:

▶ `NumSegments`: This is the number of line segments to be produced.

▶ `NumStrips`: This is the number of isolines to be produced. For this example, this should be set to one.

▶ `LineColor`: This is the color for the resulting line strip.

Set the uniform variables within the main OpenGL application. There are a total of four shaders to be compiled and linked. They are the vertex, fragment, tessellation control, and tessellation evaluation shaders.

How to do it...

To create a shader program that will generate a Bezier curve from a patch of four control points, use the following steps:

1. Use the following code for the simple vertex shader:

```
layout (location = 0 ) in vec2 VertexPosition;

void main()
{
    gl_Position = vec4(VertexPosition, 0.0, 1.0);
}
```

2. Use the following code as the tessellation control shader:

```
layout ( vertices=4 ) out;

uniform int NumSegments;
uniform int NumStrips;

void main()
{
    // Pass along the vertex position unmodified
    gl_out[gl_InvocationID].gl_Position =
            gl_in[gl_InvocationID].gl_Position;
    // Define the tessellation levels
    gl_TessLevelOuter[0] = float(NumStrips);
```

```
        gl_TessLevelOuter[1] = float(NumSegments);
    }
```

3. Use the following code as the tessellation evaluation shader:

```
layout( isolines ) in;
uniform mat4 MVP;   // projection * view * model

void main()
{
    // The tessellation u coordinate
    float u = gl_TessCoord.x;

    // The patch vertices (control points)
    vec3 p0 = gl_in[0].gl_Position.xyz;
    vec3 p1 = gl_in[1].gl_Position.xyz;
    vec3 p2 = gl_in[2].gl_Position.xyz;
    vec3 p3 = gl_in[3].gl_Position.xyz;

    float u1 = (1.0 - u);
    float u2 = u * u;

    // Bernstein polynomials evaluated at u
    float b3 = u2 * u;
    float b2 = 3.0 * u2 * u1;
    float b1 = 3.0 * u * u1 * u1;
    float b0 = u1 * u1 * u1;

    // Cubic Bezier interpolation
    vec3 p = p0 * b0 + p1 * b1 + p2 * b2 + p3 * b3;

    gl_Position = MVP * vec4(p, 1.0);

}
```

4. Use the following code for the fragment shader:

```
uniform vec4 LineColor;

layout ( location = 0 ) out vec4 FragColor;

void main()
{
    FragColor = LineColor;
}
```

5. It is important to define the number of vertices per patch within the OpenGL application. You can do so using the `glPatchParameter` function:

```
glPatchParameteri( GL_PATCH_VERTICES, 4 );
```

6. Render the four control points as a patch primitive within the OpenGL application's render function:

```
glDrawArrays(GL_PATCHES, 0, 4);
```

How it works...

The vertex shader is just a "pass-through" shader. It sends the vertex position along to the next stage without any modification.

The tessellation control shader begins by defining the number of vertices in the output patch:

```
layout (vertices = 4) out;
```

Note that this is not the same as the number of vertices that will be produced by the tessellation process. In this case, the patch is our four control points, so we use a value of four.

The main method within the TCS passes the input position (of the patch vertex) to the output position without modification. The arrays `gl_out` and `gl_in` contain the input and output information associated with each vertex in the patch. Note that we assign and read from location `gl_InvocationID` in these arrays. The `gl_InvocationID` variable defines the output patch vertex for which this invocation of the TCS is responsible. The TCS can access all of the array `gl_in`, but should only write to the location in `gl_out` corresponding to `gl_InvocationID`.

Next, the TCS sets the tessellation levels by assigning to the `gl_TessLevelOuter` array. Note that the values for `gl_TessLevelOuter` are floating point numbers rather than integers. They will be rounded up to the nearest integer and clamped automatically by the OpenGL system.

The first element in the array defines the number of isolines that will be generated. Each isoline will have a constant value for v. In this example, the value of `gl_TessLevelOuter[0]` should be one. The second defines the number of line segments that will be produced in the line strip. Each vertex in the strip will have a value for the parametric u coordinate that will vary from zero to one.

In the TES, we start by defining the input primitive type using a layout declaration:

```
layout (isolines) in;
```

This indicates the type of subdivision that is performed by the tessellation primitive generator. Other possibilities here include `quads` and `triangles`.

Within the `main` function of the TES, the variable `gl_TessCoord` contains the tessellation u and v coordinates for this invocation. As we are only tessellating in one dimension, we only need the u coordinate, which corresponds to the x coordinate of `gl_TessCoord`.

The next step accesses the positions of the four control points (all the points in our patch primitive). These are available in the `gl_in` array.

The cubic Bernstein polynomials are then evaluated at u and stored in b0, b1, b2, and b3. Next, we compute the interpolated position using the Bezier curve equation described some time back. The final position is converted to clip coordinates and assigned to the output variable `gl_Position`.

The fragment shader simply applies `LineColor` to the fragment.

There's more...

There's a lot more to be said about tessellation shaders, but this example is intended to be a simple introduction so we'll leave that for the following recipes. Next, we'll look at tessellation across surfaces in two dimensions.

Tessellating a 2D quad

One of the best ways to understand OpenGL's hardware tessellation is to visualize the tessellation of a 2D quad. When linear interpolation is used, the triangles that are produced are directly related to the tessellation coordinates (u,v) that are produced by the tessellation primitive generator. It can be extremely helpful to draw a few quads with different inner and outer tessellation levels, and study the triangles produced. We will do exactly that in this recipe.

When using quad tessellation, the tessellation primitive generator subdivides (u,v) parameter space into a number of subdivisions based on six parameters. These are the inner tessellation levels for u and v (inner level 0 and inner level 1), and the outer tessellation levels for u and v along both edges (outer levels 0 to 3). These determine the number of subdivisions along the edges of parameter space and internally. Let's look at each of these individually:

- **Outer level 0 (OL0)**: This is the number of subdivisions along the v direction where u = 0
- **Outer level 1 (OL1)**: This is the number of subdivisions along the u direction where v = 0
- **Outer level 2 (OL2)**: This is the number of subdivisions along the v direction where u = 1
- **Outer level 3 (OL3)**: This is the number of subdivisions along the u direction where v = 1
- **Inner level 0 (IL0)**: This is the number of subdivisions along the u direction for all internal values of v
- **Inner level 1 (IL1)**: This is the number of subdivisions along the v direction for all internal values of u

The following diagram represents the relationship between the tessellation levels and the areas of parameter space that are affected by each. The outer levels defines the number of subdivisions along the edges, and the inner levels define the number of subdivisions internally.

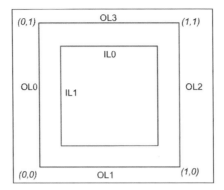

The six tessellation levels described some time back can be configured via the arrays `gl_TessLevelOuter` and `gl_TessLevelInner`. For example, `gl_TessLevelInner[0]` corresponds to **IL0**, `gl_TessLevelOuter[2]` corresponds to **OL2**, and so on.

If we draw a patch primitive that consists of a single quad (four vertices), and use linear interpolation, the triangles that result can help us to understand how OpenGL does quad tessellation. The following diagram shows the results for various tessellation levels:

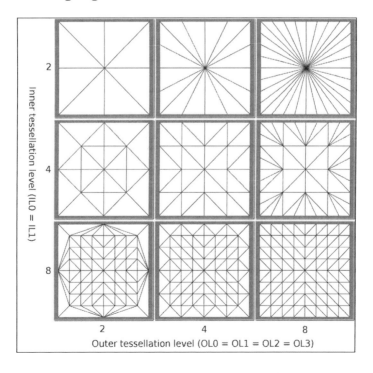

When we use linear interpolation, the triangles that are produced represent a visual representation of parameter (u, v) space. The x axis corresponds to the u coordinate and the y axis corresponds to the v coordinate. The vertices of the triangles are the (u,v) coordinates generated by the tessellation primitive generator. The number of subdivisions can be clearly seen in the mesh of triangles. For example, when the outer levels are set to 2 and the inner levels are set to 8, you can see that the outer edges have two subdivisions, but within the quad, u and v are subdivided into 8 intervals.

Before jumping into the code, let's discuss linear interpolation. If the four corners of the quad are as shown in the following figure, then any point within the quad can be determined by linearly interpolating the four corners with respect to parameters u and v.

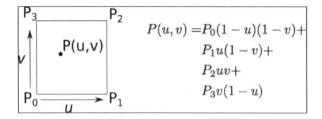

We'll let the tessellation primitive generator create a set of vertices with appropriate parametric coordinates, and we'll determine the corresponding positions by interpolating the corners of the quad using the preceding equation.

Getting ready

The outer and inner tessellation levels will be determined by the uniform variables `Inner` and `Outer`. In order to display the triangles, we will use the geometry shader described earlier in this chapter.

Set up your OpenGL application to render a patch primitive consisting of four vertices in counter clockwise order as shown in the preceding figure.

How to do it...

To create a shader program that will generate a set of triangles using quad tessellation from a patch of four vertices, use the following steps:

1. Use the following code for the vertex shader:

```
layout (location = 0 ) in vec2 VertexPosition;

void main()
{
    gl_Position = vec4(VertexPosition, 0.0, 1.0);
}
```

2. Use the following code as the tessellation control shader:

```
layout( vertices=4 ) out;

uniform int Outer;
uniform int Inner;
void main()
{
    // Pass along the vertex position unmodified
    gl_out[gl_InvocationID].gl_Position =
                gl_in[gl_InvocationID].gl_Position;

    gl_TessLevelOuter[0] = float(Outer);
    gl_TessLevelOuter[1] = float(Outer);
    gl_TessLevelOuter[2] = float(Outer);
    gl_TessLevelOuter[3] = float(Outer);

    gl_TessLevelInner[0] = float(Inner);
    gl_TessLevelInner[1] = float(Inner);
}
```

3. Use the following code as the tessellation evaluation shader:

```
layout( quads, equal_spacing, ccw ) in;

uniform mat4 MVP;

void main()
{
    float u = gl_TessCoord.x;
    float v = gl_TessCoord.y;

    vec4 p0 = gl_in[0].gl_Position;
    vec4 p1 = gl_in[1].gl_Position;
    vec4 p2 = gl_in[2].gl_Position;
    vec4 p3 = gl_in[3].gl_Position;

    // Linear interpolation
    gl_Position =
        p0 * (1-u) * (1-v) +
        p1 * u * (1-v) +
        p3 * v * (1-u) +
        p2 * u * v;

    // Transform to clip coordinates
    gl_Position = MVP * gl_Position;
}
```

4. Use the geometry shader from the recipe, *Drawing a wireframe on top of a shaded mesh*.

5. Use the following code as the fragment shader:

```
uniform float LineWidth;
uniform vec4 LineColor;
uniform vec4 QuadColor;

noperspective in vec3 EdgeDistance;   // From geom. shader

layout ( location = 0 ) out vec4 FragColor;

float edgeMix()
{
    // ** insert code here to determine how much of the edge
    // color to include (see recipe "Drawing a wireframe on
    // top of a shaded mesh").   **
}

void main()
{
    float mixVal = edgeMix();

    FragColor = mix( QuadColor, LineColor, mixVal );

}
```

6. Within the render function of your main OpenGL program, define the number of vertices within a patch:

```
glPatchParameteri(GL_PATCH_VERTICES, 4);
```

7. Render the patch as four 2D vertices in counter clockwise order.

How it works...

The vertex shader passes the position along to the TCS unchanged.

The TCS defines the number of vertices in the patch using the layout directive:

```
layout (vertices=4) out;
```

In the `main` function, it passes along the position of the vertex without modification, and sets the inner and outer tessellation levels. All four of the outer tessellation levels are set to the value of `Outer`, and both of the inner tessellation levels are set to `Inner`.

In the tessellation evaluation shader, we define the tessellation mode and other tessellation parameters with the input layout directive:

```
layout ( quads, equal_spacing, ccw ) in;
```

The parameter `quads` indicates that the tessellation primitive generator should tessellate the parameter space using quad tessellation as described some time back. The parameter `equal_spacing` says that the tessellation should be performed such that all subdivisions have equal length. The last parameter, `ccw`, indicates that the primitives should be generated with counter clockwise winding.

The `main` function in the TES starts by retrieving the parametric coordinates for this vertex by accessing the variable `gl_TessCoord`. Then we move on to read the positions of the four vertices in the patch from the `gl_in` array. We store them in temporary variables to be used in the interpolation calculation.

The built-in output variable `gl_Position` then gets the value of the interpolated point using the preceding equation. Finally, we convert the position into clip coordinates by multiplying by the model-view projection matrix.

Within the fragment shader, we give all fragments a color that is possibly mixed with a line color in order to highlight the edges.

See also

▸ The *Drawing a wireframe on top of a shaded mesh* recipe

Tessellating a 3D surface

As an example of tessellating a 3D surface, let's render (yet again) the "teapotahedron". It turns out that the teapot's data set is actually defined as a set of 4 x 4 patches of control points, suitable for cubic Bezier interpolation. Therefore, drawing the teapot really boils down to drawing a set of cubic Bezier surfaces.

Of course, this sounds like a perfect job for tessellation shaders! We'll render each patch of 16 vertices as a patch primitive, use quad tessellation to subdivide the parameter space, and implement the Bezier interpolation within the tessellation evaluation shader.

The following figure shows an example of the desired output. The left teapot is rendered with inner and outer tessellation level 2, the middle uses level 4 and the right-hand teapot uses tessellation level 16. The tessellation evaluation shader computes the Bezier surface interpolation.

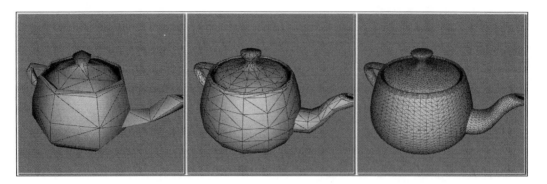

First, let's take a look at how cubic Bezier surface interpolation works. If our surface is defined by a set of 16 control points (laid out in a 4 x 4 grid) P_{ij}, with i and j ranging from 0 to 3, then the parametric Bezier surface is given by the following equation:

$$P(u, v) = \sum_{i=0}^{3} \sum_{j=0}^{3} B_i^3(u) B_j^3(v) P_{ij}$$

The instances of **B** in the preceding equation are the cubic Bernstein polynomials (refer to the previous recipe, *Tessellating a 2D quad*).

We also need to compute the normal vector at each interpolated location. To do so, we have to compute the cross product of the partial derivatives of the preceding equation:

$$\mathbf{n}(u, v) = \frac{\partial P}{\partial u} \times \frac{\partial P}{\partial v}$$

The partial derivatives of the Bezier surface boil down to the partial derivatives of the Bernstein polynomials:

$$\frac{\partial P}{\partial u} = \sum_{i=0}^{3} \sum_{j=0}^{3} \frac{\partial B_i^3(u)}{\partial u} B_j^3(v) P_{ij}$$

$$\frac{\partial P}{\partial v} = \sum_{i=0}^{3} \sum_{j=0}^{3} B_i^3(u) \frac{\partial B_j^3(v)}{\partial v} P_{ij}$$

We'll compute the partials within the TES and compute the cross product to determine the normal to the surface at each tessellated vertex.

Getting ready

Set up your shaders with a vertex shader that simply passes the vertex position along without any modification (you can use the same vertex shader as was used in the *Tessellating a 2D quad* recipe). Create a fragment shader that implements whatever shading model you choose. The fragment shader should receive the input variables TENormal and TEPosition, which will be the normal and position in camera coordinates.

The uniform variable TessLevel should be given the value of the tessellation level desired. All of the inner and outer levels will be set to this value.

How to do it...

To create a shader program that creates Bezier patches from input patches of 16 control points, use the following steps:

1. Use the vertex shader from the *Tessellating a 2D quad* recipe.

2. Use the following code for the tessellation control shader:

```
layout( vertices=16 ) out;

uniform int TessLevel;

void main()
{
    // Pass along the vertex position unmodified
    gl_out[gl_InvocationID].gl_Position =
                gl_in[gl_InvocationID].gl_Position;

    gl_TessLevelOuter[0] = float(TessLevel);
    gl_TessLevelOuter[1] = float(TessLevel);
    gl_TessLevelOuter[2] = float(TessLevel);
    gl_TessLevelOuter[3] = float(TessLevel);

    gl_TessLevelInner[0] = float(TessLevel);
    gl_TessLevelInner[1] = float(TessLevel);
}
```

3. Use the following code for the tessellation evaluation shader:

```
layout( quads ) in;
out vec3 TENormal;   // Vertex normal in camera coords.
out vec4 TEPosition; // Vertex position in camera coords
```

```
uniform mat4 MVP;
uniform mat4 ModelViewMatrix;
uniform mat3 NormalMatrix;

void basisFunctions(out float[4] b, out float[4] db, float t)
{
    float t1 = (1.0 - t);
    float t12 = t1 * t1;

    // Bernstein polynomials
    b[0] = t12 * t1;
    b[1] = 3.0 * t12 * t;
    b[2] = 3.0 * t1 * t * t;
    b[3] = t * t * t;

    // Derivatives
    db[0] = -3.0 * t1 * t1;
    db[1] = -6.0 * t * t1 + 3.0 * t12;
    db[2] = -3.0 * t * t + 6.0 * t * t1;
    db[3] = 3.0 * t * t;
}

void main()
{
    float u = gl_TessCoord.x;
    float v = gl_TessCoord.y;

    // The sixteen control points
    vec4 p00 = gl_in[0].gl_Position;
    vec4 p01 = gl_in[1].gl_Position;
    vec4 p02 = gl_in[2].gl_Position;
    vec4 p03 = gl_in[3].gl_Position;
    vec4 p10 = gl_in[4].gl_Position;
    vec4 p11 = gl_in[5].gl_Position;
    vec4 p12 = gl_in[6].gl_Position;
    vec4 p13 = gl_in[7].gl_Position;
    vec4 p20 = gl_in[8].gl_Position;
    vec4 p21 = gl_in[9].gl_Position;
    vec4 p22 = gl_in[10].gl_Position;
    vec4 p23 = gl_in[11].gl_Position;
    vec4 p30 = gl_in[12].gl_Position;
    vec4 p31 = gl_in[13].gl_Position;
    vec4 p32 = gl_in[14].gl_Position;
    vec4 p33 = gl_in[15].gl_Position;
    // Compute basis functions
    float bu[4], bv[4];   // Basis functions for u and v
    float dbu[4], dbv[4]; // Derivitives for u and v
```

```
basisFunctions(bu, dbu, u);
basisFunctions(bv, dbv, v);

// Bezier interpolation
TEPosition =
 p00*bu[0]*bv[0] + p01*bu[0]*bv[1] + p02*bu[0]*bv[2] +
 p03*bu[0]*bv[3] +
 p10*bu[1]*bv[0] + p11*bu[1]*bv[1] + p12*bu[1]*bv[2] +
 p13*bu[1]*bv[3] +
 p20*bu[2]*bv[0] + p21*bu[2]*bv[1] + p22*bu[2]*bv[2] +
 p23*bu[2]*bv[3] +
 p30*bu[3]*bv[0] + p31*bu[3]*bv[1] + p32*bu[3]*bv[2] +
 p33*bu[3]*bv[3];

// The partial derivatives
vec4 du =
 p00*dbu[0]*bv[0] +p01*dbu[0]*bv[1] +p02*dbu[0]*bv[2] +
 p03*dbu[0]*bv[3] +
 p10*dbu[1]*bv[0] +p11*dbu[1]*bv[1] +p12*dbu[1]*bv[2] +
 p13*dbu[1]*bv[3] +
 p20*dbu[2]*bv[0] +p21*dbu[2]*bv[1] +p22*dbu[2]*bv[2] +
 p23*dbu[2]*bv[3] +
 p30*dbu[3]*bv[0] +p31*dbu[3]*bv[1] +p32*dbu[3]*bv[2] +
 p33*dbu[3]*bv[3];

vec4 dv =
 p00*bu[0]*dbv[0] +p01*bu[0]*dbv[1] +p02*bu[0]*dbv[2] +
 p03*bu[0]*dbv[3] +
 p10*bu[1]*dbv[0] +p11*bu[1]*dbv[1] +p12*bu[1]*dbv[2] +
 p13*bu[1]*dbv[3] +
 p20*bu[2]*dbv[0] +p21*bu[2]*dbv[1] +p22*bu[2]*dbv[2] +
 p23*bu[2]*dbv[3] +
 p30*bu[3]*dbv[0] +p31*bu[3]*dbv[1] +p32*bu[3]*dbv[2] +
 p33*bu[3]*dbv[3];

// The normal is the cross product of the partials
vec3 n = normalize( cross(du.xyz, dv.xyz) );

// Transform to clip coordinates
gl_Position = MVP * TEPosition;

// Convert to camera coordinates
TEPosition = ModelViewMatrix * TEPosition;
TENormal = normalize(NormalMatrix * n);
}
```

4. Implement your favorite shading model within the fragment shader utilizing the output variables from the TES.

5. Render the Bezier control points as a 16-vertex patch primitive. Don't forget to set the number of vertices per patch within the OpenGL application:

```
glPatchParameteri(GL_PATCH_VERTICES, 16);
```

How it works...

The tessellation control shader starts by defining the number of vertices in the patch using the layout directive:

```
layout( vertices=16 ) out;
```

It then simply sets the tessellation levels to the value of `TessLevel`. It passes the vertex position along, without any modification.

The tessellation evaluation shader starts by using a layout directive to indicate the type of tessellation to be used. As we are tessellating a 4 x 4 Bezier surface patch, quad tessellation makes the most sense.

The `basisFunctions` function evaluates the Bernstein polynomials and their derivatives for a given value of the parameter `t`. The results are returned in the output parameters `b` and `db`.

Within the `main` function, we start by assigning the tessellation coordinates to variables `u` and `v`, and reassigning all 16 of the patch vertices to variables with shorter names (to shorten the code that appears later).

We then call `basisFunctions` to compute the Bernstein polynomials and their derivatives at `u` and at `v`, storing the results in `bu`, `dbu`, `bv`, and `dbv`.

The next step is the evaluation of the sums from the preceding equations for the position (`TEPosition`), the partial derivative with respect to `u` (`du`), and the partial derivative with respect to `v` (`dv`).

We compute the normal vector as the cross product of `du` and `dv`.

Finally, we convert the position (`TEPosition`) to clip coordinates and assign the result to `gl_Position`. We also convert it to camera coordinates before it is passed along to the fragment shader.

The normal vector is converted to camera coordinates by multiplying with the `NormalMatrix`, and the result is normalized and passed along to the fragment shader via `TENormal`.

See also

▶ The *Tessellating a 2D quad* recipe

Tessellating based on depth

One of the greatest things about tessellation shaders is how easy it is to implement **level-of-detail** (**LOD**) algorithms. LOD is a general term in computer graphics that refers to the process of increasing/decreasing the complexity of an object's geometry with respect to the distance from the viewer (or other factors). As an object moves farther away from the camera, less geometric detail is needed to represent the shape because the overall size of the object becomes smaller. However, as the object moves closer to the camera, the object fills more and more of the screen, and more geometric detail is needed to maintain the desired appearance (smoothness or lack of other geometric artifacts).

The following figure shows a few teapots rendered with tessellation levels that depend on distance from the camera. Each teapot is rendered using exactly the same code on the OpenGL side. The TCS automatically varies the tessellation levels based on depth.

When tessellation shaders are used, the tessellation level is what determines the geometric complexity of the object. As the tessellation levels can be set within the tessellation control shader, it is a simple matter to vary the tessellation levels with respect to the distance from the camera.

In this example, we'll vary the tessellation levels linearly (with respect to distance) between a minimum level and a maximum level. We'll compute the "distance from the camera" as the absolute value of the z coordinate in camera coordinates, (of course, this is not the true distance, but should work fine for the purposes of this example). The tessellation level will then be computed based on that value. We'll also define two additional values (as uniform variables) MinDepth and MaxDepth. Objects that are closer to the camera than MinDepth get the maximum tessellation level, and any objects that are further from the camera than MaxDepth will get the minimum tessellation level. The tessellation level for objects in between will be linearly interpolated.

Getting ready

This program is nearly identical to the one in the *Tessellating a 3D surface* recipe. The only difference lies within the TCS. We'll remove the uniform variable `TessLevel`, and add a few new ones that are described as follows:

- ▶ `MinTessLevel`: This is the lowest desired tessellation level
- ▶ `MaxTessLevel`: This is the highest desired tessellation level
- ▶ `MinDepth`: This is the minimum "distance" from the camera, where the tessellation level is maximal
- ▶ `MaxDepth`: This is the maximum "distance" from the camera, where the tessellation level is at a minimum

Render your objects as 16-vertex patch primitives as indicated in the recipe, *Tessellating a 3D surface*.

How to do it...

To create a shader program that varies the tessellation level based on the depth, use the following steps:

1. Use the vertex shader and tessellation evaluation shader from the recipe, *Tessellating a 3D surface*.

2. Use the following code for the tessellation control shader:

```
layout( vertices=16 ) out;

uniform int MinTessLevel;
uniform int MaxTessLevel;
uniform float MaxDepth;
uniform float MinDepth;

uniform mat4 ModelViewMatrix;

void main()
{
    // Position in camera coordinates
    vec4 p = ModelViewMatrix *
                    gl_in[gl_InvocationID].gl_Position;

    // "Distance" from camera scaled between 0 and 1
    float depth = clamp( (abs(p.z) - MinDepth) /
                    (MaxDepth - MinDepth), 0.0, 1.0 );

    // Interpolate between min/max tess levels
```

```
float tessLevel =
        mix(MaxTessLevel, MinTessLevel, depth);

gl_TessLevelOuter[0] = float(tessLevel);
gl_TessLevelOuter[1] = float(tessLevel);
gl_TessLevelOuter[2] = float(tessLevel);
gl_TessLevelOuter[3] = float(tessLevel);

gl_TessLevelInner[0] = float(tessLevel);
gl_TessLevelInner[1] = float(tessLevel);

gl_out[gl_InvocationID].gl_Position =
                gl_in[gl_InvocationID].gl_Position;
}
```

3. As with the previous recipe, implement your favorite shading model within the fragment shader.

How it works...

The TCS takes the position and converts it to camera coordinates and stores the result in the variable p. The absolute value of the z coordinate is then scaled and clamped so that the result is between zero and one. If the z coordinate is equal to MaxDepth, the value of depth will be 1.0, if it is equal to MinDepth, then depth will be 0.0. If z is between MinDepth and MaxDepth, then depth will get a value between zero and one. If z is outside that range, it will be clamped to 0.0 or 1.0 by the clamp function.

The value of depth is then used to linearly interpolate between MaxTessLevel and MinTessLevel using the mix function. The result (tessLevel) is used to set the inner and outer tessellation levels.

There's more...

There is a somewhat subtle aspect to this example. Recall that the TCS is executed once for each output vertex in the patch. Therefore, assuming that we are rendering cubic Bezier surfaces, this TCS will be executed 16 times for each patch. Each time it is executed, the value of depth will be slightly different because it is evaluated based on the z coordinate of the vertex. You might be wondering, which of the 16 possible different tessellation levels will be the one that is used? It doesn't make sense for the tessellation level to be interpolated across the parameter space. What's going on?

The output arrays gl_TessLevelInner and gl_TessLevelOuter are per-patch output variables. This means that only a single value will be used per-patch, similar to the way that the flat qualifier works for fragment shader input variables. The OpenGL specification seems to indicate that any of the values from each of the invocations of the TCS could be the value that ends up being used.

See also

- ▶ DirectX 11 Terrain Tessellation at: `http://developer.download.nvidia.com/assets/gamedev/files/sdk/11/TerrainTessellation_WhitePaper.pdf`
- ▶ The *Tessellating a 3D surface* recipe

7
Shadows

In this chapter, we will cover:

- ▶ Rendering shadows with shadow maps
- ▶ Anti-aliasing shadow edges with PCF
- ▶ Creating soft shadow edges with random sampling
- ▶ Creating shadows using shadow volumes and the geometry shader

Introduction

Shadows add a great deal of realism to a scene. Without shadows, it can be easy to misjudge the relative location of objects, and the lighting can appear unrealistic, as light rays seem to pass right through objects.

Shadows are important visual cues for realistic scenes, but can be challenging to produce in an efficient manner in interactive applications. One of the most popular techniques for creating shadows in real-time graphics is the **shadow mapping** algorithm (also called depth shadows). In this chapter, we'll look at several recipes surrounding the shadow mapping algorithm. We'll start with the basic algorithm, and discuss it in detail in the first recipe. Then we'll look at a couple of techniques for improving the look of the shadows produced by the basic algorithm.

We'll also look at an alternative technique for shadows called shadow volumes. Shadow volumes produce near perfect hard-edged shadows, but are not well suited for creating shadows with soft edges.

Rendering shadows with shadow maps

One of the most common and popular techniques for producing shadows is called shadow mapping. In its basic form, the algorithm involves two passes. In the first pass, the scene is rendered from the point of view of the light source. The depth information from this pass is saved into a texture called the shadow map. This map will help provide information about the visibility of objects from the light's perspective. In other words, the shadow map stores the distance (actually the pseudo-depth) from the light to whatever the light can "see". Anything that is closer to the light than the corresponding depth stored in the map is lit; anything else must be in shadow.

In the second pass, the scene is rendered normally, but each fragment's depth (from the light's perspective) is first tested against the shadow map to determine whether or not the fragment is in shadow. The fragment is then shaded differently depending on the result of this test. If the fragment is in shadow, it is shaded with ambient lighting only; otherwise, it is shaded normally.

The following figure shows an example of shadows produced by the basic shadow mapping technique:

Let's look at each step of the algorithm in detail.

The first step is the creation of the shadow map. We set up our view matrix so that we are rendering the scene as if the camera is located at the position of the light source, and is oriented towards the shadow-casting objects. We set up a projection matrix such that the view frustum encloses all objects that may cast shadows as well as the area where the shadows will appear. We then render the scene normally and store the information from the depth buffer in a texture. This texture is called the shadow map (or simply depth map). We can think of it (roughly) as a set of distances from the light source to various surface locations.

Technically, these are depth values, not distances. A depth value is not a true distance (from the origin), but can be roughly treated as such for the purposes of depth testing.

The following figures represent an example of the basic shadow mapping setup. The left figure shows the light's position and its associated perspective frustum. The right-hand figure shows the corresponding shadow map. The grey scale intensities in the shadow map correspond to the depth values (darker is closer).

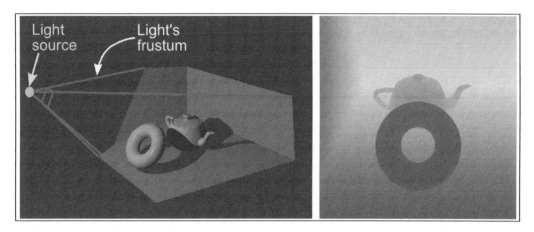

Once we have created the shadow map and stored the map to a texture, we render the scene again from the point of view of the camera. This time, we use a fragment shader that shades each fragment based on the result of a depth test with the shadow map. The position of the fragment is first converted into the coordinate system of the light source and projected using the light source's projection matrix. The result is then biased (in order to get valid texture coordinates) and tested against the shadow map. If the depth of the fragment is greater than the depth stored in the shadow map, then there must be some surface that is between the fragment and the light source. Therefore, the fragment is in shadow and is shaded using ambient lighting only. Otherwise, the fragment must have a clear view to the light source, and so it is shaded normally.

The key aspect here is the conversion of the fragment's 3D coordinates to the coordinates appropriate for a lookup into the shadow map. As the shadow map is just a 2D texture, we need coordinates that range from zero to one for points that lie within the light's frustum. The light's view matrix will transform points in world coordinates to points within the light's coordinate system. The light's projection matrix will transform points that are within the light's frustum to **homogeneous clip coordinates**.

These are called clip coordinates because the built-in clipping functionality takes place when the position is defined in these coordinates. Points within the perspective (or orthographic) frustum are transformed by the projection matrix to the (homogeneous) space that is contained within a cube centered at the origin, with each side of length two. This space is called the **canonical viewing volume**. The term "homogeneous" means that these coordinates should not necessarily be considered to be true Cartesian positions until they are divided by their fourth coordinate. For full details about homogeneous coordinates, refer to your favorite textbook on computer graphics.

The x and y components of the position in clip coordinates are roughly what we need to access the shadow map. The z coordinate contains the depth information that we can use to compare with the shadow map. However, before we can use these values we need to do two things. First, we need to bias them so that they range from zero to one (instead of -1 to 1), and second, we need to apply **perspective division** (more on this later).

To convert the value from clip coordinates to a range appropriate for use with a shadow map, we need the x, y, and z coordinates to range from zero to one (for points within the light's view frustum). The depth that is stored in an OpenGL depth buffer (and also our shadow map) is simply a fixed or floating-point value between zero and one (typically). A value of zero corresponds to the near plane of the perspective frustum, and a value of one corresponds to points on the far plane. Therefore, if we are to use our z coordinate to accurately compare with this depth buffer, we need to scale and translate it appropriately.

In clip coordinates (after perspective division) the z coordinate ranges from -1 to 1. It is the viewport transformation that (among other things) converts the depth to a range between zero and one. Incidentally, if so desired, we can configure the viewport transformation to use some other range for the depth values (say between 0 and 100) via the `glDepthRange` function.

Of course, the x and y components also need to be biased between zero and one because that is the appropriate range for texture access.

We can use the following "bias" matrix to alter our clip coordinates.

$$\mathbf{B} = \begin{bmatrix} 0.5 & 0 & 0 & 0.5 \\ 0 & 0.5 & 0 & 0.5 \\ 0 & 0 & 0.5 & 0.5 \\ 0 & 0 & 0 & 1 \end{bmatrix}$$

This matrix will scale and translate our coordinates such that the x, y, and z components range from 0 to 1 (after perspective division) for points within the light's frustum. Now, combining the bias matrix with the light's view (V_l) and projection (P_l) matrices, we have the following equation for converting positions in world coordinates (**W**) to homogeneous positions that can be used for shadow map access (**Q**).

$$Q = BP_l V_l W$$

Finally, before we can use the value of **Q** directly, we need to divide by the fourth (**w**) component. This step is sometimes called "perspective division". This converts the position from a homogeneous value to a true Cartesian position, and is always required when using a perspective projection matrix.

In the following equation, we'll define a shadow matrix (**S**) that also includes the model matrix (**M**), so that we can convert directly from the modeling coordinates (C). (Note that **W = MC**, because the model matrix takes modeling coordinates to world coordinates.)

$$Q = SC$$

Here, **S** is the shadow matrix, the product of the model matrix with all of the preceding matrices.

$$S = BP_l V_l M$$

In this recipe, in order to keep things simple and clear, we'll cover only the basic shadow mapping algorithm, without any of the usual improvements. We'll build upon this basic algorithm in the following recipes. Before we get into the code, we should note that the results will likely be less than satisfying. This is because the basic shadow mapping algorithm suffers from significant aliasing artifacts. Nevertheless, it is still an effective technique when combined with one of many techniques for anti-aliasing. We'll look at some of those techniques in the recipes that follow.

Getting ready

The position should be supplied in vertex attribute zero and the normal in vertex attribute one. Uniform variables for the ADS shading model should be declared and assigned, as well as uniforms for the standard transformation matrices. The `ShadowMatrix` variable should be set to the matrix for converting from modeling coordinates to shadow map coordinates (**S** in the preceding equation).

The uniform variable `ShadowMap` is a handle to the shadow map texture, and should be assigned to texture unit zero.

How to do it...

To create an OpenGL application that creates shadows using the shadow mapping technique, use the following steps. We'll start by setting up a **Framebuffer Object** (**FBO**) to contain the shadow map texture, and then move on to the required shader code:

1. In the main OpenGL program, set up a FBO with a depth buffer only. Declare a `GLuint` variable named `shadowFBO` to store the handle to this `framebuffer`. The depth buffer storage should be a texture object. You can use something similar to the following code to accomplish this:

```
GLfloat border[]={1.0f,0.0f,0.0f,0.0f};

//The shadowmap texture
GLuint depthTex;
glGenTextures(1,&depthTex);
glBindTexture(GL_TEXTURE_2D,depthTex);
glTexStorage2D(GL_TEXTURE_2D, 1, GL_DEPTH_COMPONENT24,
               shadowMapWidth, shadowMapHeight);
glTexParameteri(GL_TEXTURE_2D,GL_TEXTURE_MAG_FILTER,
               GL_NEAREST);
glTexParameteri(GL_TEXTURE_2D,GL_TEXTURE_MIN_FILTER,
               GL_NEAREST);
glTexParameteri(GL_TEXTURE_2D,GL_TEXTURE_WRAP_S,
               GL_CLAMP_TO_BORDER);
glTexParameteri(GL_TEXTURE_2D,GL_TEXTURE_WRAP_T,
               GL_CLAMP_TO_BORDER);
glTexParameterfv(GL_TEXTURE_2D,GL_TEXTURE_BORDER_COLOR,
                border);

glTexParameteri(GL_TEXTURE_2D,GL_TEXTURE_COMPARE_MODE,
               GL_COMPARE_REF_TO_TEXTURE);
glTexParameteri(GL_TEXTURE_2D,GL_TEXTURE_COMPARE_FUNC,
               GL_LESS);

//Assign the shadow map to texture unit 0
glActiveTexture(GL_TEXTURE0);
glBindTexture(GL_TEXTURE_2D,depthTex);

//Create and set up the FBO
glGenFramebuffers(1,&shadowFBO);
glBindFramebuffer(GL_FRAMEBUFFER,shadowFBO);
glFramebufferTexture2D(GL_FRAMEBUFFER,GL_DEPTH_ATTACHMENT,
                      GL_TEXTURE_2D,depthTex,0);
GLenum drawBuffers[]={GL_NONE};
glDrawBuffers(1,drawBuffers);
// Revert to the default framebuffer for now
glBindFramebuffer(GL_FRAMEBUFFER,0);
```

2. Use the following code for the vertex shader:

```glsl
layout (location=0) in vec3 VertexPosition;
layout (location=1) in vec3 VertexNormal;

out vec3 Normal;
out vec3 Position;

// Coordinate to be used for shadow map lookup
out vec4 ShadowCoord;

uniform mat4 ModelViewMatrix;
uniform mat3 NormalMatrix;
uniform mat4 MVP;
uniform mat4 ShadowMatrix;

void main()
{
    Position = (ModelViewMatrix *
                vec4(VertexPosition,1.0)).xyz;
    Normal = normalize( NormalMatrix * VertexNormal );

    // ShadowMatrix converts from modeling coordinates
    // to shadow map coordinates.
    ShadowCoord =ShadowMatrix * vec4(VertexPosition,1.0);

    gl_Position = MVP * vec4(VertexPosition,1.0);
}
```

3. Use the following code for the fragment shader:

```glsl
// Declare any uniforms needed for your shading model
uniform sampler2DShadow ShadowMap;

in vec3 Position;
in vec3 Normal;
in vec4 ShadowCoord;

layout (location = 0) out vec4 FragColor;

vec3 diffAndSpec()
{
    // Compute only the diffuse and specular components of
    // the shading model.
}
```

```
subroutine void RenderPassType();
subroutine uniform RenderPassType RenderPass;

subroutine (RenderPassType)
void shadeWithShadow()
{
  vec3 ambient = …;// compute ambient component here
  vec3 diffSpec = diffAndSpec();

  // Do the shadow-map look-up
  float shadow = textureProj(ShadowMap, ShadowCoord);

  // If the fragment is in shadow, use ambient light only.
  FragColor = vec4(diffSpec * shadow + ambient, 1.0);
}
subroutine (RenderPassType)
void recordDepth()
{
    // Do nothing, depth will be written automatically
}

void main() {
  // This will call either shadeWithShadow or recordDepth
  RenderPass();
}
```

Within the main OpenGL program, perform the following steps when rendering:

Pass 1

1. Set the viewport, view, and projection matrices to those that are appropriate for the light source.
2. Bind to the `framebuffer` containing the shadow map (`shadowFBO`).
3. Clear the depth buffer.
4. Select the subroutine function `recordDepth`.
5. Enable front-face culling.
6. Draw the scene.

Pass 2

1. Select the viewport, view, and projection matrices appropriate for the scene.
2. Bind to the default framebuffer.
3. Disable culling (or switch to back-face culling).
4. Select the subroutine function `shadeWithShadow`.
5. Draw the scene.

How it works...

The first block of the preceding code demonstrates how to create a FBO for our shadow map texture. The FBO contains only a single texture connected to its depth buffer attachment. The first few lines of code create the shadow map texture. The texture is allocated using the `glTexStorage2D` function with an internal format of `GL_DEPTH_COMPONENT24`.

We use `GL_NEAREST` for `GL_TEXTURE_MAG_FILTER` and `GL_TEXTURE_MIN_FILTER` here, although `GL_LINEAR` could also be used, and might provide slightly better-looking results. We use `GL_NEAREST` here so that we can see the aliasing artifacts clearly, and the performance will be slightly better.

Next, the `GL_TEXTURE_WRAP_*` modes are set to `GL_CLAMP_TO_BORDER`. When a fragment is found to lie completely outside of the shadow map (outside of the light's frustum), then the texture coordinates for that fragment will be greater than one or less than zero. When that happens, we need to make sure that those points are not treated as being in shadow. When `GL_CLAMP_TO_BORDER` is used, the value that is returned from a texture lookup (for coordinates outside the 0..1 range) will be the border value. The default border value is `(0,0,0,0)`. When the texture contains depth components, the first component is treated as the depth value. A value of zero will not work for us here because a depth of zero corresponds to points on the near plane. Therefore all points outside of the light's frustum will be treated as being in shadow! Instead, we set the border color to `(1,0,0,0)` using the `glTexParameterfv` function, which corresponds to the maximum possible depth.

The next two calls to `glTexParameteri` affect settings that are specific to depth textures. The first call sets `GL_TEXTURE_COMPARE_MODE` to `GL_COMPARE_REF_TO_TEXTURE`. When this setting is enabled, the result of a texture access is the result of a comparison, rather than a color value retrieved from the texture. The third component of the texture coordinate (the `p` component) is compared against the value in the texture at location (s,t). The result of the comparison is returned as a single floating-point value. The comparison function that is used is determined by the value of `GL_TEXTURE_COMPARE_FUNC`, which is set on the next line. In this case, we set it to `GL_LESS`, which means that the result will be `1.0` if the p value of the texture coordinate is less than the value stored at (s,t). (Other options include `GL_LEQUAL`, `GL_ALWAYS`, `GL_GEQUAL`, and so on.)

The next few lines create and set up the FBO. The shadow map texture is attached to the FBO as the depth attachment with the `glFramebufferTexture2D` function. For more details about FBOs, check out the *Rendering to a texture* recipe in *Chapter 4, Using Textures*.

The vertex shader is fairly simple. It converts the vertex position and normal to camera coordinates and passes them along to the fragment shader via the output variables `Position` and `Normal`. The vertex position is also converted into shadow map coordinates using `ShadowMatrix`. This is the matrix S that we referred to in the previous section. It converts a position from modeling coordinates to shadow coordinates. The result is sent to the fragment shader via the output variable `ShadowCoord`.

As usual, the position is also converted to clip coordinates and assigned to the built-in output variable gl_Position.

In the fragment shader, we provide different functionality for each pass. In the main function, we call RenderPass, which is a subroutine uniform that will call either recordDepth or shadeWithShadow. For the first pass (shadow map generation), the subroutine function recordDepth is executed. This function does nothing at all! This is because we only need to write the depth to the depth buffer. OpenGL will do this automatically (assuming that gl_Position was set correctly by the vertex shader), so there is nothing for the fragment shader to do.

During the second pass, the shadeWithShadow function is executed. We compute the ambient component of the shading model and store the result in the ambient variable. We then compute the diffuse and specular components and store those in the diffuseAndSpec variable.

The next step is the key to the shadow mapping algorithm. We use the built-in texture access function textureProj, to access the shadow map texture ShadowMap. Before using the texture coordinate to access the texture, the textureProj function will divide the first three components of the texture coordinate by the fourth component. Remember that this is exactly what is needed to convert the homogeneous position (ShadowCoord) to a true Cartesian position.

After this perspective division, the textureProj function will use the result to access the texture. As this texture's sampler type is sampler2DShadow, it is treated as texture containing depth values, and rather than returning a value from the texture, it returns the result of a comparison. The first two components of ShadowCoord are used to access a depth value within the texture. That value is then compared against the value of the third component of ShadowCoord. When GL_NEAREST is the interpolation mode (as it is in our case) the result will be 1.0 or 0.0. As we set the comparison function to GL_LESS, this will return 1.0, if the value of the third component of ShadowCoord is less than the value within the depth texture at the sampled location. This result is then stored in the variable shadow. Finally, we assign a value to the output variable FragColor. The result of the shadow map comparison (shadow) is multiplied by the diffuse and specular components, and the result is added to the ambient component. If shadow is 0.0, that means that the comparison failed, meaning that there is something between the fragment and the light source. Therefore, the fragment is only shaded with ambient light. Otherwise, shadow is 1.0, and the fragment is shaded with all three shading components.

When rendering the shadow map, note that we culled the front faces. This is to avoid the z-fighting that can occur when front faces are included in the shadow map. Note that this only works if our mesh is completely closed. If back faces are exposed, you may need to use another technique (that uses glPolygonOffset) to avoid this. I'll talk a bit more about this in the next section.

There's more...

There's a number of challenging issues with the shadow mapping technique. Let's look at just a few of the most immediate ones.

Aliasing

As mentioned earlier, this algorithm often suffers from severe aliasing artifacts at the shadow's edges. This is due to the fact that the shadow map is essentially projected onto the scene when the depth comparison is made. If the projection causes the map to be magnified, aliasing artifacts appear.

The following figure shows the aliasing of the shadow's edges:

The easiest solution is to simply increase the size of the shadow map. However, that may not be possible due to memory, CPU speed, or other constraints. There is a large number of techniques for improving the quality of the shadows produced by the shadow mapping algorithm such as resolution-matched shadow maps, cascaded shadow maps, variance shadow maps, perspective shadow maps and many others. In the following recipes, we'll look at some ways to help soften and anti-alias the edges of the shadows.

Rendering back faces only for the shadow map

When creating the shadow map, we only rendered back faces. This is because of the fact that if we were to render front faces, points on certain faces would have nearly the same depth as the shadow map's depth, which can cause fluctuations between light and shadow across faces that should be completely lit. The following figure shows an example of this effect:

Since the majority of faces that cause this issue are those that are facing the light source, we avoid much of the problem by only rendering back faces during the shadow map pass. This of course will only work correctly if your meshes are completely closed. If that is not the case, glPolygonOffset can be used to help the situation by offsetting the depth of the geometry from that in the shadow map. In fact, even when back faces are only rendered when generating the shadow map, similar artifacts can appear on faces that are facing away from the light (back faces in the shadow map, but front from the camera's perspective). Therefore, it is quite often the case that a combination of front-face culling and glPolygonOffset is used when generating the shadow map.

See also

▶ The *Rendering to a texture* recipe in *Chapter 4, Using Textures*

▶ The *Anti-aliasing shadow edges with PCF* recipe

▶ The *Creating soft shadow edges with random sampling* recipe

Anti-aliasing shadow edges with PCF

One of the simplest and most common techniques for dealing with the aliasing of shadow edges is called **percentage-closer filtering** (**PCF**). The name comes from the concept of sampling the area around the fragment and determining the percentage of the area that is closer to the light source (in shadow). The percentage is then used to scale the amount of (diffuse and specular) shading that the fragment receives. The overall effect is a blurring of the shadow's edges.

The basic technique was first published by *Reeves* et al in a 1987 paper (*SIGGRAPH Proceedings, Volume 21, Number 4, July 1987*). The concept involved transforming the fragment's extents into shadow space, sampling several locations within that region, and computing the percent that is closer than the depth of the fragment. The result is then used to attenuate the shading. If the size of this filter region is increased, it can have the effect of blurring the shadow's edges.

A common variant of the PCF algorithm involves just sampling a constant number of nearby texels within the shadow map. The percent of those texels that are closer to the light is used to attenuate the shading. This has the effect of blurring the shadow's edges. While the result may not be physically accurate, the result is not objectionable to the eye.

The following figures show shadows rendered with PCF (right) and without PCF (left). Note that the shadows in the right-hand image have fuzzier edges and the aliasing is less visible.

In this recipe, we'll use the latter technique, and sample a constant number of texels around the fragment's position in the shadow map. We'll calculate an average of the resulting comparisons and use that result to scale the diffuse and specular components.

We'll make use of OpenGL's built-in support for PCF, by using linear filtering on the depth texture. When linear filtering is used with this kind of texture, the hardware can automatically sample four nearby texels (execute four depth comparisons) and average the results (the details of this are implementation dependent). Therefore, when linear filtering is enabled, the result of the textureProj function can be somewhere between 0.0 and 1.0.

We'll also make use of the built-in functions for texture accesses with offsets. OpenGL provides the texture access function textureProjOffset, which has a third parameter (the offset) that is added to the texel coordinates before the lookup/comparison.

Getting ready

Start with the shaders and FBO presented in the previous recipe, *Rendering shadows with shadow maps*. We'll just make a few minor changes to the code presented there.

How to do it...

To add the PCF technique to the shadow mapping algorithm, use the following steps:

1. When setting up the FBO for the shadow map, make sure to use linear filtering on the depth texture. Replace the corresponding lines with the following code:

```
glTexParameteri(GL_TEXTURE_2D, GL_TEXTURE_MAG_FILTER,
                GL_LINEAR);
glTexParameteri(GL_TEXTURE_2D, GL_TEXTURE_MIN_FILTER,
                GL_LINEAR);
```

2. Use the following code for the shadeWithShadow function within the fragment shader:

```
subroutine (RenderPassType)
void shadeWithShadow()
{
  vec3 ambient = vec3(0.2);
  vec3 diffSpec = diffAndSpec();

  // The sum of the comparisons with nearby texels
  float sum = 0;

  // Sum contributions from texels around ShadowCoord
  sum += textureProjOffset(ShadowMap, ShadowCoord,
                           ivec2(-1,-1));
  sum += textureProjOffset(ShadowMap, ShadowCoord,
                           ivec2(-1,1));
  sum += textureProjOffset(ShadowMap, ShadowCoord,
                           ivec2(1,1));
  sum += textureProjOffset(ShadowMap, ShadowCoord,
                           ivec2(1,-1));
  float shadow = sum * 0.25;


  FragColor = vec4(ambient + diffSpec * shadow,1.0);
}
```

How it works...

The first step enables linear filtering on the shadow map texture. When this is enabled, the OpenGL driver can repeat the depth comparison on the four nearby texels within the texture. The results of the four comparisons will be averaged and returned.

Within the fragment shader, we use the `textureProjOffset` function to sample the four texels (diagonally) surrounding the texel nearest to `ShadowCoord`. The third argument is the offset. It is added to the texel's coordinates (not the texture coordinates) before the lookup takes place.

As linear filtering is enabled, each lookup will sample an additional four texels, for a total of 16 texels. The results are then averaged together and stored within the variable shadow.

As before, the value of `shadow` is used to attenuate the diffuse and specular components of the lighting model.

There's more...

An excellent survey of the PCF technique was written by *Fabio Pellacini* of *Pixar,* and can be found in *Chapter 11, Shadow Map Anti-aliasing* of *GPU Gems*, edited by *Randima Fernando, Addison-Wesley Professional, 2004*. If more details are desired, I highly recommend reading this short, but informative, chapter.

Because of its simplicity and efficiency, the PCF technique is an extremely common method for anti-aliasing the edges of shadows produced by shadow mapping. Since it has the effect of blurring the edges, it can also be used to simulate soft shadows. However, the number of samples must be increased with the size of the blurred edge (the penumbra) to avoid certain artifacts. This can, of course, be a computational roadblock. In the next recipe, we'll look at a technique for producing soft shadows by randomly sampling a larger region.

> The penumbra is the region of a shadow where only a portion of the light source is obscured.

See also

▶ The *Rendering shadows with shadow maps* recipe

Creating soft shadow edges with random sampling

The basic shadow mapping algorithm combined with PCF can produce shadows with soft edges. However, if we desire blurred edges that are substantially wide (to approximate true soft shadows) then a large number of samples is required. Additionally, there is a good deal of wasted effort when shading fragments that are in the center of large shadows, or completely outside of the shadow. For those fragments, all of the nearby shadow map texels will evaluate to the same value. Therefore, the work of accessing and averaging those texels is essentially a wasted effort.

The technique presented in this recipe is based on a chapter published in *GPU Gems 2*, edited by *Matt Pharr* and *Randima Fernando, Addison-Wesley Professional, 2005*. (*Chapter 17* by *Yury Uralsky*). It provides an approach that can address both of the preceding issues to create shadows with soft edges of various widths, while avoiding unnecessary texture accesses in areas inside and outside of the shadow.

The basic idea is as follows:

▸ Instead of sampling texels around the fragment's position (in shadow map space) using a constant set of offsets, we use a random, circular pattern of offsets

▸ In addition, we sample only the outer edges of the circle first in order to determine whether or not the fragment is in an area that is completely inside or outside of the shadow

The following figure is a visualization of a possible set of shadow map samples. The center of the cross-hairs is the fragment's location in the shadow map, and each **x** is a sample. The samples are distributed randomly within a circular grid around the fragment's location (one sample per grid cell).

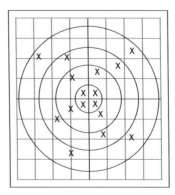

Additionally, we vary the sample locations through a set of precomputed sample patterns. We compute random sample offsets and store them in a texture prior to rendering. Then, in the fragment shader, the samples are determined by first accessing the offset texture to grab a set of offsets and use them to vary the fragment's position in the shadow map. The results are then averaged together in a similar manner to the basic PCF algorithm.

The following figures show the difference between shadows using the PCF algorithm (left), and the random sampling technique described in this recipe (right).

We'll store the offsets in a three-dimensional texture (n x n x d). The first two dimensions are of arbitrary size, and the third dimension contains the offsets. Each (s,t) location contains a list (size d) of random offsets packed into an RGBA color. Each RGBA color in the texture contains two 2D offsets. The R and G channels contain the first offset, and the B and A channels contain the second. Therefore, each (s,t) location contains a total of 2*d offsets. For example, location (1, 1, 3) contains the sixth and seventh offset at location (1,1). The entire set of values at a given (s,t) comprise a full set of offsets.

We'll rotate through the texture based on the fragment's screen coordinates. The location within the offset texture will be determined by taking the remainder of the screen coordinates divided by the texture's size. For example, if the fragment's coordinates are (10.0,10.0) and the texture's size is (4,4), then we use the set of offsets located in the offset texture at location (2,2).

Getting ready

Start with the code presented in the *Rendering shadows with shadow maps* recipe.

There are three additional uniforms that need to be set. They are as follows:

▶ OffsetTexSize: This gives the width, height, and depth of the offset texture. Note that the depth is same as the number of samples per fragment divided by two.

▶ OffsetTex: This is a handle to the texture unit containing the offset texture.

▶ `Radius`: This is the blur radius in pixels divided by the size of the shadow map texture (assuming a square shadow map). This could be considered as the softness of the shadow.

How to do it...

To modify the shadow mapping algorithm and to use this random sampling technique, use the following steps. We'll build the offset texture within the main OpenGL program, and make use of it within the fragment shader:

1. Use the following code within the main OpenGL program to create the offset texture. This only needs to be executed once during the program initialization:

```
void buildOffsetTex(int size, int samplesU, int samplesV)
{
    int samples = samplesU * samplesV;
    int bufSize = size * size * samples * 2;
    float *data = new float[bufSize];

    for( int i = 0; i< size; i++ ) {
        for(int j = 0; j < size; j++ ) {
            for( int k = 0; k < samples; k += 2 ) {
                int x1,y1,x2,y2;
                x1 = k % (samplesU);
                y1 = (samples - 1 - k) / samplesU;
                x2 = (k+1) % samplesU;
                y2 = (samples - 1 - k - 1) / samplesU;

                vec4 v;
                // Center on grid and jitter
                v.x = (x1 + 0.5f) + jitter();
                v.y = (y1 + 0.5f) + jitter();
                v.z = (x2 + 0.5f) + jitter();
                v.w = (y2 + 0.5f) + jitter();
                // Scale between 0 and 1
                v.x /= samplesU;
                v.y /= samplesV;
                v.z /= samplesU;
                v.w /= samplesV;
                // Warp to disk
                int cell = ((k/2) * size * size + j *
                            size + i) * 4;
                data[cell+0] = sqrtf(v.y) * cosf(TWOPI*v.x);
                data[cell+1] = sqrtf(v.y) * sinf(TWOPI*v.x);
                data[cell+2] = sqrtf(v.w) * cosf(TWOPI*v.z);
                data[cell+3] = sqrtf(v.w) * sinf(TWOPI*v.z);
```

```
        }
      }
    }

    glActiveTexture(GL_TEXTURE1);
    GLuint texID;
    glGenTextures(1, &texID);

    glBindTexture(GL_TEXTURE_3D, texID);
    glTexStorage3D(GL_TEXTURE_3D, 1, GL_RGBA32F, size, size,
                   samples/2);
    glTexSubImage3D(GL_TEXTURE_3D, 0, 0, 0, 0, size, size,
                   samples/2, GL_RGBA, GL_FLOAT, data);
    glTexParameteri(GL_TEXTURE_3D, GL_TEXTURE_MAG_FILTER,
                   GL_NEAREST);
    glTexParameteri(GL_TEXTURE_3D, GL_TEXTURE_MIN_FILTER,
                   GL_NEAREST);

    delete [] data;
}

// Return random float between -0.5 and 0.5
float jitter() {
  return ((float)rand() / RAND_MAX) - 0.5f;
}
```

2. Add the following uniform variables to the fragment shader:

```
uniform sampler3D OffsetTex;
uniform vec3 OffsetTexSize; // (width, height, depth)
uniform float Radius;
```

3. Use the following code for the shadeWithShadow function in the fragment shader:

```
subroutine (RenderPassType)
void shadeWithShadow()
{
  vec3 ambient = vec3(0.2);
  vec3 diffSpec = diffAndSpec();

  ivec3 offsetCoord;
  offsetCoord.xy = ivec2( mod( gl_FragCoord.xy,
                         OffsetTexSize.xy ) );

  float sum = 0.0;
  int samplesDiv2 = int(OffsetTexSize.z);
  vec4 sc = ShadowCoord;

  for( int i = 0 ; i< 4; i++ ) {
    offsetCoord.z = i;
```

```
      vec4 offsets = texelFetch(OffsetTex,offsetCoord,0) *
                          Radius * ShadowCoord.w;

    sc.xy = ShadowCoord.xy + offsets.xy;
    sum += textureProj(ShadowMap, sc);
    sc.xy = ShadowCoord.xy + offsets.zw;
    sum += textureProj(ShadowMap, sc);
  }
  float shadow = sum / 8.0;

  if( shadow != 1.0 && shadow != 0.0 ) {
    for( int i = 4; i< samplesDiv2; i++ ) {
      offsetCoord.z = i;
      vec4 offsets =
        texelFetch(OffsetTex, offsetCoord,0) *
                  Radius * ShadowCoord.w;

      sc.xy = ShadowCoord.xy + offsets.xy;
      sum += textureProj(ShadowMap, sc);
      sc.xy = ShadowCoord.xy + offsets.zw;
      sum += textureProj(ShadowMap, sc);
    }
    shadow = sum / float(samplesDiv2 * 2.0);
  }
  FragColor = vec4(diffSpec * shadow + ambient, 1.0);
}
```

How it works...

The `buildOffsetTex` function creates our three-dimensional texture of random offsets. The first parameter, `texSize`, defines the width and height of the texture. To create the preceding images, I used a value of 8. The second and third parameters, `samplesU` and `samplesV`, define the number of samples in the u and v directions. I used a value of 4 and 8, respectively, for a total of 32 samples. The **u** and **v** directions are arbitrary axes that are used to define a grid of offsets. To help understand this, take a look at the following figure:

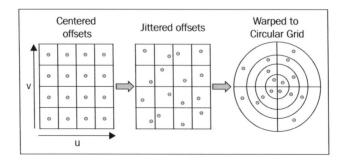

The offsets are initially defined to be centered on a grid of size `samplesU` x `samplesV` (4 x 4 in the preceding figure). The coordinates of the offsets are scaled such that the entire grid fits in the unit cube (side length 1) with the origin in the lower left corner. Then each sample is randomly jittered from its position to a random location inside the grid cell. Finally, the jittered offsets are warped such that they surround the origin and lie within the circular grid shown on the right.

The last step can be accomplished by using the v coordinate as the distance from the origin and the u coordinate as the angle scaled from 0 to 360. The following equations should do the trick:

$$w_x = \sqrt{v}\cos(2\pi u)$$
$$w_y = \sqrt{v}\sin(2\pi u)$$

Here, w is the warped coordinate. What we are left with is a set of offsets around the origin that are a maximum distance of 1.0 from the origin. Additionally, we generate the data such that the first samples are the ones around the outer edge of the circle, moving inside towards the center. This will help us avoid taking too many samples when we are working completely inside or outside of the shadow.

Of course, we also pack the samples in such a way that a single texel contains two samples. This is not strictly necessary, but is done to conserve memory space. However, it does make the code a bit more complex.

Within the fragment shader, we start by computing the ambient component of the shading model separately from the diffuse and specular components. We access the offset texture at a location based on the fragment's screen coordinates (`gl_FragCoord`). We do so by taking the modulus of the fragment's position and the size of the offset texture. The result is stored in the first two components of `offsetCoord`. This will give us a different set of offsets for each nearby pixel. The third components of `offsetCoord` will be used to access a pair of samples. The number of samples is the depth of the texture divided by two. This is stored in `samplesDiv2`. We access the sample using the `texelFetch` function. This function allows us to access a texel using the integer texel coordinates rather than the usual normalized texture coordinates in the range 0...1.

The offset is retrieved and multiplied by `Radius` and the w component of `ShadowCoord`. Multiplying by `Radius` simply scales the offsets so that they range from 0.0 to `Radius`. We multiply by the w component because `ShadowCoord` is still a homogeneous coordinate, and our goal is to use offsets to translate the `ShadowCoord`. In order to do so properly, we need to multiply the offset by the w component. Another way of thinking of this is that the w component will be cancelled when perspective division takes place.

Next, we use offsets to translate `ShadowCoord` and access the shadow map to do the depth comparison using `textureProj`. We do so for each of the two samples stored in the texel, once for the first two components of offsets and again for the last two. The result is added to `sum`.

The first loop repeats this for the first eight samples. If the first eight samples are all 0.0 or 1.0, then we assume that all of the samples will be the same (the sample area is completely in or out of the shadow). In that case, we skip the evaluation of the rest of the samples. Otherwise, we evaluate the following samples and compute the overall average.

Finally the resulting average (shadow) is used to attenuate the diffuse and specular components of the lighting model.

There's more...

The use of a small texture containing a set of random offsets helps to blur the edges of the shadow better than what we might achieve with the standard PCF technique that uses a constant set of offsets. However, artifacts can still appear as repeated patterns within the shadow edges because the texture is finite and offsets are repeated every few pixels. We could improve this by also using a random rotation of the offsets within the fragment shader, or simply compute the offsets randomly within the shader.

It should also be noted that this blurring of the edges may not be desired for all shadow edges. For example, edges that are directly adjacent to the occluder, that is, creating the shadow, should not be blurred. These may not always be visible, but can become so in certain situations, such as when the occluder is a narrow object. The effect is to make the object appear as if it is hovering above the surface. Unfortunately, there isn't an easy fix for this one.

See also

▶ The *Rendering shadows with shadow maps* recipe

Creating shadows using shadow volumes and the geometry shader

As we discovered in the previous recipes, one of the main problems with shadow maps is aliasing. The problem essentially boils down to the fact that we are sampling the shadow map(s) at a different frequency (resolution) than we are using when rendering the scene. To minimize the aliasing we can blur the shadow edges (as in the previous recipes), or try to sample the shadow map at a frequency that is closer to the corresponding resolution in projected screen space. There are many techniques that help with the latter; for more details, I recommend the book *Real-Time Shadows*.

An alternate technique for shadow generation is called *shadow volumes*. The shadow volume method completely avoids the aliasing problem that plagues shadow maps. With shadow volumes, you get pixel-perfect hard shadows, without the aliasing artifacts of shadow maps. The following figure shows a scene with shadows that are produced using the shadow volume technique.

The shadow volume technique works by making use of the stencil buffer to mask out areas that are in shadow. We do this by drawing the boundaries of the actual shadow volumes (more on this below). A shadow volume is the region of space where the light source is occluded by an object. For example, the following figures show a representation of the shadow volumes of a triangle (left) and a sphere (right).

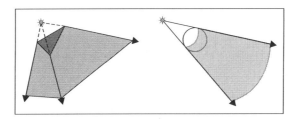

The boundaries of a shadow volume are made up of quads formed by extending the edges of the object away from the light source. For a single triangle, the boundaries would consist of three quads, extended from each edge, and triangular caps on each end. One cap is the triangle itself and the other is placed at some distance from the light source. For an object that consists of many triangles, such as the sphere above, the volume can be defined by the so-called silhouette edges. These are edges that are on or near the boundary between the shadow volume and the portion of the object that is lit. In general, a silhouette edge borders a triangle that faces the light and another triangle that faces away from the light. To draw the shadow volume, one would find all of the silhouette edges and draw extended quads for each edge. The caps of the volume could be determined by making a closed polygon (or triangle fan) that includes all the points on the silhouette edges, and similarly on the far end of the volume.

The shadow volume technique works in the following way. Imagine a ray that originates at the camera position and extends through a pixel on the near plane. Suppose that we follow that ray and keep track of a counter that is incremented every time that it enters a shadow volume and decremented each time that it exits a shadow volume. If we stop counting when we hit a surface, that point on the surface is occluded (in shadow) if our count is non-zero, otherwise, the surface is lit by the light source. The following figure shows an example of this idea:

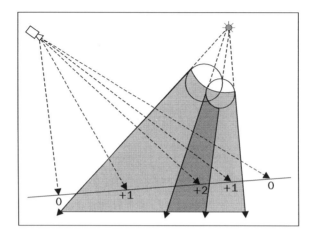

The roughly horizontal line represents a surface that is receiving a shadow. The numbers represent the counter for each camera ray. For example, the rightmost ray with value **+1** has that value because the ray entered two volumes and exited one along the way from the camera to the surface: 1 + 1 - 1 = 1. The rightmost ray has a value of zero at the surface because it entered and exited both shadow volumes: 1 + 1 - 1 - 1 = 0.

This all sounds fine in theory, but how can we trace rays in OpenGL? The good news is that we don't have to. The stencil buffer provides just what we need. With the stencil buffer, we can increment/decrement a counter for each pixel based on whether a front or back face is rendered into that pixel. So we can draw the boundaries of all of the shadow volumes, then for each pixel, increment the stencil buffer's counter when a front face is rendered to that pixel and decrement when it is a back face.

The key here is to realize that each pixel in the rendered figure represents an eye-ray (as in the above diagram). So for a given pixel, the value in the stencil buffer is the value that we would get if we actually traced a ray through that pixel. The depth test helps to stop tracing when we reach a surface.

 The above is just a quick introduction to shadow volumes, a full discussion is beyond the scope of this book. For more detail, a great resource is *Real Time Shadows* by *Eisemann* et al.

In this recipe, we'll draw our shadow volumes with the help of the geometry shader. Rather than computing the shadow volumes on the CPU side, we'll render the geometry normally, and have the geometry shader produce the shadow volumes. In the *Drawing silhouette lines using the geometry shader* recipe in *Chapter 6, Using Geometry and Tessellation Shaders*, we saw how the geometry shader can be provided with adjacency information for each triangle. With adjacency information, we can determine whether a triangle has a silhouette edge. If the triangle faces the light, and a neighboring triangle faces away from the light, then the shared edge can be considered a silhouette edge, and used to create a polygon for the shadow volume.

The entire process is done in three passes. They are as follows:

 ▶ Render the scene normally, but write the shaded color to two separate buffers. We'll store the ambient component in one and the diffuse and specular components in another.

 ▶ Set up the stencil buffer so that the stencil test always passes, and front faces cause an increment and back faces cause a decrement. Make the depth buffer read-only, and render only the shadow-casting objects. In this pass, the geometry shader will produce the shadow volumes, and only the shadow volumes will be rendered to the fragment shader.

 ▶ Set up the stencil buffer so the test succeeds when the value is equal to zero. Draw a screen-filling quad, and combine the values of the two buffers from step one when the stencil test succeeds.

That's the high-level view, and there are many details. Let's go through them in the next sections.

Getting ready

We'll start by creating our buffers. We'll use a framebuffer object with a depth attachment and two color attachments. The ambient component can be stored in a renderbuffer (as opposed to a texture) because we'll blit (a fast copy) it over to the default framebuffer rather than reading from it as a texture. The diffuse + specular component will be stored in a texture. Create the ambient buffer (`ambBuf`), a depth buffer (`depthBuf`), and a texture (`diffSpecTex`), then set up the FBO.

```
glGenFramebuffers(1, &colorDepthFBO);
glBindFramebuffer(GL_FRAMEBUFFER, colorDepthFBO);
glFramebufferRenderbuffer(GL_FRAMEBUFFER, GL_DEPTH_ATTACHMENT,
                GL_RENDERBUFFER, depthBuf);
glFramebufferRenderbuffer(GL_FRAMEBUFFER, GL_COLOR_ATTACHMENT0,
                GL_RENDERBUFFER, ambBuf);
glFramebufferTexture2D(GL_FRAMEBUFFER, GL_COLOR_ATTACHMENT1,
                GL_TEXTURE_2D, diffSpecTex, 0);
```

Set up the draw buffers so that we can write to the color attachments.

```
GLenum drawBuffers[] = {GL_COLOR_ATTACHMENT0,
                        GL_COLOR_ATTACHMENT1};
glDrawBuffers(2, drawBuffers);
```

How to do it...

For the first pass, enable the framebuffer object that we set up above, and render the scene normally. In the fragment shader, send the ambient component and the diffuse + specular component to separate outputs.

```
layout( location = 0 ) out vec4 Ambient;
layout( location = 1 ) out vec4 DiffSpec;

void shade( )
{
  // Compute the shading model, and separate out the ambient
  // component.
  Ambient = ...;    // Ambient
  DiffSpec = ...;   // Diffuse + specular
}
void main() { shade(); }
```

In the second pass, we'll render our shadow volumes. We want to set up the stencil buffer so that the test always succeeds, and that front faces cause an increment, and back faces cause a decrement.

```
glClear(GL_STENCIL_BUFFER_BIT);
glEnable(GL_STENCIL_TEST);
glStencilFunc(GL_ALWAYS, 0, 0xffff);
glStencilOpSeparate(GL_FRONT, GL_KEEP, GL_KEEP, GL_INCR_WRAP);
glStencilOpSeparate(GL_BACK, GL_KEEP, GL_KEEP, GL_DECR_WRAP);
```

Also in this pass, we want to use the depth buffer from the first pass, but we want to use the default frame buffer, so we need to copy the depth buffer over from the FBO used in the first pass. We'll also copy over the color data, which should contain the ambient component.

```
glBindFramebuffer(GL_READ_FRAMEBUFFER, colorDepthFBO);
glBindFramebuffer(GL_DRAW_FRAMEBUFFER,0);
glBlitFramebuffer(0,0,width-1,height-1,0,0,width-1,height-1,
         GL_DEPTH_BUFFER_BIT|GL_COLOR_BUFFER_BIT, GL_NEAREST);
```

We don't want to write to the depth buffer or the color buffer in this pass, since our only goal is to update the stencil buffer, so we'll disable writing for those buffers.

```
glColorMask(GL_FALSE, GL_FALSE, GL_FALSE, GL_FALSE);
glDepthMask(GL_FALSE);
```

Next, we render the shadow-casting objects with adjacency information. In the geometry shader, we determine the silhouette edges and output only quads that define the shadow volume boundaries.

```glsl
layout( triangles_adjacency ) in;
layout( triangle_strip, max_vertices = 18 ) out;

in vec3 VPosition[];
in vec3 VNormal[];

uniform vec4 LightPosition;   // Light position (eye coords)
uniform mat4 ProjMatrix;      // Proj. matrix (infinite far plane)

bool facesLight( vec3 a, vec3 b, vec3 c )
{
  vec3 n = cross( b - a, c - a );
  vec3 da = LightPosition.xyz - a;
  vec3 db = LightPosition.xyz - b;
  vec3 dc = LightPosition.xyz - c;
  return dot(n, da) > 0 || dot(n, db) > 0 || dot(n, dc) > 0;
}

void emitEdgeQuad( vec3 a, vec3 b ) {
  gl_Position = ProjMatrix * vec4(a, 1);
  EmitVertex();
  gl_Position = ProjMatrix * vec4(a - LightPosition.xyz, 0);
  EmitVertex();
  gl_Position = ProjMatrix * vec4(b, 1);
  EmitVertex();
  gl_Position = ProjMatrix * vec4(b - LightPosition.xyz, 0);
  EmitVertex();
  EndPrimitive();
}

void main()
{
  if( facesLight(VPosition[0], VPosition[2], VPosition[4]) ) {
    if( ! facesLight(VPosition[0],VPosition[1],VPosition[2]) )
      emitEdgeQuad(VPosition[0],VPosition[2]);
    if( ! facesLight(VPosition[2],VPosition[3],VPosition[4]) )
      emitEdgeQuad(VPosition[2],VPosition[4]);
    if( ! facesLight(VPosition[4],VPosition[5],VPosition[0]) )
      emitEdgeQuad(VPosition[4],VPosition[0]);
  }
}
```

In the third pass, we'll set up our stencil buffer so that the test passes only when the value in the buffer is equal to zero.

```
glStencilFunc(GL_EQUAL, 0, 0xffff);
glStencilOp(GL_KEEP, GL_KEEP, GL_KEEP);
```

We want to enable blending so that our ambient component is combined with the diffuse + specular when the stencil test succeeds.

```
glEnable(GL_BLEND);
glBlendFunc(GL_ONE,GL_ONE);
```

In this pass, we just draw a screen-filling quad, and output the diffuse + specular value. If the stencil test succeeds, the value will be combined with the ambient component, which is already in the buffer (we copied it over earlier using `glBlitFramebuffer`).

```
layout(binding = 0) uniform sampler2D DiffSpecTex;
layout(location = 0) out vec4 FragColor;

void main() {
  vec4 diffSpec = texelFetch(DiffSpecTex, ivec2(gl_FragCoord), 0);
  FragColor = vec4(diffSpec.xyz, 1);
}
```

How it works...

The first pass is fairly straightforward. We draw the entire scene normally, except we separate the ambient color from the diffuse and specular color, and send the results to different buffers.

The second pass is the core of the algorithm. Here we render only the objects that cast shadows and let the geometry shader produce the shadow volumes. Thanks to the geometry shader, we don't actually end up rendering the shadow-casting objects at all, only the shadow volumes. However, before this pass, we need to do a bit of setup. We set up the stencil test so that it increments when a front face is rendered and decrements for back faces using `glStencilOpSeparate`, and the stencil test is configured to always succeed using `glStencilFunc`. We also use `glBlitFramebuffer` to copy over the depth buffer and (ambient) color buffer from the FBO used in the first pass. Since we want to only render shadow volumes that are not obscured by geometry, we make the depth buffer read-only using `glDepthMask`. Lastly, we disable writing to the color buffer using `glColorMask` because we don't want to mistakenly overwrite anything in this pass.

The geometry shader does the work of producing the silhouette shadow volumes. Since we are rendering using adjacency information (see the *Drawing silhouette lines using the geometry shader* recipe in *Chapter 6, Using Geometry and Tessellation Shaders*), the geometry shader has access to six vertices that define the current triangle being rendered and the three neighboring triangles. The vertices are numbered from 0 to 5, and are available via the input array named VPosition in this example. Vertices 0, 2, and 4 define the current triangle and the others define the adjacent triangles as shown in the following figure:

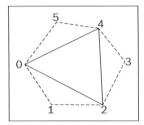

The geometry shader starts by testing the main triangle (0, 2, 4) to see if it faces the light source. We do so by computing the normal to the triangle (n) and the vector from each vertex to the light source. Then we compute the dot product of n and each of the three light source direction vectors (da, db, and dc). If any of the three are positive, then the triangle faces the light source. If we find that triangle (0, 2, 4) faces the light, then we test each neighboring triangle in the same way. If a neighboring triangle does not face the light source, then the edge between them is a silhouette edge and can be used as an edge of a face of the shadow volume.

We create a shadow volume face in the emitEdgeQuad function. The points a and b define the silhouette edge, one edge of the shadow volume face. The other two vertices of the face are determined by extending a and b away from the light source. Here, we use a mathematical trick that is enabled by homogeneous coordinates. We extend the face out to infinity by using a zero in the w coordinate of the extended vertices. This effectively defines a homogeneous vector, sometimes called a point at infinity. The x, y and z coordinates define a vector in the direction away from the light source, and the w value is set to zero. The end result is that we get a quad that extends out to infinity, away from the light source.

 Note that this will only work properly if we use a modified projection matrix that can take into account points defined in this way. Essentially, we want a projection matrix with a far plane set at infinity. GLM provides just such a projection matrix via the function infinitePerspective.

We don't worry about drawing the caps of the shadow volume here. We don't need a cap at the far end, because we've used the homogeneous trick described above, and the object itself will serve as the cap on the near end.

In the third and final pass, we reset our stencil test to pass when the value in the stencil buffer is equal to zero using `glStencilFunc`. Here we want to sum the ambient with the diffuse + specular color when the stencil test succeeds, so we enable blending, and set the source and destination blend functions to `GL_ONE`. We render just a single screen-filling quad, and output the value from the texture that contains our diffuse + specular color. The stencil test will take care of discarding fragments that are in shadow, and OpenGL's blending support will blend the output with the ambient color for fragments that pass the test. (Remember that we copied over the ambient color using `glBlitFramebuffer` earlier.)

There's more...

The technique described above is often referred to as the **z-pass** technique. It has one fatal flaw. If the camera is located within a shadow volume, this technique breaks down because the counts in the stencil buffer will be off by at least one. The common solution is to basically invert the problem and trace a ray from infinity towards the view point. This is called the z-fail technique or Carmack's reverse.

 The "fail" and "pass" here refers to whether or not we are counting when the depth test passes or fails.

Care must be taken when using z-fail because it is important to draw the caps of the shadow volumes. However, the technique is very similar to z-pass. Instead of incrementing/decrementing when the depth test passes, we do so when the depth test fails. This effectively "traces" a ray from infinity back towards the view point.

I should also note that the preceding code is not robust to degenerate triangles (triangles that have sides that are nearly parallel), or non-closed meshes. One might need to take care in such situations. For example, to better deal with degenerate triangles we could use another technique for determining the normal to the triangle. We could also add additional code to handle edges of meshes, or simply always use closed meshes.

See also

- The *Drawing silhouette lines using the geometry shader* recipe in *Chapter 6, Using Geometry and Tessellation Shaders*

8
Using Noise in Shaders

In this chapter, we will cover:

- ▶ Creating a noise texture using GLM
- ▶ Creating a seamless noise texture
- ▶ Creating a cloud-like effect
- ▶ Creating a wood-grain effect
- ▶ Creating a disintegration effect
- ▶ Creating a paint-spatter effect
- ▶ Creating a night-vision effect

Introduction

It's easy to use shaders to create a smooth-looking surface, but that is not always the desired goal. If we want to create realistic-looking objects, we need to simulate the imperfections of real surfaces. That includes things such as scratches, rust, dents, and erosion. It is somewhat surprising how challenging it can be to make surfaces look like they have really been subjected to these natural processes. Similarly, we sometimes want to represent natural surfaces such as wood grain or natural phenomena such as clouds to be as realistic as possible without giving the impression of being synthetic or exhibiting a repetitive pattern or structure.

Most effects or patterns in nature exhibit a certain degree of randomness and non-linearity. Therefore, you might imagine that we could generate them by simply using random data. However, random data such as the kind that is generated from a pseudorandom-number generator is not very useful in computer graphics. There are two main reasons:

- ▶ First, we need data that is repeatable, so that the object will render in the same way during each frame of the animation. (We could achieve this by using an appropriate seed value for each frame, but that only solves half of the problem.)

> ► Second, in order to model most of these natural phenomena, we actually need data that is continuous, but still gives the appearance of randomness. Continuous data more accurately represents many of these natural materials and phenomena. Purely random data does not have this continuity property. Each value has no dependence on the previous value.

Thanks to the groundbreaking work of Ken Perlin, we have the concept of **noise** (as it applies to computer graphics). His work defined noise as a function that has certain qualities such as the following:

- ► It is a continuous function
- ► It is repeatable (generates the same output from the same input)
- ► It can be defined for any number of dimensions
- ► It does not have any regular patterns and gives the appearance of randomness

Such a noise function is a valuable tool for computer graphics and it can be used to create an endless array of interesting effects. For instance, in this chapter, we'll use noise to create clouds, wood, disintegration, and other effects.

Perlin noise is the noise function originally defined by Ken Perlin (see `http://mrl.nyu.edu/~perlin/doc/oscar.html`). A full discussion of the details behind Perlin noise is outside the scope of this book.

To use Perlin noise within a shader, we have the following three main choices:

1. We can use the built-in GLSL noise functions.
2. We can create our own GLSL noise functions.
3. We can use a texture map to store pre-computed noise data.

At the time of writing, the GLSL noise functions are not implemented in some of the commercial OpenGL drivers, and therefore cannot be relied upon to be available, so I have decided not to use them in this chapter. As creating our own noise functions is a bit beyond the scope of this book, and because choice 3 in the preceding list gives the best performance on modern hardware, the recipes in this chapter will use the third approach (using a pre-computed noise texture).

 Many books use a 3D noise texture rather than a 2D one, to provide another dimension of noise that is available to the shaders. To keep things simple, and to focus on using surface texture coordinates, I've chosen to use a 2D noise texture in the recipes within this chapter. If desired, it should be straightforward to extend these recipes to use a 3D source of noise.

We'll start out with two recipes that demonstrate how to generate a noise texture using GLM. Then we'll move on to several examples that use noise textures to produce natural and artificial effects such as wood grain, clouds, electrical interference, splattering, and erosion.

The recipes in this chapter are meant to be a starting point for you to experiment with. They are certainly not intended to be the definitive way of implementing any of these effects. One of the best things about computer graphics is the element of creativity. Try tweaking the shaders in these recipes to produce similar results and then try creating your own effects. Most of all, have fun!

See Also...

▶ The book *Texturing and Modeling: A Procedural Approach*, by Ken Musgrave et al

Creating a noise texture using GLM

To create a texture for use as a source of noise, we need some way to generate noise values. Implementing a proper noise generator from scratch can be a fairly daunting task. Luckily, GLM provides some functions for noise generation that are straightforward and easy to use.

In this recipe, we'll use GLM to generate a 2D texture of noise values created using a **Perlin noise** generator. GLM can generate 2D, 3D, and 4D Perlin noise via the function `glm::perlin`.

It is common practice to use Perlin noise by summing the values of the noise function with increasing frequencies and decreasing amplitudes. Each frequency is commonly referred to as an **octave** (double the frequency). For example, in the following image, we show the results of the 2D Perlin noise function sampled at four different octaves. The sampling frequencies increase from left to right. The leftmost image is the function sampled at our base frequency, and each image to the right shows the function sampled at twice the frequency of the one to its left.

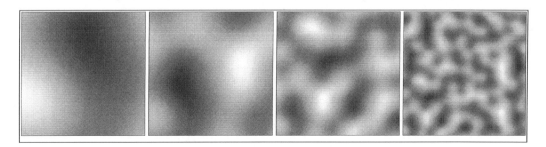

In mathematical terms, if our coherent 2D Perlin noise function is P(x, y), then each previous image represents the following equation.

$$n_i(x, y) = P(2^i x, 2^i y)$$

Here i = 0, 1, 2, and 3 from left to right.

As mentioned previously, the common practice is to sum octaves together to get the final result. We add each octave to the previous, scaling the amplitude down by some factor. So for N octaves, we have the following sum.

$$n(x, y) = \sum_{i=0}^{N-1} \frac{P(2^i ax, 2^i ay)}{b^i}$$

Where a and b are `tunable` constants. The following images show the sum of 2, 3, and 4 octaves (left to right) with a = 1 and b = 2.

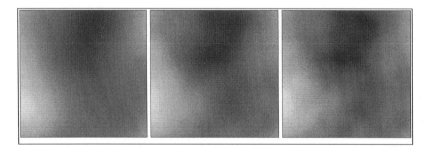

Summed noise involving higher octaves will have more high-frequency variation than noise involving only lower octaves. However, it is possible to quickly reach frequencies that exceed the resolution of the buffer used to store the noise data, so care must be taken not to do unnecessary computation. In practice, it is both an art and a science. The previous equation can be used as a starting point; feel free to tweak until you get the desired effect.

We'll store four noise values in a single 2D texture. We'll store Perlin noise with one octave in the first component (red channel), two octaves in the green channel, three octaves in the blue, and four octaves in the alpha channel.

Getting ready

Make sure you have the GLM library installed and placed in the include path.

How to do it...

To create a 2D noise texture with GLM, use the following steps:

1. Include the GLM header that includes the noise functions.

   ```
   #include <glm/gtc/noise.hpp>
   ```

2. Generate the noise data, using the previous equation:

   ```
   GLubyte *data = new GLubyte[ width * height * 4 ];

   float xFactor = 1.0f / (width - 1);
   float yFactor = 1.0f / (height - 1);

   for( int row = 0; row < height; row++ ) {
     for( int col = 0 ; col < width; col++ ) {
        float x = xFactor * col;
        float y = yFactor * row;
        float sum = 0.0f;
        float freq = a;
        float scale = b;

        // Compute the sum for each octave
        for( int oct = 0; oct < 4; oct++ ) {
          glm::vec2 p(x * freq, y * freq);
          float val = glm::perlin(p) / scale;
          sum += val;
          float result = (sum + 1.0f)/ 2.0f;

          // Store in texture buffer
          data[((row * width + col) * 4) + oct] =
                       (GLubyte) ( result * 255.0f );
          freq *= 2.0f;    // Double the frequency
          scale *= b;      // Next power of b
        }
      }
   }
   ```

3. Load the data into an OpenGL texture.

   ```
   GLuint texID;
   glGenTextures(1, &texID);

   glBindTexture(GL_TEXTURE_2D, texID);
   glTexStorage2D(GL_TEXTURE_2D, 1, GL_RGBA8, width, height);
   glTexSubImage2D(GL_TEXTURE_2D,0,0,0,width,height,
     GL_RGBA,GL_UNSIGNED_BYTE,data);

   delete [] data;
   ```

How it works...

The GLM library provides 2D, 3D, and 4D coherent noise via the `glm::perlin` function. It returns a float roughly between -1 and 1. We start by allocating a buffer named `data` to hold the generated noise values.

Next, we loop over each texel and compute the x and y coordinates (normalized). Then we loop over octaves. Here we compute the sum of the previous equation, storing the first term in the first component, the first two terms in the second, and so on. The value is scaled into the range from 0 to 1, then multiplied by 255 and cast to a byte.

The next few lines of code should be familiar. Texture memory is allocated with `glTexStorage2D` and the data is loaded in to GPU memory using `glTexSubImage2D`.

Finally, the array named `data` is deleted, as it is no longer needed.

There's more...

Rather than using unsigned byte values, we could get more resolution in our noise data by using a floating-point texture. This might provide better results if the effect needs a high degree of fine detail. The preceding code needs relatively few changes to achieve this. Just use an internal format of `GL_RGBA32F` instead of `GL_RGBA`, and don't multiply by 255 when storing the noise values in the array.

GLM also provides periodic Perlin noise via an overload of the `glm::perlin` function. This makes it easy to create noise textures that tile without seams. We'll see how to use this in the next recipe.

See also

▸   For general information about coherent noise, take a look at the book *Graphics Shaders*, by Mike Bailey and Steve Cunningham

▸   The *Applying a 2D texture* recipe in *Chapter 4, Using Textures*

▸   The *Creating a seamless noise texture* recipe

Creating a seamless noise texture

It can be particularly useful to have a noise texture that tiles well. If we simply create a noise texture as a finite slice of noise values, then the values will not wrap smoothly across the boundaries of the texture. This can cause hard edges (seams) to appear in the rendered surface if the texture coordinates extend outside of the range of zero to one.

Fortunately, GLM provides a periodic variant of Perlin noise that can be used to create a seamless noise texture.

The following image shows an example of regular (left) and periodic (right) 4-octave Perlin noise. Note that in the left image, the seams are clearly visible, while they are hidden in the right image.

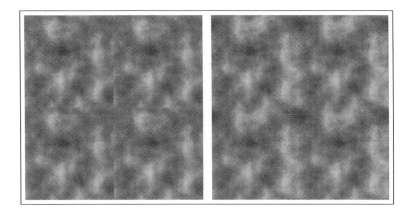

In this example, we'll modify the code from the previous recipe to produce a seamless noise texture.

Getting ready

For this recipe, we'll start with the code from the previous recipe, *Creating a noise texture using GLM*.

How to do it...

Modify the code from the previous recipe in the following way.

Within the innermost loop, instead of calling `glm::perlin`, we'll instead call the overload that provides periodic Perlin noise. Replace the statement

```
float val = glm::perlin(p) / scale;
```

with the following:

```
float val = 0.0f;
if( periodic ) {
  val = glm::perlin(p, glm::vec2(freq)) / scale;
} else {
  val = glm::perlin(p) / scale;
}
```

How it works...

The second parameter to `glm::perlin` determines the period in x and y of the noise values. We use `freq` as the period because we are sampling the noise in the range from 0 to `freq` for each octave.

See also

▸ The *Creating a noise texture using GLM* recipe

Creating a cloud-like effect

To create a texture that resembles a sky with clouds, we can use the noise values as a blending factor between the sky color and the cloud color. As clouds usually have large scale structure, it makes sense to use low octave noise. However, the large scale structure often has higher frequency variations, so some contribution from higher octave noise may be desired.

The following image shows an example of clouds generated by the technique in this recipe:

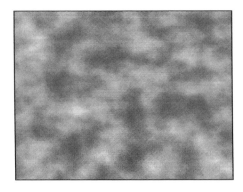

To create this effect, we take the cosine of the noise value and use the result as the blending factor between the cloud color.

Getting ready

Set up your program to generate a seamless noise texture and make it available to the shaders through the uniform sampler variable `NoiseTex`.

There are two uniforms in the fragment shader that can be assigned from the OpenGL program:

▸ `SkyColor`: The background sky color

▸ `CloudColor`: The color of the clouds

How to do it...

To create a shader program that uses a noise texture to create a cloud-like effect, use the following steps:

1. Set up your vertex shader to pass the texture coordinates to the fragment shader via the variable `TexCoord`.

2. Use the following code for the fragment shader:

```
#define PI 3.14159265

layout ( binding=0 ) uniform sampler2D NoiseTex;

uniform vec4 SkyColor = vec4 ( 0.3, 0.3, 0.9, 1.0 );
uniform vec4 CloudColor = vec4 ( 1.0, 1.0, 1.0, 1.0 );

in vec2 TexCoord;

layout ( location = 0 ) out vec4 FragColor;

void main()
{
  vec4 noise = texture(NoiseTex, TexCoord);
  float t = (cos( noise.g * PI ) + 1.0) / 2.0;
  vec4 color = mix( SkyColor, CloudColor, t );
  FragColor = vec4( color.rgb , 1.0 );
}
```

How it works...

We start by retrieving the noise value from the noise texture (variable `noise`). The green channel contains two octave noises, so we use the value stored in that channel (`noise.g`). Feel free to try out other channels and determine what looks right to you.

We use a cosine function to make a sharper transition between the cloud and sky color. The noise value will be between zero and one, and the cosine of that value will range between -1 and 1, so we add 1.0 and divide by 2.0. The result that is stored in `t` should again range between zero and one. Without this cosine transformation, the clouds look a bit too spread out over the sky. However, if that is the desired effect, one could remove the cosine and just use the noise value directly.

Next, we mix the sky color and the cloud color using the value of `t`. The result is used as the final output fragment color.

There's more...

If you desire less clouds and more sky, you could translate and clamp the value of t prior to using it to mix the cloud and sky colors. For example, you could use the following code:

```
float t = (cos( noise.g * PI ) + 1.0 ) / 2.0;
t = clamp( t - 0.25, 0.0, 1.0 );
```

This causes the cosine term to shift down (toward negative values), and the `clamp` function sets all negative values to zero. This has the effect of increasing the amount of sky and decreasing the size and intensity of the clouds.

See also

▶ Further reading on cloud generation: `http://vterrain.org/Atmosphere/Clouds/`

▶ The *Creating a seamless noise texture* recipe

Creating a wood-grain effect

To create the look of wood, we can start by creating a virtual "log", with perfectly cylindrical growth rings. Then we'll take a slice of the log, and perturb the growth rings using noise from our noise texture.

The following image illustrates our virtual "log". It is aligned with the y-axis, and extends infinitely in all directions. The growth rings are aligned with integer distances from the y-axis. Each ring is given a darker color with lighter color in between rings. Each growth ring spans a narrow distance around the integer distances.

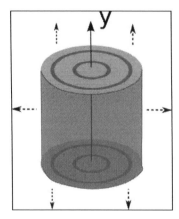

To take a "slice", we'll simply define a 2D region of the log's space based on the texture coordinates. Initially, the texture coordinates define a square region, with coordinates ranging from zero to one. We'll assume that the region is aligned with the x-y plane, so that the s coordinate corresponds to x, the t coordinate corresponds to y, and the value of z is zero. We can then transform this region in any way that suits our fancy, to create an arbitrary 2D slice.

After defining the slice, we'll determine the color based on the distance from the y-axis. However, before doing so, we'll perturb that distance based on a value from the noise texture. The result has a general look that is similar to real wood. The following image shows an example:

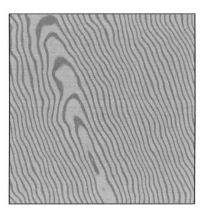

Getting ready

Set up your program to generate a noise texture and make it available to the shaders through the uniform variable `NoiseTex`.

There are three uniforms in the fragment shader that can be assigned from the OpenGL program. They are as follows:

- `LightWoodColor`: The lightest wood color
- `DarkWoodColor`: The darkest wood color
- `Slice`: A matrix that defines the slice of the virtual "log" and transforms the default region defined by the texture coordinates to some other arbitrary rectangular region

How to do it...

To create a shader program that generates a wood-grain effect using a noise texture, use the following steps:

1. Set up your vertex shader to pass the texture coordinate to the fragment shader via the variable `TexCoord`.

2. Use the following code for the fragment shader:

```
layout(binding=0) uniform sampler2D NoiseTex;

uniform vec4 DarkWoodColor = vec4( 0.8, 0.5, 0.1, 1.0 );
uniform vec4 LightWoodColor = vec4( 1.0, 0.75, 0.25, 1.0 );
uniform mat4 Slice;

in vec2 TexCoord;

layout ( location = 0 ) out vec4 FragColor;

void main()
{
   // Transform the texture coordinates to define the
   // "slice" of the log.
   vec4 cyl = Slice * vec4( TexCoord.st, 0.0, 1.0 );

   // The distance from the log's y axis.
   float dist = length(cyl.xz);

   // Perturb the distance using the noise texture
   vec4 noise = texture(NoiseTex, TexCoord);
   dist += noise.b;

   // Determine the color as a mixture of the light and
   // dark wood colors.
   float t = 1.0 - abs( fract( dist ) * 2.0 - 1.0 );
   t = smoothstep( 0.2, 0.5, t );
   vec4 color = mix( DarkWoodColor, LightWoodColor, t );

   FragColor = vec4( color.rgb , 1.0 );
}
```

How it works...

The first line of the `main` function within the fragment shader expands the texture coordinates to a 3D (homogeneous) value with a z coordinate of zero (s, t, 0, 1), and then transforms the value by the matrix `Slice`. This matrix can scale, translate, and/or rotate the texture coordinates to define the 2D region of the virtual "log".

One way to visualize this is to think of the slice as a 2D unit square embedded in the "log" with its lower-left corner at the origin. The matrix is then used to transform that square within the log to define a slice through the log. For example, I might just translate the square by (-0.5, -0.5, -0.5) and scale by 20 in x and y to get a slice through the middle of the log.

Next, the distance from the y-axis is determined by using the built-in `length` function (`length(cyl.xz)`). This will be used to determine how close we are to a growth ring. The color will be a light wood color if we are between growth rings, and a dark color when we are close to a growth ring. However, before determining the color, we perturb the distance slightly using a value from our noise texture by using the following line of code:

```
dist += noise.b;
```

The next step is just a bit of numerical trickery to determine the color based on how close we are to a whole number. We start by taking the fractional part of the distance (`fract(dist)`), multiplying by two, subtracting one, and taking the absolute value. As `fract(dist)` is a value between zero and one, multiplying by two, subtracting one, and taking the absolute value will result in a value that is also between zero and one. However, the value will range from 1.0 when `dist` is 0.0, to 0.0 when `dist` is 0.5, and back to 1.0 when `dist` is 1.0 (a "v" shape).

We then invert the "v" by subtracting from one, and storing the result in `t`. Next, we use the `smoothstep` function to create a somewhat sharp transition between the light and dark colors. In other words, we want a dark color when `t` is less than 0.2, a light color when it is greater than 0.5, and a smooth transition in between. The result is used to mix the light and dark colors via the GLSL `mix` function.

 The `smoothstep( a, b, x )` function works in the following way. It returns 0.0 when x<= a, 1.0 when x>= b and uses Hermite interpolation between 0 and 1 when x is between a and b.

The result of all of this is a narrow band of the dark color around integer distances, and a light color in between, with a rapid, but smooth transition.

Finally, we simply apply the final color to the fragment.

There's more...

A book-matched pair of boards is a pair that is cut from the same log and then glued together. The result is a larger board that has symmetry in the grain from one side to the other. We can approximate this effect by mirroring the texture coordinate. For example, we could use the following in place of the first line of the preceding `main` function:

```
vec2 tc = TexCoord;
if( tc.s > 0.5 ) tc.s = 1.0 - tc.s;
vec4 cyl = Slice * vec4( tc, 0.0, 1.0 );
```

The following image shows an example of the results:

> ▸   The *Creating a noise texture using GLM* recipe

Creating a disintegration effect

It is straightforward to use the GLSL `discard` keyword in combination with noise to simulate erosion or decay. We can simply discard fragments that correspond to a noise value that is above or below a certain threshold. The following image shows a teapot with this effect. Fragments are discarded when the noise value corresponding to the texture coordinate is outside a certain threshold range.

Getting ready

Set up your OpenGL program to provide position, normal, and texture coordinates to the shader. Be sure to pass the texture coordinate along to the fragment shader. Set up any uniforms needed to implement the shading model of your choice.

Create a seamless noise texture (see *Creating a seamless noise texture*), and place it in the appropriate texture channel.

The following uniforms are defined in the fragment shader, and should be set via the OpenGL program:

- ▶ `NoiseTex`: The noise texture.
- ▶ `LowThreshold`: Fragments are discarded if the noise value is below this value.
- ▶ `HighThreshold`: Fragments are discarded if the noise value is above this value.

How to do it...

To create a shader program that provides a disintegration effect, use the following steps:

1. Create a vertex shader that sends the texture coordinate to the fragment shader via the output variable `TexCoord`. It should also pass the position and normal to the fragment shader through the variables `Position` and `Normal`.

2. Use the following code for the fragment shader:

```
// Insert uniforms needed for the Phong shading model

layout(binding=0) uniform sampler2D NoiseTex;

in vec4 Position;
in vec3 Normal;
in vec2 TexCoord;

uniform float LowThreshold;
uniform float HighThreshold;

layout ( location = 0 ) out vec4 FragColor;

vec3 phongModel() {
   // Compute Phong shading model...
}
void main()
{
```

```
// Get the noise value at TexCoord
vec4 noise = texture ( NoiseTex, TexCoord );

// If the value is outside the threshold, discard
if ( noise.a < LowThreshold || noise.a > HighThreshold)
   discard;

// Color the fragment using the shading model
vec3 color = phongModel ();
FragColor = vec4 ( color , 1.0 );
}
```

How it works...

The fragment shader starts by retrieving a noise value from the noise texture (`NoiseTex`), and storing the result in the variable `noise`. We want noise that has a large amount of high-frequency fluctuation, so we choose four-octave noise, which is stored in the alpha channel (`noise.a`).

We then discard the fragment if the noise value is below `LowThreshold` or above `HighThreshold`. As the `discard` keyword causes the execution of the shader to stop, the following statements will not execute if the fragment is discarded.

 The discard operation can have a performance impact due to how it might affect early depth tests.

Finally, we compute the shading model and apply the result to the fragment.

See also

▶ The *Creating a seamless noise texture* recipe

Creating a paint-spatter effect

Using high-frequency noise, it is easy to create the effect of random spatters of paint on the surface of an object. The following image shows an example:

We use the noise texture to vary the color of the object, with a sharp transition between the base color and the paint color. We'll use either the base color or paint color as the diffuse reflectivity of the shading model. If the noise value is above a certain threshold, we'll use the paint color; otherwise, we'll use the base color of the object.

Getting ready

Start with a basic setup for rendering using the Phong shading model (or whatever model you prefer). Include texture coordinates and pass them along to the fragment shader.

There are a couple of uniform variables that define the parameters of the paint spatters:

- `PaintColor`: The color of the paint spatters
- `Threshold`: The minimum noise value where a spatter will appear

Create a noise texture with high-frequency noise.

Make your noise texture available to the fragment shader via the uniform sampler variable `NoiseTex`.

How to do it...

To create a shader program that generates a paint-spatter effect, use the following steps:

1. Create a vertex shader that sends the texture coordinates to the fragment shader via the output variable `TexCoord`. It should also pass the position and normal to the fragment shader through the variables `Position` and `Normal`.

2. Use the following code for the fragment shader:

```glsl
// Uniforms for the Phong shading model
uniform struct LightInfo {
   vec4 Position;
   vec3 Intensity;
} Light;

uniform struct MaterialInfo {
   vec3 Ka;
   vec3 Kd;
   vec3 Ks;
   float Shiniess;
} Material;

// The noise texture
layout(binding=0) uniform sampler2D NoiseTex;
// Input from the vertex shader
in vec4 Position;
in vec3 Normal;
in vec2 TexCoord;

// The paint-spatter uniforms
uniform vec3 PaintColor = vec3(1.0);
uniform float Threshold = 0.65;

layout ( location = 0 ) out vec4 FragColor;

vec3 phongModel(vec3 kd) {
   // Evaluate the Phong shading model
}

void main()
{
   vec4 noise = texture( NoiseTex, TexCoord );
   vec3 color = Material.Kd;
   if( noise.g> Threshold ) color = PaintColor;
   FragColor = vec4( phongModel(color) , 1.0 );
}
```

How it works...

The main function of the fragment shader retrieves a noise value from `NoiseTex`, and stores it in the variable `noise`. The next two lines set the variable `color` to either the base diffuse reflectivity (`Material.Kd`) or `PaintColor`, depending on whether or not the noise value is greater than the threshold value (`Threshold`). This will cause a sharp transition between the two colors and the size of the spatters will be related to the frequency of the noise.

Finally, the Phong shading model is evaluated using `color` as the diffuse reflectivity. The result is applied to the fragment.

There's more...

As indicated in the *Creating a noise texture using GLM* recipe using lower-frequency noise will cause the spatters to be larger in size and more spread out. A lower threshold will also increase the size without spreading over the surface, but as the threshold gets lower, it starts to look more uniform and less like random spattering.

See also

▸ The *Creating a seamless noise texture* recipe

Creating a night-vision effect

Noise can be useful to simulate static or other kinds of electronic interference effects. This recipe is a fun example of that. We'll create the look of night-vision goggles with some noise thrown in to simulate some random static in the signal. Just for fun, we'll also outline the scene in the classic "binocular" view. The following image shows an example:

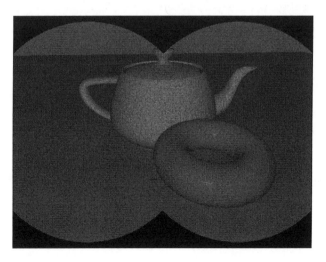

We'll apply the night-vision effect as a second pass to the rendered scene. The first pass will render the scene to a texture (see *Chapter 4, Using Textures*), and the second pass will apply the night-vision effect.

Getting ready

Create a Framebuffer Object (FBO) for the first pass. Attach a texture to the first color attachment of the FBO. For more information on how to do this, see *Chapter 4, Using Textures*.

Create and assign any uniform variables needed for the shading model. Set the following uniforms defined in the fragment shader:

- ▶ `Width`: The width of the viewport in pixels
- ▶ `Height`: The height of the viewport in pixels
- ▶ `Radius`: The radius of each circle in the "binocular" effect (in pixels)
- ▶ `RenderTex`: The texture containing the render from the first pass
- ▶ `NoiseTex`: The noise texture
- ▶ `RenderPass`: The subroutine uniform used to select the functionality for each pass

Create a noise texture with high-frequency noise, and make it available to the shader via `NoiseTex`. Associate the texture with the FBO available via `RenderTex`.

How to do it...

To create a shader program that generates a night-vision effect, use the following steps:

1. Set up your vertex shader to pass along the position, normal, and texture coordinates via the variables `Position`, `Normal`, and `TexCoord` respectively.

2. Use the following code for the fragment shader:

```
in vec3 Position;
in vec3 Normal;
in vec2 TexCoord;

uniform int Width;
uniform int Height;
uniform float Radius;
layout(binding=0) uniform sampler2D RenderTex;
layout(binding=1) uniform sampler2D NoiseTex;

subroutine vec4 RenderPassType();
subroutine uniform RenderPassType RenderPass;

// Define any uniforms needed for the shading model.
```

```
layout( location = 0 ) out vec4 FragColor;

vec3 phongModel( vec3 pos, vec3 norm )
{
  // Compute the Phong shading model
}

// Returns the relative luminance of the color value
float luminance( vec3 color ) {
  return dot( color.rgb, vec3(0.2126, 0.7152, 0.0722) );
}

subroutine (RenderPassType)
vec4 pass1()
{
  return vec4(phongModel( Position, Normal ),1.0);
}

subroutine( RenderPassType )
vec4 pass2()
{
  vec4 noise = texture(NoiseTex, TexCoord);
  vec4 color = texture(RenderTex, TexCoord);
  float green = luminance( color.rgb );

  float dist1 = length(gl_FragCoord.xy -
      vec2(Width*0.25, Height*0.5));
  float dist2 = length(gl_FragCoord.xy -
      vec2(3.0*Width*0.25, Height*0.5));
  if( dist1 > Radius && dist2 > Radius ) green = 0.0;

  return vec4(0.0, green * clamp(noise.a + 0.25, 0.0, 1.0),
      0.0 ,1.0);
}

void main()
{
  // This will call either pass1() or pass2()
  FragColor = RenderPass();
}
```

3. In the render function of your OpenGL program, use the following steps:

   1. Bind to the FBO that you set up for rendering the scene to a texture.

   2. Select the `pass1` subroutine function in the fragment shader via `RenderPass`.

   3. Render the scene.

4. Bind to the default FBO.

5. Select the `pass2` subroutine function in the fragment shader via `RenderPass`.

6. Draw a single quad that fills the viewport using texture coordinates that range from 0 to 1 in each direction.

How it works...

The fragment shader is broken into two subroutine functions, one for each pass. Within the `pass1` function, we simply apply the Phong shading model to the fragment. The result is written to the FBO, which contains a texture to be used in the second pass.

In the second pass, the `pass2` function is executed. We start by retrieving a noise value (`noise`), and the color from the render texture from the first pass (`color`). Then we compute the luminance value for the color and store that result in the variable `green`. This will eventually be used as the green component of the final color.

The next step involves determining whether or not the fragment is inside the "binocular" lenses. We compute the distance to the center of the left lens (`dist1`), which is located in the viewport halfway from top to bottom and one-quarter of the way from left to right. The right lens is located at the same vertical location, but three-quarters of the way from left to right. The distance from the center of the right-hand lens is stored in `dist2`. If both `dist1` and `dist2` are greater than the radius of the virtual lenses, then we set `green` to zero.

Finally, we return the final color, which has only a green component; the other two are set to zero. The value of `green` is multiplied by the noise value in order to add some noise to the image to simulate random interference in the signal. We add 0.25 to the noise value and clamp it between zero and one, in order to brighten the overall image. I have found that it appeared a bit too dark if the noise value wasn't biased in this way.

There's more...

It would make this shader even more effective if the noise varied in each frame during animation to simulate interference that is constantly changing. We can accomplish this roughly by modifying the texture coordinates used to access the noise texture in a time-dependent way. See the blog post mentioned in *See also* section for an example.

See also

▶ The *Rendering to a texture* recipe in *Chapter 4, Using Textures*

▶ The *Creating a noise texture using GLM* recipe

▶ This recipe was inspired by a blog post by Wojciech Toman: (`wtomandev.blogspot.com/2009/09/night-vision-effect.html`)

9
Particle Systems and Animation

In this chapter, we will cover:

- ▶ Animating a surface with vertex displacement
- ▶ Creating a particle fountain
- ▶ Creating a particle system using transform feedback
- ▶ Creating a particle system using instanced particles
- ▶ Simulating fire with particles
- ▶ Simulating smoke with particles

Introduction

Shaders provide us with the ability to leverage the massive parallelism offered by modern graphics processors. Since they have the ability to transform the vertex positions, they can be used to implement animation directly within the shaders themselves. This can provide a bump in efficiency if the animation algorithm can be parallelized appropriately for execution within the shader.

If a shader is to help with animation, it must not only compute the positions, but often we need to write the updated positions for use in the next frame. Shaders were not originally designed to write to arbitrary buffers (except of course the framebuffer). However, with recent versions, OpenGL provides the ability to do so via shader storage buffer objects and image load/store. As of OpenGL 3.0, we can also send the values of the vertex or geometry shader's output variables to an arbitrary buffer (or buffers). This feature is called **Transform Feedback**, and is particularly useful for particle systems.

In this chapter, we'll look at several examples of animation within shaders, focusing mostly on particle systems. The first example, animating with vertex displacement, demonstrates animation by transforming the vertex positions of an object based on a time-dependent function. In the *Creating a particle fountain* recipe, we create a simple particle system under constant acceleration. In the *Creating a particle system using transform feedback* recipe there is an example illustrating how to use OpenGL's transform feedback functionality within a particle system. The *Creating a particle system using instanced particles* recipe shows you how to animate many complex objects using instanced rendering.

The last two recipes demonstrate some particle systems for simulating complex real phenomena such as smoke and fire.

Animating a surface with vertex displacement

A straightforward way to leverage shaders for animation is to simply transform the vertices within the vertex shader based on some time-dependent function. The OpenGL application supplies static geometry, and the vertex shader modifies the geometry using the current time (supplied as a uniform variable). This moves the computation of the vertex position from the CPU to the GPU, and leverages whatever parallelism the graphics driver makes available.

In this example, we'll create a waving surface by transforming the vertices of a tessellated quad based on a sine wave. We'll send down the pipeline a set of triangles that make up a flat surface in the x-z plane. In the vertex shader we'll transform the y-coordinate of each vertex based on a time-dependent sine function, and compute the normal vector of the transformed vertex. The following image shows the desired result. (You'll have to imagine that the waves are travelling across the surface from left to right).

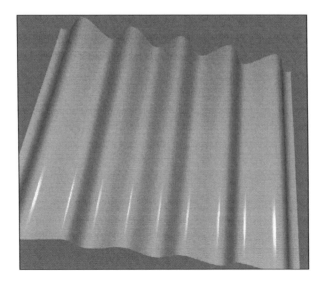

Alternatively, we could use a noise texture to animate the vertices (that make up the surface) based on a random function. (See *Chapter 8*, *Using Noise in Shaders,* for details on noise textures).

Before we jump into the code, let's take a look at the mathematics that we'll need.

We'll transform the y-coordinate of the surface as a function of the current time and the modeling x-coordinate. To do so, we'll use the basic plane wave equation as shown in the following diagram:

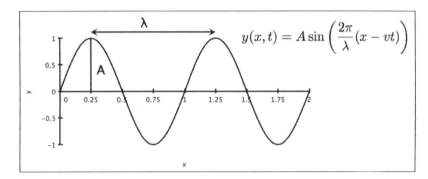

Where *A* is the wave's amplitude (the height of the peaks), lambda (λ) is the wavelength (the distance between successive peaks), and v is the wave's velocity. The previous image shows an example of the wave when $t = 0$ and the wavelength is equal to one. We'll configure these coefficients through uniform variables.

In order to render the surface with proper shading, we also need the normal vector at the transformed location. We can compute the normal vector using the (partial) derivative of the previous function. The result is the following equation:

$$\mathbf{n}(x, t) = \left(-A\frac{2\pi}{\lambda} \cos\left(\frac{2\pi}{\lambda}(x - vt)\right), 1 \right)$$

Of course, the previous vector should be normalized before using it in our shading model.

Getting ready

Set up your OpenGL application to render a flat, tessellated surface in the x-z plane. The results will look better if you use a large number of triangles. Also, keep track of the animation time using whatever method you prefer. Provide the current time to the vertex shader via the uniform variable `Time`.

The other important uniform variables are the coefficients of the previous wave equation.

> ▸ K: It is the wavenumber (2π/λ).

> ▸ Velocity: It is the wave's velocity.

> ▸ Amp: It is the wave's amplitude.

Set up your program to provide appropriate uniform variables for your chosen shading model.

How to do it...

Use the following steps:

1. Use the following code for the vertex shader:

```
layout (location = 0) in vec3 VertexPosition;

out vec4 Position;
out vec3 Normal;

uniform float Time;   // The animation time

// Wave parameters
uniform float K;          // Wavenumber
uniform float Velocity; // Wave's velocity
uniform float Amp;        // Wave's amplitude

uniform mat4 ModelViewMatrix;
uniform mat3 NormalMatrix;
uniform mat4 MVP;

void main()
{
  vec4 pos = vec4(VertexPosition,1.0);

  // Translate the y coordinate
  float u = K * (pos.x - Velocity * Time);
  pos.y = Amp * sin( u );

  // Compute the normal vector
  vec3 n = vec3(0.0);
  n.xy = normalize(vec2(-K * Amp *cos( u ), 1.0));

  // Send position and normal (in camera cords) to frag.
  Position = ModelViewMatrix * pos;
  Normal = NormalMatrix * n;

  // The position in clip coordinates
  gl_Position = MVP * pos;
}
```

2. Create a fragment shader that computes the fragment color based on the variables `Position` and `Normal` using whatever shading model you choose (see the *Using per-fragment shading for improved realism* recipe in *Chapter 3, Lighting, Shading, and Optimizations*).

How it works...

The vertex shader takes the position of the vertex and updates the y-coordinate using the wave equation discussed previously. After the first three statements, the variable `pos` is just a copy of the input variable `VertexPosition` with the modified y-coordinate.

We then compute the normal vector using the previous equation, normalize the result and store it in the variable `n`. Since the wave is really just a two-dimensional wave (doesn't depend on z), the z component of the normal vector will be zero.

Finally we pass along the new position and normal to the fragment shader after converting to camera coordinates. As usual, we also pass the position in clip coordinates to the built-in variable `gl_Position`.

There's more...

Modifying the vertex position within the vertex shader is a straightforward way to offload some computation from the CPU to the GPU. It also eliminates the possible need to transfer vertex buffers between the GPU memory and main memory in order to modify the positions.

The main disadvantage is that the updated positions are not available on the CPU side. For example, they might be needed for additional processing (such as collision detection). However, there are a number of ways to provide this data back to the CPU. One technique might be clever use of FBOs to receive the updated positions from the fragment shader. In a following recipe, we'll look at another technique that makes use of a newer OpenGL feature called transform feedback.

See also

▶ The *Using per-fragment shading for improved realism* recipe in *Chapter 3, Lighting, Shading, and Optimization*

Creating a particle fountain

In computer graphics, a particle system is a group of objects that are used to simulate a variety of "fuzzy" systems like smoke, liquid spray, fire, explosions, or other similar phenomena. Each particle is considered to be a point object with a position, but no size. Often, they are rendered as point sprites (using the GL_POINTS primitive mode), but could also be rendered as camera aligned quads or triangles. Each particle has a lifetime: it is born, animates according to a set of rules, and then dies. The particle can then be resurrected and go through the entire process again. Generally particles do not interact with other particles, or reflect light. The particle is often rendered as a single, textured, camera-facing quad with transparency.

During the lifetime of a particle, it is animated according to a set of rules. These rules often include the basic kinematic equations that define the movement of a particle that is subjected to constant acceleration (such as a gravitational field). In addition, we might take into account things like wind, friction or other factors. The particle may also change shape or transparency during its lifetime. Once the particle has reached a certain age (or position), it is considered to be "dead" and can be "recycled" and used again.

In this example, we'll implement a relatively simple particle system that has the look of a fountain of water. For simplicity, the particles in this example will not be "recycled." Once they have reached the end of their lifetime, we'll draw them as fully transparent so that they are effectively invisible. This gives the fountain a finite lifetime, as if it only has a limited supply of material. In later recipes, we'll see some ways to improve this system by recycling particles.

The following sequence of images shows several successive frames from the output of this simple particle system.

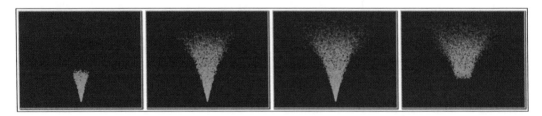

To animate the particles, we'll use the standard kinematics equation for objects under constant acceleration.

$$P(t) = P_0 + \mathbf{v}_0 t + \frac{1}{2}\mathbf{a}t^2$$

The previous equation describes the position of a particle at time **t**. $\mathbf{P_0}$ is the initial position, v_0 is the initial velocity, and a is the acceleration.

We'll define the initial position of all particles to be the origin (0,0,0). The initial velocity will be determined randomly within a range of values. Each particle will be created at a slightly different time, so the time that we use in the previous equation will be relative to the start time for the particle.

Since the initial position is the same for all particles, we won't need to provide it as an input attribute to the shader. Instead, we'll just provide two other vertex attributes: the initial velocity and the start time (the particle's time of "birth"). Prior to the particle's birth time, we'll render it completely transparent. During its lifetime, the particle's position will be determined using the previous equation with a value for _t_ that is relative to the particle's start time (`Time - StartTime`).

We'll render each particle as a textured point sprite (using `GL_POINTS`). It is easy to apply a texture to a point sprite because OpenGL will automatically generate texture coordinates and make them available to the fragment shader via the built-in variable `gl_PointCoord`. We'll also increase the transparency of the point sprite linearly with the age of the particle, to make the particle appear to fade out as it animates.

Getting ready

We'll create two buffers (or a single interleaved buffer) to store the input to the vertex shader. The first buffer will store the initial velocity for each particle. We'll choose the values randomly from a limited range of possible vectors. To create the vertical "cone" of particles in the previous image, we'll choose randomly from a set of vectors within the cone. The following code is one way to do this:

```
vec3 v(0.0f);
float velocity, theta, phi;
GLfloat *data = new GLfloat[nParticles * 3];
for( unsigned int i = 0; i < nParticles; i++ ) {
  // Pick the direction of the velocity
  theta = glm::mix(0.0f, (float)PI / 6.0f, randFloat());
  phi = glm::mix(0.0f, (float)TWOPI, randFloat());

  v.x = sinf(theta) * cosf(phi);
  v.y = cosf(theta);
  v.z = sinf(theta) * sinf(phi);

  // Scale to set the magnitude of the velocity (speed)
  velocity = glm::mix(1.25f,1.5f,randFloat());
  v = v * velocity;

  data[3*i]   = v.x;
  data[3*i+1] = v.y;
  data[3*i+2] = v.z;
```

```
    }
    glBindBuffer(GL_ARRAY_BUFFER, initVel);
    glBufferSubData(GL_ARRAY_BUFFER, 0,
                    nParticles * 3 * sizeof(float), data);
```

In the previous code the `randFloat` function returns a random value between zero and one. We pick random numbers within a range of possible values by using the GLM `mix` function, (the GLM `mix` function works the same as the corresponding GLSL function. It performs a linear interpolation between the values of the first two arguments). Here, we choose a random `float` between zero and one and use that value to interpolate between the endpoints of our range.

To pick vectors from within our cone, we utilize spherical coordinates. The value of `theta` determines the angle between the center of the cone and the outer edge. The value of `phi` defines the possible directions around the y-axis for a given value of `theta`. For more on spherical coordinates, grab your favorite math book.

Once a direction is chosen, the vector is scaled to have a magnitude between 1.25 and 1.5. This is a range that seems to work well for the desired effect. The magnitude of the velocity vector is the overall speed of the particle, and we can tweak this range to get a wider variety of speeds or faster/slower particles.

The last three lines in the loop assign the vector to the appropriate location in the array `data`. After the loop, we copy the data into the buffer referred to by `initVel`. Set up this buffer to provide data for vertex attribute zero.

In the second buffer, we'll store the start time for each particle. This will provide only a single float per vertex (particle). For this example, we'll just create each particle in succession at a fixed rate. The following code will set up a buffer with each particle created 0.00075 seconds after the previous one.

```
    float * data = new GLfloat[nParticles];
    float time = 0.0f, rate = 0.00075f;

    for( unsigned int i = 0; i < nParticles; i++ ) {
      data[i] = time;
      time += rate;
    }
    glBindBuffer(GL_ARRAY_BUFFER,startTime);
    glBufferSubData(GL_ARRAY_BUFFER, 0, nParticles * sizeof(float), data);
```

This code simply creates an array of floats that starts at zero and gets incremented by `rate`. The array is then copied into the buffer referred to by `startTime`. Set this buffer to be the input for vertex attribute one.

Set the following uniform variables from within the OpenGL program:

- ▸ `ParticleTex`: It is the particle's texture.
- ▸ `Time`: It is the amount of time that has elapsed since the animation began.
- ▸ `Gravity`: It is the vector representing one half of the acceleration in the previous equation.
- ▸ `ParticleLifetime`: It defines how long a particle survives after it is created.

Make sure that the depth test is off, and enable alpha blending using the following statements:

```
glDisable(GL_DEPTH_TEST);
glEnable(GL_BLEND);
glBlendFunc(GL_SRC_ALPHA, GL_ONE_MINUS_SRC_ALPHA);
```

You will also want to choose a reasonable size for each point sprite. For example, the following line sets it to 10 pixels:

```
glPointSize(10.0f);
```

How to do it...

Use the following code for the vertex shader:

```
// Initial velocity and start time
layout (location = 0) in vec3 VertexInitVel;
layout (location = 1) in float StartTime;

out float Transp;  // Transparency of the particle

uniform float Time;  // Animation time
uniform vec3 Gravity = vec3(0.0,-0.05,0.0);  // world coords
uniform float ParticleLifetime;  // Max particle lifetime

uniform mat4 MVP;

void main()
{
  // Assume the initial position is (0,0,0).
  vec3 pos = vec3(0.0);
  Transp = 0.0;

  // Particle doesn't exist until the start time
  if( Time > StartTime ) {
    float t = Time - StartTime;
```

```
        if( t < ParticleLifetime ) {
           pos = VertexInitVel * t + Gravity * t * t;
           Transp = 1.0 - t / ParticleLifetime;
        }
     }

     gl_Position = MVP * vec4(pos, 1.0);
}
```

Use the following code for the fragment shader:

```
in float Transp;
uniform sampler2D ParticleTex;

layout ( location = 0 ) out vec4 FragColor;

void main()
{
   FragColor = texture(ParticleTex, gl_PointCoord);
   FragColor.a *= Transp;
}
```

How it works...

The vertex shader receives the particle's initial velocity (`VertexInitVel`) and start time (`StartTime`) in its two input attributes. The variable `Time` stores the amount of time that has elapsed since the beginning of the animation. The output variable `Transp` is the overall transparency of the particle.

In the main function of the vertex shader, we start by setting the initial position to the modeling origin (0,0,0), and the transparency to `0.0` (fully transparent). The following `if` statement determines whether the particle is alive yet. If the current time is greater than the start time for the particle, the particle is alive, otherwise, the particle has yet to be "born". In the latter case, the position remains at the origin and the particle is rendered fully transparent.

If the particle is alive, we determine the "age" of the particle by subtracting the start time from the current time, and storing the result in the variable `t`. If t is greater than or equal to the lifetime for a particle (`ParticleLifetime`), the particle has already fully evolved through its animation and is rendered fully transparent. Otherwise, the particle is still active and the body of the inner `if` statement executes, which is responsible for animating the particle.

If the particle is alive, the position (`pos`) is determined using the kinematic equation described previously. The transparency is determined by linearly interpolating based on the particle's age.

```
   Transp = 1.0 - t / ParticleLifetime;
```

When the particle is born it is fully opaque, and linearly becomes transparent as it ages. The value of `Transp` is 1.0 at birth and 0.0 at the end of the particle's lifetime.

In the fragment shader, we color the fragment with the result of value of a texture lookup. Since we are rendering `GL_POINT` primitives, the texture coordinate is determined automatically by OpenGL and is available in the built-in variable `gl_PointCoord`. Before finishing, we multiply the alpha value of the final color by the variable `Transp`, in order to scale the overall transparency of the particle based on the particle's age (as determined in the vertex shader).

There's more...

This example is meant to be a fairly gentle introduction to GPU-based particle systems. There are many things that could be done to improve the power and flexibility of this system. For example, we could vary the size or rotation of the particles as they progress through their lifetime to produce different effects.

We could also create a better indication of distance by varying the size of the particles with the distance from the camera. This could be accomplished by defining the point size within the vertex shader using the built-in variable `gl_PointSize`, or drawing quads or triangles instead of points.

> While point sprites (via `GL_POINTS`) are an obvious choice for particles, they also have several drawbacks. First, hardware often has fairly low limits on point size. If particles need to be large, or change size over time, the limits might be a severe restriction. Second, points are usually clipped when their center moves outside of the view volume. This can cause "popping" artefacts when the particles have a significant size. A common solution is to draw quads or triangles instead of points, using a technique like the one outlined in *Chapter 6, Using Geometry and Tessellation Shaders*.

One of the most significant drawbacks of the technique of this recipe is that the particles can't be recycled easily. When a particle dies, it is simply rendered as transparent. It would be nice to be able to re-use each dead particle to create an apparently continuous stream of particles. Additionally, it would be useful to be able to have the particles respond appropriately to changing accelerations or modifications of the system (for example wind or movement of the source). With the system described here, we couldn't do so because we are working with a single equation that defines the movement of the particle for all time. What would be needed is to incrementally update the positions based on the current forces involved (a simulation).

In order to accomplish the previous objective, we need some way to feed the output of the vertex shader (the particle's updated positions) back into the input of the vertex shader during the next frame. This would of course be simple if we weren't doing the simulation within the shader because we could simply update the positions of the primitives directly before rendering. However, since we are doing the work within the vertex shader we are limited in the ways that we can write to memory.

In the following recipe, we'll see an example of how to use a new OpenGL feature called **transform feedback** to accomplish exactly what was just described. We can designate certain output variables to be sent to buffers that can be read as input in subsequent rendering passes.

See also

- The *Animating a surface with vertex displacement* recipe
- The *Creating a particle system using transform feedback* recipe

Creating a particle system using transform feedback

Transform Feedback provides a way to capture the output of the vertex (or geometry) shader to a buffer for use in subsequent passes. Originally introduced into OpenGL with version 3.0, this feature is particularly well suited for particle systems because among other things, it enables us to do discrete simulations. We can update a particle's position within the vertex shader and render that updated position in a subsequent pass (or the same pass). Then the updated positions can be used in the same way as input to the next frame of animation.

In this example, we'll implement the same particle system from the previous recipe (*Creating a particle fountain*), this time making use of transform feedback. Instead of using an equation that describes the particle's motion for all time, we'll update the particle positions incrementally, solving the equations of motion based on the forces involved at the time each frame is rendered.

A common technique is to make use of the **Euler method**, which approximates the position and velocity at time t based on the position, velocity, and acceleration at an earlier time.

$$P_{n+1} = P_n + \mathbf{v}_n h$$
$$\mathbf{v}_{n+1} = \mathbf{v}_n + \mathbf{a}_n h$$

In the previous equation the subscripts represent the time step (or animation frame), P is the particle position, and v is the particle velocity. The equations describe the position and velocity at frame $n + 1$ as a function of the position and velocity during the previous frame (n). The variable h represents the time step size, or the amount of time that has elapsed between frames. The term a_n represents the instantaneous acceleration that is computed based on the positions of the particles. For our simulation, this will be a constant value, but in general it might be a value that changes depending on the environment (wind, collisions, inter-particle interactions, and so on).

 The Euler method is actually numerically integrating the Newtonian equation of motion. It is one of the simplest techniques for doing so. However, it is a first-order technique, which means that it can introduce a significant amount of error. More accurate techniques include **Verlet integration**, and **Runge-Kutta integration**. Since our particle simulation is designed to look good and physical accuracy is not of high importance, the Euler method should suffice.

To make our simulation work, we'll use a technique sometimes called buffer "ping-ponging." We maintain two sets of vertex buffers and swap their uses each frame. For example, we use buffer A to provide the positions and velocities as input to the vertex shader. The vertex shader updates the positions and velocities using the Euler method and sends the results to buffer B using transform feedback. Then in a second pass, we render the particles using buffer B.

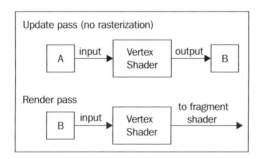

In the next frame of animation, we repeat the same process, swapping the two buffers.

In general, transform feedback allows us to define a set of shader output variables that are to be written to a designated buffer (or set of buffers). There are several steps involved that will be demonstrated, but the basic idea is as follows. Just before the shader program is linked, we define the relationship between buffers and shader output variables using the function `glTransformFeedbackVaryings`. During rendering, we initiate a transform feedback pass. We bind the appropriate buffers to the transform feedback binding points. (If desired, we can disable rasterization so that the particles are not rendered.) We enable transform feedback using the function `glBeginTransformFeedback` and then draw the point primitives. The output from the vertex shader will be stored in the appropriate buffers. Then we disable transform feedback by calling `glEndTransformFeedback`.

Getting ready

Create and allocate three pairs of buffers. The first pair will be for the particle positions, the second for the particle velocities, and the third for the "start time" for each particle (the time when the particle comes to life). For clarity, we'll refer to the first buffer in each pair as the A buffer, and the second as the B buffer. Also, we'll need a single buffer to contain the initial velocity for each particle.

Create two vertex arrays. The first vertex array should link the A position buffer with the first vertex attribute (attribute index 0), the A velocity buffer with vertex attribute one, the A start time buffer with vertex attribute two, and the initial velocity buffer with vertex attribute three. The second vertex array should be set up in the same way using the B buffers and the same initial velocity buffer. In the following code, the handles to the two vertex arrays will be accessed via the `GLuint` array named `particleArray`.

Initialize the A buffers with appropriate initial values. For example, all of the positions could be set to the origin, and the velocities and start times could be initialized in the same way as described in the previous recipe *Creating a particle fountain*. The initial velocity buffer could simply be a copy of the velocity buffer.

When using transform feedback, we define the buffers that will receive the output data from the vertex shader by binding the buffers to the indexed binding points under the `GL_TRANSFORM_FEEDBACK_BUFFER` target. The index corresponds to the index of the vertex shader's output variable as defined by `glTransformFeedbackVaryings`.

To help simplify things, we'll make use of transform feedback objects. Use the following code to set up two transform feedback objects for each set of buffers:

```
GLuint feedback[2];  // Transform feedback objects
GLuint posBuf[2];    // Position buffers (A and B)
GLuint velBuf[2];    // Velocity buffers (A and B)
GLuint startTime[2]; // Start time buffers (A and B)

// Create and allocate buffers A and B for posBuf, velBuf
// and startTime
```

```
// Setup the feedback objects
glGenTransformFeedbacks(2, feedback);

// Transform feedback 0
glBindTransformFeedback(GL_TRANSFORM_FEEDBACK, feedback[0]);
glBindBufferBase(GL_TRANSFORM_FEEDBACK_BUFFER,0,posBuf[0]);
glBindBufferBase(GL_TRANSFORM_FEEDBACK_BUFFER,1,velBuf[0]);
glBindBufferBase(GL_TRANSFORM_FEEDBACK_BUFFER,2,startTime[0]);

// Transform feedback 1
glBindTransformFeedback(GL_TRANSFORM_FEEDBACK, feedback[1]);
glBindBufferBase(GL_TRANSFORM_FEEDBACK_BUFFER,0,posBuf[1]);
glBindBufferBase(GL_TRANSFORM_FEEDBACK_BUFFER,1,velBuf[1]);
glBindBufferBase(GL_TRANSFORM_FEEDBACK_BUFFER,2,startTime[1]);
```

Similar to vertex arrays, transform feedback objects store the buffer bindings for the GL_TRANSFORM_FEEDBACK_BUFFER binding point so that they can be reset quickly at a later time. In the previous code, we create two transform feedback objects, and store their handles in the array named feedback. For the first object, we bind posBuf[0] to index 0, velBuf[0] to index 1 and startTime[0] to index 2 of the binding point (buffer set A). These bindings are connected to the shader output variables with glTransformFeedbackVaryings (or via a layout qualifier, see the *There's More* following section). The last argument for each is the buffer's handle. For the second object, we do the same thing using the buffer set B.

Once this is set up, we can define the set of buffers to receive the vertex shader's output, by binding to one or the other transform feedback object.

The uniform variables that need to be set are the following:

- ▶ ParticleTex: It is the texture to apply to the point sprites.
- ▶ Time: It defines the simulation time.
- ▶ H: It defines the elapsed time between animation frames.
- ▶ Accel: It is used to define the acceleration.
- ▶ ParticleLifetime: It defines the length of time that a particle exists before it is recycled.

How to do it...

Use the following steps:

1. Use the following code for your vertex shader:

    ```
    subroutine void RenderPassType();
    subroutine uniform RenderPassTypeRenderPass;

    layout (location = 0) in vec3 VertexPosition;
    ```

```glsl
layout (location = 1) in vec3 VertexVelocity;
layout (location = 2) in float VertexStartTime;
layout (location = 3) in vec3 VertexInitialVelocity;

out vec3 Position;    // To transform feedback
out vec3 Velocity;    // To transform feedback
out float StartTime;  // To transform feedback
out float Transp;     // To fragment shader

uniform float Time;   // Simulation time
uniform float H;      // Elapsed time between frames
uniform vec3 Accel;   // Particle acceleration
uniform float ParticleLifetime;   // Particle lifespan

uniform mat4 MVP;

subroutine (RenderPassType)
void update() {

  Position = VertexPosition;
  Velocity = VertexVelocity;
  StartTime = VertexStartTime;

  if( Time >= StartTime ) {
    float age = Time - StartTime;
    if( age >ParticleLifetime ) {
      // The particle is past its lifetime, recycle.
      Position = vec3(0.0);
      Velocity = VertexInitialVelocity;
      StartTime = Time;
    } else {
      // The particle is alive, update.
      Position += Velocity * H;
      Velocity += Accel * H;
    }
  }
}

subroutine (RenderPassType)
void render() {
  float age = Time - VertexStartTime;
  Transp = 1.0 - age / ParticleLifetime;
  gl_Position = MVP * vec4(VertexPosition, 1.0);
}

void main()
{
  // This will call either render() or update()
  RenderPass();
}
```

2. Use the following code for the fragment shader:

```
uniform sampler2D ParticleTex;
in float Transp;
layout ( location = 0 ) out vec4 FragColor;

void main()
{
   FragColor = texture(ParticleTex, gl_PointCoord);
   FragColor.a *= Transp;
}
```

3. After compiling the shader program, but before linking, use the following code to set up the connection between vertex shader output variables and output buffers:

```
const char * outputNames[] = { "Position", "Velocity",
   "StartTime" };
glTransformFeedbackVaryings(progHandle, 3, outputNames,
   GL_SEPARATE_ATTRIBS);
```

4. In the OpenGL render function, send the particle positions to the vertex shader for updating, and capture the results using transform feedback. The input to the vertex shader will come from buffer A, and the output will be stored in buffer B. During this pass we enable GL_RASTERIZER_DISCARD so that nothing is actually rendered to the framebuffer:

```
// Select the subroutine for particle updating
glUniformSubroutinesuiv(GL_VERTEX_SHADER, 1, &updateSub);

// Set the uniforms: H and Time
...

// Disable rendering
glEnable(GL_RASTERIZER_DISCARD);

// Bind the feedback obj. for the buffers to be drawn
glBindTransformFeedback(GL_TRANSFORM_FEEDBACK,
   feedback[drawBuf]);

// Draw points from input buffer with transform feedback
glBeginTransformFeedback(GL_POINTS);
glBindVertexArray(particleArray[1-drawBuf]);
glDrawArrays(GL_POINTS, 0, nParticles);
glEndTransformFeedback();
```

5. Render the particles at their updated positions using buffer B as input to the vertex shader:

```
// Enable rendering
glDisable(GL_RASTERIZER_DISCARD);

glUniformSubroutinesuiv(GL_VERTEX_SHADER, 1, &renderSub);
glClear( GL_COLOR_BUFFER_BIT );

// Initialize uniforms for transform matrices if needed
...

// Draw the sprites from the feedback buffer
glBindVertexArray(particleArray[drawBuf]);
glDrawTransformFeedback(GL_POINTS, feedback[drawBuf]);
```

6. Swap the purposes of the buffers:

```
// Swap buffers
drawBuf = 1 - drawBuf;
```

How it works...

There's quite a bit here to sort through. Let's start with the vertex shader.

The vertex shader is broken up into two subroutine functions. The `update` function is used during the first pass, and uses Euler's method to update the position and velocity of the particle. The `render` function is used during the second pass. It computes the transparency based on the age of the particle and sends the position and transparency along to the fragment shader.

The vertex shader has four output variables. The first three: `Position`, `Velocity`, and `StartTime` are used in the first pass to write to the feedback buffers. The fourth (`Transp`) is used during the second pass as input to the fragment shader.

The update function just updates the particle position and velocity using Euler's method unless the particle is not alive yet, or has passed its lifetime. If its age is greater than the lifetime of a particle, we recycle the particle by resetting its position to the origin, updating the particle's start time to the current time (`Time`), and setting its velocity to its original initial velocity (provided via input attribute `VertexInitialVelocity`).

The render function computes the particle's age and uses it to determine the transparency of the particle, assigning the result to the output variable `Transp`. It transforms the particle's position into clip coordinates and places the result in the built-in output variable `gl_Position`.

The fragment shader (step 2) is only utilized during the second pass. It colors the fragment based on the texture `ParticleTex` and the transparency delivered from the vertex shader (`Transp`).

The code segment in step 3 is placed prior to linking the shader program is responsible for setting up the correspondence between shader output variables and feedback buffers (buffers that are bound to indices of the `GL_TRANSFORM_FEEDBACK_BUFFER` binding point). The function `glTransformFeedbackVaryings` takes three arguments. The first is the handle to the shader program object. The second is the number of output variable names that will be provided. The third is an array of output variable names. The order of the names in this list corresponds to the indices of the feedback buffers. In this case, `Position` corresponds to index zero, `Velocity` to index one, and `StartTime` to index two. Check back to the previous code that creates our feedback buffer objects (the `glBindBufferBase` calls) to verify that this is indeed the case.

> `glTransformFeedbackVaryings` can be used to send data into an interleaved buffer instead (rather than separate buffers for each variable). Take a look at the OpenGL documentation for details.

The previous steps 4 through 6 describes how you might implement the render function within the main OpenGL program. In this example, there two important GLuint arrays: `feedback` and `particleArray`. They are each of size two and contain the handles to the two feedback buffer objects, and the two vertex array objects respectively. The variable `drawBuf` is just an integer used to alternate between the two sets of buffers. At any given frame, `drawBuf` will be either zero or one.

The code begins in step 4 by selecting the `update` subroutine to enable the update functionality within the vertex shader, and then setting the uniforms `Time` and `H`. The next call, `glEnable(GL_RASTERIZER_DISCARD)`, turns rasterization off so that nothing is rendered during this pass. The call to `glBindTransformFeedback` selects the set of buffers corresponding to the variable `drawBuf`, as the target for the transform feedback output.

Before drawing the points (and thereby triggering our vertex shader), we call `glBeginTransformFeedback` to enable transform feedback. The argument is the kind of primitives that will be sent down the pipeline (in our case `GL_POINTS`). Output from the vertex (or geometry) shader will go to the buffers that are bound to the `GL_TRANSFORM_FEEDBACK_BUFFER` binding point until `glEndTransformFeedback` is called. In this case, we bind the vertex array corresponding to `1 - drawBuf` (if `drawBuf` is 0, we use 1 and vice versa) and draw the particles.

At the end of the update pass (step 5), we re-enable rasterization with `glEnable (GL_RASTERIZER_DISCARD)`, and move on to the render pass.

The render pass is straightforward; we just select the render subroutine, and draw the particles from the vertex array corresponding to `drawBuf`. However, instead of using `glDrawArrays`, we use the function `glDrawTransformFeedback`. The latter is used here because it is designed for use with transform feedback. A transform feedback object keeps track of the number of vertices that were written. A call to `glDrawTransformFeedback` takes the feedback object as the third parameter. It uses the number of vertices that were written to that object as the number of vertices to draw. In essence it is equivalent to calling `glDrawArrays` with a value of zero for the second parameter and the count taken from the transform feedback.

Finally, at the end of the render pass (step 6), we swap our buffers by setting `drawBuf` to `1 - drawBuf`.

There's more...

You might be wondering why it was necessary to do this in two passes. Why couldn't we just keep the fragment shader active and do the render and update in the same pass? This is certainly possible for this example, and would be more efficient. However, I've chosen to demonstrate it this way because it is probably the more common way of doing this in general. Particles are usually just one part of a larger scene, and the particle update logic is not needed for most of the scene. Therefore, in most real-world situations it will make sense to do the particle update in a pass prior to the rendering pass so that the particle update logic can be decoupled from the rendering logic.

Using layout qualifiers

OpenGL 4.4 introduced layout qualifiers that make it possible to specify the relationship between the shader output variables and feedback buffers directly within the shader instead of using `glTransformFeedbackVaryings`. The layout qualifiers `xfb_buffer`, `xfb_stride`, and `xfb_offset` can be specified for each output variable that is to be used with transform feedback.

Querying transform feedback results

It is often useful to determine how many primitives were written during transform feedback pass. For example, if a geometry shader was active, the number of primitives written could be different than the number of primitives that were sent down the pipeline.

OpenGL provides a way to query for this information using query objects. To do so, start by creating a query object:

```
GLuint query;
glGenQueries(1, &query);
```

Then, prior to starting the transform feedback pass, start the counting process using the following command:

```
glBeginQuery(GL_TRANSFORM_FEEDBACK_PRIMITIVES_WRITTEN, query);
```

After the end of the transform feedback pass, call `glEndQuery` to stop counting:

```
glEndQuery(GL_TRANSFORM_FEEDBACK_PRIMITIVES_WRITTEN);
```

Then we can get the number of primitives using the following code:

```
GLuintprimWritten;
glGetQueryObjectuiv(query, GL_QUERY_RESULT, &primWritten);
printf("Primitives written: %d\n", primWritten);
```

Recycling particles

In this example, we recycled particles by resetting their position and initial velocity. This can cause the particles to begin to "clump" together over time. It would produce better results to generate a new random velocity and perhaps a random position (depending on the desired results). Unfortunately, there is currently no support for random number generation within shader programs. The solution might be to create your own random number generator function, use a texture with random values, or use a noise texture (see *Chapter 8, Using Noise in Shaders*).

See also

▸ The *Creating a particle fountain* recipe

Creating a particle system using instanced particles

To give more geometric detail to each particle in a particle system, we can make use of OpenGL's support for **instanced rendering**. Instanced rendering is a convenient and efficient way to draw several copies of a particular object. OpenGL provides support for instanced rendering through the functions `glDrawArraysInstanced` and `glDrawElementsInstanced`.

In this example, we'll modify the particle system introduced in the previous recipes. Rather than using point sprites, we'll render a more complex object in the place of each particle. The following image shows an example where each particle is rendered as a shaded torus.

Using instanced rendering is simply a matter of calling one of the instanced draw functions, providing the number of instances to draw. However, there is some subtlety to the way that we provide vertex attributes to the shader. If all particles were drawn with exactly the same attributes, it would be simple to draw, but would hardly be an interesting result because all particles would appear at the same location and in the same orientation. Since we'd like to draw each copy in a different position, we need some way of providing the needed information (in our case, the particle's start time) to the vertex shader separately for each particle.

The key to this is the function `glVertexAttribDivisor`. This function specifies the rate at which vertex attributes are advanced during instanced rendering. For example, consider the following setting.

```
glVertexAttribDivisor(1, 1);
```

The first argument is the vertex attribute index, and the second is the number of instances that will pass between updates of the attribute. In other words, the previous command specifies that all vertices of the first instance will receive the first value in the buffer corresponding to attribute one. The second instance will receive the second value, and so on. If the second argument was 2, then the first two instances would receive the first value, the next two would receive the second, and so on in the same way.

The default divisor for each attribute is zero, which means that vertex attributes are processed normally (the attribute advances once per vertex rather than some number per instance). An attribute is called an **instanced attribute** if its divisor is non-zero.

Getting ready

Start with a particle system as described in *Creating a particle fountain*. We'll just make a few modifications to that basic system. Note that you can also use this with transform feedback if desired, but to keep things simple, we'll use the more basic particle system. It should be straightforward to adapt this example to the transform feedback based system.

When setting up the vertex array object for your particle shape, add two new instanced attributes for the initial velocity and start time. Something similar to the following code should do the trick:

```
glBindVertexArray(myVArray);

// Set up the pointers for attributes 0, 1, and 2 (position,
//    normal, and texture coord.)
...

// Initial velocity (attribute 3)
glBindBuffer(GL_ARRAY_BUFFER, initVel);
glVertexAttribPointer(3, 3, GL_FLOAT, GL_FALSE, 0, NULL);
glEnableVertexAttribArray(3);
glVertexAttribDivisor(3, 1);

// Start time (attribute 4)
glBindBuffer(GL_ARRAY_BUFFER, startTime);
glVertexAttribPointer(4, 1, GL_FLOAT, GL_FALSE, 0, NULL);
glEnableVertexAttribArray(4);
glVertexAttribDivisor(4, 1);

// Bind to the element array buffer if necessary
```

Note the use of `glVertexAttribDivisor` in the previous code. This indicates that attributes 3 and 4 are instanced attributes (the values in the arrays are to be advanced only once per instance, rather than once per vertex). Therefore the size of the buffers must be proportional to the number of instances rather than the number of vertices in an instance. The buffers for attributes 0, 1 and 2 should (as usual) be sized in relation to the number of vertices.

> The value of the vertex attribute divisor becomes part of the vertex array object's state, so that just like the other elements of the VAO's state, we can reset it at a later point by binding to the VAO.

How to do it...

Use the following steps:

1. The vertex shader code is nearly identical to the code shown in the previous recipe *Creating a particle fountain*. The difference lies in the input and output variables. Use something similar to the following:

```
layout (location = 0) in vec3 VertexPosition;
layout (location = 1) in vec3 VertexNormal;
layout (location = 2) in vec3 VertexTexCoord;
layout (location = 3) in vec3 VertexInitialVelocity;
layout (location = 4) in float StartTime;

out vec3 Position;
out vec3 Normal;
```

2. Within the `main` function, update the position of the vertex by translating it using the equation of motion:

```
Position = VertexPosition + VertexInitialVelocity * t +
           Gravity * t * t;
```

3. Be sure to pass along the normal, and updated position (in camera coordinates) to the fragment shader.

4. In the fragment shader, implement your favorite shading model.

5. In the main OpenGL program, within the render function, render the instances using the following code:

```
glBindVertexArray(myVArray);
glDrawElementsInstanced(GL_TRIANGLES, nEls,
           GL_UNSIGNED_INT, 0, nParticles);
```

How it works...

Recall that the first three input attributes to the vertex shader are not-instanced, meaning that they are advanced every vertex (and repeated every instance). The last two (attributes 3 and 4) are instanced attributes and only update every instance. Therefore, the effect is that each instance is translated by the result of the equation of motion.

The `glDrawElementsInstanced` function (step 5) will draw `nParticles` instances of the object. Of course `nEls` is the number of vertices in each instance.

There's more...

OpenGL provides a built-in variable to the vertex shader named `gl_InstanceID`. This is simply a counter and takes on a different value for each instance that is rendered. The first instance will have an ID of zero, the second will have an ID of one, and so on. This can be useful as a way to index to texture data appropriate for each instance. Another possibility is to use the instance's ID as a way to generate some random data for that instance. For example, we could use the instance ID (or some hash) as a seed to a pseudo-random number generation routine to get a unique random stream for each instance.

See also

- ▶ The *Creating a particle fountain* recipe
- ▶ The *Creating a particle system using transform feedback* recipe

Simulating fire with particles

To create an effect that roughly simulates fire, we only need to make a few changes to our basic particle system. Since fire is a substance that is only slightly affected by gravity, we don't worry about a downward gravitational acceleration. In fact, we'll actually use a slight upwards acceleration to make the particles spread out near the top of the flame. We'll also spread out the initial positions of the particles so that the base of the flame is not just a single point. Of course, we'll need to use a particle texture that has the red and orange colors associated with flame.

The following image shows an example of the running particle system:

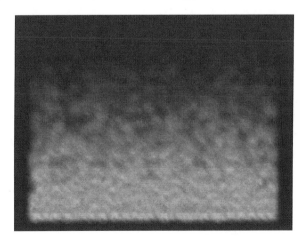

The texture that was used for the particles looks like a light "smudge" of the flame's colors. It is not shown here because it would not be very visible in print.

Getting ready

Start with the basic particle system presented in the recipe *Creating a particle system using transform feedback* earlier in this chapter.

Set the uniform variable `Accel` to a small upward value like (0.0, 0.1, 0.0).

Set the uniform variable `ParticleLifetime` to about four seconds.

Create and load a texture for the particles that has fire-like colors. Bind it to the first texture channel, and set the uniform `ParticleTex` to zero.

Use a point size of about 50.0. This is a good size for the texture that is used in this recipe, but you might use a different size depending on the number of particles and the texture.

How to do it...

Use the following steps:

1. When setting up the initial positions for your particles, instead of using the origin for all particles, use a random x location. The following code could be used:

   ```
   GLfloat *data = new GLfloat[nParticles * 3];
   for( int i = 0; i < nParticles * 3; i += 3 ) {
       data[i] = glm::mix(-2.0f, 2.0f, randFloat());
       data[i+1] = 0.0f;
       data[i+2] = 0.0f;
   }
   glBindBuffer(GL_ARRAY_BUFFER, posBuf[0]);
   glBufferSubData(GL_ARRAY_BUFFER, 0, size, data);
   ```

2. When setting up the initial velocities, we'll make sure that the x and z components are zero and the y component contains a random speed. This, combined with the chosen acceleration (see the previous code) makes each particle move in only the y (vertical) direction:

   ```
   // Fill the first velocity buffer with random velocities
   for( unsigned int i = 0; i < nParticles; i++ ) {
       data[3*i]   = 0.0f;
       data[3*i+1] = glm::mix(0.1f,0.5f,randFloat());
       data[3*i+2] = 0.0f;
   }
   glBindBuffer(GL_ARRAY_BUFFER,velBuf[0]);
   glBufferSubData(GL_ARRAY_BUFFER, 0, size, data);
   glBindBuffer(GL_ARRAY_BUFFER,initVel);
   glBufferSubData(GL_ARRAY_BUFFER, 0, size, data);
   ```

3. In the vertex shader, when recycling particles, reset the y and z coordinates, but don't change the x coordinate:

```
if( age > ParticleLifetime ) {
  // The particle is past its lifetime, recycle.
  Position = vec3(VertexPosition.x, 0.0, 0.0);
  Velocity = VertexInitialVelocity;
  StartTime = Time;
}
```

How it works...

We randomly distribute the x-coordinate of the initial positions between -2.0 and 2.0 for all of the particles, and set the initial velocities to have a y-coordinate between 0.1 and 0.5. Since the acceleration has only a y-component, the particles will move only along a straight, vertical line in the y direction. The x or z component of the position should always remain at zero. This way, when recycling the particles, we can simply just reset the y coordinate to zero, to restart the particle at its initial position.

There's more...

Of course, if you want a flame that moves in different directions, perhaps blown in the wind, you'd need to use a different value for the acceleration. In which case, our little trick for resetting particles to their initial position will no longer work. However, we only need to add another buffer to our particle system (similar to the initial velocity buffer) to maintain the initial position and re-use it when recycling particles.

See also

▶ The *Creating a particle system using transform feedback* recipe

Simulating smoke with particles

Smoke is characterized by many small particles that float away from the source, and spread out as they move through the air. We can simulate the floatation effect with particles by using a small upwards acceleration (or constant velocity), but simulating the diffusion of each small smoke particle would be too expensive. Instead, we can simulate the diffusion of many small particles by making our simulated particles change their size (grow) over time.

The following image shows an example of the results:

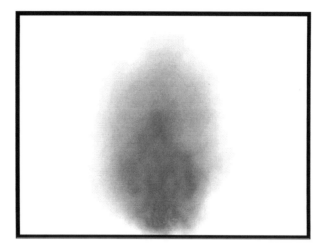

The texture for each particle is a very light "smudge" of grey or black color.

To make the particles grow over time, we'll make use of the `GL_PROGRAM_POINT_SIZE` functionality in OpenGL, which allows us to modify the point size within the vertex shader.

 Alternatively, we could draw quads, or use the geometry shader to generate the quads using the technique demonstrated in *Chapter 6, Using Geometry and Tessellation Shaders*.

Getting ready

Start with the basic particle system presented in the recipe *Creating a particle system using transform feedback*.

Set the uniform variable `Accel` to a small upward value like (0.0, 0.1, 0.0).

Set the uniform variable `ParticleLifetime` to about six seconds.

Create and load a texture for the particles that looks like just light grey smudge. Bind it to texture unit zero, and set the uniform `ParticleTex` to zero.

Set the uniform variables `MinParticleSize` and `MaxParticleSize` to 10 and 200 respectively.

How to do it...

Use the following steps:

1. Set the initial positions to the origin. Define the initial velocities in the same way as described in the recipe *Creating a particle system using transform feedback*. However, it looks best when you use a large variance in `theta`.

2. Within the vertex shader, add the following uniforms:

```
uniform float MinParticleSize;
uniform float MaxParticleSize;
```

3. Also within the vertex shader, use the following code for the `render` function:

```
subroutine (RenderPassType)
void render() {
   float age = Time - VertexStartTime;
   Transp = 0.0;
   if( Time >= VertexStartTime ) {
      float agePct = age/ParticleLifetime;
      Transp = 1.0 - agePct;
      gl_PointSize =
         mix(MinParticleSize,MaxParticleSize,agePct);
   }
   gl_Position = MVP * vec4(VertexPosition, 1.0);
}
```

4. In the main OpenGL application, before rendering your particles, make sure to enable GL_PROGRAM_POINT_SIZE:

```
glEnable(GL_PROGRAM_POINT_SIZE);
```

How it works...

The render subroutine function sets the built-in variable `gl_PointSize` to a value between `MinParticleSize` and `MaxParticleSize`, determined by the age of the particle. This causes the size of the particles to grow as they evolve through the system.

Note that the variable `gl_PointSize` is ignored by OpenGL unless `GL_PROGRAM_POINT_SIZE` is enabled.

See also

▶ The *Creating a particle system using transform feedback* recipe

10

Using Compute Shaders

In this chapter, we will cover the following recipes:

- ▸ Implementing a particle simulation with the compute shader
- ▸ Using the compute shader for cloth simulation
- ▸ Implementing an edge detection filter with the compute shader
- ▸ Creating a fractal texture using the compute shader

Introduction

Compute shaders were introduced into OpenGL with Version 4.3. A compute shader is a shader stage that can be used for arbitrary computation. It provides the ability to leverage the GPU and its inherent parallelism for general computing tasks that might have previously been implemented in serial on the CPU. The compute shader is most useful for tasks that are not directly related to rendering, such as physical simulation.

 Although APIs such as OpenCL and CUDA are already available for general purpose computation on the GPU, they are completely separate from OpenGL. Compute shaders are integrated directly within OpenGL, and therefore are more suitable for general computing tasks that are more closely related to graphics rendering.

The compute shader is not a traditional shader stage in the same sense as the fragment or vertex shader. It is not executed in response to rendering commands. In fact, when a compute shader is linked with vertex, fragment, or other shader stages, it is effectively inert when drawing commands are executed. The only way to execute the compute shader is via the OpenGL commands `glDispatchCompute` or `glDispatchComputeIndirect`.

Compute shaders do not have any direct user-defined inputs and no outputs at all. It gets its work by fetching data directly from memory using image access functions such as the image load/store operations, or via shader storage buffer objects. Similarly, it provides its results by writing to the same or other objects. The only non-user-defined inputs to a compute shader are a set of variables that determine where the shader invocation is within its "space" of execution.

The number of invocations of the compute shader is completely user defined. It is not tied in any way to the number of vertices or fragments being rendered. We specify the number of invocations by defining the number of work groups, and the number of invocations within each work group.

Compute space and work groups

The number of invocations of a compute shader is governed by the user-defined compute space. This space is divided into a number of work groups. Each work group is then broken down into a number of invocations. We think of this in terms of the global compute space (all shader invocations) and the local work group space (the invocations within a particular work group). The compute space can be defined as a 1, 2 or 3 dimensional space.

 Technically, it is always defined as a three-dimensional space, but any of the three dimensions can be defined with a size of one (1), which effectively removes that dimension.

For example, a one-dimensional compute space with five work groups and three invocations per work group could be represented as the following figure. The thicker lines represent the work groups, and the thinner lines represent the invocations within each work group.

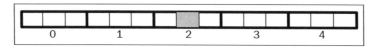

In this case, we have 5 * 3 = 15 shader invocations. The grey shaded invocation is in work group 2, and within that work group, it is invocation 1 (the invocations are indexed starting at zero). We can also refer to that invocation with a global index of 7, by indexing the total number of invocations starting at zero. The global index determines an invocation's location within the global compute space, rather than just within the work group. It is determined by taking the product of work group (2) and index number of invocations per work group (3), plus the local invocation index (1) that is 2 * 3 + 1 = 7. The global index is simply the index of each invocation in the global compute space, starting at zero on the left and counting from there.

The following figure shows a representation of a two-dimensional compute space where the space is divided into 20 work groups, four in the x direction and five in the y direction. Each work group is then divided into nine invocations, three in the x direction and three in the y direction.

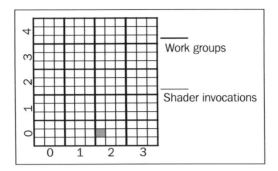

The cell that is shaded in gray represents invocation (0, 1) within work group (2, 0). The total number of compute shader invocations in this example is then 20 * 9 = 180. The global index of this shaded invocation is (6, 1). As with the one-dimensional case, this index is determined by thinking of it as a global compute space (without the work groups), and can be computed (for each dimension) by the number of invocations per work group times the work group index, plus the local invocation index. For the x dimension, this would be 3 * 2 + 0 = 6, and for the y dimension it is 3 * 0 + 1 = 1.

The same idea can extend in a straightforward manner to a three-dimensional compute space. In general, we choose the dimensionality based on the data to be processed. For example, if I'm working on the physics of a particle simulation, I would just have a list of particles to process, so a one-dimensional compute space might make sense. On the other hand, if I'm processing a cloth simulation, the data has a grid structure, so a two-dimensional compute space would be appropriate.

There are limits on the total number of work groups and local shader invocations. These can be queried (via `glGetInteger*`) using the parameters `GL_MAX_COMPUTE_WORK_GROUP_COUNT`, `GL_MAX_COMPUTE_WORK_GROUP_SIZE`, and `GL_MAX_COMPUTE_WORK_GROUP_INVOCATIONS`.

The order of execution of the work groups and thereby the individual shader invocations is unspecified and the system can execute them in any order. Therefore, we shouldn't rely on any particular ordering of the work groups. Local invocations within a particular work group will be executed in parallel (if possible). Therefore, any communication between invocations should be done with great care. Invocations within a work group can communicate via shared local data, but invocations should not (in general) communicate with invocations in other work groups without consideration of the various pitfalls involved such as deadlock and data races. In fact, those can also be issues for local shared data within a work group as well, and care must be taken to avoid these problems. In general, for reasons of efficiency, it is best to only attempt communication within a work group. As with any kind of parallel programming, "there be dragons here".

OpenGL provides a number of atomic operations and memory barriers that can help with the communication between invocations. We'll see some examples in the recipes that follow.

Executing the Compute Shader

When we execute the compute shader, we define the compute space. The number of work groups are determined by the parameters to `glDispatchCompute`. For example, to execute the compute shader with a two-dimensional compute space with 4 work groups in the x dimension and 5 work groups in the y dimension (matching the preceding figure), we'd use the following call:

```
glDispatchCompute ( 4, 5, 1 );
```

The number of local invocations within each work group is not specified on the OpenGL side. Instead, it is specified within the compute shader itself with a layout specifier. For example, here we specify nine local invocations per work group, 3 in the x direction and 3 in the y direction.

```
layout (local_size_x = 3, local_size_y = 3) in;
```

The size in the z dimension can be left out (the default is one).

When a particular invocation of the compute shader is executing, it usually needs to determine where it is within the global compute space. GLSL provides a number of built-in input variables that help with this. Most of them are listed in the following table:

Variable	Type	Meaning
gl_WorkGroupSize	uvec3	The number of invocations per work group in each dimension. Same as what is defined in the layout specifier.
gl_NumWorkGroups	uvec3	The total number of work groups in each dimension.
gl_WorkGroupID	uvec3	The index of the current work group for this shader invocation.
gl_LocalInvocationID	uvec3	The index of the current invocation within the current work group.
gl_GlobalInvocationID	uvec3	The index of the current invocation within the global compute space.

The last one in the preceding table, `gl_GlobalInvocationID` is computed in the following way (each operation is component-wise):

```
gl_WorkGroupID * gl_WorkGroupSize + gl_LocalInvocationID
```

This helps us to locate the current invocation within the global compute space (Refer to the preceding examples).

GLSL also defines `gl_LocalInvocationIndex`, which is a flattened form of `gl_LocalInvocationID`. It can help when multidimensional data is provided in a linear buffer, but is not used in any of the examples that follow.

Implementing a particle simulation with the compute shader

In this recipe, we'll implement a simple particle simulation. We'll have the compute shader handle the physics computations and update the particle positions directly. Then, we'll just render the particles as points. Without the compute shader, we'd need to update the positions on the CPU by stepping through the array of particles and updating each position in a serial fashion, or by making use of transform feedback as shown in the *Creating a particle system using transform feedback* recipe in *Chapter 9, Particle Systems and Animation*. Doing such animations with vertex shaders is sometimes counterintuitive and requires some additional work (such as transform feedback setup). With the compute shader, we can do the particle physics in parallel on the GPU, and customize our compute space to get the most "bang for the buck" out of our GPU.

The following figure shows our particle simulation running with one million particles. Each particle is rendered as a 1 x 1 point. The particles are partially transparent, and the particle attractors are rendered as small 5 x 5 squares (barely visible).

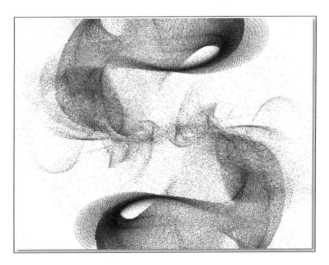

These simulations can create beautiful, abstract figures, and are a lot of fun to produce.

For our simulation, we'll define a set of attractors (two in this case, but you can create more), which I'll call the **black holes**. They will be the only objects that affect our particles and they'll apply a force on each particle that is inversely proportional to the distance between the particle and the black hole. More formally, the force on each particle will be determined by the following equation:

$$\mathbf{F} = \sum_{i=1}^{N} \frac{G_i \ \mathbf{r}_i}{|\mathbf{r}_i| \ |\mathbf{r}_i|}$$

Where **N** is the number of black holes (attractors), $\mathbf{r}_i$ is the vector between the *i*th attractor and the particle (determined by the position of the attractor minus the particle position), and $\mathbf{G}_i$ is the strength of the *i*th attractor.

To implement the simulation, we compute the force on each particle and then update the position by integrating the Newtonian equations of motion. There are a number of well studied numerical techniques for integrating the equations of motion. For this simulation, the simple Euler method is sufficient. With the Euler method, the position of the particle at time **t + Δt** is given by the following equation:

$$\mathbf{P}(t + \Delta t) = \mathbf{P}(t) + \mathbf{v}(t)\Delta t + \frac{1}{2}\mathbf{a}(t)\Delta t^2$$

Where **P** is the position of the particle, **v** is the velocity, and **a** is the acceleration. Similarly, the updated velocity is determined by the following equation:

$$\mathbf{v}(t + \Delta t) = \mathbf{v}(t) + \mathbf{a}(t)\Delta t$$

These equations are derived from a Taylor expansion of the position function about time **t**. The result is dependent upon the size of the time step (**Δt**), and is more accurate when the time step is very small.

The acceleration is directly proportional to the force on the particle, so by calculating the force on the particle (using the preceding equation), we essentially have a value for the acceleration. To simulate the particle's motion, we track its position and velocity, determine the force on the particle due to the black holes, and then update the position and velocity using the equations.

We'll use the compute shader to implement the physics here. Since we're just working with a list of particles, we'll use a one-dimensional compute space, and work groups of about 1000 particles each. Each invocation of the compute shader will be responsible for updating the position of a single particle.

We'll use shader storage buffer objects to track the positions and velocities, and when rendering the particles themselves, we can just render directly from the position buffer.

Getting ready

In the OpenGL side, we need a buffer for the position of the particles and a buffer for the velocity. Create a buffer containing the initial positions of the particles and a buffer with zeroes for the initial velocities. We'll use four-component positions and velocities for this example in order to avoid issues with data layouts. For example, to create the buffer for the positions, we might do something as follows:

```
vector<GLfloat> initPos;

... // Set initial positions

GLuint bufSize = totalParticles * 4 * sizeof(GLfloat);

GLuint posBuf;
glGenBuffers(1, &posBuf);
glBindBufferBase(GL_SHADER_STORAGE_BUFFER, 0, posBuf);
glBufferData(GL_SHADER_STORAGE_BUFFER, bufSize, &initPos[0],
            GL_DYNAMIC_DRAW);
```

Use a similar process for the velocity data, but bind it to index one of the GL_SHADER_STORAGE_BUFFER binding location.

```
glBindBufferBase(GL_SHADER_STORAGE_BUFFER, 1, velBuf);
```

Set up a vertex array object that uses the same position buffer as its data source for the vertex position.

To render the points, set up a vertex and fragment shader pair that just produces a solid color. Enable blending and set up a standard blending function.

How to do it...

Use the following steps:

1. We'll use the compute shader for updating the positions of the particles.
   ```
   layout( local_size_x = 1000 ) in;

   uniform float Gravity1 = 1000.0;
   uniform vec3 BlackHolePos1;
   uniform float Gravity2 = 1000.0;
   uniform vec3 BlackHolePos2;

   uniform float ParticleInvMass = 1.0 / 0.1;
   uniform float DeltaT = 0.0005;
   ```

```
layout(std430, binding=0) buffer Pos {
  vec4 Position[];
};
layout(std430, binding=1) buffer Vel {
  vec4 Velocity[];
};

void main() {
  uint idx = gl_GlobalInvocationID.x;

  vec3 p = Position[idx].xyz;
  vec3 v = Velocity[idx].xyz;

  // Force from black hole #1
  vec3 d = BlackHolePos1 - p;
  vec3 force = (Gravity1 / length(d)) * normalize(d);

  // Force from black hole #2
  d = BlackHolePos2 - p;
  force += (Gravity2 / length(d)) * normalize(d);

  // Apply simple Euler integrator
  vec3 a = force * ParticleInvMass;
  Position[idx] = vec4(
         p + v * DeltaT + 0.5 * a * DeltaT * DeltaT, 1.0);
  Velocity[idx] = vec4( v + a * DeltaT, 0.0);
}
```

2. In the render routine, invoke the compute shader to update the particle positions.

    ```
    glDispatchCompute(totalParticles / 1000, 1, 1);
    ```

3. Then make sure that all data has been written out to the buffer, by invoking a memory barrier.

    ```
    glMemoryBarrier( GL_SHADER_STORAGE_BARRIER_BIT );
    ```

4. Finally, render the particles using data in the position buffer.

How it works...

The compute shader starts by defining the number of invocations per work group using the layout specifier.

```
layout( local_size_x = 1000 ) in;
```

This specifies 1000 invocations per work group in the x dimension. You can choose a value for this that makes the most sense for the hardware on which you're running. Just make sure to adjust the number of work groups appropriately. The default size for each dimension is one so we don't need to specify the size of the y and z directions.

Then, we have a set of uniform variables that define the simulation parameters. `Gravity1` and `Gravity2` are the strengths of the two black holes (`G` in the above equation), and `BlackHolePos1` and `BlackHolePos2` are their positions. `ParticleInvMass` is the inverse of the mass of each particle, which is used to convert force to acceleration. Finally, `DeltaT` is the time-step size, used in the Euler method for integration of the equations of motion.

The buffers for position and velocity are declared next. Note that the binding values here match those that we used on the OpenGL side when initializing the buffers.

Within the main function, we start by determining the index of the particle for which this invocation is responsible. Since we're working with a linear list of particles, and the number of particles is the same as the number of shader invocations, what we want is the index within the global range of invocations. This index is available via the built-in input variable `gl_GlobalInvocationID.x`. We use the global index here because it is the index within the entire buffer that we need, not the index within our work group, which would only reference a portion of the entire array.

Next we retrieve the position and velocity from their buffers, and compute the force due to each black hole, storing the sum in the variable `force`. Then we convert the force to acceleration and update the particle's position and velocity using the Euler method. We write to the same location from which we read previously. Since invocations do not share data, this is safe.

In the render routine, we invoke the compute shader (step *2* in *How to do it...*), defining the number of work groups per dimension. In the compute shader, we specified a work group size of 1000. Since we want one invocation per particle, we divide the total number of particles by 1000 to determine the number of work groups.

Finally, in step *3*, before rendering the particles, we need to invoke a memory barrier to ensure that all compute shader writes have fully executed.

See also

▶ Refer to *Chapter 9, Particle Systems and Animation*, for other particle simulations. Most of these have been implemented using transform feedback, but could instead be implemented using the compute shader.

Using the compute shader for cloth simulation

The compute shader is well suited for harnessing the GPU for physical simulation. Cloth simulation is a prime example. In this recipe, we'll implement a simple particle-spring based cloth simulation using the compute shader. The following is a screenshot of the simulation of a cloth hanging by five pins. (You'll have to imagine it animating.)

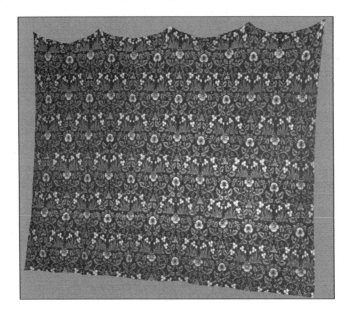

A common way to represent cloth is with a particle-spring lattice. The cloth is composed of a 2D grid of point masses, each connected to its eight neighboring masses with idealized springs. The following figure represents one of the point masses (center) connected to its neighboring masses. The lines represent the springs. The dark lines are the horizontal/vertical springs and the dashed lines are the diagonal springs.

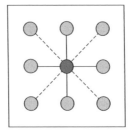

The total force on a particle is the sum of the forces produced by the eight springs to which it is connected. The force for a single spring is given by the following equation:

$$\mathbf{F} = K(|\mathbf{r}| - R)\frac{\mathbf{r}}{|\mathbf{r}|}$$

Where **K** is the stiffness of the spring, **R** is the rest-length of the spring (the length where the spring applies zero force), and **r** is the vector between the neighboring particle and the particle (the neighbor's position minus the particle's position).

Similar to the previous recipe, the process is simply to compute the total force on each particle and then integrate Newton's equations of motion using our favorite integration. Again, we'll use the Euler method for this example. For details on the Euler method, refer to the previous recipe, *Implementing a particle simulation with the compute shader*.

This particle-spring lattice is obviously a two-dimensional structure, so it makes sense to map it to a two-dimensional compute space. We'll define rectangular work groups and use one shader invocation per particle. Each invocation needs to read the positions of its eight neighbors, compute the force on the particle, and update the particle's position and velocity.

Note that in this case, each invocation needs to read the positions of the neighboring particles. Those neighboring particles will be updated by other shader invocations. Since we can't rely on any execution order for the shader invocations, we can't read and write directly to the same buffer. If we were to do so, we wouldn't know for sure whether we are reading the original positions of the neighbors or their updated positions. To avoid this problem, we'll use pairs of buffers. For each simulation step, one buffer will be designated for reading and the other for writing, then we'll swap them for the next step, and repeat.

It might be possible to read/write to the same buffer with careful use of local shared memory; however, there is still the issue of the particles along the edges of the work group. Their neighbor's positions are managed by another work group, and again, we have the same problem.

This simulation tends to be quite sensitive to numerical noise, so we need to use a very small integration time step. A value of around 0.000005 works well. Additionally, the simulation looks better when we apply a damping force to simulate air resistance. A good way to simulate air resistance is to add a force that is proportional to and in the opposite direction to the velocity, as in the following equation:

$$\mathbf{F} = -D\mathbf{v}$$

Where **D** is the strength of the damping force and **v** is the velocity of the particle.

Getting ready

Start by setting up two buffers for the particle position and two for the particle velocity. We'll bind them to the `GL_SHADER_STORAGE_BUFFER` indexed binding point at indices 0 and 1 for the position buffers and 2 and 3 for the velocity buffers. The data layout in these buffers is important. We'll lay out the particle positions/velocities in row-major order starting at the lower left and proceeding to the upper right of the lattice.

We'll also set up a vertex array object for drawing the cloth using the particle positions as triangle vertices. We may also need buffers for normal vectors and texture coordinates. For brevity, I'll omit them from this discussion, but the example code for this book includes them.

How to do it...

Use the following steps:

1. In the compute shader, we start by defining the number of invocations per work group.

```
layout ( local_size_x = 10, local_size_y = 10 ) in;
```

2. Then, define a set of uniform variables for the simulation parameters.

```
uniform vec3 Gravity = vec3(0,-10,0);
uniform float ParticleMass = 0.1;
uniform float ParticleInvMass = 1.0 / 0.1;
uniform float SpringK = 2000.0;
uniform float RestLengthHoriz;
uniform float RestLengthVert;
uniform float RestLengthDiag;
uniform float DeltaT = 0.000005;
uniform float DampingConst = 0.1;
```

3. Next, declare the shader storage buffer pairs for the position and velocity.

```
layout(std430, binding=0) buffer PosIn {
    vec4 PositionIn[];
};
layout(std430, binding=1) buffer PosOut {
    vec4 PositionOut[];
};
layout(std430, binding=2) buffer VelIn {
    vec4 VelocityIn[];
};
layout(std430, binding=3) buffer VelOut {
    vec4 VelocityOut[];
};
```

4. In the main function, we get the position of the particle for which this invocation is responsible.

```
void main() {
  uvec3 nParticles = gl_NumWorkGroups * gl_WorkGroupSize;
  uint idx = gl_GlobalInvocationID.y * nParticles.x +
             gl_GlobalInvocationID.x;

  vec3 p = vec3(PositionIn[idx]);
  vec3 v = vec3(VelocityIn[idx]), r;
```

5. Initialize our force with the force due to gravity.

```
  vec3 force = Gravity * ParticleMass;
```

6. Add the force due to the particle above this one.

```
  if( gl_GlobalInvocationID.y < nParticles.y - 1 ) {
    r = PositionIn[idx + nParticles.x].xyz - p;
    force += normalize(r)*SpringK*(length(r) -
                                   RestLengthVert);
  }
```

7. Repeat the preceding steps for the particles below and to the left and right. Then add the force due to the particle that is diagonally above and to the left.

```
  if( gl_GlobalInvocationID.x > 0 &&
      gl_GlobalInvocationID.y < nParticles.y - 1 ) {
    r = PositionIn[idx + nParticles.x - 1].xyz - p;
    force += normalize(r)*SpringK*(length(r) -
                                   RestLengthDiag);
  }
```

8. Repeat the above for the other three diagonally connected particles. Then add the damping force.

```
  force += -DampingConst * v;
```

9. Next, we integrate the equations of motion using the Euler method.

```
  vec3 a = force * ParticleInvMass;
  PositionOut[idx] = vec4(
      p + v * DeltaT + 0.5 * a * DeltaT * DeltaT, 1.0);
  VelocityOut[idx] = vec4( v + a * DeltaT, 0.0);
```

10. Finally, we pin some of the top verts so that they do not move.

```
  if( gl_GlobalInvocationID.y == nParticles.y - 1 &&
      (gl_GlobalInvocationID.x == 0 ||
       gl_GlobalInvocationID.x == nParticles.x / 4 ||
       gl_GlobalInvocationID.x == nParticles.x * 2 / 4 ||
```

```
        gl_GlobalInvocationID.x == nParticles.x * 3 / 4 ||
        gl_GlobalInvocationID.x == nParticles.x - 1)) {
    PositionOut[idx] = vec4(p, 1.0);
    VelocityOut[idx] = vec4(0,0,0,0);
  }
}
```

11. Within the OpenGL render function, we invoke the compute shader such that each work group is responsible for 100 particles. Since the time step size is so small, we need to execute the process many times (1000), each time swapping the input and output buffers.

```
for( int i = 0; i < 1000; i++ ) {
  glDispatchCompute(nParticles.x/10, nParticles.y/10, 1);
  glMemoryBarrier( GL_SHADER_STORAGE_BARRIER_BIT );

  // Swap buffers
  readBuf = 1 - readBuf;

  glBindBufferBase(GL_SHADER_STORAGE_BUFFER,0,
                    posBufs[readBuf]);
  glBindBufferBase(GL_SHADER_STORAGE_BUFFER,1,
                    posBufs[1-readBuf]);
  glBindBufferBase(GL_SHADER_STORAGE_BUFFER,2,
                    velBufs[readBuf]);
  glBindBufferBase(GL_SHADER_STORAGE_BUFFER,3,
                    velBufs[1-readBuf]);
}
```

12. Finally, we render the cloth using the position data from the position buffer.

How it works...

We use 100 invocations per work group, 10 in each dimension. The first statement in the compute shader defines the number of invocations per work group.

```
layout( local_size_x = 10, local_size_y = 10 ) in;
```

The uniform variables that follow define the constants in the force equations and the rest lengths for each of the horizontal, vertical, and diagonal springs. The time step size is DeltaT. The position and velocity buffers are declared next. We define the position buffers at binding indexes 0 and 1, and the velocity buffers at indexes 2 and 3.

In the main function (step 4), we start by determining the number of particles in each dimension. This is going to be the same as the number of work groups times the work group size. Next, we determine the index of the particle for which this invocation is responsible. Since the particles are organized in the buffers in row-major order, we compute the index by the global invocation ID in the y direction times the number of particles in the x dimension plus the global invocation ID in the x direction.

In step 5, we initialize our force with the gravitational force, `Gravity` times the mass of a particle (`ParticleMass`). Note that it's not really necessary here to multiply by the mass since all particles have the same mass. We could just pre-multiply the mass into the gravitational constant.

In steps 6 and 7, we add the force on this particle due to each of the eight neighboring particles connected by virtual springs. For each spring, we add the force due to that spring. However, we first need to check to see if we are on the edge of the lattice. If we are, there may not be a neighboring particle (see the following figure). For example, in the preceding code, when computing the force due to the spring/particle above, we verify that `gl_GlobalInvocationID.y` is less than the number of particles in the y dimension minus one. If that is true, there must be a particle above this one. Otherwise, the current particle is on the top edge of the lattice and there is no neighboring particle above. (Essentially, `gl_GlobalInvocationID` contains the particle's location in the overall lattice.) We can do a similar test for the other three horizontal/vertical directions. When computing the force for the diagonally connected particles we need to check that we're not on a horizontal and a vertical edge. For example, in the preceding code, we're looking for the particle that is above and to the left, so we check that `gl_GlobalInvocationID.x` is greater than zero (were not on the left edge), and that `gl_GlobalInvocationID.y` is less than the number of particles in the y direction minus one (were not on the top edge).

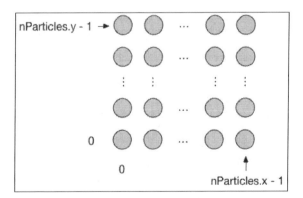

Once we verify that the neighboring particle exists, we compute the force due to the spring connected to that particle and add it to the total force. We organized our particles in row-major order in the buffer. Therefore, to access the position of the neighboring particle we take the index of the current particle and add/subtract the number of particles in the x direction to move vertically, and/or add/subtract one to move horizontally.

In step 8, we apply the damping force that simulates air resistance, by adding to the total force `DampingConst` times the velocity. The minus sign here assures that the force is in the opposite direction of the velocity.

In step 9 we apply the Euler method to update the position and velocity based on the force. We multiply the force by the inverse of the particle mass to get the acceleration, then store the results of the Euler integration into the corresponding positions in the output buffers.

Finally, in step 10, we reset the position of the particle if it is located at one of the 5 pin positions at the top of the cloth.

Within the OpenGL render function (step 11), we invoke the compute shader multiple times, switching the input/output buffers after each invocation. After calling `glDispatchCompute,` we issue a `glMemoryBarrier` call to make sure that all shader writes have completed before swapping the buffers. Once that is complete, we go ahead and render the cloth using the positions from the shader storage buffer.

There's more...

For rendering, it is useful to have normal vectors. One option is to create another compute shader to recalculate the normal vectors after the positions are updated. For example, we might execute the preceding compute shader 1000 times, dispatch the other compute shader once to update the normals, and then render the cloth.

Additionally, we may be able to achieve better performance with the use of local shared data within the work group. In the above implementation the position of each particle is read a maximum of eight times. Each read can be costly in terms of execution time. It is faster to read from memory that is closer to the GPU. One way to achieve this is to read data into local shared memory once, and then read from the shared memory for subsequent reads. In the next recipe, we'll see an example of how this is done. It would be straightforward to update this recipe in a similar way.

See also

 ▶   The *Implementing an edge detection filter with the compute shader* recipe

Implementing an edge detection filter with the compute shader

In the *Applying an edge detection filter* recipe in *Chapter 5, Image Processing and Screen Space Techniques*, we saw an example of how to implement edge detection using the fragment shader. The fragment shader is well suited for many image processing operations, because we can trigger execution of the fragment shader for each pixel by rendering a screen-filling quad. Since image processing filters are often applied to the result of a render, we can render to a texture, then invoke the fragment shader for each screen pixel (by rendering a quad), and each fragment shader invocation is then responsible for processing a single pixel. Each invocation might need to read from several locations in the (rendered) image texture, and a texel might be read multiple times from different invocations.

This works well for many situations, but the fragment shader was not designed for image processing. With the compute shader, we can have more fine grained control over the distribution of shader invocations, and we can make use of local shared memory to gain a bit more efficiency with data reads.

In this example, we'll re-implement the edge detection filter using the compute shader. We'll make use of local (work group) shared memory to gain additional speed. Since this local memory is closer to the GPU, memory accesses are faster than they would be when reading directly from the shader storage buffers (or textures).

As with the previous recipe, we'll implement this using the Sobel operator, which is made up of two 3 x 3 filter kernels shown as follows:

$$\mathbf{S}_x = \begin{bmatrix} -1 & 0 & 1 \\ -2 & 0 & 2 \\ -1 & 0 & 1 \end{bmatrix} \quad \mathbf{S}_y = \begin{bmatrix} -1 & -2 & -1 \\ 0 & 0 & 0 \\ 1 & 2 & 1 \end{bmatrix}$$

For details on the Sobel operator, please refer to Chapter 5, *Image Processing and Screen Space Techniques*. The key point here is that in order to compute the result for a given pixel, we need to read the values of the eight neighboring pixels. This means that the value of each pixel needs to be fetched up to eight times (when processing the neighbors of that pixel). To gain some additional speed, we'll copy the needed data into local shared memory so that within a work group, we can read from the shared memory rather than fetching from the shader storage buffer.

 Work group shared memory is generally faster to access than texture or shader storage memory.

In this example, we'll use one compute shader invocation per pixel, and a 2D work group size of 25 x 25. Before computing the Sobel operator, we'll copy the corresponding pixel values into local shared memory for the work group. For each pixel, in order to compute the filter, we need to read the values of the eight neighboring pixels. In order to do so for the pixels on the edge of the work group, we need to include in our local memory an extra strip of pixels outside the edges of the work group. Therefore, for a work group size of 25 x 25, we'll need storage of size 27 x 27.

Getting ready

Start by setting up for rendering to a **Framebuffer Object** (**FBO**) with a color texture attached, we'll render the raw pre-filtered image to this texture. Create a second texture to receive the output from the edge detection filter. Bind this latter texture to unit 0. We'll use this as the output from the compute shader. Bind the FBO texture to image texture unit 0, and the second texture to image texture unit 1 using `glBindImageTexture`.

Next, set up a vertex/fragment shader pair for rendering directly to the FBO, and for rendering a full-screen texture.

How to do it...

Use the following steps:

1. In the compute shader, as usual, we start by defining the number of shader invocations per work group.

   ```
   layout (local_size_x = 25, local_size_y = 25) in;
   ```

2. Next, we declare uniform variables for our input and output images and for the edge detection threshold. The input image is the rendered image from the FBO, and the output image will be the result of the edge detection filter.

   ```
   uniform float EdgeThreshold = 0.1;
   layout(binding=0, rgba8) uniform image2D InputImg;
   layout(binding=1, rgba8) uniform image2D OutputImg;
   ```

3. Then we declare our work group's shared memory, which is an array of size 27 x 27.

   ```
   shared float
       localData[gl_WorkGroupSize.x+2][gl_WorkGroupSize.y+2];
   ```

4. We also define a function for computing the luminance of a pixel called `luminance`. Since the same function was used in several previous recipes, this need not be repeated here.

5. Next, we define a function that applies the Sobel filter to the pixel that corresponds to this shader invocation. It reads directly from the local shared data.

   ```
   void applyFilter()
   {
   ```

```
uvec2 p = gl_LocalInvocationID.xy + uvec2(1,1);

float sx = localData[p.x-1][p.y-1] +
           2*localData[p.x-1][p.y] +
           localData[p.x-1][p.y+1] -
           (localData[p.x+1][p.y-1] +
           2 * localData[p.x+1][p.y] +
           localData[p.x+1][p.y+1]);
float sy = localData[p.x-1][p.y+1] +
           2*localData[p.x][p.y+1] +
           localData[p.x+1][p.y+1] -
           (localData[p.x-1][p.y-1] +
           2 * localData[p.x][p.y-1] +
           localData[p.x+1][p.y-1]);
float g = sx * sx + sy * sy;

if( g > EdgeThreshold )
  imageStore(OutputImg,
     ivec2(gl_GlobalInvocationID.xy), vec4(1.0));
else
  imageStore(OutputImg,
     ivec2(gl_GlobalInvocationID.xy), vec4(0,0,0,1));
}
```

6. In the main function, we start by copying the luminance for this pixel into the shared memory array.

```
void main()
{
  localData
  [gl_LocalInvocationID.x+1][gl_LocalInvocationID.y+1] =
  luminance(imageLoad(InputImg,
            ivec2(gl_GlobalInvocationID.xy)).rgb);
```

7. If we're on the edge of the work group, we need to copy one or more additional pixels into the shared memory array in order to fill out the pixels around the edge. So we need to determine whether or not we're on the edge of the work group (by examining gl_LocalInvocationID), and then determine which pixels we're responsible for copying. This is not complex, but is fairly involved and lengthy, due to the fact that we also must determine whether or not that external pixel actually exists. For example, if this work group is on the edge of the global image, then some of the edge pixels don't exist (are outside of the image). Due to its length, I won't include that code here. For full details, grab the code for this book from the GitHub site.

8. Once we've copied the data for which this shader invocation is responsible, we need to wait for other invocations to do the same, so here we invoke a barrier. Then we call our `applyFilter` function to compute the filter and write the results to the output image.

```
barrier();

// Apply the filter using local memory
applyFilter();
}
```

9. In the OpenGL render function, we start by rendering the scene to the FBO, then dispatch the compute shader, and wait for it to finish all of its writes to the output image.

```
glDispatchCompute(width/25, height/25, 1);
glMemoryBarrier(GL_SHADER_IMAGE_ACCESS_BARRIER_BIT);
```

10. Finally, we render the output image to the screen via a full-screen quad.

How it works...

In step 1, we specify 625 shader invocations per work group, 25 in each dimension. Depending on the system on which the code is running, this could be changed to better match the hardware available.

The uniform `image2D` variables (step 2) are the input and output images. Note the binding locations indicated in the layout qualifier. These correspond to the image units specified in the `glBindImageTexture` call within the main OpenGL program. The input image should contain the rendered scene, and corresponds to the image texture bound to the FBO. The output image will receive the result of the filter. Also note the use of `rgb8` as the format. This must be the same as the format used when creating the image using `glTexStorage2D`.

The array `localData` is declared in step 3 with the shared qualifier. This is our work group's local shared memory. The size is 27 x 27 in order to include an extra strip, one pixel wide along the edges. We store the luminance of all of the pixels in the work group here, plus the luminance for a strip of surrounding pixels of width one.

The `applyFilter` function (step 5) is where the Sobel operator is computed using the data in `localData`. It is fairly straightforward, except for an offset that needs to be applied due to the extra strip around the edges. The luminance of the pixel that this invocation is responsible for is located at:

```
p = gl_LocalInvocationID.xy + uvec2(1,1);
```

Without the extra strip of pixels, we could just use `gl_LocalInvocationID`, but here we need to add an offset of one in each dimension.

The next few statements just compute the Sobel operator, and determine the magnitude of the gradient, stored in g. This is done by reading the luminance of the eight nearby pixels, reading from the shared array `localData`.

At the end of the `applyFilter` function, we write to `OutputImg` the result of the filter. This is either (1,1,1,1) or (0,0,0,1) depending on whether g is above the threshold or not. Note that here, we use `gl_GlobalInvocationID` as the location in the output image. The global ID is appropriate for determining the location within the global image, while the local ID tells us where we are within the local work group, and is more appropriate for access to the local shared array.

In the main function (step 6), we compute the luminance of the pixel corresponding to this invocation (at `gl_GlobalInvocationID`) and store it in the local shared memory (`localData`) at `gl_LocalInvocationID + 1`. Again, the + 1 is due to the additional space for the edge pixels.

The next step (step 7) is to copy the edge pixels. We only do so if this invocation is on the edge of the work group. Additionally, we need to determine if the edge pixels actually exist or not. For details on this, please refer to the code that accompanies the book.

In step 8, we call the GLSL barrier function. This synchronizes all shader invocations within the work group to this point in the code, assuring that all writes to the local shared data have completed. Without calling the barrier function, there's no guarantee that all shader invocations will have finished writing to `localData`, and therefore the data might be incomplete. It is interesting (and instructive) to remove this call and observe the results.

Finally, we call `applyFilter` to compute the Sobel operator and write to the output image.

Within the OpenGL render function, we dispatch the compute shader such that there are enough work groups to cover the image. Since the work group size is 25 x 25, we invoke width/25 work groups in the x dimension and height/25 in the y. The result is one shader invocation per pixel in the input/output image.

There's more...

This is a straightforward example of the use of local shared memory. It is only slightly complicated by the fact that we need to deal with the extra row/column of pixels. In general, however, local shared data can be used for any type of communication between invocations within a work group. In this case, the data is not used for communication, but is instead used to increase efficiency by decreasing the global number of reads from the image.

 Note that there are (sometimes stringent) limits on the size of shared memory. We can use GL_MAX_COMPUTE_SHARED_MEMORY_SIZE (via glGetInteger*) to query the maximum size available on the current hardware. The minimum required by the OpenGL specification is 32 KB.

See also

▸ The *Applying an edge detection filter* recipe in *Chapter 5, Image Processing and Screen Space Techniques*

Creating a fractal texture using the compute shader

We'll wrap up this chapter with an example that makes use of the compute shader to produce an image of a fractal. We'll use the classic Mandelbrot set.

The Mandelbrot set is based on iterations of the following complex polynomial:

$$z_{n+1} = z_n^2 + c$$

Where **z** and **c** are a complex numbers. Starting with the value **z** = 0 + 0i, we apply the iteration repeatedly until a maximum number of iterations is reached or the value of z exceeds a specified maximum. For a given value of **c**, if the iteration remains stable (z doesn't increase above the maximum) the point is inside the Mandelbrot set and we color the position corresponding to **c** black. Otherwise, we color the point based on the number of iterations it took for the value to exceed the maximum.

In the following figure, the image of the Mandelbrot set is applied as a texture to a cube:

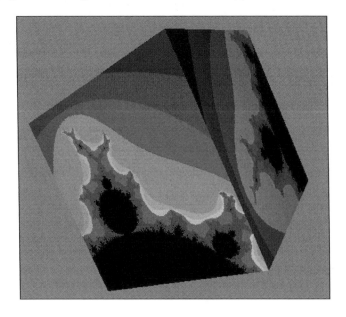

We'll use the compute shader to evaluate the Mandelbrot set. Since this is another image-based technique, we'll use a two-dimensional compute space with one compute shader invocation per pixel. Each invocation can work independently, and doesn't need to share any data with other invocations.

Getting ready

Create a texture to store the results of our fractal calculation. The image should be bound to the image texture unit 0 using `glBindImageTexture`.

```
GLuint imgTex;
glGenTextures(1, &imgTex);
glActiveTexture(GL_TEXTURE0);
glBindTexture(GL_TEXTURE_2D, imgTex);
glTexStorage2D(GL_TEXTURE_2D, 1, GL_RGBA8, 256, 256);
glBindImageTexture(0, imgTex, 0, GL_FALSE, 0, GL_READ_WRITE,
                   GL_RGBA8);
```

How to do it...

Use the following steps:

1. In the compute shader, we start by defining the number of shader invocations per work group.

   ```
   layout( local_size_x = 32, local_size_y = 32 ) in;
   ```

2. Next, we declare the output image as well as some other uniform variables.

   ```
   layout( binding = 0, rgba8) uniform image2D ColorImg;
   #define MAX_ITERATIONS 100
   uniform vec4 CompWindow;
   uniform uint Width = 256;
   uniform uint Height = 256;
   ```

3. We define a function to compute the number of iterations for a given position on the complex plane.

   ```
   uint mandelbrot( vec2 c ) {
     vec2 z = vec2(0.0,0.0);
     uint i = 0;
     while(i < MAX_ITERATIONS && (z.x*z.x + z.y*z.y) < 4.0) {
       z = vec2( z.x*z.x-z.y*z.y+c.x, 2 * z.x*z.y + c.y );
       i++;
     }
     return i;
   }
   ```

4. In the main function, we start by computing the size of a pixel in the complex space.

```
void main() {
    float dx = (CompWindow.z - CompWindow.x) / Width;
    float dy = (CompWindow.w - CompWindow.y) / Height;
```

5. Then we determine the value of c for this invocation.

```
vec2 c = vec2(
        dx * gl_GlobalInvocationID.x + CompWindow.x,
        dy * gl_GlobalInvocationID.y + CompWindow.y);
```

6. Next we call the `mandelbrot` function and determine the color based on the number of iterations.

```
uint i = mandelbrot(c);
vec4 color = vec4(0.0,0.5,0.5,1);
if( i < MAX_ITERATIONS ) {
  if( i < 5 )
        color = vec4(float(i)/5.0,0,0,1);
  else if( i < 10 )
        color = vec4((float(i)-5.0)/5.0,1,0,1);
  else if( i < 15 )
        color = vec4(1,0,(float(i)-10.0)/5.0,1);
  else color = vec4(0,0,1,0);
}
else
    color = vec4(0,0,0,1);
```

7. Finally, we write the color to the output image.

```
imageStore(ColorImg,
            ivec2(gl_GlobalInvocationID.xy), color);
}
```

8. Within the render function of the OpenGL program, we execute the compute shader with one invocation per texel, and call `glMemoryBarrier`.

```
glDispatchCompute(256/32, 256/32, 1);
glMemoryBarrier( GL_SHADER_IMAGE_ACCESS_BARRIER_BIT );
```

9. Then we render the scene, applying the texture to the appropriate objects.

How it works...

In step 2, the uniform variable `ColorImg` is the output image. It is defined to be located at image texture unit 0 (via the `binding` layout option). Also note that the format is `rgb8`, which must be the same as what is used in the `glTexStorage2D` call when creating the texture.

MAX_ITERATIONS is the maximum number of iterations of the complex polynomial mentioned above. CompWindow is the region of complex space with which we are working. The first two components CompWindow.xy are the real and imaginary parts of the lower left corner of the window, and CompWindow.zw is the upper right corner. Width and Height define the size of the texture image.

The mandelbrot function (step 3) takes a value for c as the parameter, and repeatedly iterates the complex function until either a maximum number of iterations is reached, or the absolute value of z becomes greater than 2. Note that here, we avoid computing the square root and just compare the absolute value squared with 4. The function returns the total number of iterations.

Within the main function (step 4), we start by computing the size of a pixel within the complex window (dx, dy). This is just the size of the window divided by the number of texels in each dimension.

The compute shader invocation is responsible for the texel located at gl_GlobalInvocationID.xy. We compute the point on the complex plane that corresponds to this texel next. For the x position (real axis), we take the size of the texel in that direction (dx) times gl_GlobalInvocationID.x (which gives the distance from the left edge of the window), plus the position of the left edge of the window (CompWindow.x). A similar calculation is done for the y position (imaginary axis).

In step 6, we call the mandelbrot function with the value for c that was just determined, and determine a color based on the number of iterations returned.

In step 7, we apply the color to the output image at gl_GlobalInvocationID.xy using imageStore.

In the OpenGL render function (step 8), we dispatch the compute shader with enough invocations so that there is one invocation per texel. The glMemoryBarrier call assures that all writes to the output image are complete before continuing.

There's more...

Prior to the advent of the compute shader, we might have chosen to do this using the fragment shader. However, the compute shader gives us a bit more flexibility in defining how the work is allocated on the GPU. We can also gain memory efficiency by avoiding the overhead of a complete FBO for the purposes of a single texture.

Index

compute shader
about 345, 346
compute space 346, 347
edge detection filter, implementing
with 361-365
executing 348
particle simulation, implementing
with 349-353
used, for creating fractal texture 366-369
using, for cloth simulation 354-360
work groups 346, 347
compute space 346, 347
const qualifier 74
convolution filter 164, 165
core profile
about 9
vs, compatibility profile 9
C++ shader program class
building 52-56
cube map
about 137
used, for simulating reflection 136-143
used, for simulating refraction 143-147
cubic Bezier curve
about 243
drawing, tessellation shader used 243-248
CUDA 345

D

data
sending, to shaders using uniform
variables 37-41
sending, to shaders using vertex
attributes 25-30
sending, to shader using vertex buffer
objects 25-31
debug messages
getting 49-52
deferred shading
about 164, 196
using 196-201
deprecation model 9
depth shadows. *See* **shadow mapping**
depth test
configuring 113, 115
diffuse component 65

diffuse reflectivity 61
diffuse shading
implementing, with single point
light source 60-64
directional light source
about 70, 95
shading with 95-97
DirectX 11 Terrain Tessellation
URL 262
discard keyword 59, 86
disintegration effect
creating 306-308

E

edge detection filter
about 164
applying 164-170
implementing, with compute shader 361-365
element arrays
using 33, 34
emitEdgeQuad function 291
environment mapping 136
Euler method 326

F

fire
simulating, with particle system 339-341
fixed-function pipeline 8
flat shading
about 79
implementing 79, 80
fog effect
camera distance, computing 112
simulating 110-112
forward compatible 9
fractal texture
creating, compute shader used 366-369
fragment shader
about 58, 59
discarding, to create perforated look 86-89
fragment shader output 33
Framebuffer Object (FBO) 118, 155, 268, 362
Freeimage
URL 122
Fresnel equations 148

instanced rendering 335
instance name
  using, with uniform blocks 47
interleaved arrays 34

L

layout qualifiers
  using 334
  using, with uniform blocks 48, 49
level-of-detail (LOD) algorithm
  about 219
  implementing, with tessellation
    shader 259-261
light attenuation 71
link function 55
Lua
  about 10
  URL 10
lua command 11
luminance 362
luminance function 170

M

mandelbrot function 368
multiple light sources
  shading with 92, 94
multiple texture
  applying 124-127
multisample anti-aliasing
  about 191
  using 191-195

N

night-vision effect
  creating 311-314
noise 294
noise texture
  creating, using GLM 295-298
non-local viewer
  about 70
  using 70
normal mapping 130
normal maps
  using 130-136

NVIDIA
  URL 150, 233

O

object local coordinate system 131
OIT
  about 203
  implementing 202-212
OpenCL 345
OpenGL
  GLM types, using 15
  shaders 57
  URL, for documentation 34
  version, determining 15-17
OpenGL 3.2
  compatibility profile 9
  core profile 9
OpenGL 4 117
OpenGL 4.2 118
OpenGL application binary interface (ABI) 10
OpenGL Extension Wrangler. *See* GLEW
OpenGL functionality
  accessing, GLLoadGen used 10, 11
OpenGL Loader Generator. *See* GLloadGen
OpenGL Mathematics. *See* GLM
OpenGL Shading Language. *See* GLSL
OpenGL version 1.1 10
OpenGL Version 4.3
  about 58
  compute shader 345, 346
  fragment shader 58, 59
  vertex shader 58, 59
optimization technique 170
Order Independent Transparency. *See* OIT
Outer level 0 (OL0) 248
Outer level 1 (OL1) 248
Outer level 2 (OL2) 248
Outer level 3 (OL3) 248

P

paint-spatter effect
  creating 309, 311
particle simulation
  implementing, with compute shader 349-353

update function 332
use function 55

V

Verlet integration 327
vertex array object (VAO) 30
vertex attributes
format 31, 32
used, for sending data to shaders 25-30
vertex buffer objects
used, for sending data to shaders 25-30
vertex displacement
surface, animating with 316-319
vertex shader 58, 59
view matrix (V) 149

W

wireframe
drawing, on shaded mesh 225-233
wood grain effect
creating 302-305
work groups 346, 347

Z

z-pass technique 292

Thank you for buying
OpenGL 4 Shading Language Cookbook *Second Edition*

About Packt Publishing

Packt, pronounced 'packed', published its first book "*Mastering phpMyAdmin for Effective MySQL Management*" in April 2004 and subsequently continued to specialize in publishing highly focused books on specific technologies and solutions.

Our books and publications share the experiences of your fellow IT professionals in adapting and customizing today's systems, applications, and frameworks. Our solution based books give you the knowledge and power to customize the software and technologies you're using to get the job done. Packt books are more specific and less general than the IT books you have seen in the past. Our unique business model allows us to bring you more focused information, giving you more of what you need to know, and less of what you don't.

Packt is a modern, yet unique publishing company, which focuses on producing quality, cutting-edge books for communities of developers, administrators, and newbies alike. For more information, please visit our website: www.packtpub.com.

About Packt Open Source

In 2010, Packt launched two new brands, Packt Open Source and Packt Enterprise, in order to continue its focus on specialization. This book is part of the Packt Open Source brand, home to books published on software built around Open Source licences, and offering information to anybody from advanced developers to budding web designers. The Open Source brand also runs Packt's Open Source Royalty Scheme, by which Packt gives a royalty to each Open Source project about whose software a book is sold.

Writing for Packt

We welcome all inquiries from people who are interested in authoring. Book proposals should be sent to author@packtpub.com. If your book idea is still at an early stage and you would like to discuss it first before writing a formal book proposal, contact us; one of our commissioning editors will get in touch with you.

We're not just looking for published authors; if you have strong technical skills but no writing experience, our experienced editors can help you develop a writing career, or simply get some additional reward for your expertise.

Android Native Development Kit Cookbook

ISBN: 978-1-84969-150-5   Paperback: 346 pages

A step-by-step tutorial with more than 60 concise recipes on Android NDK development skills

1. Build, debug, and profile Android NDK apps

2. Implement part of Android apps in native C/C++ code

3. Optimize code performance in assembly with Android NDK

jMonkeyEngine 3.0 Beginner's Guide

ISBN: 978-1-84951-646-4   Paperback: 352 pages

Develop professional 3D games for desktop, web, and mobile, all in the familiar Java programming language

1. Create 3D games that run on Android devices, Windows, Mac OS, Linux desktop PCs and in web browsers—for commercial, hobbyists, or educational purposes.

2. Follow end-to-end examples that teach essential concepts and processes of game development, from the basic layout of a scene to interactive game characters.

3. Make your artwork come alive and publish your game to multiple platforms, all from one unified development environment.

Please check **www.PacktPub.com** for information on our titles

Augmented Reality with Kinect

ISBN: 978-1-84969-438-4   Paperback: 122 pages

Develop your own handsfree and attractive augmented reality applications with Microsoft Kinect

1. Understand all major Kinect API features including image streaming, skeleton tracking, and face tracking

2. Understand the Kinect APIs with the help of small examples

3. Develop a comparatively complete Fruit Ninja game using Kinect and augmented Reality techniques

Learning Raphaël JS Vector Graphics

ISBN: 978-1-78216-916-1   Paperback: 130 pages

Over 70 code examples to create vector graphics and data visualizations!

1. Create impressive vector graphics and data visualizations in your browser

2. Add animation and interactivity to your web applications

3. Work with native SVGs to create complex vector graphics

4. Develop cross-browser vector graphics solutions

Please check **www.PacktPub.com** for information on our titles

Made in the USA
Lexington, KY
18 March 2015